Also by Michael Scheuer

Imperial Hubris:
Why the West Is Losing the War on Terror

Through Our Enemies' Eyes:
Osama bin Laden, Radical Islam, and the Future of America

MARCHING
TOWARD
HELL

AMERICA AND ISLAM
AFTER IRAQ

MICHAEL SCHEUER

FREE PRESS
New York   London   Toronto   Sydney

FREE PRESS
A Division of Simon & Schuster, Inc.
1230 Avenue of the Americas
New York, NY 10020

First Free Press trade paperback edition February 2009

FREE PRESS and colophon are trademarks of Simon & Schuster, Inc.

For information about special discounts for bulk purchases,
please contact Simon & Schuster Special Sales at 1-800-456-6798
or business@simonandschuster.com

Manufactured in the United States of America

3   5   7   9   10   8   6   4

The Library of Congress has cataloged the hardcover edition as follows:

Scheuer, Michael.
Marching toward hell : America and Islam after Iraq / Michael Scheuer.
p.   cm.
Includes bibliographical references and index.
1. Islamic countries—Foreign relations—United States.   2. United States—Foreign
relations—Islamic countries.   3. United States—Politics and government—2001–
4. Afghan War, 2001–   5. Iraq War, 2003–   6. Islam—21st century.   I. Title.
DS35.74U6S34   2008
327.73056—dc22   2007043814
ISBN-13: 978-0-7432-9969-5
ISBN-10:   0-7432-9969-8
ISBN-13: 978-0-7432-9971-8 (pbk)
ISBN-10:   0-7432-9971-X (pbk)

As always, for Beth and Bernice, those aging but still lovely cowhands, and for the three beautiful, bouncing Beth'ettes. Happy trails to all of you.

For my sage and exacting Korean taskmasters, Amly and Elik, with all my love and sincere thanks for graciously permitting me to chauffeur you around everywhere . . . each day . . . all day . . . everyday . . . endlessly.

For L.B., a kind, brilliant, and generous man, who, if he is not careful, may begin to give lawyers a good name.

For Lillian, a master teacher of humility, perseverance, and patience.

And for America's best, the U.S. Marine Corps and CIA's clandestine service, men and women who know that the prayer "May God bless America" must always be completed with the earnest plea, "and may He damn and help me destroy her enemies."

Acknowledgments

In writing this book, I had the indispensable help of several new and much-valued friends. My book agent, Stuart Krichevsky, runs an impressively tight business ship but is never too busy to talk through problems or compare notes about the joys and agonies of watching our respective sons learn to play the astoundingly difficult game of baseball. My publicist, Jenny Powers, is a marvel at gently but effectively putting importuning journalists in their place, as well as in getting me to the right place at the right time, and doing so with a smile even when my forgetfulness is driving her to distraction. At Free Press, Dominick Anfuso and Maria Bruk Aupérin worked with me patiently to tame a good deal of vituperative prose that otherwise might well have prevented the arguments of an already very much nonmainstream analysis from getting a decent hearing. I offer my sincere thanks to each of them.

I also wish to thank a number of writers, historians, and commentators—most of whom I have never met—who have had the moral courage to argue that the status quo in U.S. foreign and military policy toward the Islamic world is not adequately protecting America and must be changed. I do not agree with all of what these men write, and, I am very confident, none of them will agree with all I have written here, and several will disagree with a good deal of it. But be that as it may, I have consistently learned from these men, they have caused me to rethink my own positions many times, and they are driving a debate that may yet save America and the West from their governing elites' mulish, self-serving, and ultimately self-immolating devotion to the status quo. May I offer my thanks and admiration, then, to Ralph Peters, Mark Steyn, Tony Blankley, Abd al-Bari Atwan, Peter Bergen, T. X. Hammes, Patrick Buchanan, Bruce Hoffman, Martin van Creveld, Robert Pape, Robert D. Hormats, Omar Nasiri, Samuel Huntington, Marc Sageman, and Walter A. McDougall.

Acknowledgments

And after spending a career focused on foreign states and entities, I am slowly relearning and trying to apply the lessons taught by America's founders and their constructive successors—especially by George Washington, Alexander Hamilton, Thomas Paine, Abraham Lincoln, and William T. Sherman—and by the two Europeans who best taught Americans about the great difficulties in founding and then enduringly protecting a republic, Niccolò Machiavelli and Alexis de Tocqueville. The lessons these men taught are timeless; we ignore them at our own and our children's peril.

Finally, I alone am responsible for all that follows.

Contents

Contents

Part IV: Where to from Here?

Introduction to the Paperback Edition:

The More Things Change . . .

The paperback version of this book is being published as Americans slowly recover from their two-year obsession with the 2008 presidential election campaign, during which they paid even less than the minimal attention they usually pay to foreign affairs. Sadly, they will find that America's war against Osama bin Laden, al-Qaeda, their Islamist allies, and those they inspire is going very badly. As the campaign wore on, Americans may have been reassured by the almost-always-wrong social scientists and so-called expert journalists who argued that al-Qaeda is dead and only "home-grown" Islamist militants warrant attention.[1] They have also heard that the words of isolated and at times incarcerated anti-al-Qaeda Islamists are destroying bin Laden's organization and personal appeal,[2] and that the "surge" has yielded victory in Iraq.[3] But the truth is Americans have quite a number of shocks awaiting them as post-campaign reality comes into view, and these will be in addition to the current economic crisis.

They will find that the influence of bin Laden and al-Qaeda is spreading, the Salafist sect to which they belong also is "gaining in numbers and influence across the Middle East," and that the organization itself remains the single most dangerous threat to the continental United States.[4] Indeed, al-Qaeda remains the most likely perpetrator of a nuclear attack on America. This nuclear threat is growing, thanks to the failure of the Clinton and Bush administrations to completely secure the Former Soviet Union's nuclear arsenal and the unwillingness of Republicans and Democrats to control borders for fear of losing the Hispanic vote.[5] Only in contemporary America could senior political leaders believe that effectively controlling national borders is not integral to maintaining the nation's sovereignty and providing for its defense.

Americans will also find that because Osama bin Laden was not killed by Bill Clinton (who as president had ten chances to do so from May 1998 to May 1999) or George Bush (who had one chance, in December 2001), the tall Saudi has steadied, rebuilt, and expanded his organization after it was whacked hard by the U.S.-led coalition in 2001–2002. He also has facilitated the growing military capabilities of the Taliban and its Afghan allies, who now have the military initiative in Afghanistan against NATO forces, the impact of which appears to be crumbling the resolve of the alliance's leaders.[6] Even now, NATO's Afghan military effort is rapidly reverting to the twentieth-century Anglo-American standard for really hard military tasks: the United States, Canada, Britain, and Australia are, as always, shouldering the greatest share of the financial costs, manpower commitments, and casualties.

For all intents and purposes, the Afghan War is lost. Afghan president Hamid Karzai's government is powerless, incompetent, and corrupt, and even now NATO commanders are planning to reposition their sparse forces nearer to Kabul because the mujahedin threaten the capital's security. And when during the presidential campaign one heard Senator John McCain and Senator Barack Obama pledge to send two more U.S. brigades to Afghanistan to "finish the job," one had to wonder if either man or his senior advisers ever looked at a map of the country.[7] There are about 6,000 soldiers in two U.S. combat brigades and probably only about half of them are combatants—shooters, if you will. Afghanistan is as big as Texas and shares a 2,600-kilometer border with Pakistan. The Taliban can use about a third of Pakistan's territory—the Pashtun tribal region—for safe-haven, training, and launching operations against NATO forces. This tribal area, moreover, is now the scene of a small but fierce war between the Pakistani Taliban— joined by its Afghan and Arab allies—and the Pakistani army, a fight Islamabad correctly fears could lead to a civil war and the dissolution of the country as a viable political entity.[8] What, then, could the two senators have been thinking? Were they both ignorant of the geographical facts? Were they demonstrating how fully their thinking is still controlled by such obsolete Cold War axioms as finding proxies—in this case then-president Pervez Musharraf's Pakistan—to do America's dirty work?[9] Or were they simply trying to put off delivering to voters the news that saving Washington's Afghan nation-building project would require 200,000 or more troops and then would still have only the slightest chance of succeeding? In all likelihood, President-elect Obama will be forced by on-the-ground realities to choose between giving up Afghanistan to the Taliban and losing both Afghanistan and nuclear-armed Pakistan to the Islamists. There is, of course, only one genuine option: Afghanistan must be cut loose.

In Iraq, the deeply cynical political charade known as "the surge" began to unravel even before the presidential election. This process has been marked by the re-infiltration of al-Qaeda into parts of the countryside and some cities, and, more recently, by a steadily rising number of suicide bombings, especially in Baghdad.[10] The latter is now run by a Shia central government, military, and security service, thanks to the blind eye Washington turned toward Iraqi policies meant to drive the Sunni population out of the city.[11] That said, the now-sainted surge did what U.S. politicians hoped it would do: It kept Iraq off the front pages and television screens during the presidential campaign. This allowed Senator McCain to claim the surge had worked and victory was near, and permitted Senator Obama to soft-pedal withdrawal. Obama also avoided appearing as a surrender advocate because the largely pro-Democratic media was almost silent on the issue.

Once Inauguration Day's revelry is past, Americans will begin to see the bill of goods they have been sold on Iraq. Prime Minister Nouri al-Maliki's Shia regime already is hunting down members of the Sunni Awakening Councils, who had been trained, armed, and then abandoned by the U.S. military, and now are an obvious threat to the goal of Shia ascendancy.[12] As this nascent civil war expands, al-Qaeda will be welcomed back to the country by Iraq's greatly outnumbered Sunnis, and both will be clandestinely supported with funds and ordnance by the Gulf's Sunni states.[13] As this scenario unfolds, moreover, Americans will receive a salutary reminder of just how closely aligned are the foreign policy goals of al-Qaeda, Saudi Arabia, and the other major Sunni states. Indeed, the only problem Riyadh and its Arabian Peninsula neighbors have ever had with al-Qaeda is the group's attacks on the peninsula, and then only because the killing was not limited to non-Muslims.

In their new president's first year in power, Americans will also find that President George W. Bush and his neoconservative cohorts have given them a gift that will keep giving, one that they will keep paying for in taxes and the blood of their soldier-children. The war in Iraq that was instigated by U.S. citizen Israel-firsters and their evangelical Christian allies—whose names one day will be found heading the list of signatures on Israel's death warrant—has not only failed to create a secular democracy in Iraq, it has created a well-armed, anti-Israel Shia state that is unable and probably unwilling to control the al-Qaeda and mujahedin bleed-through across Iraq's western border into the Levant states, a process that has been under way since 2003. Lebanon, Jordan, and Syria are now each afflicted to varying degrees by increasingly violent domestic Islamist militants who aim to both undermine those regimes and establish bases on territory as close to Israel as possible. The threat that is being created by this bleed-through will before long make Washington and its Israeli masters long for the halcyon days when Saddam Hussein ruled Iraq and Hafiez al-Assad ruled Syria.[14]

Given this evolving situation, a withdrawal of most U.S. forces from Iraq would eliminate the only major obstruction to the accelerating bleed-through of al-Qaeda and other Islamist mujahedin.[15] And guess what? Because both U.S. political parties are wholly owned subsidiaries of the American Israel Public Affairs Committee (AIPAC) and the Israeli government, there is no large-scale U.S. military withdrawal from Iraq in the cards under President-elect Obama's administration or even in the foreseeable future. If you doubt this, keep in mind the name Rahm Emanuel. Slated to be the president-elect's chief of staff, Mr. Emanuel has labored as a volunteer for AIPAC's various anti-U.S. causes, strove to ensure the defeat of anti–Iraq War Democratic congressional candidates in 2006, and in 1991, as a 32-year-old U.S. citizen, chose to serve with the Israeli Defense Forces rather than volunteer to fight for the United States in the war against Saddam's Iraq.[16]

As if this is not enough bad news, Americans need to accept that Afghanistan, Pakistan, Iraq, and the Levant states are not the only areas of rising al-Qaeda-associated influence and military activity. In Algeria, al-Qaeda-in-the-Islamic-Maghreb has revitalized its forces and is executing attacks that limit the number of innocent Muslims killed. It is again threatening the autocratic Algerian regime by focusing on government, military, and energy-industry infrastructure targets, and has run operations in Chad, Morocco, and Mauritania. In 2008, its leaders also pledged to stage attacks in France and Spain.[17] In Somalia, the Islamic Courts Union and its military wing, al-Shabab, have reorganized and refitted. They are on the offensive against the UN-backed interim government, the Organization of African Unity's (OAU) peacekeeping force, and the occupying Ethiopian army, and are beginning to use remotely controlled roadside bombs similar to those used in Iraq. In addition, Kenya, Tanzania, and, it appears, large and small cargo vessels plying the waters off the coast of east Africa are beginning to feel the violent impact of mujahedin bleed-out from Somalia.[18] In Yemen, a former bin Laden secretary, Nasir al-Wahayshi, who escaped from a Yemen prison in early 2006, has rebuilt al-Qaeda's organization in the country. He has assumed a more offensive military posture, and is employing a new and sophisticated media production unit—as are most al-Qaeda components worldwide—to extend the organization's popular appeal. It now, for example, publishes a regularly issued electronic journal, *The Echo of Epic Battles*. Under al-Wahayshi, Yemeni al-Qaeda's target list has included oil industry infrastructure on land and sea, foreign tourists, and, in September 2008, the U.S. embassy in Sana.[19] And in China and India, the pace of Islamist insurgent and terrorist activities is growing. Muslim minority communities in those countries have begun to respond violently to what they regard as their longtime status as second-class citizens who are persecuted by favored, non-Muslim populations—the Han Chinese in China and the Hindus in India.[20]

The Islamist movement's growth in India is particularly intriguing because the West, until the November 26–29, 2008, attacks in Mumbai, had taken almost no notice of it, notwithstanding India's role as an important engine of economic globalization and a major site for U.S. and other foreign investment. Since 9/11, India has been the target of more destructive Islamist terrorist attacks than any other nation on earth. The attacks have been increasingly lethal, professional, and technologically sophisticated in execution. As many as seventeen bombs have been detonated in series via timers or remote control in a single attack. In addition, post-9/11 terrorist operations in India have seen a large increase in the participation of Indian Muslims. Although India's knee-jerk reaction is to blame all its domestic terrorism on Pakistan—a position usually supported by the West—the fact is India is now facing a violent and growing internal Islamist movement motivated by New Delhi's treatment of Indian Muslims as second-class citizens, its support for the U.S. war on terror, its flamboyant relationship with Israel, and its tolerance for the anti-Muslim agendas of the country's Hindu nationalist political parties. In a worst-case scenario, the accelerating Islamist terror campaign in India could lead to catastrophic intercommunal violence and/or a nuclear confrontation between Islamabad and New Delhi. Either conflict would cause enormous human casualties and strike a severe blow against the now-weakening international economy.[21]

Beyond the foregoing nations, the hardcover edition of this book also examined six locations where there appeared to be emerging Islamist and/or energy-related problems: Somalia, the North Caucasus, Nigeria, Thailand, Bangladesh, and Europe.[22] The Islamist challenge in each place has grown since the hardcover's publication. As noted above, the Somali Islamists are regaining public support and have seized the military initiative: they are again threatening Mogadishu and they are being reinforced by al-Qaeda and other non-Somali Muslim fighters from elsewhere in Africa and the Islamic world. "I want to make it clear to you," a senior Somali Islamist commander told the media in October 2008, "that [Muslim] foreigners are among us [and] fighting alongside us." Because Ethiopia has decided to withdraw its troops from Somalia before the end of 2008, it is a near certainty the Islamists will rule Somalia before 2009 is over.[23] In the North Caucasus, the forces of the Islamic Emirate—formed by Islamist groups from the six Russian republics and led by Dokka Umarov—also have taken the initiative: the tempo of their insurgent operations is up across the region and that offensive is driving much of the ethnic Russian population—the region's best and brightest—out of the North Caucasus. In addition, insurgent pressure has prevented Russia from withdrawing any of its forces, and they are suffering steady casualties. Moscow's surrogate local regimes lack political credibility—locals view them as Russia's lackeys and hired guns—and their personnel are being killed in steadily rising numbers. Finally, foreign Muslim fighters, from Egypt, Jordan, Saudi Arabia, and elsewhere, appear to be joining the North Caucasus's jihad, and overall the region appears to be slipping from Moscow's control.[24] In Nigeria, violent confrontations keep occurring between Muslims and Christians, and the Movement for the Emancipation of the Niger Delta (MEND) is continuing its low-level insurgency against Nigerian government, military, and security targets, as well as against the mostly foreign-owned oil industry, especially against expatriate oil workers, pipelines, and production platforms located up to 120 kilometers offshore. The MEND's effectiveness is seen in the fact that it cut Nigeria's total oil production by 25 percent for the period 2006–2008.[25] In 2012, the United States will be receiving 20 percent of its crude oil imports from the Niger Delta. MEND leaders are well aware of this and have publicly warned that their fighters' actions will have "ripple effect[s]" that will "continue to speak volumes beyond the Nigerian shores."[26]

In Asia, Islamist movements are also gaining ground. In Thailand, Islamist insurgents in the country's southern provinces—Yala, Pattani, Narathiwat, and Songkla—have continued their attacks on Thai military and security personnel, as well as on Buddhist citizens who are employed by the Bangkok regime as teachers and civil servants. The Thai regime has been unable to make any substantial progress in quelling the insurgency, although it has deployed 30,000 troops in the southern provinces, and in mid-2008, it abandoned a long and stubbornly held position that it would not negotiate with the insurgents. The two sides met in August 2008, in Bogor, Indonesia, in a conference mediated by Indonesian vice president Jusuf Kalla. The conference yielded little, and the media claim Bangkok has decided to restore its focus on achieving a military solution to the insurgency. For now, fighting in southern Thailand continues amid reports that the insurgents are using roadside-bomb and sniping tactics similar to those used in Iraq, and that an increasing number of foreign Muslims are arriving in Thailand to train the Islamist insurgents there.[27] In Bangladesh, the country is still governed by a military-backed, interim administration that was installed in January 2007; parliamentary elections have been repeatedly delayed and are now set for late December 2008. According to the media, Bangladeshi Islamist organizations have continued to grow under the interim regime. There are now four major Islamist groups and there may be up to 125 smaller ones operating in the country, and some have opened or expanded training camps in the country's southwest along the border with the Indian states of Assam, West Bengal, and Tripura. In addition to training Bangladeshi militants, the media reports, the camps provide training to Burmese Muslims and some Thai Islamists. The country's main Islamist group appears to be the Harakat-ul-Jamaat-Islami-Bangladesh (HUJI-B), whose leader signed bin Laden's 1998 fatwa and which runs several camps. HUJI-B has long-standing ties to al-Qaeda, the Afghan Taliban, and Pakistan's Inter-Services Intelligence Directorate. New Delhi has accused HUJI-B of being a key player since 2006 in attacks on major Indian cities such as Mumbai, Ahmedabad, Hyderabad, and Jaipur. In March 2008, the U.S. government listed the HUJI-B as an international terrorist organization.[28]

Finally, Islamist militancy continues to grow across Western Europe, and most critically for U.S. interests, in Great Britain. In October and November 2008, senior officials of the British Security Services (MI5) publicly warned Britons that the Islamist threat in the United Kingdom is reaching critical proportions—"the severe end of severe," they said. The authorities said there are "some thousands" of domestic Islamist extremists who mean to attack in Britain, and that there are particularly heavy concentrations of these individuals in London, Birmingham, and Luton. The threat is so serious, they added, security and police services are operating at "full stretch" and even the safety of the government's central zone—which includes Whitehall and the houses of Parliament—cannot be considered safe. Given this personnel shortage, the recent decision by Air Chief Marshal Sir Jock Stirrup, the UK's Chief of Defense Staff, to send British troops leaving Iraq in 2009 home to rest and refit rather than to Afghanistan to join a U.S.-led "surge," may also be designed to support domestic police and security forces if there is a major Islamist attack.[29]

Thus the battlefield on which the Islamists operate has grown geographically while Americans elected a president. If there is to be an ongoing "war on terror," it will henceforth be fought in many more countries and perhaps on the oceans as well. In addition, U.S. and Western politicians, social scientists, and journalists will be able to take less solace in Muslim anger over attacks that kill innocent Muslims. In Algeria, India, China, Afghanistan, and the North Caucasus, Islamist insurgents have adjusted their attack plans to begin limiting casualties among Muslims, unless they have compromised their "innocent" status by willingly working or fighting for non-Muslim or apostate governments.[30] Bin Laden himself has recognized that the only genuine post-9/11 strategic threat to al-Qaeda was that posed by Abu Musab al-Zarqawi's indiscriminate slaughter of Shia and Sunni Muslims in Iraq. Bin Laden implicitly expressed regret to the Muslim world for those deaths,[31] and by sending a veteran Egyptian mujahid named Abu Hamza al-Muhajir to lead Al-Qaeda-in-Iraq he set in motion an effort to recoup lost ground among Iraqi Sunnis—an effort being aided by Maliki's harsh treatment of the Awakening's leaders—and to affirm al-Qaeda's traditional role of quietly supporting and not leading foreign Islamist insurgencies.

Americans will soon find that the recent presidential election did nothing to change U.S. foreign policy in the Middle East, and thus did nothing that will even begin to sap the motivation and growth of our Islamist enemies. The campaign itself was a model of foreign-policy deceit: both Senator Obama and Senator McCain and their surrogates—especially fierce Israel-firster Senator Joseph Lieberman—stuck to the old lie about how al-Qaeda and its Islamist allies are attacking because they hate America's freedoms, gender equality, movies, and elections. And now, with the Democrats controlling the White House and Congress, it will not be long before Americans begin to hear the old saw about how terrorism is caused by poverty, unemployment, bad health, illiteracy, and hopelessness and how a huge, taxpayer-funded "New Deal" for the Muslim world will solve the problem. All of these contentions are, of course, nonsense and the product of the minds of the moral cowards who populate America's bipartisan political elite. The Islamist enemies are not irrational, illiterate, and fanatic nihilists with bad teeth. They are pious, rational, patient, adaptable, and Internet-loving men who are motivated by what the United States government has done in the Muslim world for more than thirty-five years, and not by what Americans believe and how they live and behave at home. Though it seems unlikely that any U.S. politician will pay heed, Islamists are motivated by the same U.S. interventionist foreign policies that motivated them even before 1996, when Osama bin Laden enumerated those policies in al-Qaeda's declaration of war on the United States:

- U.S. military and civilian presence on the Arabian Peninsula

- U.S. exploitation of Muslim energy resources

- Unqualified U.S. support for Israel

- The U.S. military presence in Muslim lands outside the Arabian Peninsula

- U.S. support for anti-Muslim nations, especially India, Russia, and China

- U.S. protection of Arab tyrannies, especially Saudi Arabia and Egypt[32]

Training in rocket science is not required to understand the motivation of al-Qaeda and its allies—they have described it in a flood of statements, books, essays, and interviews—nor is it needed to understand that more than three-quarters of Muslims worldwide share bin Laden's perception that U.S. foreign policy is meant to undermine or destroy Islam.[33] It is Washington's prolonged bipartisan interventionism in the Muslim world—in forms ranging from armed invasion to Christian proselytizing to feminist imperialism—not the lifestyle of Americans, that has landed the United States today in a war it is losing across the board.

And, tragically, President-elect Obama's foreign-policy comments over the past year seem to foreshadow a proclivity for war-causing, interventionist policies in places where the United States has no discernible national interests at risk. During the campaign, for example, Obama—like McCain—could not contain his enthusiasm for more U.S. overseas involvement. The Illinois senator welcomed the independence of Kosovo, thus joining McCain, other leaders in both parties, and the quite mad Europeans in lighting the fuse to the next Balkans' war and committing America to resist an inevitable and justifiable Serbian invasion to reclaim that country's most politically sacred territory. After the Russia-Georgia war, he also agreed with McCain and most of the U.S. political elite that getting Georgia into NATO ought to be a priority, as if all of them are willing to sacrifice U.S. soldiers for an unfulfillable security guarantee like the one Britain gave Poland in 1939. And like all AIPAC-influenced U.S. politicians, Obama spent the last six months of the campaign dancing the Tel Aviv Two-Step, pledging in essence to protect and support Israel as if it were a state in the American union—this to secure Jewish votes and campaign contributions. He thereby built on President George W. Bush's policy of ensuring that Americans will pay with their taxes and children's lives to be involved in the Israel-Arab religious war, in which no genuine U.S. national security concern is at stake.

At this point, then, President-elect Obama seems to have all the sorry status quo attributes of a war-causing interventionist. He appears largely ignorant of the nature of the threat America faces from Islamist militancy and seems uninterested in first learning what motivates al-Qaeda, et al., and then explaining what he has learned to the American people so a substantive debate can begin over the goals of U.S. foreign policy. And even if Obama surprises and decides to acquire that knowledge—and all Americans should pray that he does—his effort would be undermined by the fact that he has surrounded himself with Israel-firsters like Rahm Emanuel. He also will have to contend with the pro-Israel U.S. media and U.S. foreign policy and defense bureaucracies; devoted interventionists like Hillary

Clinton; generals who betray their troops by saying "there is no military solution to this or that problem" whenever their political masters decide, for public relations reasons, to prevent the U.S. military from winning a war;[34] and some of the same Arab-royalty-loving, white-feather-wearing national security bureaucrats who facilitated the 9/11 attacks by ardently working to block the killing of Osama bin Laden during President Clinton's two administrations.

Locked in willful ignorance about our Islamist enemy's motivation, advised by any number of unreformed Cold Warriors such as Zbigniew Brzezinski and Vice-President-elect Joe Biden, and surrounded by Clinton-era Israel protectors, interventionists, political generals, and cowardly-lion bureaucrats, President-elect Obama has his work cut out for him just to get a vision of the world as it is and not as he and his colleagues want it to be.

On Inauguration Day 2013, then, the odds are America will be in a worse mess in the Muslim world than it is today, and that mess will be of its own making. Long before winning the presidency in 1860, Abraham Lincoln made a statement that President-elect Obama would do well to consider. "If destruction be our [America's] lot," Mr. Lincoln said in early 1838, "we must ourselves be its author and finisher. As a nation of free men we must live through all time or die by suicide."[35] By God's favor, the Union Army's skill and blood, and Mr. Lincoln's steady hand, heart, and mind, America lived through its first attempt at suicide during four years of civil war. Today, we again appear to be ready to author our own destruction. By willfully ignoring the Islamists' motivation for fifteen-plus years, and by treating our foreign policy as unalterable divine writ, we have left ourselves almost no options that promise victory, a situation no nation of free men should tolerate. And so we move inexorably toward defeat at the hands of a four-foot-tall enemy who has been made into a ten-foot-tall behemoth due to our political leaders' sanctimony, self-deception, and moral cowardice. As long as this status quo remains, we in America neither can expect nor do we really deserve to live through all time as free men.

Preface

The South could have won the Civil War, could have won at Gettysburg. On the human level alone, there was no inevitability. But the South had lived too long on illusion and would not see to fight. [James] Longstreet, a critical patriot, was considered anti-Southern after the War, just as critical patriots are accused of being "un-American" now—and out of the same fearful frame of mind. People perish from a lack of vision.

Kent Gramm, 1994

Perhaps the easiest task in today's America would be to write a book maintaining America's current illusions by assigning President George W. Bush's administration responsibility for all of America's international troubles since September 11, 2001, and then advance the delusional argument that all will be well once Mr. Bush returns permanently to his ranch in Crawford, Texas. Such a misinterpretation is superficially supportable because several moments in Mr. Bush's presidency will forever reside in the thankfully small compartment of U.S. history reserved for the infamous. The unprovoked invasion of Iraq surely is one such event, as is Vice President Dick Cheney's reptilian contention that Americans who criticize U.S. foreign policy are "validating the strategy of the terrorists."[1] In addition, the thought of what history will say about Donald Rumsfeld's tenure at the Department of Defense ought to make his relatives shudder down to their latest generation.

There is a great danger, however, in simply heaping abuse on Mr. Bush and his lieutenants because it was on their watch that the much ballyhooed and nearly beatified "bipartisan approach" to post–Cold War foreign policy played out its string and collapsed. Rather than crafting a paradigm appropriate to the new era in America's foreign relations, President Bush—always his father's son—launched a last, desperate, and ultimately futile attempt to keep the Cold War–era policy consensus on track and running toward a revamped version of his dad's vague but clearly silly vision of a New World Order. No effort was spared before the 2003 Iraq war. All the traditional buttons were pressed—prewar congressional support, extensive UN consultations, and intricate coalition-building—but to no avail. The fact that this effort now lies in smoldering ruins has less to do with the competence of President Bush and his colleagues (although, to be sure, competence was not the administration's common virtue) and more to do with the reality that America's bipartisan governing elite is both unprepared and unwilling to deal with the world as it is, rather than as they want it to be or think it should be. Because of their profound and willful ignorance—there is no kinder or gentler description that applies—America has traveled a path that has seen the lethal nuisance originally presented by Sunni militants transformed into an existential threat that is poised to strike at the core of our social and civil institutions in a way that could change our collective lifestyle for many decades, perhaps forever.

For the purposes of this book the term *bipartisan governing elite* is used to describe the inbred set of individuals who have influenced, contributed ideas to, drafted, and conducted U.S. foreign policy for the past thirty-five years. Within that group there are politicians, journalists, academics, civil servants, military officers, pundits, preachers, and untold numbers of thespians, philanthropists, and do-good organizations. Some are Republicans, others Democrats; some are evangelicals, others atheists; some are militarists, others pacifists; some are purveyors of Western civilization, others are multiculturalists. Our bipartisan governing elite's social, political, economic, and religious philosophies are numerous and diverse. But they all conduce to one motivating factor: an unquenchable ardor to have the United States intervene abroad in all places, situations, and times. Some of the elite prefer diplomatic intervention, others military; some prefer humanitarian activities, others covert action; and some prefer foreign aid mixed with Christian proselytizing, others prefer aid meant to break down traditional religious conventions, such as funds for family planning in conservative Muslim states. From Hillary Clinton to Franklin Graham, from John McCain to George Soros, and down to the elite's lowest-ranking man or woman, all share in one near-religious belief in the role of the United States in the world. The mix of philosophies and tools brought to an intervention may vary, but unrelenting intervention itself is the lodestone of America's bipartisan governing elite.

Because of our elite's allegiance to intervention and its intense aversion to substantive change—do not confuse their "embrace the change" rhetoric with a desire for genuine change—America today lives in what can be described as a prolonged Cold War hangover, an environment in which our elites' perception of the world seems to have frozen stiff on the day the Berlin Wall fell. On that day, though perhaps not for much longer, the United States did indeed stand as the world's only superpower, ready to undertake the elder Mr. Bush's dream of building the New Jerusalem. Sadly and inexplicably, the first Mr. Bush and his two successors failed to see that with the Cold War's end, the major keeper of world peace and order—the U.S.-USSR rivalry, and especially the sainted doctrine of Mutually Assured Destruction (MAD)—had exited the scene, ushering in a steadily rising tide of pervasive international disorder that has deposited the world in a new age of barbarity. It is now clear that MAD provided much of the world with a halcyon half-century of substantial peace and gradually increasing prosperity—Pax Atomica, if you will—as well as with the glittering, still-dominant, but utterly fatuous illusion of a coming age of eroding nationalism and increased international cooperation and comity. We now are living through the last stages of Pax Atomica's peace and prosperity, but America's governing elite has thus far done its best to patch up and maintain the illusion that the old girl still has lots of life in her. She does not.

U.S. politicians, generals, academics, and pundits can, I think, be forgiven for being a bit intoxicated and Pollyanna-ish during the first, heady post-Soviet years. The emotional and psychological release from the end of a fifty-year nuclear standoff unavoidably gave birth to a certain reality-defying giddiness. But who would have expected this normal reaction to harden into an apparently permanent mindset? Well, Osama bin Laden apparently did.

In September of the fifth post–Cold war year this lanky and quiet Saudi Arabian declared war on the United States. Bin Laden's Anglo-American–like formal declaration of war—an action the U.S. Congress has found passé since 1941, notwithstanding quaint but indisputable constitutional requirements—received little notice in Washington's halls of power.

In his treatise bin Laden provided a well-honed needle that ought to have deflated the West's post-Soviet/New World Order balloon. Without so much as a courteous apology to the history-ending Francis Fukuyama, bin Laden, in twelve densely written pages, carefully explained that history had resumed, that the Muslim religion was alive, thriving, and angry, that the Cold War's limits to worldwide conflict had been sundered, and that war-to-the-finish had reassumed its traditional and proper station in human affairs. In short, bin Laden announced that many Muslims were less interested in building a New Jerusalem than in conquering Israeli-occupied Old Jerusalem. Bin Laden's declaration should have been required reading for all U.S. policymakers and citizens (it did not become widely available to the latter for almost a decade), and it should have been compared and contrasted with Fukuyama's *The End of History and the Last Man*.[2] Bin Laden had the better, more historically accurate, and commonsense end of the debate then; he dominates the debate now.

While bin Laden delivered the clear and substantive message that the war he was initiating against the United States, and the countries choosing to take its side, was a defensive reaction to specific U.S. foreign policies and their impact in the Muslim world, American leaders have since 1996 floundered around almost comically in trying to defend elements of American life that are not under attack—liberties, freedoms, and elections. Indeed, their campaign to defend these unattacked elements of America's political and social life is one of the strongest indicators of the still-dominant Cold War mindset: these were the things we defended against the hated Bolsheviks; therefore they must be under attack again. The absurdity of the debate between bin Laden and U.S. policymakers is palpable and generally unfolds as follows: Bin Laden issues a starkly specific attack on a U.S. foreign policy, and Washington responds with defiant words defending a right or liberty that bin Laden has not mentioned and that has nothing to do with his assertion. Thus, bin Laden says: Get U.S. forces out of the Arabian Peninsula; Washington responds: You will not prevent our women from going to school. Bin Laden says: Stop supporting Russia's genocidal war in Chechnya; Washington responds: You will not disrupt our elections. Bin Laden says: Stop supporting the tyrannical Arab police states that oppress and torture; Washington says: Freedom is on the march for Arabs. While bin Laden and his lieutenants must shake their heads in frustration over the blatant deafness of U.S. and Western leaders, they have taken full advantage of that self-imposed and possibly fatal handicap.

This book, then, is not an attempt to minutely analyze each event of America's post-9/11 war with Islamist militancy. It rather seeks, first, to reconstruct how the United States found itself with an untenable set of foreign policies and national-security strategies on the day of the attacks on New York and Washington. And second, it tries to understand, explain, and assess the costs of the U.S. government's stubborn and obviously losing rearguard action to maintain these catastrophically deficient policies and strategies. This book began life entitled *From Pandora's Box: America and Islam After Iraq.* I chose the title because I initially thought there was something credible to the claim that the disaster that has occurred in Iraq—and Afghanistan as well—amounted to a set of amazing, unintended, and unpredictable consequences. Well before I completed researching, however, it was clear to me that while I was definitely telling a story of unintended consequences, it most assuredly was not a tale of unpredictable consequences. A person and a nation may not intend to cause untoward consequences by their actions, but only a fool assumes that the consequences of all his actions can only be positive for everyone concerned. Enter America's bipartisan governing elite.

In reviewing the years since 1973, and especially those since the 9/11 attacks and the March 2003 invasion of Iraq, it will, I believe, become clear that the negative events that have unfolded for America may have been unintended but were in no sense unforeseeable. The unwinnable insurgencies we now face in Afghanistan and Iraq, the rock-solid hatred of U.S. foreign policy among a huge majority of Muslims and many non-Muslims as well, the flood of heroin entering the West from Southwest Asia, the rising tide of militancy across the Islamic world—surely none of these were the intentions or expectations of U.S. policymakers. Only madmen and perhaps a few neoconservatives and Israel-firsters would have sought these consequences, but anyone with an average knowledge of history could have foreseen most of them.

Given predictable consequences, and assuming no malign intent, U.S. political leaders and policymakers from both parties between 1996 and 2007 must stand guilty of willful historical ignorance, a paucity of common sense, and, as I have argued before, a disastrous degree of intellectual hubris. The interlocking of this historical ignorance, sparse common sense, and galloping hubris is in all individuals, countries, and eras a fatal combination. America's full-bore war with the Islamic world today is the result of exactly that combination of attributes in our bipartisan governing elite. Since 9/11 there has been a war between two opponents. On one side are the Islamists, fighting in deadly earnest for fully explained reasons and limited objectives; on the other is the United States, grandly assuming inevitable victory over a foe that exists only in its mind. It was this stark reality that prompted me to retitle the book *Marching Toward Hell.*

One final word. This book is about pointing fingers at the unnecessary and self-defeating U.S. mistakes—political, diplomatic, military, and intellectual. As such it is a fairly unrelenting discussion and analysis of negatives. America has, of course, scored victories since 9/11, but almost all have been of a tactical nature and redound to the credit not of U.S. leaders but of the military and intelligence personnel, men and women, who serve, in military terms, at the level of colonel and below. These individuals have shown initiative, courage, and a deep and abiding concern for the security of Americans and their country. They have taken life-risking actions that more senior careerists would have avoided like grim death. They have helped defend America but have not advanced their careers. There surely is a story to be told about these heroic individuals who spent their blood to buy time for America, but it will not be told here. Why? Because their undeniable substantive and admirable tactical victories have not advanced America's strategic position in the war against al-Qaeda and the Islamists since they have occurred within the context of a national-security strategy, which is the common handiwork of the first Bush, Clinton, and current Bush presidencies, that creates enemies faster than they can be killed and that finds America in a worse position today than it was on 9/11. Indeed, the lives of those who died on 9/11 and all those who have since died battling al-Qaeda–led forces have been squandered uselessly because of the arrogance- and ignorance-powered failure of their leaders. It is the story of that failure that this book will tell.

Introduction

[E]vents started by human folly link themselves in a sequence which no sagacity can foresee and no courage can break through.

Joseph Conrad, 1911

It is painful enough to discover with what unconcern they speak of war and threaten it. I have seen enough of it to make me look upon it as the sum of all evils.

Major General T. J. Jackson, 1862

In two previous books and numerous articles, I have tried to explain and defend my conclusion that U.S. political leaders from both parties and American citizens generally have misunderstood the motivation of Osama bin Laden, al-Qaeda, and their steadily increasing number of Islamist allies. My argument, simply stated, was and is that Islamist militants are attacking America because of what it does in the Islamic world and not because of the way America's people think, vote, behave, and believe or not believe in God. I readily acknowledge that many of the Islamists confronting us detest our society and lifestyle and would never duplicate them in any country they would govern. Clearly, there would be nothing akin to MTV, gender equality, or quadrennial presidential elections in an al-Qaeda–run Saudi Arabia.

But granting that reality, I argued that it was a profound and unnecessary mistake, an instance of what Conrad called "human folly," to believe that the Islamist militants' animosities for the accoutrements of our society were the main motivating and unifying factors behind their hatred and willingness to wage war against the United States. Such an error, moreover, would cause U.S. leaders and citizens to grossly underestimate the threat

1

they faced from the Islamists, lead them to deploy insufficient military force, and stand pat on untenable foreign policies, thereby leading to America's defeat. It would be better, I argued, to face the unpleasant reality head on and recognize that the forces led and personified by Osama bin Laden are motivated and united by an ever-deepening hatred for the impact of U.S. foreign policy in the Muslim world. Unqualified support for Israel, a half-century of protecting and nurturing Muslim police states, and a military presence in Muslim lands—these were the tangible, physical manifestations of U.S. foreign policy that are perceived by most—yes, definitively, most—Muslims as a concerted and deliberate attempt to destroy Islam and its followers. This formulation was meant to alert Americans to what I saw as an existential threat to the United States that was in some ways greater than that which had been posed by the Soviet Union. It was more dangerous because it came from an opponent that was far less easy to define, one who, unlike the USSR, had virtues and a thoroughly human and egalitarian theology, and one that was all but impossible to contain and deter.

My arguments were not meant to be a condemnation of U.S. leaders, policymakers, and their foreign policy as mad, evil, or imperialistic. My goal was simply to suggest that our foreign policies toward the Muslim world had been in place for a very long time, some for more than thirty years, and had run out of gas; that they were not doing the only thing U.S. foreign policies must do: ensure the protection and promote the expansion of liberty and freedom at home, keep America as safe as possible from external attack, and serve as a model of responsible and humane self-government for those abroad who might choose to emulate it.

More often than not my writings were used by pundits as prime examples of raw America-hating, cowardly appeasement, anachronistic isolationism, and fierce anti-Semitism. Well, so be it. If putting forward a belief that holds U.S. national security interests to be a limited and narrowly defined set of life-and-death issues wins for me such ugly and meant-to-be debate-halting monikers so prized by the U.S. governing elites, I will listen, dismiss them, and press on.

In deciding to research and write a third book that falls into the category of the United States versus the forces led and inspired by Osama bin Laden, I became increasingly interested in and finally fixed on a single question: "Is the protection of U.S. interests and American citizens, and the maintenance of American sovereignty, independence, and freedom of action, any longer the primary, overriding concern of the U.S. federal government?" The answer should obviously be an emphatic yes, at all times and on every issue. And yet the more I read, researched, and encountered the discrepancy between the words and deeds of U.S. leaders, and especially the vast gulf between their description of the world and the world as I perceived it, the more I became doubtful that the answer to the pivotal question above could be even a timid yes.

In the obsession with national security that has consumed Americans and their leaders since the 9/11 attacks on New York and Washington, we seem to have fallen into the belief not only that the world changed forever on that date but also that nothing before that date contributed to the events of 9/11 or those that have ensued. In part this is because, as I noted above, we have refused to frankly assess whether the cumulative impact of thirty-plus years of U.S. foreign policies in the Muslim world may have helped to motivate the Islamists who attacked on 9/11 in the name of defending their faith and brethren.[1] In this regard, and to paraphrase the venerable Satchel Paige, our elites seem afraid to look over their shoulders because the truth might be gaining on them. Also contributing to this situation is the fact that most Americans have a difficult time imagining they are anything but good-hearted and benign, or that their impact on the world is anything but generous and uplifting. Cynically, our governing elites use this ingrained predisposition to condemn and defame those who suggest that U.S. policies helped to encourage our enemies on their path to 9/11 and beyond. Our elites, after all, have been the craftsmen, purveyors, and defenders of these policies for three-plus decades, and it is much less dicey in terms of unpleasant domestic political repercussions to savage those critical of their policies by dismissing them as blame-America-firsters.

Still, even accepting that our national self-esteem and our political leaders' political fortunes are most easily protected by maintaining the foreign-policy status quo, this did not seem a satisfactory excuse for what my research suggested was a deepening reluctance to make the protection of U.S. interests and citizens the federal government's top priority, and an almost blasé acceptance of war for purposes unconnected to America's national interests. And *reluctance* is not even the right word to use; it seems rather a combination of shame, embarrassment, and fear of employing American resources to protect Americans. The more I read and reflected on my own two-plus decades of service at the Central Intelligence Agency (CIA), the more likely it seemed that the answer to the question, "Does protecting Americans come first?" is very plainly no. The organizing concept of the federal government is no longer, as the Founders intended, the protection and expansion of freedom, liberty, and the rule of law at home, with a foreign policy, backed when necessary by military force, designed to ensure the maintenance of that domestic environment. "The Founding Fathers," the brilliant historian Walter A. McDougall has reminded his fellow citizens, "flatly denied that the United States ought to be in the business of changing the world, lest it only change itself—for the worse. . . . [T]hey saw foreign policy as an instrument for the preservation and expansion of American freedom and warned that crusades would belie our ideals, violate our true interests, and sully our freedom."[2] Today, however, the federal government's organizing principle flows directly from the country's pop culture; namely, the federal government, under Republican or Democratic control, does what is easiest, most expedient, least risky, politically correct and opportune, and most sellable. In the present case, these actions are anchored in neither the Founders' intent nor any significant knowledge of American history or the history of the Muslim world.

In essence, U.S. independence and safety are now threatened by our elites consistently asking the wrong question about national-security policy. Instead of asking what could happen if we do not respond in a timely manner and eliminate a particular threat to the United States—that is, what will the failure to act cost America in lives and treasure?—U.S. governing elites ask what will happen if they do act to defend America. The answer to the first question is very substantive and specific. For example, if President Bill Clinton fails to kill Osama bin Laden in the late 1990s, and if President George W. Bush fails to kill Abu Musab al-Zarqawi before March, 2003, both will live to have the chance to execute the deadly actions against the United States they repeatedly promised. Thus, it seems to be only common sense to say that it is better to try to kill bin Laden and al-Zarqawi and fail than not to try at all. The answer to the second question is usually another set of questions from U.S. political leaders and senior bureaucrats that stress the negative political costs that could accrue to U.S. leaders who authorize such actions when the actions subsequently fail to achieve their aim. Using the case of bin Laden, these questions include: "What will the world think of us if we attack and miss? Won't the Europeans view us as hip-shooters? If innocents get killed, won't we alienate Europeans, Muslims, or fill-in-the-blank others around the world?"[3] Summing the answers to such questions usually yields paralysis or an action that is ineffective and that allows—and sometimes encourages—those behind the danger at hand to become more confident, bolder, and increasingly lethal.

I refer here to the bin Laden and al-Zarqawi cases because I am familiar with them on a direct, first-hand basis, but it is easy to see what inaction or ineffective action has yielded in the cases of North Korea and Iran and in the failure to annihilate Saddam Hussein's Iraq in 1991. In short, the reason the U.S. federal government does not put the protection of America first is that our governing elites do not believe the United States is worth defending if the world audience they are playing to will criticize the actions they take in America's interests. Our current elite—including the second Bush administration, which talks tough but refuses to kill the numbers of enemies needed to win America's wars—takes its guidance on how and when to protect America from its estimate of how the liberal Western media will react and National Public Radio's pacifist theory of international relations, not from *The Federalist Papers* or Washington's Farewell Address.

This reality, I think, goes far toward explaining the series of unmitigated overseas disasters that America has experienced since September 11, 2001. In an almost mindless way, the making of U.S. national security and defense policy for much of the past three decades has followed the path of least resistance, which happened likewise to be the path of least effectiveness. The single, awe-inspiring exception to the rule was Ronald Reagan's decision to use his best judgment to buck the status quo politicians, diplomats, intelligence officers, academics, and pundits and try to terminate the seemingly endless Cold War by using the truth and the wondrously productive U.S. economy to break Mikhail Gorbachev and the Soviet Union. This effort stands out even more starkly because Mr. Reagan's administration in many ways was not much different from its predecessors and successors in choosing the paths of least resistance for its overall foreign policy, especially in such traditional stand-pat areas as Israel, energy policy, and support for Arab tyrannies.

Introduction

Mr. Reagan, more than any other American leader in our lifetime, recognized and exploited the enormous gap between the hardworking, insular, can-do, tough, and goal-oriented American people and their soft, fearful, and antinationalist bipartisan elites. Reagan's rhetoric and personal rapport with Americans intimidated the perpetually fearful elites and allowed him to reach past them and carry Americans with him as he successfully attained the end-state that is so foreign, feared, and lacking in sophistication to our elite—the scoring of a complete and utter victory for America by annihilating the USSR. Reagan's personal courage was such that at the Reykjavik Summit he simply stood up and walked away from a disbelieving Mikhail Gorbachev when the latter's take-it-or-leave-it offer failed to protect U.S. security; he knew full well that the Western media and elites would rake him mercilessly over the coals for not wanting peace at any price. So out of character was such decisiveness, integrity, and clarity of thought and purpose in post-Vietnam U.S. politics—and so appalled were our elites by the risks Reagan prudently but cheerfully took—that the professorate has spent the last twenty years trying to prove Reagan never really existed, that the out-of-luck, nuclear gangster Gorbachev was the real hero of the moment, or that both sides held equal moral responsibility for the Cold War. Bosh. Reagan won for America hands down; he said the only acceptable outcome of the Cold War was "we win and they lose," and he delivered that end-state. Indeed, so definitive and durable was Reagan's victory that it has taken twelve years of Bush presidencies and eight years of Clintonism to completely squander Reagan's achievement and legacy.

The high point of Reagan's presidency—destroying Gorbachev and the Bolsheviks—stands in stark contrast to the general conduct of non–Cold War specific U.S. foreign policy since 1973. From that year until 2001, U.S. foreign policy was conducted on the basis of political expediency: popularity maintained, with few risks taken, little offense given, and none but the Soviet threat eliminated. U.S. national-security interests in the era were frequently proclaimed, discussed, and legislated, but they were seldom defended. During these thirty-plus years, the U.S. government disinvested in national security by assuming that the status quo in which its foreign policies operated was permanent, refusing to destroy the emerging Islamist threat to the nation, and consistently expanding the list of pseudo–national-security interests to include such American domestic priorities but hardly life-and-death foreign-policy issues as human rights, spreading democracy, religious freedom, nation-building, and women's rights. By 2001, when the stage was set for al-Qaeda to attack New York and Washington, the United States was bound by a series of commitments that all but negated its freedom of maneuver and left it facing a slate of long-ignored, festering threats, armed with an outdated and innovation-restricting set of foreign policies. As a result, the 9/11 attacks found America so hobbled that its government was unable to draft and implement a focused, coherent, and effective response that promised victory. America is today less secure than it was on what al-Qaeda refers to as "the Tuesday of God's glory" because its post-1973 leaders, as Machiavelli wrote in 1513, never "reflected in tranquil times that there might come a change (and it is human nature when the seas are calm not to think of storms)."[4]

Author's Note

Which is more blameworthy, those who will see and steadily pursue
their own interests, or those who cannot see, or seeing will not act
wisely?

George Washington, 1790

It is truly unfortunate that those engaged in public affairs so rarely
make notes of transactions passing within their knowledge. Hence
history becomes fable instead of fact. The great outlines may be true,
but the incidents and colouring are according to the faith and fancy
of the writer.

Thomas Jefferson, 1814

In two earlier books I tried to lay out for Americans what I saw as the dangers we faced from Osama bin Laden and his al-Qaeda organization, as well as from the growing Sunni Islamist militant movement they led and inspired.[1] My method in both was as simple and straightforward as my prose style allowed: I let bin Laden and his lieutenants speak for themselves. I then took those words and tried to do two things with them. First, I sought to place their words in the context of fourteen-plus centuries of Islamic history, and second, I attempted to assess how these men matched their words to their deeds. My bottom line in both books was that in their public remarks bin Laden and the other Islamist leaders had been extraordinarily precise in stating the motivations that drove them to war; that bin Laden was a master of Islamic history and had structured his narrative for war against the United States in a manner that was fully consistent with the causes for defensive jihads throughout Islamic history, thus resonating positively with Muslims worldwide; and that the correlation between the words and deeds of bin Laden, his lieutenants, and their allies was close to perfect—if they said they were going to do something, they were much more than likely to try to do it. Their record in this regard puts Western leaders to shame.

Based on these findings, I argued in both books that there was no inherent reason why U.S. presidents and others in the American governing elite could honestly misunderstand the motivation of our Islamist enemies and the centrality of U.S. foreign policy to that motivation and to mobilizing support for the Islamists in the Muslim world. I was wrong about their ability to misunderstand, but I still do not believe that they can do so honestly. With President Washington, I believe that they see the Islamist problem but do not act wisely. So instead of trying to explain once more what is plainly obvious to me—and I suspect it is being sensed by growing numbers of Americans, given Washington's recent overseas setbacks—I thought a better tack was to try to understand what makes U.S. leaders resist following Sun Tzu's commonsense advice to "know your enemy" when it comes to the war against al-Qaeda.

I am the first to admit that this book is eclectic, impressionistic, and at times idiosyncratic. In examining the stubborn wrongheadedness of U.S. leaders, for example, I found that part of the answer lies in decisions taken twenty years before almost any American ever heard the name Osama bin Laden. Washington's decisions to keep America dependent on foreign energy suppliers, and its unquestioning, joined-at-the-hip policy of supporting Israel and Saudi Arabia, are the two most obvious 1970s-vintage policies that would turn out to be sources of strength for militant Islam. The U.S. governing elite's failure to change any significant part of its Cold War–era view of the world and how it works also has contributed greatly to America's so-far-losing performance against the Islamists. This inability to change with the times is apparent in the failure of U.S. leaders to recognize the abrogation of the Cold War's implicit limits on how much military violence could be applied in a given situation to ensure the nuclear threshold would not be crossed. America now faces an enemy who recognizes no such limits, cannot be deterred, and since 1992 has been seeking a nuclear device to use in the continental United States. Nonetheless, U.S. and Western leaders generally behave as if Cold War rules are still functioning and as if shock-and-awe attacks that smash concrete but kill few will cow our enemies.

My research also found a basis for our current predicament vis-à-vis Islam in the at-best-mediocre presidential leadership Americans have been afforded since the Cold War's end. On the whole, George H.W. Bush, Bill Clinton, and George W. Bush did virtually nothing to educate Americans about a world that is increasingly threatening to America and at the same time is less predictable, controllable from Washington, and tolerant of U.S. orders, advice, direction, or—most of all—intervention. The first Mr. Bush's twaddle about a New World Order led and managed by the United States still dominates the thinking of the federal government's executive and legislative branches. It also blinds many in and out of government to the fact that the United States can no longer dictate much of anything in the world. The most recent example of this blindness is clearly evident in *The Iraq Study Group Report*.[2] In an era that is fraught with war, strident nationalisms, ethnic chauvinism, and intensifying religious militancy, the commission chaired by James Baker III and Lee Hamilton issued a report that is written by and for U.S. leaders who still operate as if none of this is true, as if they are still the Cold War masters of the ballet of international politics, and as if unfolding or unexpected international events can be managed according to U.S. preferences and timetables.[3]

The second Mr. Bush's obsession with building debilitating coalitions and alliances to respond to attacks solely directed at America is another good example of an unhelpful modus operandi left over from the U.S.-Soviet confrontation. The time consumed by Mr. Bush and Secretary of State Colin Powell in building the coalition for Afghanistan would have been far better spent killing Taliban and al-Qaeda fighters before they were fully dispersed. In many ways both Mr. Bushes, although they greatly differ in the tone and wording of their rhetoric, are still Cold War–style leaders who are unable to recognize that neither time, tide, nor those who threaten us will wait for Washington to dot each "i" and cross each "t" before it acts.

And Mr. Clinton, of course, was and is the personification of all that was worst in Cold War America, a man embarrassed by the unsophisticated nature of American life and so armed with a passionate thirst to be loved and applauded by European and Hollywood elites; holding deep-seated animosity toward the U.S. military and intelligence services; and displaying a willingness to sacrifice American lives and interests to protect his standing as "the world's president" and keep earning the applause of the young, callow, inexperienced, and anti-American. No single individual could have done more than Mr. Clinton to neutralize much of the Islamist threat that today threatens America's survival. No other individual could have conceivably achieved less in that regard.[4]

Beyond looking at the legacy of foreign policy and leadership that brought America to 9/11, the Iraq war, and the abyss toward which it is now slipping, my other intention in writing this book is to try to undo some of the disservice rendered to Americans by the eleven-member 9/11 Commission, cochaired by former New Jersey Republican governor Thomas H. Kean and former Indiana Democratic congressman Lee H. Hamilton. That set of commissioners had a signal opportunity to examine, identify, and begin to fix all the problems with worldview, policy, and leadership listed above. Yet they not only failed, they knowingly shirked their responsibility to do so. By failing to find an individual culpable for anything that occurred on or before September 11, 2001 (in their words, "our aim has not been to assign individual blame"[5]) the commissioners uncovered a first in human history: a first-order military disaster that was caused by an inanimate organizational structure, that of the U.S. Intelligence Community (IC), and not by the failures of the men and women who were charged with running the organization. By refusing to point fingers, the commissioners did not tell Americans the truth that two presidents, the National Security Council, and senior IC leaders were not passive, helpless observers of an organizational structure run amok but negligent individuals who preferred not to rock the bureaucratic boat or offend the U.S. media and international opinion and so provided Osama bin Laden a much smoother and safer road to 9/11 than he had any right to expect.

Also left unexamined and unchallenged by the commissioners were the U.S. foreign policies that are at the core of America's growing confrontation with the Muslim world. While some would argue that the 9/11 commissioners had no writ to comment on U.S. foreign policy, I believe that to carry out their task of revitalizing the IC, the commissioners at a minimum had to voice this reality and note that no matter how much the IC's organization was improved, the pending war with Islam would continue to increase in the threat that it posed to America as long as the foreign-policy status quo remained. The commissioners and their staffers certainly recognized that the traditional role of the IC to support and implement U.S. foreign policy faced a unique problem: the more the IC succeeded in its traditional role, the stronger America's Islamist enemies became. For example, the more the IC effectively supported Israel against the Palestinians and the Saudis against domestic Islamist insurgents, the more leaders like bin Laden could persuade the Muslim world that Washington allowed Israel to kill Muslims at will and that the al-Saud regime was simply America's agent for destroying the mujahedin. Between finding no individual culpable and refusing to comment on the biggest problem facing the U.S. intelligence community—the impact of U.S. foreign policy—the Kean-Hamilton commissioners seem certain to go down in history as men and women who made a long war and a worse-than-9/11 attack inside America all but inevitable.

This point leads me to make a few comments on the source materials used in this book. The bulk of those materials are the works of Western, Muslim, and Islamist journalists, scholars, and strategists, and they are listed in the book's endnotes and bibliography. As in my earlier work, I have tried to use easily accessible source materials in an effort to demonstrate that Americans can learn and then think about this threat for themselves and do not need to depend solely on their leaders' views. In Chapter 7 I have also drawn on readily available materials to show how easily bin Laden and other Islamist leaders can exploit America's open society to learn about, understand, and find the vulnerabilities of their U.S. enemy. In this regard, of course, the battlefield is sharply titled in favor of the Islamists, who would have even less excuse than ourselves for not knowing their enemy.

In this book, however, much of the text also is informed by my experiences and observations over the course of a career at the CIA that ran from September 19, 1982, until November 12, 2004. For the final nineteen of those twenty-two-plus years I served in the Directorate of Operations and managed covert-action operations in the Middle East and Southwest Asia. In December 1995 I formed the CIA's bin Laden unit and ran it until June 1999. I finished my career as the special adviser to the chief of a much bigger, post-9/11 bin Laden department. Even with my professional curriculum vitae in mind, the correct question for any diligent reader to ask is: "Why should I believe what a former federal bureaucrat has to say, especially if it runs counter to claims made and explanations provided in books authored by presidents, generals, secretaries of state, DCIs, and ambassadors?" That is an excellent, pertinent question and one that I certainly cannot answer to the satisfaction of all. I faced it before while a serving member of the CIA's Senior Intelligence Service, however, and it may help the current reader if I explain how I then tried to be credible to my audience using much of the same material that informs this book.

On the day of the 9/11 attacks it was clear that the CIA and the other IC components would be investigated for their "failures." As it turned out, I and my CIA colleagues participated in three such investigations: one by the CIA's inspector general; another by a joint congressional panel cochaired by then-senator Bob Graham (D-Florida) and then-congressman Porter Goss (R-Florida); and the independent investigatory commission headed by Governor Kean and Congressman Hamilton. Faced with these investigations, the veteran CIA officers who were most closely involved in tracking bin Laden and providing the White House with opportunities to capture or kill him, decided that their testimony—whether under oath or not—would be useless if they could not provide documents to back up what was told to the commissioners and their staffers.[6] Cognizant of our imperfect memories, and well aware of the always-overriding desire of such postdisaster investigatory commissions to flay the lowest-ranking civil servants,[7] those of us at the center of operations against bin Laden and al-Qaeda collectively decided to provide official documents to support testimony whenever possible. We naïvely believed that if the commissioners had been sent to protect the leaders of both parties and their lieutenants in the bureaucracy, they could ignore what we said—chalking it up to hearsay—but that they would be hard pressed, in the context of three thousand dead Americans, to ignore what was contained in official documents. We were wrong.

Let me here part company with my former CIA colleagues and say that henceforth I am speaking only for myself. Most of my colleagues are still working at the CIA and are therefore forbidden from speaking publicly about the issues raised in this book. If they did so, they would be subject to disciplinary action or dismissal. I also must add that nothing I have written in this book is based on any conversation with any officer still employed by the CIA or other IC component that occurred after the effective date of my resignation, November 12, 2004. Let me say it clearly: I alone am responsible for *all* of the contents of this book and it contains *no* information from any still-serving U.S. intelligence officer.[8]

As I was preparing to brief, answer questions, or give testimony to the trio of 9/11 investigatory panels, I wanted to be able to tell the truth as I knew it and as the documents showed it. To that end, I prepared a compilation of between 480 and 500 pages of official documents to take along with me whenever I was appearing before either commissioners or staffers. The documents included cables to and from CIA facilities overseas, internal CIA memoranda, e-mail messages between and among CIA officers, after-action reports, and a smattering of official documents from other government agencies.[9]

The binder in which I placed my documents, I must stress, did not contain notes I wrote down from memory long after the events, but rather contemporary, official, and electronically retrievable documents that would either support or not support what I had to say. To make the process work as smoothly as possible for the Kean-Hamilton commission, I decided to pass the entire binder to those commissioners and their staffers so it would be in front of them whenever we spoke.[10] It took me three attempts to get it passed to the 9/11 Commission through the clearinghouse that DCI George Tenet established in the CIA for the transfer of such material. I do not know why the first two attempts were unsuccessful, but on the third try I numbered each page by hand and consecutively with a black indelible marker, then telephoned the commission's executive director, Philip Zelikow, to confirm that it was in his hands. Mr. Zelikow confirmed that the binder had arrived, but I was never again called on to testify to or brief the commission.

I go into this detail to emphasize that the CIA thoroughly screened the documents in my binder, redacted them appropriately to protect sources and methods, and forwarded them to the 9/11 Commission. The documents therefore have no potential for damaging U.S. national security or for compromising the CIA's past or ongoing operations. Indeed, they were cleared of sensitive data by the CIA for the express purpose of allowing their use to help Americans understand why the 9/11 attacks occurred. The documents do, however, hold significant potential for embarrassing senior U.S. officials—elected, appointed, and civil service—but CIA regulations state that embarrassment does not constitute grounds for censoring. These documents, others, and the testimony held by the 9/11 Commission identify those who did not act to protect Americans and their interests; shows Americans the truth about foreign enemies, like Saudi Arabia, that U.S. leaders have for decades consistently identified as friends and allies; and shames each 9/11 commissioner for failing to give Americans a complete accounting of the events preceding 9/11.

I contend that if the commission had published at least some of the documents in my binder, Americans would have a far better fix on how very well the CIA performed, as well as a better understanding of the many senior officials in the federal government who had been knowingly negligent in not making sure everything possible was done to protect Americans and U.S. interests. This strikes me as particularly essential in the aftermath of President Clinton's petulant, over-the-top, and nationally televised insistence in September 2006 that he took advantage of every opportunity he had to eliminate Osama bin Laden—an assertion I know to be untrue. In addition, the importance of publishing these and the other redacted documents and sworn testimonies held by the 9/11 Commission has taken on increased importance because of two factors. First, the inability of the U.S. government to determine with any precision the number or content of the documents stolen from the National Archives by Samuel Berger, President Clinton's last national security adviser, and subsequently destroyed. Mr. Berger's self-admitted criminal behavior adds urgency to getting the full documentary record published because his plea agreement with the Department of Justice denied him security clearances for only three years. In other words, if the Democrats win the presidential election in 2008, there is every chance that Mr. Berger will receive a position of trust from the new president; indeed, he is already advising Senator Clinton on foreign policy. From that position, Mr. Berger could not only strike back at the critics of his crime and his incompetent, derelict performance as national security adviser against al-Qaeda, but also ensure the complete destruction of whatever incriminating documents his felonious scissors missed the first time around.[11]

The second factor is former DCI George Tenet's recent book, *At the Center of the Storm*.[12] As I will note below, there are other books about the pre-9/11 period that have been, from my perspective, deliberately misleading, Richard Clarke's *Against All Enemies* being—until Mr. Tenet's book—the first among equals in this regard.[13] Mr. Tenet's book, however, is much more dangerous than Mr. Clarke's and the others in terms of distorting history because Mr. Tenet served as the DCI—a nonpartisan position from which senior U.S. political leaders are told the truth about foreign affairs and threats to America—and yet he has no qualms about misleading Americans about the role Saudi Arabia played in hobbling U.S. efforts against bin Laden and al-Qaeda[14]; deceiving Americans about the chances to capture or kill bin Laden before 9/11[15]; and urging Americans not once but twice to blindly trust their bipartisan governing elite because they are all good people whose "motives" should not be questioned.[16] The documents I and many others provided to the 9/11 Commission would surely tell against the veracity of Mr. Tenet on these points.

Most disturbing, however, is Mr. Tenet's seemingly deliberate attempt to lay the groundwork for blaming President George W. Bush's administration, rather than Mr. Clinton's, if al-Qaeda detonates a nuclear device inside the United States. Mr. Tenet claims that such an attack is his biggest worry and argues, "Our nation ought to be moving heaven and earth to get a handle on all the deadly fissile material currently unaccounted for."[17] Now, no one can disagree with the former DCI on this point, but it is worth noting that Mr. Tenet claims that it was not until President Bush's watch in February 2001 that "al-Qaeda's pursuit of WMD became clear . . . [when] Jamal Ahmad al-Fadl, described how, as far back as 1993, he helped bin Laden try to obtain uranium in Sudan to be used in some type of nuclear device."[18] Thereafter, Mr. Tenet asserts, "the only responsible course of action [for the U.S. government] was to do whatever was necessary to rule out any possibility that the terrorists could get their hands on fissile material."[19] Again, no one can disagree with Mr. Tenet on this point, but Americans might like to know that the documents provided to the 9/11 Commission irrefutably show that Mr. al-Fadl's very specific and worrying information was not new in 2001 but rather had been first acquired by the U.S. from Mr. al-Fadl after he "walked in" to a U.S. embassy in Africa in the fall of 1996 and that it was available to Mr. Clinton and his National Security Council from that point until the end of the Democratic administration. Mr. Tenet's valid assertion that Mr. al-Fadl's information required the U.S. government "to do whatever was necessary" to eliminate the nuclear threat raises the question of why President Clinton and his national security advisers never acted to capture or kill the sponsor and manager of the nuclear threat, Osama bin Laden, when they had ten chances to do so between May 1998 and May 1999. Notwithstanding Mr. Tenet's attempt to make sure that Mr. Bush and the Republicans take the blame if a mushroom cloud one day appears over an American city, the documents in the 9/11 Commision's archive clearly show that all the political fallout, as well as direct responsibility for the accompanying deaths and economic catastrophe, will fall on Mr. Clinton, his national security team, and needless to say, the duplicitous Mr. Tenet.

Finally, I would like to remind readers that when I refer to the documents in my binder, I am doing so from memory. I studied those documents so closely and for so long, however, that I am confident that I am paraphrasing them correctly. For those interested in pursuing further study on these issues, I believe that I have described the binder (a black, four-or-five-inch, three-ring, government-issue binder) well enough to permit a fairly accurate Freedom of Information Act request for the material, which again has already been redacted by the CIA to eliminate all the concerns the CIA had in regard to the possible compromise of sources and methods. This is one case where the paucity of documents by government officials lamented by Jefferson is not a problem. Indeed, I think that many of these documents could be described as what Jefferson called on another occasion "morsel[s] of history" which are things "so rare always to be valuable."[20] And their publication, along with other documents and testimony held by the 9/11 Commission, might begin to negate the effort of the George W. Bush administration and our overall governing elite to "dissuade Americans from peering too deeply at the events of 9/11. Were they to do so, they might just pose discomfiting questions about the competence of our leaders, the organization and purposes of government, and the rationale of U.S. foreign policy."[21]

PART I

GETTING TO 9/11

If the liberties of America are ever completely ruined . . . it will in all probability be the consequence of a mistaken notion of prudence, which leads men to acquiesce in measures of the most destructive tendency for the sake of present ease.

Samuel Adams, 1771

On September 11, 2001, history began exacting revenge from America's bipartisan governing elite for thirty years of ill-considered, path-of-least-resistance decisions and policies that had disinvested in U.S. security, as well as for its inability to alter the worldview that forms the basis for U.S. national-security policy—even as they chanted that the Cold War was over and fresh foreign-policy thinking was required. The 9/11 attacks found U.S. leaders ignorant both of America's lack of options that had been created by a quarter-century of decisions taken "for the sake of present ease," and of the dimensions and power of the Islamist foe their policies had nurtured. They also were boundlessly confident that the approaches that brought victory in the Cold War would ensure the quick and utter destruction of the forces led, inspired, and instigated by Osama bin Laden and al-Qaeda.

Between 1973 and 9/11, U.S. foreign policy in the Muslim world committed Americans to the untenable position of supporting and protecting the viability of an endless religious war-to-the-death between Israelis and Arabs. In economic policy, moreover, Washington ignored the warning shot fired by the Saudi Arabia–led 1973 oil embargo and decided to let the

U.S. economy remain dependent on energy supplies from a group of foreign nations that had used oil as an anti-U.S. weapon. This steady and deliberate disinvestment in U.S. national security also encouraged the growth of Islamist militancy by allowing Islamist leaders to demonstrate to their audiences that America was an extraordinary and malignant hypocrite, rhetorically championing democracy and liberty for all peoples, while specializing in the killing and brutal oppression of Muslims, supporting Israel in the former and Muslim police states like Saudi Arabia in the latter.

Between 1996 and 9/11, Washington compounded the damage caused by its prolonged security disinvestment with an equally debilitating failure to shuck off Cold War thinking and accept that history had resumed with a vengeance. For the U.S. governing elite, the Islamists were not a threat to U.S. national security but a lethal nuisance that could be defeated at the pace and moment and with means decided by the United States. Washington was about to learn that security disinvestment and a Cold War hangover left it to confront Islamism with few good options, and so, to paraphrase what Mr. Lincoln once said in another losing situation: If there is a place worse than hell in 2008, Americans are now in it.[1]

CHAPTER 1

Readying bin Laden's Way:

America and the Muslim World, 1973–1996

The future always comes as a surprise, but political wisdom consists
in attempting at least some partial judgment of what that surprise
might be. And for my part I cannot but believe that a main unexpected thing of the future is the return of Islam.

> Hilaire Belloc, 1938

My young friends, history is a river that may take us where it will.
But we have the power to navigate, to choose the direction, and
make our passage together.

> Ronald Reagan, April 1984

It has become a commonplace to argue that the world changed forever on
September 11, 2001. Only rarely in history, however, can a specific date be
pointed to with accuracy as such a landmark. Generally, important events
that happen on specific days—July 4, Austrian Archduke Franz Ferdi-
nand's 1914 assassination, and Fort Sumter's surrender—are points of
culmination, the end-points of lengthy series of events that occurred over
years prior to the date that came to be seen as a historical breaking point.
Independence Day was the culmination of a quarter-century of increasing
alienation between Great Britain and her American colonies; the archduke's murder triggered a war between two rival military alliances that had
been rapidly arming and bumping against each other for a decade or more;
and the cannonading of Fort Sumter capped two decades of political jockeying, acrimonious sectional partisanship, and finally a crisis over the
westward extension of slavery.

If the world did change fundamentally for America on and after 9/11—and I tend to think that it did, and greatly for the worse—the change was caused not by the attack but by the foreign-policy decisions taken and implemented over the preceding three-plus decades. During that period, I will argue, the federal government, under both parties, steadily disinvested in U.S. national security vis-à-vis the Muslim world, both by the things it did and by those that it did not do. While Washington had invested heavily, and by the end of 1991 successfully, in defeating the Soviet Union in the Cold War, its ability to protect the country against other threats had simultaneously withered. Washington's mindset seemed to be that the United States was vulnerable only to the USSR and that none of the other wars, problems, and threats in the international system would ever reach the status of endangering national security. The term *national-security threat,* for purposes of this book, is defined in the narrow (and I suppose old-fashioned) sense of a life-and-death threat to the nation's survival. In turn, the term *national interest* is used herein to denote an issue of utmost importance because it involves the survival of the United States. Dependence on anti-U.S. energy-supplying states is a national security threat to the United States, for example, and therefore ending that debilitating dependence is a national interest of the United States. Establishing U.S.-like women's rights regimes abroad, on the other hand, is an admirable ambition, but the lack thereof is not a national security threat to the United States, and by definition, the creation of such regimes overseas cannot be deemed a national interest.

As noted above, the discussion that follows will strike some as eclectic and even eccentric in its choice of the 1973–96 foreign-policy issues on which it focuses. In response I can only say that the topics covered in this chapter are those that, at least in my estimate, contributed substantially and directly to the unwitting but almost systematic elimination of U.S. foreign-policy options in regard to the transnational Islamist groups that began finding their legs in the years after Israel defeated its multiple Arab-state attackers in 1973. Some of the issues discussed below did not immediately sound alarms about the nascent Islamist threat, but over time they have proven to be nearly immovable obstacles in the path of America's ability to plot a course that will deliver victory over that threat. No better examples of the ever-tightening shackles on America's ability to maneuver and defend itself against the Islamist threat can be found, for example, than the policies Washington set in 1973 toward Israel, Saudi Arabia, and energy policy. In addition, several of the topics in this chapter have not received much public discussion, such as the enduring negative impact for America of the Clinton administration's military response to Saddam Hussein's 1993 attempt to kill former president George H.W. Bush. I have included lesser-known topics because I believe they contributed to the mess in which we now find ourselves mired in the Muslim world, and because I had first-hand exposure to how U.S. leaders perceived and handled the problems.

For Americans, I believe, their country's current quandary is founded on the failure of its governing elite to study U.S. and world history and perhaps, even more, to recognize that their faith in American exceptionalism does not equate to America being exempt from the lessons, warnings, and wisdom acquired by studying history. How much less dangerous would America's current confrontation with the Islamists be, for example, had its leaders simply followed the most important advice for foreign-policy makers available in the canon of Western political science and philosophy? "I am not ignorant that many have been and are of the opinion that human affairs are so governed by Fortune and by God, that man cannot alter them by any prudence of theirs, and indeed have no remedy against them," Niccolò Machiavelli wrote in 1513, "and for this reason have come to think that it is not worthwhile to labor much about anything, but that they must leave everything to be determined by chance.

> Often when I turn the matter over, I am in part inclined to agree with this opinion . . . Nevertheless, that our free will be not wholly set aside, I think it may be that Fortune is the mistress of one half our actions, and yet leaves the control of the other half, or a little less, to ourselves. And I would liken her to one of those wild torrents which, when angry, overflow the plains, sweep away trees and houses, and carry off soil from one bank to throw it sown upon another. Everyone flees before them, and yields to their fury without the least power to resist. And yet, though this be their nature, it does not follow that in the seasons of fair weather, men cannot, by constructing weirs and moles, take such precautions as to cause them when again in flood to pass off by some artificial channel, or at least prevent their course from being so uncontrolled and destructive. And so it is with Fortune, who displays her might where there is no organized strength to resist

her, and directs her onset where she knows there is neither barrier nor embankment to confine her.[1]

From 1973 to this day I would argue that U.S. policymakers have done little to prepare for changes of what Machiavelli called "Fortune" in the Muslim world. As will be seen, U.S. policies were based on the assumption of an unchanging status quo and were designed to follow the path of least resistance. When war with the Islamists came, therefore, the United States had no policy options other than the status quo and had built no "weirs or moles" with which to deflect or channel the Islamists' violence back toward its primary targets, Muslim regimes and Israel. This lack of prudent common sense left the United States adrift and in a state where reacting to the actions of others was the order of the day. "And so when occasion requires the cautious man to act impetuously," Machiavelli wrote in words that exactly mirror the optionless reality faced by U.S. policymakers on 9/11, "he cannot do so and is undone; whereas, had he changed his nature with time and circumstances, his fortune would have been unchanged."[2]

1973: Israel, Saudi Arabia, and Oil—America's Shackles

In 1973, America confronted two major challenges in the Middle East, and while it did not suffer an immediate outright defeat in dealing with either, both would prove to be paralyzing burdens on the United States when it moved to respond to the 9/11 attacks.

America's first major 1973 challenge flowed from the Arab-Israeli war of that year. Under President Richard Nixon and Secretary of State Henry Kissinger, the U.S. government went to Israel's rescue during the Yom Kippur War by providing unlimited financial support and military equipment, as well as by standing toe-to-toe with the Soviet Union—risking nuclear war—to prevent Moscow's all-out support for Israel's Arab foes. After the superb and U.S.-resupplied Israeli military rallied to defeat the Arab armies, U.S. aid proved to be, not a stopgap, wartime measure, but the opening of a spigot through which would flow unlimited, no-strings-attached financial, military, and diplomatic support for Israel. As the level of this support grew, so too did efforts by pro-Israel Americans in both parties and large parts of academia, the media, and Hollywood—complemented by what can only be described as superbly effective covert political action by Israel's intelligence services[3]—to entwine U.S. support for Israel ever more deeply and inextricably into U.S. domestic politics. Indeed by the morning of the 9/11 attacks, unquestioning U.S. support for Israel was as much a domestic political issue—exactly the same kind of politically sacrosanct "third rail" as Social Security—as it was a foreign-affairs matter. Of all the foreign policy issues that have come before the American people in their history, support for Israel was and is perhaps the only one that is certainly immune to challenge or change and very nearly exempt from comment, criticism, or debate. And Israel, of course, is not the real problem here. Reasonable people can disagree over what the nature of U.S. support for Israel—if any—should be. The problem lies, rather, in the reality that such disagreement and the debate it would naturally engender are not possible in America because critics of the relationship are shouted down as anti-Semites by the bipartisan governing elite and Israel's U.S.-citizen acolytes and agents.

The inauguration and domestication of the U.S.-Israel relationship surely ranks as one of the least debated and most undemocratic watershed events in American history, one that is now costing us both blood and treasure and will cost us much more of each in the future. The U.S. federal government, without any initial authorization save the president's decision, tied America's future relations with the Islamic world to an ever-tightening, one-way relationship with the state of Israel, a country devoid of any natural, political, or geographic resources needed by the United States; virtually undefendable against a united foe; and then as now absolutely irrelevant and manifestly counterproductive to the national-security interests of the United States. All of President Nixon's successors and all successive Congresses have tied the United States more closely and expensively to Israel, to the extent that an attack of any sort on Israel is responded to by Washington as if an enemy had reached out and smashed Delaware or some other state of the Union.

While Nixon risked nuclear war with Moscow for Israel's sake, today America, as the unquestioning superpower supporter of anything and everything that Israel does, confronts more than a billion Muslims. One cannot help but wonder what the Founders would have thought of such an absurd situation, one in which Americans and their future are put increasingly at risk to further the interests of a state that contributes nothing to

America's economic welfare or strategic security but rather is a drain on both. Reflect for a moment on George Washington's advice to his countrymen on the occasion of his retirement from the presidency, then decide for yourself if America's current relationship with Israel is in the national interest. In foreign policy, Washington wrote,

> a passionate attachment of one Nation for another produces a variety of evils. Sympathy for the favorite nation, facilitating the illusion of an imaginary common interest, in cases where no real common interest exists, and infusing into one the enmities of the other, betrays the former into a participation in the quarrels and Wars of the latter, without adequate inducement or justification. It leads also to concessions to the favorite Nation of privileges denied to others, which is apt doubly to injure the Nation making the concessions; by unnecessarily parting with what ought to have been retained; and by exciting jealousy, ill will, and a disposition to retaliate, in the parties from whom eql. [equal] privileges are withheld. And it gives to ambitious, corrupted, or deluded citizens (who devote themselves to the favorite Nation) facility to betray, or sacrifice the interests of their own country, without odium, sometimes even with popularity; gilding with the appearances of a virtuous sense of obligation a commendable deference for public opinion, or a laudable zeal for public good, the base or foolish compliances of ambition, corruption or infatuation.[4]

Is there a better description of the dangers America faces because of its governing elite's "passionate attachment" to Israel? Is not our adversarial relationship with the Palestinians and Muslims generally an example of the "infusing" into America of the "enmities" of Israel? And what better definition of the double standard that our Islamist foes cite is there than the "concessions to the favorite Nation of privileges denied to others" in the form of the constant U.S. veto of any UN resolution condemning Israeli actions?

It is fashionable in these days to regard Washington—and America's other Founders, who will be cited periodically throughout this book—as irrelevant, as dead white men, as antiquated, and as morally abhorrent because some of them owned black slaves. This attitude is a mistake for any American to take. The Founders remain vitally relevant to the conduct of American domestic politics and foreign policy, not because they could

26

see the impact of such future developments as transcontinental railroads, the cell phone, ballistic missiles, Social Security, and nuclear weapons. They clearly could not, and so have little value to us as soothsayers. The Founders' eternal relevance for Americans is based on their study and knowledge of human beings, of how human beings act and interact, and of the manifest imperfectibility of human beings. When the Founders met in 1787 in Philadelphia to write the American constitution, as the brilliant professor Daniel Robinson has said, they drew on the totality of the "political life of early America [which itself] is an extended treatise on the nature of human nature, informed by scripture, informed by Christian apologists, informed by philosophers."[5] The Founders' wisdom must remain in the forefront of American thinking not because they were demigods but because they were, by their own admission, flawed human beings who used that knowledge about themselves and others to shape a nation capable of an ongoing effort to build an equitable society, preventing the growth of tyrannical power at home, and savvy enough to survive in a world of competitive nation-states and frequent wars.

Let me pause here to note that my attitude toward Israel—and almost all other nations—turns solely on its usefulness, or lack thereof, to the United States. I always have argued that Israel should and must do whatever it believes is necessary to protect its citizens and territorial integrity from its Muslim enemies. I have no quarrel with Israel's actions; nor am I arrogant enough to make recommendations for policy changes for the Israeli people. My criticism is not for Israel but for U.S. governments that have knowingly put America at risk on Israel's behalf. Nothing in America's relationship with Israel rises to the level of a U.S. national interest as defined above. Given this reality, it is dangerous and ultimately self-defeating to confuse the tremendous emotional attachment some U.S. citizens and most of the American governing elite have for Israel—with the campaign contributions of many of the former often cementing the support of many of the latter— with the actual existence of a genuine U.S. national security interest in the survival of Israel. No such interest exists, and what substantive ties do exist hardly justify the contribution they make to what is becoming an endless war between the United States and the Muslim world.

Much of the unreality in U.S. attitudes toward Israel is the result of ahistorical arguments that Israel has "the right to exist." Clearly, no nation has the "right" to exist; Darwinian logic applies to nation-states as well as

27

to the other components of the animal kingdom. If there was such a right, the nations of the world would be working to resuscitate the Soviet Union, Sparta, Hannibal's Carthage, and the Latin Kingdom of Jerusalem. Nations exist as long as they can defend themselves, contain internal societal rot at nonfatal levels, maintain economic viability, and do not gratuitously make a constellation of more powerful enemies. This truism applies equally to all: the United States has no more right to exist than does Israel, Palestine, Bolivia, Saudi Arabia, Belgium, or Russia. "You form your country, and you take your chances" is a pretty good synopsis of history over the past several millennia. In regard to Israel, the U.S. governing elite—especially its neoconservative and liberal elements—have compounded the right-to-exist doctrine with a demand that Israel's enemies accept that right to exist before there can be talks or negotiations. The fairly and democratically elected Hamas government therefore must accept Israel's "right to exist" before talks between the two can begin and before Hamas can receive Western economic aid. In other words, Hamas must renounce a large part of the basis for its election—a willingness to fight and defeat Israel—and accept Israel's right to exist to avoid being economically strangled by the West. In this context, it is clear that the recognition of a state's "right to exist" is based not on a right at all but on one side's ability to coerce abject surrender from the other. Supporting Israel's "right to exist" is especially ahistorical when it is advocated by Americans, as it is a "right" they have never insisted on for their own nation. If they had, we would have never talked or negotiated with the Soviets after Premier Nikita Khrushchev promised that the USSR would "bury" the United States—surely a failure to acknowledge America's right to exist if there ever was one.

The second great challenge faced by the United States in 1973 was the oil embargo imposed by Saudi king Faisal to damage the U.S. economy in retaliation for Nixon's all-out support for Israel against the Arab armies. Although the rise in 1973 pump prices seems distant and inconsequential compared to the inflated prices in 2005–7, the shock to the U.S. economy and Americans' confidence thereon was nonetheless substantial. If common sense had prevailed or had even been in the general neighborhood, the embargo would have ignited a massive, federal government–led financial and brainpower investment in domestic oil and gas deposits, alternative energy sources, the design and manufacture of much more efficient automobile engines, and the development and proliferation of safer nuclear-power plants.

Sadly, as in the case of Washington signing up for automatic war when Israel is at war, neither common sense nor General Washington's guidance was anywhere to be found. Nearly thirty-five years after the first Saudi oil embargo, we have the same energy dependence, a reality that is made worse by lingering memories of ill-heated federal buildings and by the irritating recollection of President Jimmy Carter wearing Captain Kangaroo's cardigan while whimpering about the malaise in which American citizens were mired. No national energy policy has been forthcoming, although such a policy has been much talked about whenever prices at the pump begin to creep up. Whenever anyone has had the political courage to say that energy supply is an issue of national security as much as or more than a matter of economic policy and so should not be left to the crapshoot of market forces, he or she was shouted down by two groups. Both political parties' gun-for-hire economists, especially from the Republican side, would babble some economic jargon about oil being a "fungible commodity," the supply of which would be adequately allocated by international cooperation and market forces.[6] Any rejoinder arguing that unless the United States greatly reduced its energy independence, Americans would be in the economic thrall of foreigners and would eventually fight wars to ensure oil supplies, was greeted with contempt and derision: "Does the speaker not know that our close and loyal friends, the Saudis, would make sure America has adequate oil supplies?" Few seemed to recall that it was a Saudi king who authored the 1973 embargo, and fewer still seemed to recall the words of General Washington—words that hauntingly warn against decisions that make U.S. security dependent on so-called friendly nations. With relevance as strong today as in 1796, Washington warned his countrymen that wisdom lies in

> constantly keeping in view that it is folly in one nation to look for disinterested favors from another; that it must pay with a portion of its independence for whatever it may accept under that character; that, by such acceptance, it may place itself in the condition of having given equivalents for nominal favors, and of yet being reproached for not giving more.

There can be no greater error than to expect or calculate upon real favors from nation to nation. It is an illusion, which experience must cure, which a just pride ought to discard.[7]

The other attack on the advocates of increased energy independence came from America's ultimate elitists—the environmentalist purists, whose fanaticism undermines the ability to promote reasonable and much-needed environmental-protection measures in America. Phoning their congressmen from Volvos plastered with Ralph Nader and save-the-whale bumper stickers, these folks let it be known that they were all in favor of energy conservation and independence, as long as no Arctic hare was disturbed, and exotic shrimp and ferns could multiply in peace and comfort atop forever-untappable energy deposits on the floor of the Gulf of Mexico. In essence, the environmentalist elite much prefers to have U.S. Marines killed in overseas wars for oil—as is happening today—than to lose a species of aquatic plant life or a potentially succulent candidate for a tasty plate of shrimp scampi.

U.S. national security, therefore, suffered two enormous and slowly accelerating defeats in 1973, the cost of which would become increasingly clear in succeeding years, especially after 9/11. While rescuing Israel in 1973 might have made sense for the United States in Cold War terms, there seems to have been no sober second thought in Washington after the Yom Kippur War ended; no one asked the question, "What is America's real interest in an alliance with Israel?" One would have thought that the near-sinking of the U.S. naval ship *Liberty* by the Israeli air force might have caused someone to ask what sort of ally we were aligning ourselves with, but such was not the case. And if the near-destruction of the *Liberty* did not prompt the question, King Faisal's embargo clearly should have, by its display of both the depth of Arab-Israeli hostility and the potential price the Arabs had the capability to exact from Israel's supporters. But wariness and smarts in Washington were in short supply, and the Nixon administration signed up America on both sides of a religious war-to-the-finish between Israel and the Arab states. By cementing the U.S. relationship with Israel and turning the other cheek to King Faisal's attempt to destroy the U.S. economy, Washington made itself the abject servant of two unforgiving masters. Henceforth the political party in power in Washington gave Israel free rein to do as it liked because of the domestic political disaster that pro-

Israeli Americans could inflict on politicians who did not equate the protection of Israel with that of America, and it genuflected toward the Arab tyrants in Riyadh and elsewhere in the Gulf to ensure the steady oil supply that the U.S. economy needed to prosper and that, in turn, kept pump prices low and helped them to hold office.

Thus 1973 saw the start of a series of decisions that ran directly counter to one of the chief goals of any country's foreign policy, that of keeping open the greatest number of options so that the government maintains flexibility when the time comes to confront unexpected events. And no 20/20 hindsight is needed to draw this conclusion. The decisions Washington made regarding Israel, Saudi Arabia, and oil voluntarily gave strategic hostages to fortune and that was clear at the time; shortsightedness, negligence, and stupidity were and are blatant in Washington's decisions to tie U.S. national security to that of another nation-state, and to acquiesce in ceding to the anti-American Saudis control over U.S. access to the strategic commodity of oil. On and after 9/11, it would become clear that Washington's 1973 decisions on Israel and oil left the George W. Bush administration with virtually no room to maneuver in the Muslim world, though it must be said that the ideological rigidity and close oil-industry ties of Bush and his cabinet were such that they may have perceived no need for maneuverability. These shackles constricting America launched Uncle Sam into bin Laden's well-laid trap. "It is easy to make acquaintances," General Washington wrote in 1783 in words applicable to America's relationships with Israel and Saudi Arabia today, "but very difficult to shake them off, however irksome and unprofitable they are found, after once we have committed ourselves to them."[8]

1982: Watching the Mujahedin Assembly Line

While the U.S. defeats of 1973 resulted from conscious if ill-considered decisions and then their blithe perpetuation, 1982 ushered in an era of nondecisions in which the U.S. government and its major allies would simply stand by and idly watch the growth of a worldwide infrastructure of paramilitary training camps that specialized in training young Islamists as insurgents and terrorists. I chose 1982 as a starting point not because the first camps were organized in that year—Yassir Arafat's PLO and other secular, non-U.S.-threatening groups in the Muslim world and elsewhere had opened camps before then—but because Lebanese Hezbollah was formed in that year and soon thereafter began building its training camps in Lebanon's Biqa Valley. These camps became the world's flagship training installations for religiously motivated Shia militants. The Hezbollah camps were internationally known; they were condemned and threatened from every political rostrum in the United States and Western Europe; and they were left absolutely undisturbed. In the years after 1982, similar and often better-quality training camps began to be built for Sunni militants in places like Afghanistan, Iran, Iraq, Kashmir, Mindanao, Somalia, Sudan, Syria, and Yemen. Diverse Islamist groups, adhering to differing versions of Islam, received various kinds of military training in these camps. The camps themselves, moreover, ranged widely in quality from facilities that were the equal of camps used by nation-state militaries to ones that resembled home-made obstacle courses. The one commonality of all of these camps was that they operated without hindrance from the United States.

Washington and its European allies were watching the camps, however. In the decades since Hezbollah's birth, for example, mutiple components of the U.S. Intelligence Community have used their collection capabilities to annually assemble a review of all the known terrorist training camps in the world. The community also drew heavily on open-source material that surprisingly contained a good deal of detail, much of it provided by fighters who attended the camps. It seems frivolous to call this report a "yearbook," but in essence that is what it was. Growing in length with each passing year, these annual reports contained a separate section on each camp's attributes. The sections were updated each year (few camps were ever closed), and new sections were written to cover any new camps that had been discovered or built since the last issue of the yearbook. We could never be certain that we knew about all the camps that existed, but from Iraq's Salman Pak camp to Afghanistan's al-Faruq and Khaldun camps, to the bevy of camps run by Sudan's Popular Defense Forces, the CIA and the U.S. Intelligence Community kept a steady, inquisitive, and increasingly knowledgeable eye on these facilities.

The work of the CIA, its sister U.S. agencies, and foreign intelligence services, alas, proved to be an exercise in counterterrorist voyeurism; we collected intelligence for the sake of collecting intelligence. Until the

U.S.-led invasion of Afghanistan in October 2001, neither the United States nor any of its allies made a serious, systematic, and sustained effort to destroy the camps in even one of the countries in which they were located. Not even Hezbollah's camps in the Biqa Valley—the targets of immense martial ranting by Western leaders for more than two decades but still operating in 2008—were ever destroyed. Why? Two reasons, really. First, from the 1980s to this day Western governments talk a good game about the threat posed to national security by transnational entities (terrorists, narcotics traffickers, nuclear proliferators, etc.) but seldom demonstrate through their actions that they genuinely believe their own rhetoric. In this attitude the policymakers were often abetted by military officials who dismissed the camps as "jungle gyms" built of "rope ladders."[9] America builds weapons systems, fleets of aircraft carriers and submarines, strategic bombers, sophisticated satellites, and specialized military units to deploy against threats posed by nation-states, but it drafts not much more than angry words to deploy against transnational threats. Between 1982 and 2001 the universe of terrorist training camps was assailed only with harsh words, which did not harm them a lick.

The second reason terrorist camps lay undisturbed for nearly twenty years is that there were always other "nuances" in international politics that made it inconvenient for U.S. officials to take definitive military or covert action against camps that trained Islamist fighters to kill the citizens of America and its allies. We could not hit Hezbollah's camps, for example, because it might disrupt one of the always recurring and always false positive trends in Arab-Israeli relations; we could not take out camps on the island of Mindanao because it might complicate negotiations between the Philippine government and one or another of the groups of militant Moro Muslims; and we could not attack Salman Pak camp because Iraq was a Soviet client and an attack might disrupt détente or then perestroika. During my career, no senior U.S. official was better at using the nuance dodge than Richard A. Clarke, the NSC's longtime chief of counterterrorism. In his memoir Mr. Clarke delivers a perfect depiction of how the nuance argument works, showing how that even after the USS *Cole* was nearly sunk, Washington found it more important to help the Israelis than to bomb the al-Qaeda camps where some of the 9/11 attackers may well have been training. "Time was running out on the Clinton administration," Clarke wrote of the weeks after the attack on the *Cole*,

There was going to be one last major national security initiative and it was going to be a final try to achieve an Israeli-Palestinian agreement. It really looked like the long-sought goal was possible. The Israeli Prime Minister had agreed to major concessions. I would have liked to try both, Camp David and blowing up the al-Qaeda camps. Nonetheless, I understood. If we could achieve a Middle East peace much of the popular support for al-Qaeda would evaporate overnight [sic]. *There would be another chance to go after the camps.*[10]

If you work in the U.S. Intelligence Community, you become very familiar with the "nuance" argument; it comes up almost without fail each and every time an opportunity is developed or chanced upon to use military force or covert action to attack and destroy a threat to American citizens. When intelligence officers produce a black and white option such as "Here is a training camp; it is producing men who will kill Americans; this is how it can be destroyed," they are more often than not congratulated for fine detective work by senior IC officials and the senior grandees of the National Security Council. These individuals take the information and then wrap themselves in the sophisticated cloak of nuance, arguing that the intelligence is excellent but the officers who gathered it simply do not understand how an attack at this particular time, on this or that specific training camp, would be detrimental to maintaining a balance beneficial to the United States in the "ballet of international politics." The yield from this process is always the same: the Nuancers emerge victorious, no action is taken, and the final score is nuance 1, American security 0. The net result: the CIA's archives hold a lengthy shelf of terrorist training camp yearbooks featuring mind-numbing levels of detail on camps that were never attacked.[11]

Why is this important? Well, there are those reasons that most senior policymakers and bureaucrats find trivial: men and women from the CIA and other U.S. agencies risk their lives to acquire data about the camps, and American taxpayers pay extortionate taxes to make sure their government acquires the information needed to protect them and their children. And still, clear threats to the United States are left free to operate and strengthen. Leaving these trivialities aside, the story of the unmolested training camps is important because between 1982 and late 2001 those facilities produced tens of thousands of well-trained terrorists and insurgents, and those outside of eastern and southeastern Afghanistan are still producing fighters. The rough and open-source-based estimates for the total number of men trained in just the best-known Afghan training camps—al-Faruq, Darunta, Khaldun, Khowst, etc.—range between 40,000 and 100,000. Looking at the camps the U.S. government knew of—and remember, it is certain that Washington did not identify all of them—total numbers may well be five or ten times higher than the figure for those trained at the Afghan camps. That is, in the worst case, there could have been up to a million Islamists trained in camps around the world during the two decades after 1982.[12]

If that is not bad enough, it must be recalled that most of the world's Islamist training camps were created not only to train indigenous fighters—as in Afghanistan, Lebanon, and Sudan—but also to welcome nonlocal Muslims for training and perhaps some actual combat experience. These nonlocals were then sent home to undertake military action there. On returning, they did indeed undertake military operations, but they also set about training those who could not afford the cost (or procure the travel documents needed) to travel to a training camp abroad. And it is a sure bet that those trained at home by those trained abroad then went on to train others at home. Therefore the total number of fighters produced by the training camps increased geometrically, and there is yet no study that suggests a plausible methodology for pegging even a ballpark total figure. This brief look at the geometric expansion of the body of trained Islamist fighters over two decades, however, suggests that claims made by senior commanders in the U.S.-led coalitions in Iraq and Afghanistan to have killed four thousand in the former and three to four thousand in the latter amount to a barely discernible dent in the cadre trained since 1982.[13]

And what kind of paramilitary training did these fighters receive? Well, it varied from camp to camp, but a recent book by a former al-Qaeda fighter suggests that, at least in bin Laden's camps, the training was well suited to produce the formidable mujahedin that U.S. forces are now encountering around the world. Describing his mid-1990s training at al-Qaeda's Khaldun camp, Omar Nasiri explains that he learned to use "a huge variety of weapons."

> Abu Suhail [a senior al-Qaeda trainer] introduced me to guns I had never seen before. Most were German and Russian weapons from World War II

35

[Tokarov, Makarov, Walther PKK, SIG-Sauer, and Luger pistols] . . . Once I learned those, Abu Suhail taught me how to use the larger machine guns. First I trained on the Uzi . . . After that I trained on two more Soviet military guns: the Degtyarev DP, a light machine gun from the 1920s, and the RPD, which was introduced much later. It is a belt-fed machine gun with a built-in bipod. Abu Suhail finally taught me the legendary weapons invented by Mikhail Kalashnikov. First the Kalashnikov AK-47, a gas-operated rifle . . . And then I learned how to use the famous PK and PKM. These are fully automatic machine guns, fed from an ammunition belt . . . Finally, we moved on to larger artillery [sic]. First, we learned the Dushkas: the DShK and the DSkKM 12.7 [caliber machine guns] . . . After the Dushkas, we learned the RPGs, an early version first used in the 1960s, and then the RPG-18, a lighter, short-range version, which was easier to carry because it was collapsible. Finally, we learned how to use the RPG-22, a version invented in the 1980s. It is so powerful it can penetrate a meter of concrete or four hundred millimeters of armor. We had all these weapons at Khaldun, and were able to practice on every one of them . . . We never had to conserve ammunition, and there was always something new to try.[14]

While there remains much unclear and much to learn about the camps and their training regimens, it is a rock-solid certainty that those elected to protect Americans since 1982 (and their counterparts in Western Europe, Australia, New Zealand, and Canada) did nothing to halt the geographic spread and continual operation of terrorist training camps. Since 9/11 only the most prominent training camps in Afghanistan have been destroyed, and media reporting clearly suggests that their loss has been made good by camps that have been built in the tribal areas along Pakistan's western border.[15] The issue of training camps, I think, shows that very often the failure to act to protect Americans is just as damaging as making decisions that disinvest in U.S. national security. The mujahedin units that the armed forces of the United States and its allies face today, as well as the insurgents' massive reserves of trained manpower, are the responsibility of elected U.S. policymakers and their senior diplomatic and intelligence officials. These men and women decided to study the nuances and dance the ballet of international politics rather than make the protection of American lives their first priority. They sat, they watched, and—

wrapped in their own self-importance and worldly sophistication—they did nothing.[16] Oddly, the post-9/11 investigatory commissions found no fault with those individuals who allowed the uninterrupted operation of training camps, and the contribution they made to the growth of al-Qaeda's capabilities. Indeed, the Kean-Hamilton commission could not find the moxie even to comment when Richard Clarke, who had watched but not generated action against the camps for all of the 1990s, condemned the George W. Bush administration for not attacking the al-Qaeda camps after it took office. Clarke told the 9/11 commissioners that he could not understand "why we continue to allow the existence of large-scale al Qida [sic] bases where we know people are being trained to kill Americans."[17] Could it be that the Bush team was simply following Mr. Clarke's decade-long demonstration of supine behavior?

1989: Afghanistan—Intervening to Ensure Disaster

On February 15, 1989, there began a process that was destined to prove the incompetence of U.S. officials in conducting overseas political interventions, as well as the futility of making the "building of democracies" a central goal of U.S. foreign policy. On that date the world witnessed the last Soviet military commander in Afghanistan walk over the Friendship Bridge spanning the Amu Darya River and step onto the soil of the then-Soviet republic of Uzbekistan. That general's footfall marked the Red Army's defeat by the Afghan mujahedin and their non-Afghan allies— among which were both Muslims and such infidel entities as the U.S. Treasury and the CIA. The Afghan Islamists had defeated a superpower, and the glory and honor of that victory belongs exclusively to them. Western journalists and politicians have since made an industry out of the concept of "Afghan blowback," the supposed rise and radicalization of Islamist militants because of U.S. support for the Afghan mujahedin, but this was and is nonsense.[18]

Undeniably the United States supplied billions of dollars in cash, military equipment, ordnance, and the other sinews of war in what became the largest and most successful covert-action program ever conducted by the CIA under the president's orders. And I had the great honor of being a bit player in that effort from 1985 until early 1992. From the perspective I had, and as history shows, the CIA did an extraordinary job in making sure that the Afghans could kill Soviet soldiers as quickly and efficiently as possible using AK-47s and other arms from World War II and the Korean War (with the important exception of Stinger missiles), instead of the Lee-Enfield rifles and even muzzle-loaders left over from Britain's imperial Afghan misadventures in the nineteenth and early twentieth centuries. As long as the Soviets occupied Afghanistan, the focus and goals of the U.S. covert-action program were clear: help the Afghans kill increasing numbers of Soviet military personnel until Moscow decided to throw in the towel. For the CIA, the heroes of the Afghan program were its financial and logistics officers, who ensured the mujahedin had the wherewithal to keep Soviet blood flowing, and its clandestine officers in the field who made sure that most U.S. arms and cash went to the Afghan Islamist leaders who were actually in the field killing Soviets and not to the so-called "moderate" Afghans who fought their war dressed in three-piece suits and battled each other for Western media attention and bigger cuts of the U.S.- and Saudi-provided swag.

And then the Soviets withdrew, and the roof caved in for the United States and the West generally. As the Afghan Islamist groups who beat the Red Army saddled up to undertake the fighting that remained to defeat Afghan Communist leader Najibullah's Soviet-supported regime in Kabul, U.S. and Western diplomats, most of whom had turned up their noses while the CIA and other intelligence services did a decade of the dangerous work of arming the mujahedin, spotted a chance to go a-nation-building. The task of defeating Najibullah's regime turned out to take thirty-eight months and concluded in April 1992. During this period the Afghan Islamists fought the Afghan Communists, were bedeviled by Pakistani authorities who, searching for a quick victory, pushed them into several bloody defeats in semiconventional battles, fought with each other with increasing ferocity, and unknowingly were led to lose all they had gained by the feckless intervention and interference of U.S. and Western diplomats.

Through all of this post-Soviet-withdrawal mayhem, U.S. and Western policymakers made another massive disinvestment in their nations' long-term national security. Instead of running as fast and as far as they could from Afghanistan (the advice offered by Thomas Twetten and Frank Anderson, then respectively the CIA's deputy director for operations and chief of the Near East Division), Washington, London, the UN, and other

NATO foreign ministries deployed and detonated the West's most powerful weapon of mass destruction: diplomats obsessed with building Western-style, secular democracies in places where they are not wanted, especially in Islamic cultures that view them as an affront to God. Instead of leaving the Afghans to recover their own political balance after nearly fifteen years of war and the dire social and economic costs of the barbarous Soviet occupation, the U.S.-led West joined the UN to send diplomats to teach the Afghans how to govern themselves, as if the Afghans were brand new to politics and not a political culture that was already well and stubbornly established when Alexander the Great and his army invaded nearly four hundred years before Christ's birth. A bevy of U.S. diplomats of ambassadorial rank, among them Peter Tomsen, Robert Oakley, Zalmay Khalilzad, and Phyllis Oakley, arrived in Afghanistan to lead the great unwashed mass of Afghan Muslims in the creation of a secular and democratic Afghan Monticello on the banks of the Kabul River.

These smart, talented, good-hearted, and well-intentioned men and women never had a chance and in the end did a great deal more harm than good for U.S. interests, a self-inflicted fiasco that their successors are repeating and deepening today in Afghanistan and Iraq at a time when the stakes are much greater for America. U.S. diplomats, U.S. AID officials, and hundreds of Western nongovernmental organizations flooded the Afghan playing field armed with large amounts of money and expectations entirely inapplicable to those of the people they were trying to help. Ambassador Tomsen, for example, spoke often about building a Hamiltonian federal system in Afghanistan,[19] and Ambassador Phyllis Oakley brought in groups of American lawyers (as if the Afghans had not suffered enough under the Soviets) to lecture Afghan tribesmen on the niceties of due process, human rights, and the rule of law. Simultaneously, Ambassadors Robert Oakley and Zalmay Khalilzad spent untold hours trying to teach Afghan resistance leaders the ins and outs of parliamentary government, fiscal responsibility, and the protection of minority rights. Always polite, patient, and hospitable, the Afghans listened intently to their professorate of ambassadors, took the money that was on offer, and proved themselves unable and more often unwilling to implement anything they were taught. Why? Because the U.S., Western, and UN diplomats wanted to deal with Afghans like those who had fled to overseas exile during the war against the Soviets or who belonged to resistance groups that talked but did not fight. They wanted to deal with people who resembled themselves in style and temperament, men who were mannered, well-coiffed, wore suits, spoke English or French, were educated in India or the West, and were at most nominal Muslims—after all, no polity needs too much of that religion stuff. In short, the West preferred to deal with those Afghans who had played a minor role in the struggle against the Red Army or had safely spent the war abroad.

To the surprise of Western diplomats but not of anyone with common sense, the Afghan leaders who had fought the Red Army had no intention of ceding control of their country to a government installed, paid for, and protected by foreigners. By deliberately leaving the Islamist Afghan mujahedin on the outside looking in, the West ensured that no weak but coherent Afghan central government would emerge (the only type of central government the Afghans will tolerate) and that the civil war that began to take shape as the Soviet withdrawal was completed would evolve into a nationwide Hobbesian conflict of all against all.

The upshot of this democracy-spreading U.S.-Western involvement, then, was not the now-dominant urban legend of Western abandonment after Soviet withdrawal but an involvement that guaranteed that post-jihad Afghanistan would not find a way toward either the anathema of secular democracy or the political stability potentially possible through the use of the tools and practices of a two-millennia-old, tribal-dominated polity. Indeed, the Western spanner in the Afghan works helped to foster a national environment of intertribal strife, crime, banditry, narcotics trafficking, and ethnic animosity so dire that the rise of the harsh Koran-based rule of the Taliban would be welcomed because it brought reliable law and order in its train. Thus 1989 marked the start of a period in which the West missed a chance to let the Afghans find their own political equilibrium and resume their traditional, intense insularity. By seeking to install a secular democracy, it ensured that Afghanistan would grow from a nonthreat to the United States to the home of bin Laden and al-Qaeda. Sadly, the 1989 effort in Afghanistan would not be the last time U.S. governing elites would embark on attempts to install democracy abroad and succeed only in killing Americans and bleeding their wealth.[20]

1990–91: More Steps on the Road to Defeat

If there were ever turning-point years for the United States, setting the stage for almost everything negative that occurred to it after 9/11, they are surely 1990 and 1991. Responding in panic to Iraq's invasion of Kuwait in August, 1990, Saudi king Fahd coerced his bought-and-paid-for clerics into defying the Prophet Muhammad's prohibition against the presence of non-Muslims on the Arabian Peninsula. Warned by many dissenting Saudi clerics and prominent citizens—including Osama bin Laden—that once U.S. forces arrived on the peninsula they would never leave, King Fahd nonetheless approved the U.S. deployment and foolishly accepted Washington's word that U.S. forces would be withdrawn after Iraq was defeated. Poor, silly Fahd, he did not know that Washington went to war without the slightest intention of winning, and so U.S. forces are still on the peninsula today, seventeen years later. The now-dead king's lasting legacy to the Saudi state will be that his decision to allow deployment marked the first step toward the final destruction of the al-Saud regime.

As 1990 became 1991, the Saudi Arabia–based, U.S.-led coalition bombed the daylights out of Iraq's infrastructure; the U.S. military stupidly televised its killing of Muslims to the entire Islamic world, then drove Iraqi ground forces out of Kuwait in one hundred hours and won—nothing. Saddam survived, his military and intelligence forces survived, the societies of Iraq, Kuwait, Saudi Arabia, and the other Arabian Peninsula states began a journey toward Islamic radicalization, and the many bureaucrats who masquerade as U.S. generals actually believed they had won a decisive victory and would henceforth be able to conduct wars with virtually no casualties.

What the 1991 U.S.-led war against Iraq did was to prove to Saddam and our other enemies in the Islamic world (nation-states and transnational actors) that U.S. presidents and officials would speak loudly, rattle sabers endlessly, and then apply their mighty club with resolute daintiness so the world—and especially the European elites they so much admired—would not think too badly of those in power in Washington. In 1991, as in 2003, we let nearly a half-million Iraqi military personnel not only survive but also flee to safety with their guns, thereby living to fight and kill U.S. soldiers and Marines another day. President George H. W. Bush's contention

41

that destroying Iraq's ground forces and dethroning Saddam would have meant capturing Baghdad, and thereby destabilizing the Middle East, was and is a false rationalization serving to disguise moral cowardice. Then-general Colin Powell (before he degenerated into just one more tacking, pragmatic politician) was right: once we decided on war, the job at hand was to surround the Iraqi army, kill all of it, and let the chips fall where they might. Generals Norman Schwarzkopf and Barry McCaffrey accomplished the surrounding requirement of Powell's doctrine, but Bush and his cabinet decided to let those they had identified as the enemies of America survive, escape, re-form, and reequip. As I write, nearly 3,900 service personnel have died in Iraq because the first President Bush and his team did not have the courage of their convictions to destroy Saddam's state when they had the chance.

The first U.S.-Iraq war also provides a good example of the "fog of war," in which unexpected and seemingly unrelated matters can be exceedingly costly. After the Iraqi invasion of Kuwait there was a good deal of informal discussion and debate within the U.S. Intelligence Community about whether President Bush would use enough U.S. military power to definitively eliminate the Saddam problem. Bush was well liked in the U.S. Intelligence Community—especially in the CIA, where he had been DCI under President Gerald Ford—but he did not inspire the same confidence as had Ronald Reagan. Reagan left the constant impression that he was out to protect America, first, last, and always. Bush and his closest advisers, on the other hand, were clearly what I have referred to as "nuancers" and "ballet of international politics" men, people who would make international affairs so complex and interconnected that the result was often either paralysis and no action or half-measures that left threats undefeated and simmering, ready to boil another day. And so it seemed likely to be the case in Iraq. Recognizing this eternally temporizing potential, some in the IC took comfort in the thought that Bush and his team would be kept up to mark because there was at least one manly, decisive leader in the Iraq war coalition—British prime minister Margaret Thatcher. Having watched Mrs. Thatcher conduct the Falklands war, break relations with Syria on the terrorism issue, and face down and then smash Britain's labor unions, she seemed likely to keep Bush from "going wobbly" and leaving a half-fought, eventually-to-be-resumed war in Iraq.

Alas, however, such was not to be the case. As the war opened, a now deservedly forgotten Tory politician named Michael Heseltine led a successful party revolt and unseated Mrs. Thatcher, although he did not win the premiership. At precisely the instant President Bush and company were collapsing with wobbliness, Mrs. Thatcher was no longer on hand to provide the Oval Office with the requisite spine. And on such pedestrian events do great disasters pivot. Without the Iron Lady at his side, President Bush proved to be very much a man meant for turning. Quailing before the bloodbath that would have permanently protected America, Israel, the West, their allies, and the Iraqi people against Saddam, Bush, Baker, and Scowcroft joined hands and danced the nuancers' minuet and explained away their lack of concern for Americans by dilating on the complex and unpredictable impact that annihilating Iraq's military would have on regional and world affairs. To paraphrase a 1790s American who hated the diplomat John Jay for not adequately protecting U.S. trade from Britain, every American parent who has lost a son or a daughter in Iraq since 1990, and every Iraqi who lost a child because of the UN sanctions that became necessary because Bush and his dance partners refused to destroy Saddam's regime, should once a day express their contempt by saying: "Damn George Bush! Damn everyone who won't damn George Bush! Damn everyone that won't put lights in their windows and sit up all night damning George Bush!"[21]

The second momentous event of 1991 was the fall of the Berlin Wall and the dissolution of the Soviet Union. This event was, of course, a great victory for the United States and a singular achievement for the determination and vision of Ronald Reagan. Unfortunately, Mr. Reagan was not president when the great moment came, and instead America was led by a very good man and a very bad politician, George H. W. Bush. While the fall of the wall was certainly an occasion to celebrate the victory of America and Mr. Reagan, President Bush turned out to be something of a weepy, dreamy Adlai Stevenson/Henry Wallace clone, talking endlessly about the arrival of what Noël Coward once called "the age of peace and plenty," and the "New World Order" that the U.S. government would build from it.

Well, the elder-Bush-designed and -managed New Jerusalem never arrived, but we went on speaking as if it had for the rest of the 1990's and to this day—recall Madeleine Albright's delusion that America is "the indispensable nation."[22] The major result of terminating the USSR was the destruction of the fairly well-ordered and world war–less international environment we had enjoyed for nearly half a century. In many ways the Cold War–era's U.S.-USSR standoff had amounted to a genuine New World Order, but that framework of stability and peace was shattered by the American victory, and the world thereafter began a steady descent toward a new era of barbarity, an era whose arrival would be hastened by the happy talk and silly democracy-spreading notions of Messrs. Bush, Clinton, and Bush. While these three gentlemen put protecting Americans on the back burner in favor of occupying an office the U.S. Constitution does not provide for—President of the World—the forces that attacked us on 9/11 peacefully and quite openly, as noted above, gathered, trained, and prepared for war. Barbarism arrived to kill Americans, while our presidents were busy seeking the world's applause, admiration, and cultural amalgamation.

1993: An Unshared Revelation, Another Pulled Punch

In February 1993 Ramzi Ahmed Yusuf and a team of minimally talented and intelligent individuals spent about twenty thousand dollars on explosives and other materials and detonated a bomb that came within an ace of collapsing the two towers of the World Trade Center (WTC) in New York City. If it had been completely successful, the attack would have killed many times more Americans than died on 9/11. After the bombing, Yusuf scurried out of the United States and continued to roam the world looking for U.S. targets to attack. In January 1994, Yusuf barely escaped from Philippine police in Manila but was captured the next month in Pakistan in an operation led by Pakistani security officers. The effort yielded Yusuf in chains and the opportunity for the FBI to falsely claim credit for the success. This claim established a now-hallowed FBI tradition regarding its efforts against Osama bin Laden and al-Qaeda: claiming credit for other agencies' successes. Such claims now amount to a fabricated litany of Bureau "successes" that probably explains why the FBI continues to be involved in counterterrorist operations. There is no other plausible reason. Without these claims of overseas successes, the FBI could do no more than its standard operating procedure: find some addled U.S. Muslims, recruit a slightly brighter Muslim, and then use the latter to frame the former in a sting operation that makes them look like terrorists. We all have seen this method of operation in practice in such places as Lodi, Minneapolis, Albany, and Miami.[23]

Anyway, Yusuf's near-miss attack on the WTC should have persuaded U.S. officialdom that one icily brilliant Islamist militant and his retinue of mostly half-baked colleagues had demolished the doctrine of deterrence, as it had come to be known during the Cold War. Al-Qaeda would later publish a brilliantly written essay explaining the strategic importance of the 9/11 attacks and claiming that the attack had destroyed the three pillars of U.S. security policy: early warning, preemption, and deterrence.[24] Al-Qaeda was wrong. What the attack on 9/11 did was definitively drive home for U.S. political leaders and policymakers the great lesson of Ramzi Yusuf's failed 1993 attack; namely, that deterrence was useless against religiously motivated nonstate actors, and that our ability to detect and preempt them before they attacked was extremely limited.

One of the senior U.S. government officials who seemed to intuitively grasp this reality was Richard A. Clarke, then the National Security Council's chief for transnational issues. In the spring of 1995, I headed the unit at CIA headquarters that was responsible for managing worldwide operations against Sunni militants, and the pursuit and capture of Yusuf and his associates fell under that unit's mandate. After Yusuf's arrest in Peshawar by U.S. and Pakistani officials, I briefed Mr. Clarke several times on the operation and on the hard-copy and electronic materials that were confiscated from Yusuf and his subordinates in Manila, Bangkok, and Peshawar. One of the most troubling discoveries made during the examination of a computer seized from Yusuf's apartment in Manila was a file that contained a detailed plan (Yusuf had code-named the plan "Bojinka") to down a dozen or so U.S. commercial airliners in midflight over the Pacific Ocean. The planes were to be brought down by the detonation of liquid-explosive bombs brought onto them at their points of origin by Yusuf's operatives. The explosives and the necessary electrical components would be concealed in carry-on luggage as innocuous-looking items—contact-lens-solution bottles, compact disk players, wristwatches, etc. During the first leg of the flight, the attacker would assemble the bomb, position it in the cabin, set the timer to detonate on the aircraft's second leg over the Pacific, and then deplane. The Bojinka attacks were not to be suicide operations.

U.S. government forensics specialists examined the formula for the liquid explosive, as well as the schematic for the electric-detonating system, and concluded that the bomb would have worked. Then, after interrogations of Yusuf and his colleagues, we learned that the bomb had already been used once. Yusuf himself had boarded a Japanese airliner in Manila that was flying to Sebu, in the Philippines, and then on to Tokyo. He successfully smuggled the components on board in Manila, assembled and set the bomb on the flight's first leg, and deplaned in Sebu. The bomb detonated over the Pacific, killing one Japanese national. Yusuf later said that he used only a small amount of explosives on this trial run because there were not enough Americans on board to justify destroying the aircraft.[25]

When briefing Mr. Clarke on this information, it was clear that he "got it" immediately. Men like Yusuf, he said, could not be deterred. As important, Mr. Clarke ruminated that if Yusuf been successful in bringing down the World Trade Center towers and/or a dozen U.S. airliners flying Pacific routes, the United States—by that time the world's only superpower—would have suffered a massive, costly, and humiliating defeat. Worse, Washington would have had absolutely nothing against which to militarily respond. The superpower and its massive military machine would have been seen looking at the ruins, quivering with rage, pressed by a population eager for revenge, and yet impotent to respond in any meaningful way. Mr. Clarke clearly saw what many CIA counterterrorism officers saw: Yusuf had irrevocably ended the comfortable era of Cold War deterrence by proving it irrelevant to at least the transnational threat posed by Islamist militants. Mr. Clarke's effectiveness in conveying to the Oval Office this vital, Yusuf-taught lesson about a new kind of national-security threat demanding preemption is unclear. I do know though that from the spring of 1995 until I temporarily left the CIA's bin Laden operations, Mr. Clarke and his superiors turned down every opportunity provided by the U.S. clandestine service to conduct a preemptive covert-action or military attack against bin Laden. But while the Clinton administration was fatally slow on the pickup, Osama bin Laden and al-Qaeda learned Professor Yusuf's lesson by heart.

The other event that would have lasting impact on the perceptions of America's Islamist foes involved the Iraqi Intelligence Service's (IIS) reliably clumsy and ham-fisted attempt to kill former president George H. W. Bush during his visit to Kuwait in February 1993. The attack was preempted by Kuwaiti security officials, who initially tried to hide their success for fear that its publication would cause the visit's cancellation. In this judgment, the Kuwaitis clearly were ignorant of the enormous personal courage of that fine gentleman.

After the CIA acquired the information from the Kuwaitis about the disrupted attack, an intense multiweek and multiagency effort ensued to prove what was obvious before the investigation began: Saddam had ordered his security service to murder Mr. Bush. By reason of my position at the time, I and several other CIA officers—analysts, lawyers, and operations officers—worked with FBI and Department of Justice (DoJ) officials to prepare a paper for the National Security Council and President Clinton assessing whether Iraq was culpable for the attempted assassination. This was a testy and at times acrimonious process. The CIA knew who conducted the attack: the human intelligence and physical evidence were complete and the forensic evaluation was conclusive. The FBI and DoJ officials, however, were looking for court-quality evidence and were decidedly gun-shy about vouching for the validity of information acquired by the clandestine service and the Kuwaitis. At one point, I recall, a very senior FBI official threw his pen across the conference table at the CIA team out of frustration over the fact that CIA reporting contained so much detail, some of which might be exculpatory if used in a courtroom situation. As he launched the pen, he barked something like "if one of my officers ever wrote down that much of what a source told him, he would find himself packed off to the FBI office in Juneau." Refraining from firing a return volley of Paper Mates, we simply told our FBI counterpart that CIA officers are trained to write down exactly what their assets tell them, whether or not U.S. judges, law enforcement officials, or policymakers want to hear it.[26]

We eventually put together a paper that brought us all the way back to where we began—Saddam had ordered the assassination attempt. The NSC and President Clinton accepted the paper's conclusion and ordered the U.S. military to prepare a retaliatory cruise-missile attack on IIS headquarters in Baghdad. While preparations for the raid were ongoing, I was assigned the task of traveling to New York to brief the then-U.S. ambassador to the UN Madeleine Albright on the paper's conclusions, as well as to explain the nature and quality of the evidence that supported them. The goal was to prepare Ambassador Albright to present UN members with an explanation and justification for the cruise-missile strike we were about to launch on Iraq. The briefing did not begin until almost midnight on a Saturday evening in the ambassador's residence, but Ms. Albright proved to be a very quick study and asked pointed questions; indeed, she struck me as the sharpest, toughest, and most aggressive individual I had so far encountered in the Executive Branch while dealing with this issue. This was, of course, before Ms. Albright's champagne-glass-clinking days with Kim Jong Il. In any event, the next day Ambassador Albright delivered an excellent briefing to the assembled UN grandees and received virtually no pushback from anyone.

When I returned to CIA headquarters the next morning, I learned that the White House had launched the cruise-missile strike against Saddam's intelligence headquarters in the middle of the night so as to limit casualties.[27] Thus the hard and contentious work of the U.S. Intelligence Community was completely wasted. Saddam's regime had tried to murder a former American president, and the mightiest military power the earth had ever seen responded by breaking some cheap Iraqi concrete and cinderblock and killing a few members of the janitorial staff and a very unlucky female Iraqi poet who lived nearby. What was the point? Well, here was another instance where the nuancers and "ballet of international politics" sermonizers—this lot from the Democratic Party's ranks—easily persuaded themselves that protecting Americans and U.S. interests was not really their top priority. President Clinton and his advisers pulled their punch because they did not want to upset Moscow, which still had a strong relationship with Iraq; they did not want to be seen to deliver a militarily disproportionate response to what, after all, had been an unsuccessful attempt on Mr. Bush's life, if we did so, they fretted, the Europeans and Muslims would be angry with them; and they reliably dragged out that traditional bipartisan Executive Branch excuse for moral cowardice and not protecting Americans—they wanted to limit collateral damage. In this case, of course, the last justification was absurd because the timing of the attack ensured that only innocent Iraqis sweeping floors, cleaning toilets, and composing verse would be killed.

All these justifications amounted to just one thing—pure hooey. The sum of this useless raid on IIS headquarters totaled one probable and one definite loss for U.S. security and the safety of Americans. The probable loss: Saddam's grip on power might have been undermined. It depended in large measure on the strength and loyalty of his intelligence service, a brutal, murderous, and effective internal-security service if there ever was one. Had the U.S. military been ordered to strike the intelligence headquarters in Baghdad in the late morning of a workday, there is every chance that many hundreds of Iraq's intelligence officers, including some of the service's senior leaders, would have been killed. In thereby tearing a large human chunk out of the Iraqi service (and breaking up some concrete to boot), we would have denigrated the capabilities and manpower of one of the main instruments Saddam relied on to maintain power. Such an eminently positive and valuable slaughter would have merited Machiavelli's praise for well-used cruelty [28] and might have had the added benefit of causing Iraqi intelligence officers to begin thinking about whether Saddam was worth keeping around if his personal desire for revenge against former president Bush earned such a retaliatory massacre. While a coup probably was too much to expect, CIA operators surely would have found a few candidates for recruitment as penetrations of Saddam's regime among IIS officers worried about the possibility of another surprise visit by a cruise missile on their headquarters. [29] In wartime, as a general rule, the steady application of intense violence produces increased opportunities for the collection of high-quality intelligence. [30]

In the definite-loss category, our Islamist enemies went to school on this feckless, noncasualty-causing U.S. military raid. Al-Qaeda and its allies live in a police state-dominated culture whose lingua franca is the sturdy and remorseless application of power. While we in the West detest that reality because it does not mesh with our fantasy that all cultures and societies have equal value, the routine, arbitrary, and excessive use of force is a fact of everyday life for Muslims who live under the tyrannies that America supports and that govern much of the Islamic world. Thus what our foes saw was that Saddam Hussein had tried to kill the former U.S. president, in a manner that made little or no effort to hide Iraq's hand. Indeed, Saddam expected the attack to succeed and wanted the world to know that he was responsible for exacting revenge against his persecutor. In response, the Clinton administration loudly rattled the American saber and reduced a mass of cinder-blocks and concrete to gravel. The lesson drawn by al-Qaeda was that the U.S. response to an attack was liable to be wordy but weak. The nuancers had again triumphed, and Richard Clarke later wrote that the cruise missile sent a message to Saddam that brought cessation of Iraqi terrorist attacks on U.S. interests. The reality is that there was no sustained Iraqi terrorist campaign against the United States before the cruise-missile strike, and Mr. Clarke's claim is just part of his book-length apologia for the ineffective Clinton national-security team of which he was a key member.[31] When ineffective U.S. military attacks are used to "send messages" to our Muslim and Islamist enemies, a message is indeed delivered. Unfortunately, the message delivered causes mirth, not trepidation. The message read by the Islamists is: "The Americans are stupid, they have the strongest military in history and are afraid or embarrassed to use it; we can, with prudence, do what we want." That is the message delivered by Washington's military half-measures, and it is heard by all but those in the White House who are too busy congratulating themselves for successfully modulating the use of violence so as not to disrupt the sophisticated ballet of international politics.

Summing Up, 1973–96: Gulliver Recklessly Binds Himself

In the years between 1973 and 1996, then, U.S. leaders—the elected and unelected of both parties and their senior civil servants—made a number of decisions that severely limited America's foreign policy options and military credibility by the time the 9/11 attacks occurred. The pattern of these decisions also encouraged al-Qaeda and other Islamists to strongly suspect that Washington would not respond with all the power at its command no matter what sort of attack was launched against the United States.

It would be foolish of course to argue that U.S. policymakers should have made none of the decisions discussed above in anticipation of the emergence of a foe like Osama bin Laden. Many things can and should be demanded of policymakers, but 20/20 foresight is not one of them. There was no way to anticipate the rise of a unique and history-altering figure like bin Laden, although the path he trod to that emergence was clear long before U.S. policymakers accepted the seriousness of the developments they were watching. Two remarkable points about the decisions, however, must cause one to wonder whether the foregoing decisions made any kind of common sense for the national-security interests of the United States and its citizens.

The decisions that bound America to very public, bipartisan, and unquestioning support for anti-Arab Israel, to a less public but just as firm support for the anti-Israeli Arab police states, and to our enduring acquiescence in allowing the latter to hold the life-and-death energy lever over the U.S. economy surely must be open to question solely on the basis of common sense, without any reference whatsoever to bin Laden and the Islamist threat. By unstintingly supporting both sides in the Arab-Israeli conflict U.S. policymakers consciously gave a set of potentially lethal hostages to fortune that were and are almost entirely beyond U.S. control. One-sided support for Israel in the conflict not only increasingly alienated the Muslim world but especially alienated Saudi Arabia, whose king's status as the Protector of the Two Holy Mosques gives the kingdom at least symbolic leadership in the Arab war against Israel. Saudi Arabia, in turn, was and is the world's key oil producer and as such constantly keeps at least a theoretical pistol trained on the head of the U.S. economy.

These two policy decisions allied us with the theocracies in Israel and Saudi Arabia—surely a vastly ironic situation for the secular American republic and its taxpayers, who are in effect forced to pay to support the regimes of religions to which almost none of them belong. The policies have made us responsible for the survival of two mortal enemies, one of which has developed a large undocumented, unmeasured, and uninspected arsenal of weapons of mass destruction (WMD), and the other of which could bring the U.S. economy and military to a grinding halt in less than a year by closing the oil spigot.[32] Both likewise know that they can play havoc with U.S. domestic politics, Israel via its powerful lobby, covert political action, and propaganda machine, and Riyadh via its own potent lobby, ability to hike prices at the pump, and holding of vast amounts of U.S. government securities. Because each holds a whip-hand over all presidential administrations, Israel feels free to do as it pleases vis-à-vis Palestine, and Saudi Arabia makes little effort to disguise the massively expensive and successful campaign it is running to spread a particularly virulent anti-American and anti-Western form of Islam worldwide, nowhere more aggressively than in the United States.

In addition, both of these de facto alliances traduce much of what the Founders intended America to stand for. America has been bound to a self-professed "Jewish state" and equally to self-professed "Islamic states," neither of which is open to the kind of freedom the Founders envisioned, not even to the Protestant Christianity that so thoroughly informs America's constitution, and the only faith on which the Founders believed the republic could endure. "Our Constitution," John Adams wrote in October 1798, in reference to that Protestant Christianity, "was made only for a moral and religious people. It is wholly inadequate to the government of any other."[33] Washington's resolute, bipartisan maintenance of these alliances, with countries renowned for political intolerance, religious bigotry, and studied duplicity, has done more than anything else to undercut the Muslim world's perception of America as a model for fair-minded and tolerant self-government. Our willing, abject, and seemingly permanent surrender to a dependence on foreigners for the energy needed to keep our economy functioning, moreover, would have appalled the Founders, who prized the maintenance of foreign-policy options and complete American independence on the decision of peace or war. On energy, quite simply, Washington has voluntarily ceded control over our economic destiny to barely disguised enemies, and committed the nation to war in their defense if energy supplies are threatened.

The other set of decisions saw the U.S. government steadily develop the habit of pulling its punch whenever it was forced to formulate a military response to an attack on U.S. interests and citizens. These decisions likewise cannot be blamed on the failure to envision the emergence of militant Islam. But our now firmly ingrained reluctance—even fear—to respond with overwhelming force when attacked provided those who later formed al-Qaeda and its allies the loud-and-clear lesson that they had little to fear from U.S. military retaliation. Long before 9/11, the Islamists had pegged the United States as a super-talker rhetorically and as a super-diddler militarily.

Taken together, these two sets of decisions framed the conclusion in the minds of Osama bin Laden and our other Islamist foes that America is in a box of its own making, from which it will be hard put to extricate itself. Bin Laden and other Islamists believe that because of the American public's unwarranted emotional guilt over the Holocaust, the wealth and resultant political influence of pro-Israeli figures and organizations in U.S. domestic politics, and Israel's superb covert action inside the United States—which has created a situation where Americans damn other Americans for questioning the U.S.-Israel relationship and try to limit their willingness to speak out by slinging the anti-Semite slur—U.S. foreign policy is all but welded to support Israel without limit. Bin Laden and his like

52

were and are confident that, of all the U.S. policies they could use as foils, America's ties to Israel was among the most difficult for Washington to change or even to recognize as being in need of change.

Bin Laden also has come to count on the durability of Washington's path-of-least-resistance willingness to see its economy, and those of its allies, stay dependent on oil produced on the Arabian Peninsula. This, in turn, binds Washington to its longstanding policy of supporting tyrannical governments in Saudi Arabia, elsewhere on the peninsula, and across the Muslim world, thereby discrediting Western calls for democracy for Muslims and creating ever more discontent toward America and the West among Islamic peoples who believe that U.S. support for their governments is an endorsement of the tyranny and repression imposed on them.

Believing that America has locked itself into nearly irreversible policies—ones that are simple to compellingly advertise as anti-Islamic—the icing on the cake for the Islamists is America's repeated failure to annihilate enemies when opportunities arise. In the period between bin Laden's 1996 declaration of war and the 9/11 attacks, bin Laden, his lieutenants, and their allies experienced on a first-hand basis further validation of these conclusions via a series of U.S. actions and nonactions that seemed to prove that Washington's worldview was still dominated by a Cold War mindset that worked well against nation-state opponents but has yielded almost no positive results against transnational threats such as those posed by the Islamists.

CHAPTER 2

Fighting Islamists with
a Blinding Cold War Hangover,
1996–2001

The National Commission on Terrorism . . . issued its report last
week. . . . It vastly exaggerates the terrorist threat [to the United
States]. . . . On average, more Americans have died annually over the
last five years from venomous snake or scorpion bites than at the
hands of international terrorists.

Larry Johnson, 2000

The dogmas of the quiet past are inadequate to the stormy present.
The occasion is piled high with difficulty, and we must rise with the
occasion. As our case is new, so must we think anew and act anew.
We must disenthrall ourselves, and then we shall save our country.

Abraham Lincoln, 1862

How many times have Americans heard the leaders of political parties, as
well as senior bureaucrats, pundits, generals, and academics, mimic Mr.
Lincoln by solemnly proclaiming that "the Cold War is over," that the
"long nuclear nightmare has ended," and that the post–Cold War world
requires "new thinking" or (that most detestable, incorrect, and repellent of
catch-phrases) "thinking outside the box." In all likelihood, the endless rep-
etition of these stock cant phrases is about the only thing that has outpaced
the long-ignored training camps' production of professional Islamist insurgents and terrorists. The "Cold War is over" phrases and the mujahedin,

however, do have at least one thing in common: they both have the potential to defeat the United States.

I must admit up front that I am neither an expert on the Cold War nor one of those CIA officers who had the honor to spend his career in the ultimately successful, Ronald Reagan–capped effort to destroy the Soviet Union. Indeed, I made a decision early in my career to try to avoid any assignments that primarily focused on either Israel or the Soviet Union, both of which were intertwined in the general ambit of Cold War issues when I joined the Agency in 1982. I avoided Israel because the U.S. relationship with that state was clearly and inexorably drawing America into a religious war—Muslim versus Jew—in which we had no plausible interest and to which there was no imaginable solution. "Unlike most wars," the conservative commentator Armstrong Williams wrote in summing up this dark reality in 2000, "which are rooted in territorial disputes, the unrest in the Middle East is, at bottom, a religious struggle. For either side—Jewish or Muslim—to compromise would be to commit suicide on those core values that endows each culture with its unique meaning."[1] I also steered clear of the Israeli account because the pro-Israel orientation of every presidential administration under which I worked was so pervasive that there was no call from or tolerance among policymakers and senior IC bureaucrats for intelligence (reports from the field or formal intelligence assessments) that pointed to the massive, obvious, and deadly handicap Washington's succoring of Israel posed for U.S. interests in the Islamic world. Whenever such information surfaced, which was frequently, the administration of the day deployed the all-purpose, Cold War–era defense: no matter what the cost, America's vital national interests demand that we must support Israel because it is an island of democracy in a region threatened by Soviet expansionism. This defense survived the fall of the Berlin Wall, with its champions simply deleting "Soviet" and replacing it with the now fashionable and deliberately misleading term "Islamofascist terrorists." It is no more true to say that U.S. national security depends on the survival of an Israeli democracy—itself an oxymoronic term—than to say America is threatened only by a small number of Muslims, who are terrorists and criminals, who hate our freedoms, who have nothing to do with religion, and who in no way speak for any significant part of the Islamic world. When analyzed, each argument conduces to lethal nonsense. Israel's survival is not essential to U.S. security, and the threat America faces from

Islamist militancy is huge, growing, and motivated by a faith that perceives itself under attack by U.S. foreign policy, part of which is seen as U.S. subservience to Israel.[2]

I also tried to avoid working on the Soviet Union because after serving as a CIA analyst for a few years it became apparent that the overall attitude of senior Agency managers was (notwithstanding Reagan's clearly stated goal of defeating the USSR) that the Soviet Union had a lot of life in it and that the Cold War would be perking along long after all current CIA employees had tottered off into retirement. Like many Americans, I have a fairly short attention span, and I had no intention whatsoever of working on an issue that had been in play for thirty-seven years when I joined the Agency and that all my betters believed would be in full swing on the day I was slipped a gold watch. The closest I came to working on the Soviet Union was to do all I could to help the Afghan mujahedin kill as many Soviet military personnel as possible. I accepted this job in late 1985 because I was weary of working in the Directorate of Intelligence on the stultifying issue of the ballet of Cold War politics in Western Europe—my first and last purely analytic assignment—and because I thought the Soviets deserved to die, and because the Afghans were doing America's work for us by trying to give them their just deserts. It also was a job that provided a strong suggestion that the federal bureaucracy had a tendency to be "protective" regarding the Soviet Union,[3] and that at least some officers working on the USSR tended toward a view that attributed a rough moral equivalency to the two superpowers. In addition, I took the job because working on covert-action wars at the CIA is great fun and brought two other possibilities—infamy if the war went badly, promotion if the war progressed or was won. Because the Afghans won, helping them to kill Russians was definitely a career enhancer and I hope in some very small way helped Reagan's effort to overcome an Intelligence Community bureaucracy that was largely happy and content with the Cold War status quo.

I say all this in prelude to a discussion of what seems to me to be Cold War leftovers (ways of thinking about and perceiving the world) that continue to this day to plague the conduct of U.S. foreign policy. Unless, as Mr. Lincoln said, U.S. leaders disenthrall themselves from this Cold War hangover, they will never formulate a precisely accurate estimate of the threat posed by the Islamist forces led and inspired by bin Laden and al-Qaeda. Again, I claim no Kissinger- or Richard Pipes-like experience or expertise on either Cold War history or the USSR as a political entity, but I can at least claim to be an informed observer of both, and a bit-better-than-average student of America's steadily worsening confrontation with the Islamic world.

Sense of Time: After the Soviet Union acquired a nuclear capability and the means of delivering it to the continental United States, the Cold War settled in and, certainly by the mid-1950s, took on the appearance of permanence. Decade after decade the Cold War continued and, aside from an occasional harrowing blip that brought the world to the brink of nuclear war (the Berlin blockade, the Cuban missile crisis, the 1973 Yom Kippur War, and the tense 1983–84 period), U.S. elected officials and their senior foreign-policy bureaucrats planned policy based on a vision that saw no end to the Cold War. And once the policy of Mutually Assured Destruction (MAD) kicked in, the Cold War's nuclear-standoff scenario seemed to be mankind's earthly destiny.

This reality came to be accepted as the definition of normality, and time moved for politicians and policymakers at a steady and relatively undisturbed pace. To say that the Cold War world was a nine-to-five affair with weekends off for the U.S. politicians, civil servants, and military personnel managing the U.S.-Soviet relationship would be an exaggeration, but it would not be much of one. If, for example, U.S. intelligence found that the Soviets had begun designing a new military aircraft, such information would cause a flurry of activity, debate, staff work, and decision-making. That activity would yield a U.S. program to design a better aircraft that could be fielded in the same time frame as the Soviet plane. The decision was an important one for U.S. security, but the time line for accomplishing its goal was quite a few years in the future. So while the discovery of Soviet intentions was essential, and immediate remedial action was required, most Cold War "emergencies" allowed response times numbered in years and not in months, weeks, days, or hours.

Cold War–era military conflicts also tended to last for years: Vietnam, 1963–75; Afghanistan, 1979–92; and Korea, 1950–today, the last outliving the Cold War itself. Once begun, these conflicts of course needed to be managed and decisions had to be made, but the decisions were intended to calibrate the pace of the ongoing conflict, not to make a final decision where victory or defeat hung in the balance. And decisions about these wars were never taken in the context of having to prevent an imminent attack on U.S. territory. Superpower arms-control negotiations also went on for multiple decades in Geneva, during U.S.-Soviet summits, and at the United Nations, as did the talks pertaining to the Arab-Israeli conflict, each side of which had a superpower supporter. These gab-athons seldom yielded surprises or results, and decisions could be made when the time was right—or not made at all—at these forums; indeed, success was often defined as the continuation of discussions without much eagerness or even hope for a culmination.

Also allowing a steady, close-to-relaxed pace of events was the variety of sophisticated detection systems that American industry and the U.S. military and intelligence services designed and implemented to reduce the chance that U.S. political and bureaucratic leaders would be surprised by an entirely unforeseen threat from the Soviet Union or any other nation-state. From human intelligence to satellite imagery to X-15s to instruments for detecting electronic and chemical emissions, U.S. leaders could be confident that they would know if any sudden change in the Soviet threat required their immediate attention. Thus there was a large element of predictability in the Cold War world that allowed time for thought, study, and measured response, not to mention tennis after work, golf on the weekends, and plans for long summer vacations that rarely if ever had to be scrapped at the last moment. Though always fraught with a slim chance of nuclear catastrophe, and punctuated sporadically by periods of high stress, the Cold War environment for U.S. leaders was mostly calm, civil, and unhurried. Very few and far between were the occasions when life-and-death decisions had to be made on issues laid on the table only hours earlier.

The times and their tenor changed with the 1991 collapse of the USSR and the simultaneous ascendance of the United States to the rank of the world's greatest power. The military capabilities of other nation-states remained of concern to U.S. policymakers and generals, but none posed a threat even faintly resembling that posed by Moscow in its prime. In some ways, the first few years of unchallenged American dominance resembled what the Harvard historian Charles S. Maier described as the "few blissful years" between the annihilation of Imperial Japan and Hitler's Germany and Russia's acquisition of nuclear weaponry.[4] The latter obviously ended America's era of bliss and invulnerability, and Washington took notice, responded accordingly, and the Cold War was on.

In retrospect, it is hard to detect a point at which Washington similarly woke up during the period between the end of the Soviet threat and the attacks of 9/11, though such wake-up calls were loud and frequent. The gradual emergence of a set of transnational threats to U.S. security—terrorism, narcotics trafficking, organized crime, and nuclear proliferation—had been recognized even before the Cold War's end, but in that era they were the cats and dogs of America's international concerns, regarded as lethal nuisances not national-security threats. While presidents George H. W. Bush and Bill Clinton waxed eloquent between 1991 and 9/11 about the New World Order, the positive benefits accruing to all from the progress of globalization, and the irreversible narrowing of differences between peoples of all creeds, cultures, ethnicities, and colors, the United States military was embarrassed by and then driven from Somalia, the World Trade Center was nearly destroyed, two U.S. military facilities were attacked in Saudi Arabia, Osama bin Laden declared war on America in Islam's name, two U.S. embassies were simultaneously destroyed in East Africa, bin Laden declared war on the United States for the second time, U.S. interests and citizens at home and abroad were barely saved when al-Qaeda's millennium-eve plot was foiled, and a billion-dollar U.S. Navy destroyer was nearly sunk in Aden, Yemen. The gap between the glories-of-globalization rhetoric and reality was never bridged in this period: Washington spoke as if the Cold War had been won and no serious threat were on the horizon, and all the while increasing portions of the world's largest religion were mobilizing to wage or support war against America.

From my perspective, there is no clearer evidence that U.S. policymakers were still operating on Cold War time between 1991 and 2001 than the manner in which they addressed the need to capture or kill Osama bin Laden and destroy his organization. After bin Laden's summer of 1996 declaration of war on the United States, and even after the clandestine service had definitively established by that year's end that al-Qaeda had in 1992 established a specific unit to seek weapons of mass destruction,[5] the U.S. government's approach was still characterized by an attitude something akin to: "There is always time to take care of things, and so we can wait until we have better intelligence about the threat." It was as if Washington were competing with the Soviets in producing a more sophisticated and potent fighter plane, a competition whose outcome could be confidently predicted and whose pace was leisurely. The deadly shortcoming in maintaining this approach after 1991 was that there was no balance of nuclear power vis-à-vis al-Qaeda, no mutually assured destruction if bin Laden's team acquired and then used a purchased, fabricated, or stolen nuclear device inside the United States.[6]

Our failure to shake this patient approach can also be seen in the Clinton administration's refusal to try to capture or kill Osama bin Laden. Between May 1998 and May 1999 the CIA presented President Clinton with two chances to capture bin Laden and eight chances to kill him using U.S. military air power. Mr. Clinton and his team decided against action on each occasion.[7] This was of course Mr. Clinton's rightful decision as commander in chief, but it is interesting to note that Mr. Clinton and his colleagues told the Hamilton-Kean 9/11 Commission that the intelligence available on each of these opportunities was not "good enough" to take action.[8] Implicit in these decisions was the Cold War notion that there was time to sit and wait for better intelligence and then act with more confidence of accuracy and success, and in any event our massive military will protect us from any unpleasant surprises. Wrong. America had—and has—no dependable deterrent against al-Qaeda and its allies. Our only defenses against al-Qaeda-ism are changes in foreign policy and military or covert-action preemption, a notion that amounts to what was in Cold War thinking the then-morally repugnant idea of the first strike. Because of this reality the most senior U.S. political leaders and policymakers must abandon the leisurely Cold War approach to national security and learn to decide quickly, on less-than-perfect intelligence, and then act to protect Americans. They must accept that this is necessary against the transnational threat and that if they miss and cause other deaths or physical damage—so what? There is no coequal great power from whom we need fear military retaliation, we can endure criticism from the international community and simply prepare to try again to defend America.

Proxies: Beyond the doctrine of Mutually Assured Destruction, the best method the United States and the Soviet Union found to ensure that the red line drawn just in front of nuclear calamity would not be crossed was to make sure that their own forces never directly fought each other. Both Washington and Moscow knew that even a small engagement between the Red Army and U.S. forces or U.S.-led NATO forces had the potential to escalate into cataclysm. From Germany's Fulda Gap to Korea's 38th parallel, therefore, the lines of confrontation between the opposing forces were precisely demarcated and intensely monitored so that no unexpected skirmish could erupt that might quickly escalate to a nuclear catastrophe.

But humans are hardwired for war, and so there was still fighting to be done all around the Cold War world. Moscow had to assist those in foreign countries trying to smooth the supposedly inevitable triumph of Marxism-Leninism (a noninevitable inevitability that ought to give pause to the ideologues of democratization and globalization), and the United States was determined to help those trying to resist or roll back that inevitability. The superpowers could not openly use their own forces, for reasons noted above, and found that the next best option was to use proxy forces as the instrument and symbol of their supportive intentions. In places like Nicaragua, Afghanistan, Cambodia, and Namibia, Moscow and Washington squared off against each other, never losing a drop of their own blood and never creating a *casus belli* for a nuclear exchange. In each of these arenas, the superpowers' surrogates fought for years on end in wars that did not directly impact genuine U.S. or Soviet national-security interests—excepting Afghanistan, of course, where Afghan courage and Soviet stupidity combined to cause domestic economic and societal damage that contributed marvelously to the USSR's implosion. The goal of each superpower was simply to bleed the other and, if possible, to extend the sway of its lifestyle, political ideology, and the number of countries counted as its allies. If such extension by one side was not possible, blocking the advance of the other was sufficient. In essence, the Cold War's proxy conflicts resembled the jockeying over slavery extension in 1850s America, and the world was lucky enough to have the bad guys in the struggle collapse before a nuclear Fort Sumter brought calamity.

Since the demise of the USSR it is has been hard to assess what lessons the former Soviets took from their, on balance, losing experiences in proxy wars.[9] Russian premier Vladimir Putin's continuing wars in the North Caucasus suggest that he and his colleagues have not learned that Russians do not do well fighting Muslims in cold and mountainous lands. It is now, however, obvious that America took the wrong lesson and has yet to unlearn it. As noted, proxy wars were generally undertaken by one superpower to stop the other's expansion. Neither superpower sought or demanded total victory; as long as the enemy was bleeding and the would-be expansion could not be solidified, both sides judged the game well played. These were not national-security issues in the life-and-death sense, and without some almost unimaginable blunder by one side or the other, the conflicts were not going to trigger superpower war. I recall while working in the CIA's Afghan covert-action program in the 1980s, for example, that Pakistani president Zia ul-Haqq was eager to carry the Afghan jihad into Soviet Central Asia and began sending the mujahedin there to conduct sabotage operations and disseminate the Koran and other Islamist literature translated into the local languages. Washington was startled at this initiative, fearing Moscow would not tolerate such U.S.-supported activities on its own soil and so sent then-DCI William Casey to Pakistan to persuade Zia to halt the endeavors in the name of preventing Afghanistan from becoming a potential nuclear flashpoint.[10]

Moving into the post–Cold War period, the fixation of U.S. leaders and policymakers on the use of proxies continued and even intensified. We seemed to forget the most important points about the Cold War use of proxies: first, that the proxies were fighting for issues that were life-and-death matters for themselves as they were not for their superpower-backer, and, second, that proxies were almost exclusively people who needed America to do things that they could not do for themselves.[11] The proxies were never our agents or creatures, and we had almost no command-and-control over them. As noted, the U.S. role was heavily logistical and financial, coupled with the provision of diplomatic support at the UN and other multinational fora that sought to mediate these conflicts. For the most part, we made our proxies better trained and more proficient killing machines. At day's end, however, Washington's proxies were doing their work first and America's dirty work secondarily. None of the proxies would have been in the field solely to further U.S. national-security interests.

After 1991, however, the world changed not only in terms of the sudden absence of the superpower rivalry but also in the United States' justifications for involving itself in other peoples' wars—there were no Soviets to roll back—and in the need for or even the willingness of foreign armed groups or nation-states to do Washington's lethal bidding. Nonetheless, right up to and since the 9/11 attacks, U.S. administrations under both parties have looked for others to do our dirty work. Peruvians, Colombians, and Mexicans are to solve our narcotics problems; the IAEA is to handle nuclear proliferation; corrupt incompetents like Ahmed Chalabi were to unseat Saddam; and a galaxy of Arab and Muslim intelligence services, from Morocco to Indonesia, were to defeat the Islamist militants bent on attacking America. This quest for proxies even extends to the domestic front, as Washington allows the self-appointed Minutemen to try to staunch the flow of illegal immigrants across U.S. borders. Even against Osama bin Laden and al-Qaeda—the only entity to declare war on the United States since Hitler's underappreciated folly of December 11, 1941—Washington has relied on the CIA's human assets, UN conferences, the late Ahmed Shah Masood's Northern Alliance, reluctant NATO allies, and currently, the Pakistani intelligence and military services. Indeed, so far as we know, voodoo dolls are about the only proxy Washington has not tried to use to kill bin Laden.

In this panoply of post–Cold War proxies and surrogates, not a single one's interests are identical to those of the United States, and unlike the Cold War era, most of the issues against which we are now trying to use proxies are preeminently life-and-death issues for U.S. national security. The Cold War's end, in short, ushered in an era in which proxies are much less useful and reliable because they are being asked to fight and die for our interests, not their own. We are no longer simply paying them to allow us to hitch a ride along a road they were already traveling for their own purposes; we are asking them to undertake the trip and risk their lives, wealth, and, in the case of nation-states, stability for our sakes. Currently, Pakistan is the best example of this reality. Pakistani president Pervez Musharraf has assisted us in the war against al-Qaeda and the Taliban in a manner that has weakened his country's stability and runs counter to its genuine national interests. Musharraf has done about all he can for the United States without risking civil war in his country, and yet U.S. leaders continue pushing him to do more. In February 2007, Vice President Cheney went to Islamabad specifically to press for more Pakistani help against bin Laden, and in fall 2007 Washington pressed Musharraf to allow Benazir Bhutto back in to Pakistan's political mix, a destabilizing move that caused him to declare a state of emergency. Six years after 9/11 and sixteen-plus after the USSR's demise, we are still looking for others to do our dirty work; we are, in essence, actively in the market for mercenaries, while forgetting Machiavelli's warning that mercenaries "are useless and dangerous . . . and bring nothing but loss." Machiavelli's solution? "Experience has shown that only princes and republics achieve solid success." In other words, use your own military forces to do your own dirty work.[12]

Antinational Organizations: The Cold War decades gave birth to any number of political, legally oriented, and humanitarian organizations that manifested an abiding dislike of the nation-state and an unwavering belief in a coming age of a true international community in which national identities and nation-specific interests would be increasingly submerged and powerful supranational authorities would proliferate. Helen Caldicott and the unilateral disarmers; Amnesty International, with its hydralike ability to facilitate the proliferation of other human-rights groups; Greenpeace and other environmentalists; the National Organization for Women (NOW) and other women's rights groups; and host of U.S. and European nongovernmental organizations (NGOs) that now clog battlefields worldwide are just a few examples of the antinationalist organizations born during the Cold War. Even such useful international organizations as the International Crisis Group, whose analytic reports on world trouble spots may be without peer in the private sector, become burdens on national governments because of their unquenchable thirst for Western intervention and for telling other countries, cultures, and governments how to improve themselves by secularizing and democratizing. These organizations have three main features: an inability to perceive reality; a dedication to international law administered by supranational authorities that trump national governments; and a belief that carnivores no longer stalk the earth, or rather, that the good guys who won the Cold War are now the only carnivores they need to slay. These features flourish in such organizations because their leaders' pacifism and anti-Americanism is often expressed through irresponsible rhetoric, equating Western leaders with Bolsheviks, American presidents with Hitler, and U.S. soldiers with the Gestapo.

At day's end, these antinational organizations are the arrogant and self-righteous engines of Western imperialism and intervention abroad; their power results from their fanatically religious conviction of their right to impose secular values around the world, their ability to win allies in the media and academia, and their talent for pushing cowardly politicians to embark on overseas misadventures rather than risk the votes of the ironically small electoral constituencies that the antinationalists represent. Today one of the best examples of the antinationalists' poisonous influence on U.S. interests can be found in their persuading Senator John McCain (R-Arizona) to champion U.S.-British military intervention in the Darfur region of Sudan, a place where no U.S. interests are involved and where a military action can only waste American lives and money, worsen the civil war, and again validate the Islamists' contention that Washington intends to destroy the Sudanese and all Muslim regimes that will not do its bidding.[13]

These antinationalist groups grew in Western societies not only because speech is free but also because the U.S.-led West's ideological confrontation with the Soviet Union depended in part on constantly juxtaposing Western liberty and the freedom to dissent against the Soviet's brutal political repression, one-party government, gulags, and comprehensive state censorship. The U.S. government and its NATO allies were therefore forced not only to acquiesce in the existence of these groups but also at times to pretend that unrealistic folks like the unilateral nuclear disarmers had a point of view worth both respect and consideration. Most of the antinationalist organizations wasted the time and energy of any adult with common sense and served as political obstacles to be overcome, but Western governments had to pat them on the head as worthy, thoughtful participants in public debate because of the need to keep the demarcating line between Western liberty and Soviet tyranny as starkly drawn as possible.

Unfortunately, these groups took root in Western societies, survived the Cold War, and now stand as hardy political institutions in their own right, allied with many in the media and especially in academia. Indeed, their enervating and detrimental impact on common sense in the West today is largely due to their hold on the Western professorate, which is now indoctrinating its third generation of students in such nonsense as religion is dead, the nation-state is an anachronism, all conflicts can be settled by negotiation and compromise, and the coming age will be one of denationalized international cooperation. All of this at a time when, as the brilliant Gertrude Himmelfarb clearly has pointed out, the post–Cold War world finds itself at a "bloody crossroads" where it is "confronting a lethal combination of nationalism and religion—and not in one region but all over the globe."[14]

Who would have thought that political leaders who had the realism and moral courage to stare down the nuclear-armed Soviets for half a century would be intimidated, after Moscow's demise, by organizations that offered nothing but tripe and wasted time? But that is exactly what has happened. Organizations that were impediments to the political unity of nation-states but useful free-speech ornaments in defeating the Soviet Union (by ensuring that the Bolshevik model appealed to no one outside Western universities) became in the post–Cold War era serious obstacles to the national security of the United States by handicapping its ability to use military force effectively to defend itself. Today, for example, when U.S. ground forces deploy abroad for combat, the terrain is occupied not only by the enemy but also by any number of NGOs who assist the enemy's survival by making more difficult the rapid and direct movement of military units and whose presence on the battlefield often makes impossible the immediate application of firepower on targets. This is not to say that NGOs do not do good work; many obviously run first-rate humanitarian relief operations, although large numbers of Western NGOs manifest a strong antimilitary and anti-U.S. bias. But they have no place on a battlefield. If there are NGOs in a theater of operations as war begins, they should quickly evacuate of their own accord or be forced out as combat commences. If they choose to stay and resist eviction, they should be treated as expendables and take whatever firepower comes their way. The only mercy in wartime is quick and utter victory, and U.S. forces should not be slowed in their quest for victory by the foolish stubbornness of NGOs.

A worse impediment to defending U.S. national security, however, is the interlocking network of human-rights organizations. No other organizations on earth are more anti-American or have less balance and contact with reality. When American forces deploy these days, they are not only confronted by the enemy and encumbered by NGOs, but every U.S. service person—man and woman, private and general—must, as they seek to kill the enemy in whatever numbers necessary to prevail, operate under the prying, biased, busybody, and war-crimes-litigation-eager eyes of human-rights groups, monitors, and advocates. Our military, as a result, now operates under rules of engagement that make them more targets than killers. I am not arguing that these organizations have no right to exist; our system is worth fighting for because it protects dissent by and debate among both the reasonable and the irrational. The human-rights mafia, however, has no standing to prevent America from defending itself, which in wartime means quickly annihilating the enemy and its support networks, whatever the niceties of Cold War–era human rights accords, treaties, and conventions that were designed specifically for a world of nation-states and an environment in which a war for survival was unlikely to occur.

In the 1996–2001 period these antinational organizations continued to be taken as seriously by U.S. leaders as they were during the Cold War era, perhaps even more so. The end of the Soviet Union saw the reemergence of a much more Hobbesian world; nation-states proliferated, transnational threats grew, religious militancy intensified, and the lack of a central existential threat made individual nations more insistent on pursuing their own interests and much less willing to subordinate them for the common Western good. While not yet a case of all against all, the trend line is in that direction. U.S. leaders took no notice, however, and instead of reverting to form and acting as a national government ought to act—that is, in a timely manner to protect its citizens and interests—they continued to heed the international law and norms of behavior established during the Cold War and most suitable for a world where nation-states are the main actors. More than that, these leaders continued to be intimidated by the groups noted above.

The absurdity of giving these groups and their often-celebrity spokespersons a telling voice at the table of government was apparent to the CIA officers working against bin Laden and al-Qaeda after their return to Afghanistan from Sudan in May 1996. Shortly thereafter the Taliban regime consolidated power over most of Afghanistan and offered bin Laden and his fighters the status of protected guests. There was, to be fair, never much chance that Washington could have negotiated with the Taliban to secure bin Laden's arrest and extradition. No people are more protective of their guests than Afghans, and none is less likely to abide by the coercively phrased demands of a foreign power. Still, the Taliban did want Washington to recognize it as the legitimate government of Afghanistan, and it was no threat to the United States except that it hosted bin Laden and al-Qaeda. The Clinton administration underscored this reality with its ardor for a deal with the Taliban to allow Union Oil Company of California (UNOCAL) to build a natural gas pipeline through southern Afghanistan while bin Laden was resident there.[15] For those of us working the issue, therefore, it seemed reasonable that Washington should use all the levers of its power to seek bin Laden's turnover and to avoid giving the Taliban more reasons to refuse.

But such a commonsense approach was foreclosed by the voice and influence of a woman named Mavis Leno, the comedian's wife, and her Hollywood sisters-in-feminism. While sitting around the pool, Mrs. Leno et al. apparently decided that social and political rights for Afghan women would be their cause-of-the-moment, and they had no problem getting a hearing in the White House given President Clinton's adolescent passion for winning the admiration of the young and inexperienced and the applause and dollars of media celebrities; one might call it the Lewinsky-Streisand syndrome. Mrs. Leno, the chair of the Feminist Majority Foundation, and the leaders of NOW forced the Senate to pass a resolution (SR 68, May 5, 1999) calling on the president not to recognize the Taliban unless rights for women were secured.[16]

Thus, eliminating the threat from bin Laden and al-Qaeda—the most important U.S. national-security goal in Afghanistan—was encumbered by a second demand on which the Taliban was just as hard-over: Western-style rights for Afghan women. By allowing Mrs. Leno and her sisters-in-the-cause to shape U.S. Afghan policy in favor of an issue that is not remotely a genuine U.S. national interest, Clinton and his lieutenants blithely forfeited the admittedly small chance that Washington had to resolve the bin Laden issue with the Taliban before 9/11. I can think of about six thousand American families who today believe that it might have been better for Mr. Clinton to have told Mrs. Leno to stage a letter-writing campaign to Taliban chief Mullah Omar while Mr. Clinton pulled out the stops in using all the federal government's powers and options to try to eliminate bin Laden.

Soft Power and Public Diplomacy: There has been no better description of what America's brand of soft power should be than that proposed by Secretary of State John Quincy Adams in a speech made on July 4, 1821. In the speech Adams advised his countrymen that when the world asks "what has America done to benefit mankind? Let our answer be this:

America with the same voice that spoke herself into existence as a nation, proclaimed to mankind the inextinguishable rights of human nature, and the only lawful foundations of government. America, in the assembly of nations, since her admission among them, has inevitably, though often fruitlessly, held forth to them the hand of honest friendship, or equal freedom, or generous reciprocity . . . She has uniformly spoken among them, though often to heedless and often to disdainful ears, the language of equal liberty, equal justice, and of equal rights . . . Wherever the standard of freedom and independence has been or shall be unfurled, there will her heart, her benedictions, and her prayers be.

But she goes not abroad in search of monsters to destroy. She is the well-wisher to the freedom and independence of all. She is the champion and vindicator only of her own.[17]

This is the sort of mind-our-own-business soft power that the Founders envisioned America using: the positive example of a republic's disciplined self-government and the visible benefits derived from it by Americans. During the Cold War soft power provided the core of U.S. public diplomacy and was a key component of Washington's comprehensive anti-Soviet policy. But the influence of such soft power in the defeat of the USSR has come to be greatly overestimated in the period since that happy event. U.S. soft power operated and did its work under the overall umbrella of a nuclear balance that all but negated the chance of world war save via an almost unimaginable set of miscalculations. Once this balance was established, U.S. soft power was unchallenged, less because of its self-evident purity and beneficence than because its Bolshevik opponent had virtually nothing to offer in the soft-power category—freedom was pitted against tyranny, faith against atheism, meritocracy against nepotism, and material plenty against chronic shortages. For U.S. and Western appliers of soft power it was like shooting ducks in a barrel of vodka. As the historian Charles S. Maier has written, those in the West's camp accepted "American hegemony because it had provided a defense against a rival and a far more oppressive domination." Rather than persuasive soft power, Maier notes, "Washington's fundamental asset was the capacity to threaten the use of nuclear weapons."[18]

Once the Soviet system dissolved, America's practitioners and advocates of soft power—often they are one and the same—took all too much credit for victory and began to see soft power as a potential future war winner. Truth to tell, had U.S. hard power and Moscow's belief that Washington would use it not existed, U.S. soft power would not have been worth Cactus Jack Garner's bucket of warm spit. In the post–Cold War world, U.S. soft power no longer has a corrupt, sclerotic, and sordid nation-state to attack, and moreover nationalism and religious faith have been reinvigorated with a vengeance. As a result, many nations, groups, and peoples—especially in the Muslim world—grew slowly resistant and then directly hostile to American soft power, seeing its attributes as something not to aspire to but to ward off for reasons of faith or national identity or both. Under both Democratic and Republican administrations, however, Washington continued pushing the Cold War–era soft-power product as if the world had not changed after 1991, an effort at self-delusion that is supported by that tireless proponent of soft power, Harvard's Joseph Nye.[19]

In addition, U.S. leaders either did not notice or lacked the courage to admit that large components of traditional American soft power were fast decaying. With the end of the Soviet threat, for example, both Western and Third World peoples became more acutely aware of the lethal hypocrisy inherent in a soft-power approach that preached democracy, individual rights, and liberty, while the U.S. and Western purveyors of that approach ever more handsomely kept police states on doles funded by their taxpayers. Over time funding, protecting, and apologizing for the likes of Mubarak, the al-Sauds, and other tyrants eroded the moral suasion the Founders intended their disciplined, self-governing polity to exude. In John Quincy Adams's words, Washington was still able to "commend the general cause [of liberty] by the countenance of her voice" but because of her close ties to tyrants could no longer evoke popular support by "the benignant sympathy of her example."[20] Nowhere was this truer than in the Muslim world, where U.S.- and Western-backed dictators have suppressed their peoples since 1945 and have thereby built a wide and responsive audience for Osama bin Laden's demand for liberation from those tyrants. America's governing elite also failed to acknowledge—this they could not have missed—that the popular-culture component of U.S. soft power was becoming increasingly malodorous. Indeed, since the fall of the Berlin Wall American popular culture has come to stand in the same relationship to the Western canon of literature, music, and art as untreated sewage to potable water. Professor Nye has written that soft power "is the ability to get what you want by attracting others to adopt your goals," but in an era of worldwide religious revival the combination of hatred for U.S. foreign policy and revulsion toward our increasingly pagan culture is a heavy and in the long run unsupportable burden for soft power to bear and still hope to "attract" Muslims.[21]

Between 1996 and 2001 Washington's use of soft power was still very much based on the Cold War model. U.S. public diplomacy sang a never-ending hymn about the glories of secular democracy, yet has demonstrated an absolute willingness to ensure the survival of tyrannies that are either useful to us or hold us in their thrall. There is no better example than Washington's alliance with the Kingdom of Saudi Arabia. In the period between December 1995 and June 1999, I was the chief of the CIA unit charged with collecting intelligence to help the U.S. government understand the threat posed by Osama bin Laden and to track, locate, and eliminate that threat.[22] As one of the unit's first actions in early 1996, we requested that the Saudis provide the CIA with basic information about bin Laden. That request remained unfulfilled on September 11, 2001, and when I resigned from CIA on November 12, 2004. The Saudis, moreover, refused to provide any sort of other help in regard to bin Laden and al-Qaeda. As a sign of the influence the Saudi regime wields within the U.S. government our continued requests to the Saudis were ultimately not supported by senior U.S. political and diplomatic officials in the Clinton administration. Clearly, the Saudis were not helping the United States to eliminate the man and organization that had declared war on America, but because of their close ties to the U.S. governing elite and their crucial role in providing energy to the United States and its allies, Washington continued to pretend they were our friends.

Thus the U.S. government knowingly put itself in a no-win position. At one and the same time we publicly supported a brutal, medieval Arab tyranny—denigrating the soft-power potential of championing democracy—and took no action against a government that helped ensure that bin Laden and al-Qaeda remained beyond the reach of the United States throughout the pre-9/11 years. Even today, the Saudis know they have taken our measure and are eager to show they have nothing but contempt for both soft and hard U.S. power. In November 2007, for example, Saudi Prince Bandar—former ambassador to the United States and now the Saudi king's national security adviser—told Al-Arabiya television that Saudi intelligence was "actively following" most of the 9/11 plotters "with precision" and "[i]f U.S. security authorities had engaged their Saudi counterparts in a serious and credible manner, in my opinion, we would have avoided what happened [the 9/11 attacks]." Incredibly, not a single U.S. government official or politician of either party challenged, let alone denied, what I would evaluate as Bandar's fabrication; instead, by their silence, all condoned Bandar's implicit claim that U.S. negligence alone prevented the preemption of the 9/11 attacks. If the Saudis knew the bombers and were following them before 9/11 and did not tell us, Bandar and the Saudi ruling clique withheld information that makes them culpable for the 3,000 Americans who died on 9/11 and all the others that have died in war since.[23]

Nation-State Fixation: Of all the aspects of the U.S. governing elite's post–Cold War hangover, its fixation on threats from nation-states is the most understandable: America's half-century face-off against the USSR was preeminently a state-vs.-state confrontation. The durability of the fixation was obvious in both Bush administrations' wars against Iraq: the elder Mr. Bush echoed World War II rhetoric about thwarting aggression against Kuwait, while the younger Mr. Bush and his advisers looked for a nation-state to assign culpability for 9/11. It can also be seen in the war drums that both Republicans and Democrats beat more or less regularly vis-à-vis the supposed threats from Iran and North Korea. And this focus is not misplaced, only myopia-inducing. The just-mentioned states, plus Russia and China, do to a greater or lesser degree threaten America. The nation-state threat has not disappeared, but for the moment it is eminently containable.

But the nation-state threat invariably remains at the head of the line in Washington's formulation of foreign and defense policies. While the last three administrations have talked the talk of transnational threats, the walk they have walked—from weapons systems and NATO expansion, to wars, air strikes, and economic sanctions on Iraq—is nation-state centric. This reality is very marked in regard to al-Qaeda and its threat to use weapons of mass destruction inside the United States. As noted, bin Laden made this threat before 9/11, and the U.S. Intelligence Community has consistently told the Executive Branch that in 1992 al-Qaeda formed a special unit—staffed by engineers, technicians, and hard scientists—to try to build, steal, or purchase such weapons. Indeed, the U.S. government held first-hand reporting from an individual who had participated in a failed al-Qaeda attempt to purchase uranium. Then after the 2001 invasion of Afghanistan U.S. personnel recovered documents showing that al-Qaeda's deputy chief, Ayman al-Zawahiri, had been running two programs to develop chemical weapons, each of which was compartmented from the other and proceeding on different paths. Finally in May 2003 al-Qaeda secured a treatise from an important Saudi Islamic scholar that sanctioned the use of nuclear weapons in the United States and set the upper limit of religiously permissible American casualties at ten million.[24] Americans can take minor comfort, I suppose, in the fact that bin Laden must go back to the clerics and win their approval if he plans to kill more than ten million Americans. They should take no comfort, however, from the fact that the Saudi authorities "persuaded" the cleric to recant the approval expressed in his treatise. Such recantations are produced by Riyadh and other Arab regimes simply to deceive Western governments and publics. Few Muslims, radical or otherwise, put stock in such reversals because their prevailing and probably accurate assumption is that the individual's reversal of view was prompted by threats or physical punishment directed at him or his family.

One can agree or disagree about whether al-Qaeda has a nuclear device, as well as about whether it would know how to detonate one, but it is impossible to argue that bin Laden is not pursuing such a weapon or that al-Qaeda would not use it if acquired. And yet that is exactly how the Clinton and George W. Bush administrations have behaved. They have not been bashful about warning Americans about this possibility, but twelve years after bin Laden declared war, and six-plus years after 9/11, U.S. borders remain porous to the point of being wide open. Instead of seeing border control as perhaps the single most vital element of homeland security, our governing elite have turned it into a political issue with which to court Hispanic voters, a tactic that can only be seen as meaning our leaders value their offices more than the lives of Americans. More disastrously, sixteen years after the fall of the Berlin Wall, the three post-1988 U.S. presidential administrations have failed to push to conclusion the U.S.-Russian program to secure the 22,000 nuclear devices that form the former USSR's nuclear arsenal. The Clinton and George W. Bush administrations, in fact, have cut funding and manpower for the program.[25] Open borders and unaccounted-for nuclear devices are a dangerous combination, especially because al-Qaeda and America's other enemies have been on the trail of the latter since 1992.

How to explain such criminal negligence? One possible answer is that our leaders are still of a mind that genuine national-security threats come only from nation-states. But that seems unlikely given that post–Cold War Democratic and Republican administrations have specialized in undermining U.S. national security by ludicrous actions or inactions toward nation-states: not pushing Russia to secure its nuclear weapons; allowing Saudi Arabia to continue to hold the energy hammer over the head of the U.S. economy; and encouraging China to hold a percentage of U.S. debt that could be used as a kind of WMD in its own right. Unable or unwilling to recognize the threat posed by al-Qaeda and other transnational threats, and actively disinvesting in U.S. security by surrendering strategic advantages to ill-disposed nation-states, perhaps the best explanation is simple incompetence and a dearth of common sense.

Just-War Theorists: Like antinationalist organizations and soft-power advocates, the just-war theorists flourished under the umbrella of U.S. and Soviet nuclear forces and have grown livelier and more dangerous to U.S. national security since the end of the Cold War. Tracing their roots back to Saint Augustine, the just-war theorists have become ever more strident in their rhetoric and ever more influential with their doctrines, especially that of proportional and discriminate response—a theory that usually leaves America in an ineffective, tit-for-tat military response mode against its enemies.[26]

Like other antinationalist groups, the just-war theorists were abetted by U.S. and Western political leaders during the Cold War and have become even more popular with those political leaders since 1991. Indeed, the influence of the just-war theorists has increased in direct proportion to the downturn in the quality of political leadership that the West has experienced since the end of the Reagan-Thatcher era. The moral cowardice that is rife among today's Western leaders makes them eager to use just-war doctrine and its totem of proportional response to avoid the popular opprobrium inherent in the effective use of military power. Today weak and ineffective military responses to attacks on or threats to the United States are not mistakes; they are rather evidence that elected leaders and too many U.S. strategists and generals have listened to the just-war theorists and are conducting war in a "civilized" manner.

Hogwash. The antinational and antihumanity triumph of the just-war theorists can be seen in the dozen half-fought, waiting-to-be-resumed wars that litter the world. Proportional and discriminate responses are the recipe for only one sure thing: wars that are never finished and enemies who always have the time and calm in which to regroup, reequip, and fight another day. From Haiti to the Balkans, and from Somalia to Afghanistan, proportional response has left America's enemies intact and biding their time for another round. Half a millennium ago the Italian political philosopher Niccolò Machiavelli reminded his readers that a nation cannot use patience and goodness to subdue enemies; it must exact vengeance through punitive actions that annihilate present enemies and make their successors think twice before pursuing attacks that risk the same response.[27] Perhaps more pertinent words for Americans, though harsher sounding, are those of the Civil War era's General Philip H. Sheridan. "The main thing in true strategy is simply this," Sheridan wrote in his memoirs. "First deal as hard blows at the enemy's soldiers as possible, and then cause so much suffering to the inhabitants of a country that they will long for peace and press their government to make it. Nothing should be left to the people but eyes to lament the war." Al-Qaeda and its allies, of course, do not govern or possess countries, so the populations among which they live and hide will have to be punished until they will no longer allow the Islamists to base among them.[28]

The period between 1996 and 2001 demonstrated in detail how damaging the doctrine of proportional response was to U.S. interests, and how it simultaneously allowed our Islamist enemies to not only survive but also to proliferate, to train, and to believe as an article of faith that America would never use its military power effectively. We already have seen how both President George H. W. Bush and President Clinton fretted about what the world would think if they used the military power that Americans have paid for to protect their country. That thought process again carried the day in the summer of 1998. On August 7, 1998, al-Qaeda destroyed the U.S. embassies in Nairobi, Kenya, and Dar es Salaam, Tanzania, in attacks that occurred less than ten minutes apart. Several hundred people were killed, and more than five thousand were wounded.

In response, President Clinton ordered the U.S. military to prepare cruise-missile attacks on al-Qaeda-related training facilities near Khowst, in southeastern Afghanistan, and against a pharmaceutical factory in Khartoum, Sudan. Intelligence reporting showed that the latter was handling precursor materials for chemical weapons, and the plant appeared to be part of the Sudanese government's effort to develop weapons of mass destruction. On August 20, 1998, the U.S. military launched about one hundred cruise missiles at the two targets. Both attacks occurred after dark when few people would be in the vicinity. The end result was (as in the 1993 attack on Iraq's intelligence headquarters) few enemy casualties and a lot of broken bricks and concrete. The U.S. military had begun using million-dollar-a-copy missiles to do the work of day laborers armed with thirty-dollar sledgehammers.

The bigger of the two raids was focused on the Khowst training facilities because several intelligence sources reported that bin Laden was going to meet other senior mujahedin leaders there on August 20, 1998. As it turned out, according to Abu Jandal, the al-Qaeda chief's former bodyguard, bin Laden decided at the last minute to skip the trip to Khowst and go to Kabul instead.[29] Interestingly, even if bin Laden had been there, it would have taken a good deal of luck to kill him. The camp facilities at Khowst are fairly extensive and cover a substantial piece of ground. So the best chance we had of killing bin Laden was to pinpoint the main mosque that would be used for the evening prayers; wherever he and the other mujhaedin chiefs were in the Khowst complex, they were (given what we knew about their behavior) very likely to gather at the mosque to pray. The White House, however, did not order the missile strike to occur at evening prayer time but rather several hours afterward.[30] Why? Because even if it meant severely degrading the chances of killing the man who a fortnight earlier had caused nearly six thousand casualties in east Africa, U.S. leaders thought it was more important to avoid offending the Muslim world (and, of course, Europe's elites) than to use the disproportionate force that might have ensured the death of bin Laden, even at the cost of hundreds of other Islamist fighters at prayer, many of whom surely had not been involved in the embassy bombings. The application of the just-war theorists' concept of "proportionate response," in short, almost certainly would have spared bin Laden's life had he been at Khowst that night, leaving him alive to plan—as he did—the attacks on the USS *Cole,* New York, and Washington.

Ahistorical Thinking: The Cold War, I think, was a historical anomaly; in many ways, it was a fifty-year, out-of-the-box experience that absolutely required out-of-the-box thinking. For the first time in human history, national leaders had the ability to kill many tens of millions of people over the course of twenty-four hours, while simultaneously making large swaths of the world uninhabitable for generations if not centuries. Indeed, these leaders theoretically held in their hands the potential for ending human life on earth. The task of managing this just-around-the-corner Armageddon had no precedent; U.S. leaders learned as they went, and all praise and honor is due to them for their success. But in many ways these leaders enjoyed a luxury that their predecessors and successors did not and do not enjoy. The leaders of the Cold War era worked in an environment where the balance of contending forces, the doctrine of Mutually Assured Destruction, and the development and deployment of multiple technologies to provide early warning more or less deleted unexpected threats, surprise attacks, and the need to stage preemptive attacks from their list of things to lose sleep over in regard to other nation-states.

What should have struck the Cold War's elected leaders, policymakers, bureaucrats, and generals was that they were living through an ahistorical era. In few periods of modern history were the chances lower of surprise attack and total war between great powers. These individuals should have reveled in the great good luck they enjoyed in serving America during Pax Atomica, but they should have likewise been consistently reminding themselves that their luck might someday run out. More important, they should have been mentoring their successors, to the point of hectoring, that history suggested that such good fortune could not last forever and that the much more unpredictable pre–Pax Atomica world would someday return and with it the requisite resumption of thinking inside the historical box. Our leaders did not perform this reality check on themselves; nor apparently did they press it upon their subordinates. The result in the 1996–9/11 period was that history resumed while the U.S. governing elite continued to think about and perceive the world as if the out-of-the-box Cold War era were still moving along in full swing. "The problem . . . that unpleasantly confronts us here at the beginning of the 21st century," Georgetown University scholar Joshua Mitchell has argued, is that the Cold War's end removed "the temporary masking of those darker aspirations in the human heart: order, honor, and tribal affiliation . . . The people of the Middle East know nothing of the victory of freedom and the end of history. That myth is ours, not theirs."[31]

Proof of this failure can be found most eloquently in the words of the cochairmen of the 9/11 Commission and the NSC's counterterrorism chief under President Clinton and George W. Bush, Messrs. Lee Hamilton, Thomas Kean, and Richard Clarke. Each of these gentleman led off his post-9/11 evaluation of what went wrong before al-Qaeda's attacks by claiming that U.S. policymakers, politicians, generals, and senior intelligence officers had suffered a "failure of imagination" about what al-Qaeda and Islamist militants intended to do to the United States. There was, this troika (and many other graybeards) claimed, not enough out-of-the-box thinking about the Islamist threat to America.[32]

These assertions irrefutably prove that even after 9/11 these gentlemen all remained firmly rooted in the historically anomalous, outside-the-box, Cold War experience. The years from 1996 to 9/11 were chock-a-block with evidence that history had resumed with great gusto. Granted, the reality of a powerful, transnational entity like al-Qaeda took some getting used to, but its attributes were easy to learn, and the fact that the blessed peace and predictable world of the MAD era was over should have shocked U.S. leaders down to their shoes. Al-Qaeda declared war twice, attacked U.S. targets a half-dozen times, and regularly and publicly described the kind of increasingly lethal wringer it intended to put the United States through until Washington changed its foreign policies toward the Muslim world. The failure of the U.S. governing elite to take heed of these things and unleash U.S. forces to wipe out their authors root and branch is the best possible proof that they collectively failed to imagine that the world could ever leave Pax Atomica behind. Warned repeatedly by working-level military, intelligence, and State Department officials that the al-Qaeda threat was genuine, imminent, and potentially devastating, the governing generation, of which Hamilton, Kean, and Clarke are deservedly distinguished members, continued to think in the anomalous, patient, outside-the-box, nonpreemptive, worry-about-European-opinion manner—and three thousand Americans died on 9/11. They were still seeking to manage rather than eliminate the threats to America, believed that there was always enough time to handle problems at our own pace, and counted the likelihood of unexpected threats and surprise attacks as minimal and acceptable. None seemed to realize that with the demise of the ahistorical Pax Atomica, history had resumed, and with that resumption came those troubling things with which the statesmen of centuries past had had to contend—limited time in which to make life-and-death decisions, the rapid and unexpected emergence of smart, flexible, and adaptable enemies, and the likelihood of surprise attack. What Messrs. Kean, Hamilton, and Clarke and so many others failed to see after 1991 was that U.S. national security required a return to the inside-the-box historical thinking that is pertinent to the unpredictable and often uncontainable threats that have dominated human history on either side of the Cold War.

Exiles, Expatriates, and Ethnic Experts: For most of its history, the United States has benefited from the advice and assistance of individuals who voluntarily came from abroad to help us wage war or who were themselves exiled from the country or countries at which we were at war. At America's birth, Casimir Pulaski and Baron von Steuben came from Europe to train and lead Washington's soldiers in our revolutionary war against Britain; Thomas Paine's pamphlet *Common Sense* inspired Americans to seek independence and reminds us today how much of our independence we have surrendered to foreigners. In the 1930s Albert Einstein, Enrico Fermi, and many other European scientists came to America and helped develop the atomic bombs that America so effectively used to smash Imperial Japan into final defeat. During the Cold War Aleksandr Solzhenitsyn, Andrei Sakharov, and other external and internal exiles of the Soviet Empire bravely spoke the truth about a monumentally criminal system and helped the West to understand the threat and hold on until Ronald Reagan arrived and brought victory. All of these individuals helped America prevail against its enemies, and they did so in the name of liberty and freedom, in a common effort to defeat tyrannies that threatened the United States.

In our war against Islamist militancy, however, more exiles, expatriates, and ethnic experts than ever before are helping less than any of their predecessors. Why? The most important reason for this reversal, I think, is that the exiles we deal with today are unrepresentative of the great mass of Muslims across the Islamic world. They have been displaced by revolutions or hounded by security services, were ineffectual in insurgencies, or were philosophically so far out of touch with their countrymen that they chose to emigrate. These men and women talk the talk of freedom but at bottom want the United States to do something that they themselves cannot do. And that phrasing is important because from Ahmed Chalabi to Fareed Zakaria to Zalmay Khalilzad to the late Shah of Iran's son to Walid Phares, the current roster of these types of experts have argued that America should act to install secular democracies in Muslim lands—without a shred of evidence that such an action would be welcomed by anyone except the experts and their Westernized friends. Indeed, the distinguishing characteristic of the current crew of such advisers is that they have been dead wrong in almost all of the recommendations for policy that they have made to the U.S. governing elite. They seem, moreover, ashamed and embarrassed by the reality that the great bulk of their brethern want no truck with secularism, and they project their own ambitions for their homelands as achievable foreign policy goals for the United States. As Abdel Bari Atwan, editor in chief of *Al-Quds Al-Arabi,* has written, the George W. Bush administration "listened to Arabs or so-called Arab 'experts' who gave it advice and studies to fit its anti-Arab and anti-Muslim strategy and not the advice or studies that reflected reality."[33]

Complexity: The Cold War's edge-of-Armageddon nuclear standoff created an environment in which U.S. leaders of all kinds—political, military, academic, and media—were able to create in their minds a world of stunning complexity, one that was far more complex than the reality that existed. Because Mutually Assured Destruction protected Americans against everything save the ultimate catastrophe (the chance of which the same doctrine likewise reduced to near zero), U.S. leaders lost track of the only organizing principle that is essential for the conduct of U.S. foreign policy: protect Americans, their liberties, and independence; maintain a domestic environment that cultivates liberty and equality of opportunity; and let no domestic interests or foreign countries stand as an obstacle to those objectives. This view of what the U.S. government should be about is singular, not simplistic; it simply follows George Washington's sage advice, "We ought not to convert trifling difficulties into insuperable obstacles."[34] It would encourage our governing elite to always use a clear and inflexible priority when formulating national-security policy by simply asking and answering the question: "Where do America's interests lie in this or that issue?" This query automatically would put a brake on the enduring Cold War propensity to make the setting of national-security policy unnecessarily difficult and complex. When this Cold War leftover predominates, the American people see—and some unreflectively come to share—a number of odd and self-defeating ideas. For example, U.S. leaders, even in wartime, equate the life of an American with that of a foreigner, even an enemy and his supporters; the U.S. response to attacks on American citizens and interests becomes proportionate, leaving the enemy intact and ready to kill again; and the U.S. government goes to war not against peoples, groups, or countries but against individuals like Milosevic, Saddam, bin Laden, and Qaddafi. This is the nuanced, international-ballet-of-politics approach to U.S. foreign policy. Since 1991 the men and women who practice this sort of diplomacy have produced policies that have consistently yielded dead Americans, undefeated U.S. enemies, and new crops of foes for the United States. These individuals are the enemies of common sense and the security of Americans that David Brooks identified as "bourgeoisophobes."

> Diplomacy is highly formal, highly elitist, highly civilized. Most of all, it is complex. Complexity is catnip to the etherealized bourgeoisophobes. It paralyzes brute strength, and justifies subtle and basically immobile gestures, calibrations, and modalities. Bourgeoisophobes have a simpleminded faith that whatever the problem is, the solution requires complexity.[35]

In the period between 1996 and 2001, the Clinton administration's nuanced-ballet-of-politics crowd was an example par excellence of Brooks's "bourgeoisophobes" in their approach to foreign policy: they used the idea of the horrendously complex international political arena as a shield behind which to hide their moral cowardice. On the snowy Sunday before Christmas in 1998, for example, I accompanied Director of Central Intelligence George Tenet and Deputy Director of Central Intelligence General John Gordon (USAF) to the White House operations center where Mr. Tenet was to present to the NSC's Counterterrorism Steering Group (NSC/CSG) a chance to kill Osama bin Laden in Khandahar, Afghanistan. The method of attack would be military, using the cruise missiles on U.S. submarines then on station in the Indian Ocean. CIA officers and their assets on the ground had located the building and the room in which bin Laden was to spend the night, and Tenet was to describe this information, detail the manner in which it was acquired, and (as he told us before we left CIA headquarters) remind his listeners, once again, that the intelligence was not likely to become any better or more reliable than that which we had at the moment. Tenet went into the meeting alone, leaving General Gordon and myself to wait and watch the football game unfolding on the operations center's television sets.

Mr. Tenet came out of the room after about an hour and, saying little, signaled it was time to return to CIA headquarters. Riding back through the snow on the George Washington Parkway, Tenet said that the administration had decided not to attempt to kill bin Laden. The reason? The house in which bin Laden was staying the night was located in the proximity of a mosque, and the White House did not want to take the chance of "offending opinion in the Muslim world" by shooting and having some shrapnel from the attack hit, mar, or destroy the mosque and thereby cause a violent response in the Muslim world that would endanger Americans overseas. No, the NSC was not worried about wounding or killing innocent worshippers at the mosque; the attack, after all, would have occurred in the middle of the night. What they had worried themselves into paralysis over was the potential that some stone in the mosque might get scraped or broken up, thereby making more Muslims hate us and perhaps kill U.S. tourists.[36]

Well, truth to tell, by December 1998 Muslims could not have hated U.S. actions much more than they already did, and the impact of an ephemeral event like damaging a mosque's structure with shrapnel would have been negligible. Polls by Gallup, Zogby, the Pew Trust, and the BBC were then showing eighty-plus percent majorities in many Muslim countries hating the same U.S. foreign policies that bin Laden had identified and condemned as attacks on Islam. In addition, the administration's decision again demonstrated its papable ignorance of the Islamic world; with a few major exceptions—the mosques in Mecca, Medina, and Jerusalem, for example—Sunnis do not put nearly as much value on structures as do Christians and Shias. Indeed for many Sunnis treating mosques as shrines smacks of the idol worship of polytheism.[37] Thus Washington's reason for not killing bin Laden on that snowy Sabbath does not hold water and was at base stupid—and the NSC/CSG members certainly knew that. They simply were grasping at straws to find a justification not to shoot to protect Americans and—if one was cynical—so as not to disturb their plans for the coming Christmas season.

Even more questionable was their other reason for not shooting: that enraged Muslims might take to the streets and kill Americans or other Westerners. Now, here we had a Democratic administration—those paragons of antiracism and champions of multiculturalism—assigning to Muslims a kind of genetic madness that would cause them to rise up en masse and mindlessly slaughter non-Muslims left, right, and center if a mosque in Khandahar was damaged by shrapnel. Could the CSG members really see headlines in their minds that read "Thousands of Westerners Slain by Muslims Enraged by Scratched Stone!" If they could, they were racists of the worst sort.

No, neither stupidity nor racism is the likeliest answer to why Washington did not try to kill bin Laden on that Sunday. Part of the answer lies simply in our elites' eagerness to make things vastly more complicated than they are. Yes, Muslims might be upset about an attack on bin Laden in a Muslim country. Yes, Pakistan might yelp if U.S. missiles flew over its territory with little or no notice. Yes, we might not kill bin Laden and some innocents might be killed in the raid. And yes, the Pavlovian European political-and-media elites would go into a knee-jerk, well-lathered anger over the irresponsible gun-slinging American cowboys. All of these issues surely weighed on the minds of the CSG members that Sunday and led to their paralysis, but only because they did not put U.S. interests first, work through the problem from that starting point, and then recognizing the likely downsides, ask the right question—"So what?" What were all those angry folks going to do in response to a U.S. military action meant to protect Americans? Well, they surely would intensify the scurrilous epithets they routinely throw at the United States, but they were not going to invade Alabama, blockade our ports, or reject the military protection and economic aid that U.S. taxpayers provide. All of them together could do nothing more than shout and pout. So who cared? The fillip to U.S. national security provided by a dead bin Laden far outweighed any offense the whiners could have imposed on our ears. And silently and smugly, government leaders from Paris to Riyadh and from Islamabad to Kuala Lumpur would have rejoiced over the elimination of Osama bin Laden and the fact that the Americans took the heat and they did not have to take action themselves.

The final reason for the no-shoot decision was simple moral cowardice. Though the Soviet threat is long gone, U.S. leaders in both parties still foist on Americans the Cold War tune about the massive complexities involved in managing the ballet of international politics. Inured by a half-century of this Cold War rhetoric, Americans buy it much too readily, losing sight of the fact that they pay exorbitant taxes for the protection of their families, not to have their government worry about the tender feelings or lives of foreigners—especially those who abet U.S. enemies. Mr. Clinton et al. did not try to kill bin Laden on that and several other occasions because they did not want to sacrifice the world's admiration for something so petty and commonplace as protecting Americans. On numerous occasions Mr. Clinton proved that claims about the daunting complexity of international affairs are an extremely effective shield behind which to hide moral cowardice.

War Within Bounds: So reliably peaceful was the halcyon era of Mutually Assured Destruction that U.S. officialdom—and its counterparts in NATO countries, Japan, and Australia—came to believe that wars could be managed, and that relatively low upper limits on their intensity and destructiveness could be established and maintained. As noted, each superpower's use of paramilitary proxies worldwide lent documented credibility to this belief; none of the proxy wars of the Reagan years came close to spinning out of control. Those wars, like the superpower relationship, were managed. Then came the first U.S.-led war against Iraq in 1991, which, as Andrew Bacevich has written, taught the American governing elite "that war can be—and ought to be—virtually bloodless. As with an idea so stupid only an intellectual can believe it, the imperative of bloodless war will strike some as so bizarre that only a bona fide Washington insider (or a techno-geek soldier) could take it seriously."[38] But contra common sense, Washington insiders went for the concept of virtually bloodless war like lemmings go for the sea.

The evidence for the U.S.'s predilection for bloodless war can be seen over and over again. Two al-Qaeda declarations of war on America were discounted or ridiculed as the rhetoric of fanatics, and multiple attacks on U.S. citizens, facilities, and interests were responded to with precise and precisely useless discrimination and proportionality—so unashamedly hawked by the just-war flim-flammers—or not at all, like the 1995 attack in Riyadh, the 1996 attack in Dhahran, Saudi Arabia, and the October 2000 attack on the USS *Cole.* Each al-Qaeda attack was more destructive than the last, as bin Laden had promised in 1996, and long before 9/11 he had promised to use a nuclear device or other mass-destruction weapon against the United States as soon as he could acquire one.

Well before 9/11, then, it was clear that the only limits bin Laden would respect on the destructiveness of his attacks on the United States were those he himself established: just enough violence to make America change its policies toward the Muslim world and leave the Middle East, but ever-increasing violence until both goals were accomplished. When Washington deigned to respond to al-Qaeda's pre-9/11 attacks, it sought to match him in violence rather than to kill him and eliminate his organization's ability to conduct additional attacks. Indeed, U.S. policymakers continued to use the Cold War's means of sending messages through the modulated use of force, as in: "This or that amount of violence will send a message to the enemy that we are serious and will, in turn, intimidate them." Well, the message al-Qaeda received was that U.S. leaders were afraid and unwilling to use America's power in more than a tit-for-tat manner and did not believe al-Qaeda was willing to use any amount of violence it could obtain and deploy. And the tepid post-9/11 U.S. military performances in Iraq and Afghanistan—temperate, compassionate, punch-pulling, and therefore enemy-preserving—suggest that, for all its warrior rhetoric, the George W. Bush administration still believes that the enemy can be intimidated and dissuaded through the application of moderate force that sends a "do not mess with us" message made effective because of the awesome potential military power we theoretically could deploy. This is Cold War deterrence thinking, but the USSR is not there to get the messages Washington is sending. Al-Qaeda not only does not fear U.S. escalation, it intends to escalate its own violence as far as necessary to win.

In his posthumously published novel *Islands in the Stream,* Ernest Hemingway presents a scene via the story's narrator, Thomas Hudson, that perfectly captures America's current quandary in its fight with al-Qaeda and the overall Islamist movement. In the scene, a youthful gentleman from New York City, who is a well-trained boxer and standing on his yacht, loudly demeans and threatens a slovenly-looking writer friend of Hudson's named Roger. Roger tells the gentleman to take his pick: quiet down or get up on the dock and fight. The gentleman chooses the latter tack, and once the fight begins, Roger proves to be a street-fighter who is unconcerned with the pugilistic niceties the unnamed gentleman had learned in his New York gym and administers to him a bare-knuckled thrashing.

Roger was holding the man [from New York] again with his thumbs pushing in against the tendons at the base of the biceps. Thomas Hudson was watching the man's face. It had not been frightened at the start; just mean as a pig's is; a really mean boar. But it was really completely frightened now. He had probably never heard of fights that no one stopped.[39]

Well, prior to the anomalous Cold War era, "fights that no one is going to stop" were not rare, and they are not going to be rare on this side of that anomaly. Al-Qaeda is Roger and America is the gentleman boxer from New York. The U.S. government has issued warnings and threats, called bin Laden and his lieutenants names—gangsters, nihilists, psychopaths, killers, fanatics, etc.—and applied moderately, at most, the world's fittest, best-trained armed forces. But America is still being thrashed by al-Qaeda's Roger-style street fighters. Why? I suspect, as I've mentioned, it's because the U.S. government is still in the Cold War mindset; the U.S. military fought no fights to the finish between 1945 and 1991, and as a result, many U.S. officials have "probably never heard of fights no one stopped." Hemingway writes that the gentleman was "ruined" in the fight and his servants "picked him up from where he lay on his side . . . and carried him sagging heavily."[40] Unless U.S. leaders begin to recognize that they are in a fight with al-Qaeda that no one is going to stop, they better hope there is someone left to pick America up—"sagging heavily"—after al-Qaeda detonates a nuclear device inside the United States.

Revolution in Military Affairs: Even before the Berlin Wall's last cement block hit the ground, America's defense establishment—bureaucrats, think tankers, and the U.S. defense industry's reliable allies in both houses of Congress, such as Duncan Hunter (R-California) and legions of others— was already touting the need for American taxpayers to fund all-out U.S. participation in what they called the "Revolution in Military Affairs (RMA)." Weakness and vulnerability, they argued, would naturally flow from any failure by Washington to spend untold billions of dollars on ever-more sophisticated technology and smart weapons. Federal government–funded studies proliferated, and most were framed in words that suggested that the RMA was a unique historical phenomenon. While it is true that enormous changes had occurred repeatedly in the past, and that weaponry and military communications had obviously evolved toward ever-greater sophistication since the introduction of the longbow and encoded handwritten letters, the studies asserted that the current pace of technological advance was such that this new edition of the RMA was utterly unique and dangerous.

Well, no. The RMA was both a failure and a hoax. "Its dishonest claims," wrote Ralph Peters in his magnificently sulphurous prose, "was concocted by theoreticians unburdened by practical experience and by defense contractors whose greed can never be satisfied.

> The RMA claimed to substitute technology for flesh and blood on the battlefield, replacing soldiers with the satellite. It was not only going to change the nature of warfare fundamentally, but also would lead us into bloodless wars so swift they would be painless. The gory hand of man would give way to precision weapons, robotics, and, eventually non-lethal weapons to inaugurate a military version of the Age of Aquarius.
>
> The claims were not merely lies. They were among the most expensive lies in history.
>
> The nature of warfare *never* changes, only its superficial manifestations. Joshua and David, Hector and Achilles would recognize the combat that our soldiers and Marines have waged in the alleys of Somalia and Iraq. The uniforms evolve, bronze gives way to titanium, arrows may be replaced by laser-guided bombs, but the heart of the matter is still killing your enemies until any survivors surrender and do your will.[41]

In the sixteen-plus years since the dissolution of the Soviet Union, Colonel Peters's analysis has been validated by the discrepancy between what the champions of the RMA predicted and the military reality that U.S. soldiers and Marines are confronting on the battlefield, a gap that has widened to astounding dimensions. U.S. military forces find themselves in Iraq and Afghanistan fighting insurgents who are armed with a smattering of modern weaponry—shoulder-fired anti-aircraft missiles and mortars aimed with the help of Global Positioning System satellites—but who overwhelmingly depend on weapons and ordnance in use during World War II and the Korean War; ordnance on which, of course, they were trained in the paramilitary camps that Washington and its allies ignored for two decades. Our Islamist enemies today are using the same armaments used by the Afghan mujahedin against the Red Army's troops between 1979 and 1989: crew-served 12.7mm and 14.5mm machine guns, recoilless rifles, AK-47 assault rifles, mortars of various calibers, and explosive materials and captured artillery shells that are used to build improvised explosive devices (IEDs). And while there are certainly Islamic insurgents who employ sophisticated communications systems—such as INMARSAT radios, encrypted computer-to-computer Internet communications, and satellite telephones—a good portion of their battlefield communications still depend on 1950-or-earlier vintage high-frequency and push-to-talk radios. For the Islamist insurgents, moreover, these effective weapons and communication tools have the additional advantage of being in production, cheap, extremely durable, available everywhere, and nearly maintenance free—unlike the host of U.S. precision weapons, which are maintenance intensive, touchy on the battlefield, and so expensive that plentiful they are not.

The problem is not that the RMA advocates were wrong in predicting quantum advances in the sophistication of some military equipment and communications gear—such an advance is occurring, primarily in the arena of potential state-vs.-state conflicts—but rather that they refused to pay more than lip service to the continuing usefulness against U.S. forces of what they considered archaic military equipment. And they never believed for a moment that such equipment, if used by our enemies, would pose a serious problem for the U.S. military's thoroughly RMA-ified arsenal. Their error, in other words, was not in anticipating the RMA but rather in arrogantly believing that the RMA made all earlier military weaponry not only obsolete but also unusable, and that the only thing they had to prepare for was the ever-modernizing threat. They were wrong because they did not take account of enemies who had a different target to prepare to fight and defeat. "The 'revolutions in military affairs' so prominent in our discussion of defense today were not revolutions at all," Colonel Thomas X. Hammes (USMC, Ret.) accurately concludes. "Rather they were the culmination of practical men seeking practical solutions to the tactical and operational problems of their day."[42] America's Islamist opponents are exactly the "practical men seeking practical solutions" Colonel Hammes describes, and the solutions they have settled on just happen to be massively less than state-of-the-art. Just a few examples suffice to show how wrong the RMA advocates have been in places like Iraq and Afghanistan: the high levels of man-to-man combat[43] and the limited usefulness of precision weaponry; insurgents armed with early Cold War weaponry but savvy enough in their use of modern tools to deny us the "information dominance" that U.S. military doctrine requires; and a foe adaptable enough to bleed the most technologically sophisticated military in history into paralysis with roadside bombs made of World War II–vintage 155mm artillery shells detonated with timers from washing machines.

So completely forward-looking were the RMA'ers in the 1996-to-9/11 period that they helped to make sure that bin Laden stayed alive to kill Americans. When I was chief of CIA operations against bin Laden and al-Qaeda, the National Security Council's (NSC) instructions were to pinpoint bin Laden's location, either to permit an effort to capture him or to give the U.S. military the opportunity to try to kill him. This task the clandestine service accomplished repeatedly,[44] but the NSC and DCI Tenet always wanted to be more certain of the intelligence before deciding to act. These demands for more and better corroboration are, parenthetically, yet more evidence of the policymakers' Cold War hangover. Transnational terrorists, insurgents, narcotics traffickers, and WMD proliferators are by definition dispersed around the globe; they have few or no fixed targets against which to focus intelligence-collection operations, as well as no Soviet-like communication hubs, headquarters buildings, missile sites, airfields, barracks, arms-production factories, navies, or strategic bombers. Access to intelligence on transnational Islamist organizations, therefore, is likely to always be less complete and confidence-inspiring than was the intelligence we acquired against the USSR or any of today's nation-states.

Taking his cue from his timid NSC masters, Mr. Tenet decided that the trouble in targeting bin Laden was that the clandestine service was providing only what he described as "single-threaded intelligence," meaning, I think, that it came from only one asset or set of assets.[45] Well, that was not the case. The information about bin Laden's location was being provided by an asset that had been working with the CIA and had a proven track record. In addition to having the asset's eyes on bin Laden with some regularity, the information they reported was further corroborated by technical means.[46] Thus, for an effort to collect data on the world's most-wanted man, in a country run by an anti-U.S. regime, where the Executive Branch adamantly demanded the more difficult operation—capture not assassination[47]—and would not allow CIA officers to be deployed inside Afghanistan in support of an actual operation, the information was about as good as it could possibly be. Mr. Tenet repeatedly told CIA officers that he consistently described this reality to the NSC but that they always insisted on further corroboration—they needed "double-threaded intelligence."

This was, of course, nonsense, but orders are orders, and we began to look for ways to acquire "double-threaded intelligence"—that is, intelligence from a greater number of sources. At this point, we ran into the obtuseness of the RMA's champions. The quickest and easiest way to acquire the second thread was to try to collect against the tactical-communications gear used by the al-Qaeda and Taliban fighters who provided security for bin Laden and his residences, offices, and in-country travel. I use the word *easiest* not because it was a simple or safe undertaking, but because at the time bin Laden's security personnel were mostly using World War II–era communications gear, high-frequency (HF) radios, and push-to-talk radios or walkie-talkies. Because the forerunners of the National Security Agency (NSA) had been collecting against these types of electronic communications since the happy days of Wehrmacht-smashing, the bin Laden unit and CIA technical officers believed that this sort of collection would produce the required second thread. The NSA's collection and reporting of signals intelligence (SIGINT) has the added benefit—much beloved by clandestine service officers—of possessing a far greater power to persuade policymakers than is warranted. At times policymakers will not believe the most reliable, ironclad, manifestly true human intelligence (HUMINT) report, but if they receive even the flimsiest piece of SIGINT to complement it, the HUMINT becomes close to divine revelation for the policymakers. In essence, if the NSA had collected SIGINT to corroborate the CIA's close-to-definitive HUMINT on bin Laden's location, an effort would have been made—unless Mr. Tenet and the NSC decided they needed a third thread—either to capture bin Laden or to have the U.S. military spread him in tiny pink bits over the desert landscape of southern Khandahar province.

Alas, it proved impossible to collect the SIGINT that would have produced the NSC-demanded double-threaded intelligence. Why? Well, it was not because the NSA could not collect it; it was because the NSA would not collect it. In response to the CIA's request for SIGINT collection against Hitler-era communications gear, the NSA grandees looked down their noses at the CIA and sniffed something akin to: "How quaintly passé you HUMINT fellows are! Haven't you heard of the Revolution in Military Affairs? We simply do not do anything as old-fashioned as HF and push-to-talk collection. Our job is to support the Pentagon in defending America against the most technologically sophisticated threats from nation-states. We collect against satellites, encrypted computers and telephones, and underground fiber optic cables. We have no time for HF, for goodness sake."

Hearing this answer and tugging my forelock in deference to the SIGINT mandarins, I pointed out that they would be surprised by how little underground fiber-optic cable there was in Khandahar in the spring of 1998. All to no avail. NSA refused to collect against the Islamists' obsolete equipment; DCI Tenet, as always, refused to use the extensive powers of his office to force the NSA to do the collection; and the NSC did not get the superfluous but, to their minds, requisite second thread of intelligence. Bin Laden? He kept his life because he was not using communications gear that the RMA'ers respected and would collect against. And yes, this is yet another episode that was detailed and documented for the 9/11 commissioners. Just do not look for it in their report.

Coalition Love and Common Interests: The Cold War taught U.S. leaders to ignore the Founders' warning against becoming involved in what Jefferson described as "entangling alliances." After the Soviet threat emerged and solidified, the United States took charge of forming and then leading a galaxy of multilateral organizations meant to help protect the West politically, economically, and militarily, as well as to wisely create an environment in which U.S. economic interests would thrive. Among them were NATO, CENTO, the European Economic Community, SEATO, the UN, the Organization of American States, the World Bank, and the International Monetary Fund. On and on the list grew until a point was reached where unilateralism was not only seldom used but also was routinely ridiculed and opposed by the Anglo-American-European governing elite.

This interlocking web of multilateral military alliances, financial institutions, and political and humanitarian organizations moved slowly and timidly and stressed the necessity of unanimity before acting. Under the umbrella of Pax Atomica, the inbred and ever-deepening lethargy of these groups was frustrating but tolerable; the Soviet Union's own set of alliances and international organizations were, if anything, even more sclerotic. The Cold War was the heyday for alliance-building, and as it turned out, U.S. leaders and policymakers were unable to kick the habit once Mr. Reagan dished the Bolsheviks.

Through the 1996-to-9/11 period, Washington's involvement in multilateral alliances and organizations did much to prevent it from moving quickly, unilaterally, and effectively to protect America by destroying her enemies. As noted, Washington's response to Saddam's attempt to kill the first president Bush was conditioned by its desire to avoid offending one or another of our European allies, a desire that trumped the chance to slaughter a significant segment of Iraq's intelligence service. The al-Qaeda attacks in Riyadh in 1995, Dhahran in 1996, and on the USS *Cole* in 2000 were never responded to at all. And again, the military response to the East Africa bombings in August 1998 was designed more to avoid the condemnation of world opinion than to wreak havoc on al-Qaeda's leadership and organization.

America's Cold War coalitions were, of course, not organizations that should have been immediately abandoned as the last Berlin Wall brick hit the ground. As with all human institutions that have long existed and achieved positive results, they should not be abandoned until it is clear that their usefulness is spent. That said, the fall of the USSR did remove the raison d'être for many of the alliances—especially NATO—while simultaneously creating an international environment in which transnational threats prospered and proliferated. And although the cant-spreaders have preached that Islamist extremism is an equal threat to all "civilized nations," that is a lie on its face. The most lethal attacks by al-Qaeda and its allies have been on U.S. interests, not on those of our allies in the alliance network. In addition, our NATO allies, save for the U.K. and Italy, have recognized this fact and much prefer to keep the United States on al-Qaeda's bull's-eye and so take counterterrorism actions only as needed to frustrate attacks in their own countries. One of the most important post-9/11 lessons that U.S. leaders have yet to learn is that al-Qaeda poses threats to many countries, but the United States currently is its main target, and most of our Cold War alliance partners like it that way.

Thus, there is a strong element of Cold War hangover in Washington's belief in the absolute need for alliance support or coalition-building when America is faced with the need to defend its national security. The Clinton administration was palsied by this hangover, forgoing numerous chances to

93

capture or kill bin Laden out of fear of what our allies might say and responding to direct attacks on U.S. interests and citizens in an ineffective but politically correct military manner—when it responded at all. The Bush administration too ensured America's eventual defeat in Afghanistan by taking more than a month to coalition-build before attacking the Taliban and al-Qaeda, allowing most of their fighters and military supplies to be dispersed and hidden. The history of U.S. foreign policy since 1991 teaches a clear lesson: maintaining rigid dependence on Cold War alliances and delaying military actions in favor of forming ad hoc coalitions kills Americans and let the enemy survive. But perhaps Americans should not feel too bad about their government's self-inflicted failure to unilaterally eliminate their enemies because several just-war theorists think such delay is just peachy. "There were no immediate reprisals for the attacks of 'Nine-Eleven,' " rejoiced two distinguished scholars of just war, "an extremely good sign that patience did rule the day—and plans were made for exactly how the U.S. would respond." That bin Laden, al-Zawahiri, and most al-Qaeda and Taliban fighters escaped because of Washington's delay and are now waging an insurgency that is defeating America in Afghanistan is apparently a small price to pay for having played by the rules of just war.[48]

Multiculturalism: Much as they fostered antinationalist organizations and just-war advocates, Western governments facilitated and abetted the growth and influence of the multiculturalists in the context of their ideological struggle with the Soviet Union. In that confrontation, Moscow controlled its bloc at the point of a gun and the prospect of a gulag, and the West controlled its by U.S. military power, shared philosophical inheritance, economic growth, and fear of the USSR. The Cold War's hearts-and-minds contest therefore was played out in the Third World. The Soviets did their best, but for the most part Russian chauvinism shone through, and a shared Marxism-Leninism between Moscow and its clients was not enough to suppress the ill feelings it caused. The Russians were not all that keen about their allies in the Warsaw Pact, so nonwhite Afghans, Nigerians, Egyptians, and Indians were not likely to win either empathy or treatment as equals. For better or worse, the Soviets thought they had life right—economically, ethnically, socially, and politically—and did not think there was much to learn from others.

For the United States and the West, on the other hand, the search for Third World hearts and minds was a genuine effort—at least to the extent that we wanted the Third Worlders to steer clear of Moscow—and while Western governments supplied funding, Western academic, humanitarian, and Christian missionary organizations took the lead. Somewhere along the line, however, a postmodern incarnation of Lewis Carroll ushered the United States and the West through the multicultural looking glass. Suddenly the silliest ideas were not only in vogue but accepted as eternal truths. All cultures are equal in quality and ability to peacefully coexist; nationalism and religion are not only dead but evils in their own right; there are no absolute values or virtues; enforcing immigration laws is racism; the West has much to learn from illiterate brutal native societies; and a host of other idiocies for which there is neither scientific, empirical, nor common-sense grounding but that came to be accepted as correct and indeed immutable tenets of Western politics. As long as the Cold War continued, this sort of nonsense was maddening but tolerable because the multiculturalists could be patted on the head, shown off as evidence of the Free World's tolerance and open-mindedness, and left to conduct field investigations abroad and at home to ruin the ability of college students to employ logic and common sense.

But no good thing lasts. The Cold War ended, history resumed, and wars, religion, ethnic animosities, tribalism, and nationalism came roaring back to dominate human affairs. And arm in arm as a team both at home and in Europe, multiculturalists and antinational organizations rendered U.S. self-defense excruciatingly difficult. In both Europe and America, borders remained open to allow in noble Third Worlders who had no chance whatsoever of fitting into their new societies, and indeed brought with them the practices of corruption and other forms of criminal behavior that were not only rife but culturally acceptable and economically necessary for survival in their homelands. Assimilation—that wonderful process that allowed twentieth-century America to become history's only durable and equitable multicultural society—was disowned as a form of racism whose champions had the nerve to insist that Americans had the right and a duty to preserve the society that they had fought and bled for centuries to build. And strictly from an intelligence officer's perspective, the European Community—that pluperfect type of godless, bureaucratic, and quasi-socialist society that the multiculturalists and antinationalists hope to create—produced a safe haven for proven Sunni Islamist extremists, terrorists, and insurgents. In their utopian lust to make the EC the temple of human rights, humane law enforcement, atheism, and multiculturalism, EC leaders refused to extradite convicted or wanted Sunni fighters back to their home countries if those countries had the death penalty. These Islamist enemies of Europe and the United States gladly accepted this mindless, Pollyanna-ish hospitality, took up residence, signed up for the dole, and quietly expanded their military, economic, proselytizing, and logistics networks. As always, Western leaders who operate on the belief that man is perfectible benefit only the enemies of the people they represent.

PART II

SIX YEARS OF WAR,
2001–2007

For there has never been a protracted war from which the country benefited . . . Hence what is essential in war is victory, not prolonged operations.

> Sun Tzu

Every attempt to make war easy and safe will result in humiliation and disaster.

> William T. Sherman, 1875

The colonel says I may go if and if; and warning me of the hazards, etc., etc., shirking all responsibility. It is ridiculous in war to talk this way. If a thing ought to be done according to the lights we have, let us go and do it, leaving events to take care of themselves. This half-and-half policy; this do-less waiting for certainties before action, is contemptible.

> R. B. Hayes, 1862

On October 7, 2001, the U.S. government launched its "Global War on Terror" with the invasion of Afghanistan, following it up eighteen months later with the invasion of Iraq. Both were dubbed "new types of war," but they were new only in the sense that they differed radically from the conflicts that had occurred during the nearly half-century-long Cold War. Without exception, U.S. political leaders, Republican and Democratic, approached the wars with Cold War assumptions: America was the sole superpower, undefeatable, and was fighting on behalf of the civilized world; the wars would be localized, short, and minimally bloody; precision weapons would intimidate and eliminate a transnational enemy that was not a nation-state, small in number, lacking in popular support, and therefore not a life-and-death national security threat to the United States; most of the fighting and bleeding would be done by U.S. proxies; and liberated populations would joyously welcome invasion, occupation, and the installation of secular democracy. Our bipartisan governing elite was wrong on every count.

They were also ignorant of the malodorous foreign-policy baggage they brought with them to the wars in the Muslim world and, as important, of the fact that those policies had been used masterfully by Osama bin Laden to lay a trap for the United States among Muslims and marshal their support. Bin Laden's frequently repeated six-point indictment of U.S. foreign policy—U.S. presence on the Arabian Peninsula; military presence in Muslim lands; unqualified support for Israel; support for Russia, China, and India against Muslims; theft of Muslim oil; and protection of Muslim tyrannies—was known by few American leaders and was largely dismissed, when read, as a madman's irrational ravings.

Thus, U.S. leaders launched their wars with burdens that were both terrific substantive handicaps and virtual unknowns to themselves and, especially, to American citizens. The arrogance, hubris, and risk aversion of America's governing elite set the stage for self-imposed tragedies of unplanned-for length and Shakespearean proportions.

CHAPTER 3

Afghanistan–A Final Chance to Learn History Applies to America

America is her own mistress and can do what she pleases.
Thomas Paine, 1778

America is a new character in the universe. She started with a cause divinely right.

Thomas Paine, 1782

The cause of America is in great measure the cause of all mankind.
Thomas Paine, 1776

Paine thought more than he read.
Thomas Jefferson, 1824

Thomas Paine was one of the most incisive and decisive writers of the American revolutionary era. He wrote with startling clarity and rare brevity and in most cases with a historically informed mind. Paine's brilliant essay *Common Sense* resonates with American readers to this day. And unfortunately, so does Paine's blind spot about America and its place and role in the world. Paine's arguments that America is "a new character in the universe" and can "do what she pleases" are ahistorical in the extreme, but they have been adopted wholesale by the post–World War II U.S. governing elite. In 1998, for example, Secretary of State Madeleine Albright echoed Paine and her peers in both parties when she said: "If we have to use force, it is because we are America. We are the indispensable nation. We stand tall. We see further into the future." Our elite's allegiance to the most ill-informed aspect of Paine's legacy has caused the United States to incur endless troubles and costs because it conceals the reality that history's lessons do apply to America—and painfully so.[1]

The continuing negative impact of Paine's lapse from common sense struck me forcefully on October 22, 2006, when I was driving home from Mass with my teenage son and listening to C-SPAN's simulcast of *Washington Journal* on the radio. The call-in program—a species of broadcast at which C-SPAN excels—featured a commentator who the host described as an expert on Afghanistan. In the course of answering callers, the expert said that the resurgence of the Taliban and al-Qaeda since the fall of 2005 had "sharply surprised" everyone, and that U.S. generals, NATO commanders, and the government of Afghan president Hamid Karzai were scrambling to cope with and eventually defeat it. She also told her listeners across the country that no one had expected to see either the number of fighters the Taliban is now fielding or the range of effective military training and plentitude of ordnance they were displaying.[2] My son, as is his wont, was taking his post-Mass snooze in the passenger seat and gave no sign of hearing me when I turned to him and said that C-SPAN's expert was dead wrong, and that I and dozens of other members of the U.S. Intelligence Community had predicted that the Taliban was not defeated and would eventually return (to paraphrase what was once said of Richard Nixon) tanned, rested, and ready for jihad.

As soon as the words were out of my mouth, I was glad my son was dozing. To his ears they would have had an arrogant "I told you so" sound, which was not my intent. What caused my snappish words was simply the fact that C-SPAN's expert was giving Americans the impression that the now-evolving disaster for U.S. and Western interests in Afghanistan had come as a complete surprise, that U.S. leaders and their Western and Afghan allies had done their best but were caught short by a resiliency in the Taliban and al-Qaeda that no human being could have predicted. What made the C-SPAN expert's commentary even worse was that it echoed precisely what U.S. political leaders from both parties, U.S. general officers, and their counterparts in NATO and the Kabul regime were telling their electorates.

Clearly, what is happening today in Afghanistan was predictable and had been predicted. And making the prediction required nothing more than a reading of history and a review of the U.S. government's CIA-led covert-action program (1979–92) that supported the Afghan mujahedin. I made the prediction in two books,[3] and individuals much smarter and more experienced than myself in both Afghan history and covert-action operations, such as Sir John Keegan[4] and Milt Bearden,[5] made the same prediction, the former with more erudition and better prose, and the latter with insight from in-the-field experience. The bottom line is that the U.S. governing elite must not be let off the hook for the approaching calamity for U.S. interests in Afghanistan. Rather than a surprise, the pending defeat is the direct result of their shortsightedness, willful historical ignorance, political correctness, and inability to change patterns of thought created for and nurtured by the Cold War. As Jefferson wrote about Paine, the leaders of America's bipartisan governing elite think and speak without reading enough history. They try to make history without bothering to understand it.

Going to War

Now well past his thirtieth year as the premier court historian for both Democratic and Republican administrations, the *Washington Post*'s Bob Woodward did Americans an inestimable service by writing his book about the Afghan conflict, *Bush at War*.[6] One can almost see the White House–authorized troop of CIA officers and other U.S. government officials climbing the stairs to Mr. Woodward's home, ready to disgorge state secrets in support of the Bush administration's cynical manipulation of Woodward to disseminate its distorted first-cut of history. The White House–sanctioned leaking allowed the publication of a book that made Messrs. Bush, Rumsfeld, Cheney, Tenet, Franks, Powell, and Wolfowitz, as well as Ms. Rice, appear to have designed and run a near-perfect war, one that reflected their clear brilliance and mastery of the world stage and the ballet of politics occurring thereon. The book's publication, moreover, came even before all guns were silenced, so certain were senior U.S. officials that the war was irreversibly won. This timing, in itself, says much about the administration's ignorance of their foe and Afghanistan's history and geography. The insurgent forces of the Taliban and al-Qaeda had not stood and fought to the death; they had rather done what all successful insurgents throughout history have done—they dispersed into the almost impenetrable topography of South Asia to fight another day. While the administration mistook this interlude for victory and rushed to get its glittering but faux triumph published under Mr. Woodward's imprimatur, the Taliban and al-Qaeda were pursuing the traditional—and well-documented—Afghan strategy that was described by the senior al-Qaeda commander Sayf al-Adl. "We say to those who want a quick victory," al-Adl explained in March 2003, "that this type of war waged by the mujahedin employs a strategy of [the] long-breath and the attrition and terrorization of the enemy, and not the holding of territory."[7]

The amateurish ad hoc'ery of the U.S. military's going to war in Afghanistan was also painfully apparent, and it underscored the truth of Dr. Richard K. Betts's pithy but all-too-gentle comment: "Only in America could the nation's armed forces think of direct defense of national territory as a distraction."[8] Notwithstanding al-Qaeda's 1996 and 1998 declarations of war on the United States,[9] at least three major attacks on U.S. targets since 1996, and repeated Intelligence Community warnings of a pending al-Qaeda attack in the first half of 2001, the U.S. military had no retaliatory or expeditionary plans on the shelf to present to President Bush on 9/11 or any of the next few days. Stuck in the Cold War mindset that non–nation-state threats can be handled when America is ready to do so, the Pentagon's negligence cost America the chance of destroying any significant segment of al-Qaeda and Taliban forces before they dispersed.[10] So inadequate were the U.S. military's plans to attack America's attackers that even stationary targets in Afghanistan stood unmolested until the aerial bombardment began on October 7, 2001. By the time U.S. military personnel were ready to hit the ground in Afghanistan, CIA officers had cleared landing zones, recruited Afghan proxies, set up tents, and had the coffee brewing.

Adding to the lethargy of the going-to-war effort was Washington's controlling Cold War impulse: build a coalition to join America in waging war. While the unprepared U.S. military prepared, President Bush, Secretary of State Colin Powell, National Security Adviser Condoleezza Rice, and Vice President Dick Cheney directed, like carnival barkers, cries at the international audience: "Come on down! Join us for Operation Enduring Freedom!"[11] Because of the shocking nature of the 9/11 attack, the old Cold War juju worked, and allies galore came forward to sign up in the context of the glib and silly French headline "We are all Americans now." Even Colin Powell—he of the surround-and-kill-the-Iraqi-army doctrine of 1990–91—turned into what Claude Rains would have called a "rank sentimentalist," telling President Bush that the 9/11 attack "is not just an attack on America, this is an attack on civilization and an attack against democracy."[12] Buried amid weepiness, behind-the-scenes coercion,[13] and the confident expectations of a quick victory that drove the rapid growth of the nascent coalition, several key facts were forgotten: that it was the United States that had been attacked, that the U.S. military could and should have taken care of al-Qaeda by itself, and that the motley group of allies that signed up for the Hindu Kush adventure would do only two things: limit the amount of savagery America could use to annihilate its foe, and agitate for leaving before the job was done. We surely needed access to Afghanistan from Pakistan, Uzbekistan, and the Persian Gulf, but the only place where a genuine need for on-the-ground military partners existed was in our leaders' Cold War–dominated imaginations.[14]

Another consequence of Cold War thinking on America's Afghan War was, of course, the irony that the George W. Bush administration found itself confronted with the necessity of fighting it. The war would not have had to be fought if the Clinton administration had not been so palsied by its Cold War hangover that it failed to kill bin Laden when it had multiple chances to do so. Former President Clinton injected this issue into the 2006 congressional elections by telling Fox News's Chris Wallace that his administration had taken every opportunity presented to it to eliminate Osama bin Laden and the threat he posed.[15] Mr. Clinton lied in this regard[16] but correctly admitted that he failed. He then added, however, that his national-security team had left the incoming Bush administration a complete master plan for the invasion of Afghanistan, the defeat of the Taliban, and the elimination of bin Laden and al-Qaeda. Mr. Clinton described this plan as "a comprehensive anti-terrorism strategy."[17] Now, intelligence officers like myself are always acutely aware that there are things they do not know, even in areas for which they are directly responsible. They are trained, moreover, not to question the veracity of the commander in chief. In this case, however, I believe that America heard that rarity—a deliberate, knowing lie from Mr. Clinton. To the best of my knowledge, there was no master plan left behind by the Clinton administration for the incoming Bush administration.[18]

After the October 12, 2000, al-Qaeda attack on the USS *Cole,* the National Security Council ordered the CIA and other appropriate IC components to establish and maintain an up-to-date list of Taliban and al-Qaeda targets in Afghanistan that could be struck by the U.S. military if bin Laden again attacked U.S. interests. You will note that the NSC directive was predicated on the concept of "if al-Qaeda attacks U.S. interests *again,*" which clearly suggests that the members of Mr. Clinton's NSC team who dealt with counterterrorism at least recognized al-Qaeda's culpability for the *Cole* attack. I can say with confidence that CIA working-level officers had no doubt about who had authored the attack on the *Cole*—al-Qaeda's fingerprints were visible from the moment the water-borne bomb was detonated. Whatever the reason Mr. Clinton decided not to militarily respond to the near-sinking of the *Cole,* it was not due to a lack of intelligence pointing to al-Qaeda's culpability. It may well have been that DCI Tenet and senior FBI officials who were dealing with Mr. Clinton and his staff on the issue sensed that the White House did not want to attack Afghanistan in the midst of the presidential election and so those officials maintained a false sense of ambiguity through Election Day. If so, however, their motivation could only have been sycophancy, not genuine uncertainty.[19]

In any event, at the time of the *Cole* bombing I was the chief of counternarcotics operations in Southwest Asia, and several of my officers were assigned to be part of the team that was drawn from the CIA, the Defense Intelligence Agency (DIA), the NSA, and U.S. Central Command (CENTCOM) to create and maintain the NSC-mandated target list that existed from late October 2000 to 9/11. The target list included airfields, training camps, military storage facilities, infrastructure targets, heroin factories,[20] and other physical assets of the Taliban and al-Qaeda. So far as I know, this target list was the full extent of the master plan for the annihilation of the Taliban and al-Qaeda left behind by Mr. Clinton and his advisers for Mr. Bush's team. Obviously, such a list was not meant to serve as the basis for an invasion that would put paid to the Taliban and al-Qaeda. Rather, it was designed for the kind of operation so beloved of our Cold War–addled governing elite, particularly those of the Democratic persuasion: a punitive air attack with precision weapons, which is always ineffective and indecisive but allows us to preempt most international criticism of a disproportionate and indiscriminate response and that reduces the domestic political problems that would be caused by American battlefield casualties.

As minimal as was Mr. Clinton's post-*Cole* planning, however, the new Bush administration, in its first of many acts of self-immolating arrogance, threw out the Clinton-era target list before day's end on 9/11, thereby voluntarily abandoning the only well-prepared basis for immediate U.S. retaliation. When the new Rumsfeldian target list appeared, the heroin factories were not included. Much to the relief of the world's richest and most militarily adept heroin traffickers—and to the chagrin of our British allies, whose country's crime problem is mostly driven by Afghan heroin entering its borders—Mr. Rumsfeld left in place the cultivated fields and production infrastructure that has made Afghanistan in 2008 the largest heroin manufacturer in the history of mankind. And in a case of tragic poetic justice, the U.S. Drug Enforcement Agency reported in January 2007 that Afghan heroin is for the first time beginning to enter the United States in significant quantities.[21]

A final element that did not seem to cross the minds of U.S. leaders and policymakers as they undertook the invasion of Afghanistan was that the country is but one part of a bigger whole known as the Islamic world. This had not always been the case. Prior to the 1979 Soviet invasion, Afghanistan was on the periphery of the Islamic world—and was perceived so by Arabs; it practiced an easygoing brand of Islam that was heavily informed and moderated by tribal traditions and mores. The Afghan-Soviet war changed that, however, and the practice of Islam in Afghanistan today has moved closer to the Arab model; as important, both Afghans and non-Afghan Muslims see Afghanistan as a much more integral part of the Islamic world than ever before. While in no way comparable to the centrality of a heartland Muslim country like Iraq in the minds, imagination, and historical consciousness of Muslims, Afghanistan is still seen as an important part of the ummah (the community of believers), one that, having given all Muslims hope by defeating the invading atheist Soviets in 1989, is once again occupied and oppressed by infidel invaders. Thus, Washington should have been aware at some point soon after the U.S.-led invasion of Afghanistan that the Muslim world's view of that action would transition quickly from a grudging tolerance of it as a perhaps necessary act of self-defense to a conclusion that its prolonged and open-ended nature is another example of malignant U.S. intent toward Islam and Muslims.[22]

Waging the Afghan War, a Macro View:
Time, Topography, and Democratic Fantasies

One central, vital, and unavoidable fact is essential for any non-Muslim military force planning to invade Afghanistan to keep in mind—the welcome you receive will be limited and will begin to decay from the moment the first soldier's boot touches Afghan soil. The welcome, moreover, will be beguiling because those who most warmly welcome the non-Muslims will be those whose only chance of gaining and keeping power depends on being installed by foreign bayonets and being protected by the invaders as they evolve into occupiers. This group of infidel-welcoming Afghans has never been large or ruthless enough to hold and administer the country after the invaders were defeated and sent packing by their countrymen. The very fact that we remain in Afghanistan seventy-five months after our arrival underscores our ignorance on this point and, more important, shows that our leaders still believe we can operate on Cold War time, taking whatever time we need to work things out to our satisfaction and secure our intended accomplishments and implicitly assuming that our enemies will allow us that time. The best example of this thinking, of course, was the decision by U.S. generals that resulted in bin Laden's 2001 escape from Tora Bora. In making that decision, they stuck hard to the Cold War script: U.S. casualties are unpopular at home so do not risk troops; protect U.S. troops by using Afghan mujahedin proxies to go into the mountains after bin Laden, and employ Pakistani military proxies to close the border and block bin Laden's escape; and try to get him, but if you fail another chance will occur.[23]

Then, too, we have conducted the Afghan war with a startlingly cavalier disregard for geographic realities. Look at the map of Afghanistan. It is a country that is as big as Texas, hosts many of the highest mountains on earth, and shares borders of varying length with five nations whose populations are overwhelmingly Muslim, some militantly so. A good deal of the topography along the Pakistan-Afghanistan border—from Konar in the north to Baluchistan in the south—is incompletely mapped, a fact that makes planning military or clandestine operations extraordinarily difficult. During the 1979–92 CIA covert-action program to support the Afghan mujahedin against the Soviets, for example, we were forced to use U.S. military maps that were more than twenty years old and incomplete, captured Russian military maps, and sketch maps made by the Afghan insurgents whose talents bore no resemblance to those of Rand-McNally. When we invaded Afghanistan in 2001, we were using the same U.S. military maps, a more modern set of Russian-made maps, and maps drawn in the nineteenth century by British and Indian military engineers and clandestine cartographers—the legendary *pandits*—working for the Viceroy of India. The latter, not surprisingly, are the best of the lot. Satellite photography does, of course, help U.S. personnel to understand the topography, but there is no adequate substitute for reliable topographic maps for the military or clandestine-service officer operating there on the ground.

And how many troops do the United States and NATO have in Afghanistan to defeat an accelerating insurgency and install a Western-style secular democracy? About fifty thousand at this writing. Yes, no kidding, fifty thousand. And in that total there are contingents—Germans and Danes, for example—whose rules of engagement make their primary tasks school-building, police-training, and well-digging, not combat meant to kill insurgents. Even among the national contingents most aggressively fighting the Taliban—Americans, Canadians, British, and Australians—one has to be concerned about the number of fighters that can actually be fielded. In this era of the increasing electronic sophistication of conventional military forces—computers, communications gear, precision weapons, etc.—the number of support personnel today must be a larger percentage of the total force than was the case with the 120,000-man contingent that the Soviet Union fielded in Afghanistan between 1979 and 1989. This is especially the case because Moscow's forces were equipped with small arms, rocket-launchers, tanks, artillery, and armored vehicles that were first produced during and just after World War II. It always has surprised me that no one in the U.S. media ever asks the U.S. secretary of defense or the chairman of the Joint Chiefs of Staff what the "tooth-to-tail ratio" is for U.S. and NATO forces in Afghanistan, or in Iraq for that matter. I suspect that the number of actual combat troops that can be fielded on any given day is only a fraction of the fifty-thousand-man total and smaller than the reciprocal total for the Taliban, al-Qaeda, and their allies. A truthful answer to this question would, I think, shock Americans with how much their leaders are asking to be done by so few U.S. and NATO soldiers.

So, faced with a waning welcome, hamstrung by geographical ignorance, and using a combat force probably not large enough to occupy and control a country the size of South Carolina, the U.S.-led coalition then proceeded to behave as if it were fighting a traditional nation-state: it invaded, took Kabul and the other major Afghan cities, and declared victory. Western leaders mistakenly interpreted the joy of Kabulis over the arrival of their occupiers (Kabul is the least representative Afghan city; it was a haven for Western hippies in the 1960s and was Communist-run in the 1970s and 1980s) and projected that belief over the rest of the country and settled in to reconstruct and democratize the country.[24] Meanwhile the Taliban and al-Qaeda evacuated across open borders at all four points of the compass to fight another day, and the rural Afghan population—that is, the poorest and most religious of the country's people—began to feel the deterioration of law and order that accompanied the temporary overthrow of the Taliban regime. The truth is that Afghans missed the Taliban almost before they were gone because of the postinvasion resurgence of banditry in rural Afghanistan.

Believing that the Afghan war was over, the U.S.-led coalition began holding elections, rebuilding damaged structures and roads, and fielding Provincial Reconstruction Teams to build schools, inoculate children, and refurbish irrigation systems. In addition, hundreds of Western NGOs raced to get to Kabul and then to the countryside, thereby reinforcing a growing perception among Afghans that their country was again in the hands of non-Muslim conquerors. At this point we again run into one of those quaint and always-wrong assumptions that the West operates on when it intervenes in a Muslim country. Whether in Washington, London, or The Hague, the most basic assumption of nation-building is that if poor, illiterate, unhealthy Muslims are given potable water, schooling, prenatal care, and voting booths, they will abandon their faith, love Israel, demand visits by Salman Rushdie, and encourage their daughters to be feminist with a moral sense alien to most of the Islamic world—that is, they will try to become Europeans.

This, of course, has never occurred in the wake of a Western intervention in a Muslim country. Islam invariably becomes more, not less, important to the inhabitants of an invaded Muslim country, and while improvements in water, disease resistance, and schoolbooks are appreciated, they are not religiously transforming. We simply end up with Muslims who are better educated, healthier, and more militantly Islamic. This has happened in countries (Somalia, Afghanistan, Iraq, and several of the Balkan states) and in prison camps; in Guantanamo Bay, for example, we are building a truly dedicated and virulently anti-U.S. mujahedin battalion, the members of which will have the best-cared-for teeth in the Islamic world. But through it all, U.S. and Western leaders, the UN, and untold numbers of NGO spokespersons continue to sell shopworn lies to Western electorates—that nation-building will yield secularists who will desire only to live in peace with their Western conquerors. This type of thinking will ultimately prove calamitous for the United States and Europe because it assumes Muslims can be bribed from their faith by imposed material improvements and because it continues to ignore the source of Muslim animosity toward the West: the impact of our foreign policies and our increasing military presence in the Islamic world. In essence, Muslims see the secular Western mores brought to the poor and illiterate of the Islamic world as the baggage of infidel invaders, and it is more likely to produce Islamist enemies than postmodern, European-like atheistic hedonists.[25] Ask yourself, for example, how much the comprehensive system of social-welfare benefits in the European Union has stopped or even slowed the growth of Islamist militancy across Europe.

Waging the Afghan War, a Micro View:
If Only U.S. Leaders Knew History!

Since I resigned from the CIA in November 2004, the question I have been most often asked is "Why have we not captured or killed bin Laden?" My answer is seldom fully satisfactory to the questioner, as I try to explain that bin Laden takes advantage of mountainous terrain; stays with welcoming and protecting tribes that regard him as a guest and an Islamic hero; has nearly a quarter-century of experience living and fighting in the region; has a record of standing by the Afghans in their war against the USSR; and has scarce U.S. forces on the ground looking for him. I sometimes add that America is paying the price for its Republican and Democratic leaders' decisions not to kill bin Laden when they had repeated chances to do so. This last comment, however, often leads to acrimony, as some questioners assume I am either a Clinton-basher or a Bush-detractor (I am both on their failure to defend America) and that such partisanship makes me a shill for one or the other party, or an intelligence officer trying to find political scapegoats to blame for the CIA's failure to collect intelligence good enough to allow bin Laden to be eliminated.[26]

The best answer to the question, however, would be that we have not captured or killed bin Laden and are losing the war in Afghanistan because U.S. leaders and generals here blithely ignored that country's two-plus millennia of history. As noted, scholars and retired intelligence officers far smarter than I am have explained that Afghan history teaches that the country cannot be successfully invaded and controlled. In advice meant for the Bush administration and U.S. military leaders, the eminent British historian and great friend of the United States Sir John Keegan wrote on September 20, 2001, that Afghanistan is "unstable, fractious, and ultimately ungovernable" and urged Washington to steer well clear of a "general war and of policies designed to change the society or government in Afghanistan."[27] Sir John was not arguing that America should refrain from attacking Afghanistan—9/11 was an act of war—but rather that its focus should be on its only true objective: to quickly kill bin Laden, al-Zawahiri, Mullah Omar, and as many of their lieutenants and foot-soldiers as possible. History, Sir John said, held the key for the United States.

> Efforts to occupy and rule [Afghanistan] usually ended in disaster. But straightforward punitive expeditions . . . were successful on more than one occasion. It should be remembered that, in 1878, the British did indeed succeed in bringing the Afghans to heel [with a punitive expedition]. Lord Roberts' march from "Kabul to Khandahar" was one of Victoria's celebrated wars. The Russians, moreover, foolishly did not try to punish rogue Afghans, as Roberts did, but to rule the country. Since Afghanistan is ungovernable, the failure of their [1979–92] effort was predictable . . . America should not seek to change the regime, but simply to find and kill the terrorists. It should do so without pity.[28]

Get in fast, kill faster, and get out still faster, was Sir John's sage advice. And for anyone caring to read a bit of history, these recommendations were seconded by the very British general to whom Sir John referred, Lord Roberts of Khandahar. "It may not be very flattering to our *amour propre*," Roberts wrote to his military and political superiors after the success of his 1878 punitive expedition, "but I feel sure that I am right when I say that the less the Afghans see of us the less they will dislike us. Should Russia in future years attempt to conquer Afghanistan, or invade India through it, we should have a better chance of attaching the Afghans to our interests if we avoid all interference with them in the meantime."[29] Notwithstanding the ready availability of such sound advice from a distinguished pro-U.S. scholar, as well as a general who is perhaps the only infidel military practitioner who was ever successful in Afghanistan, U.S. leaders said, Thanks for the comments, but history does not pertain to America, and we will—like Sinatra—do it our way. They did, and they will suffer a calamitous loss in Afghanistan because of it.

Beyond failing to read history, U.S. leaders have conducted the hunt for Osama bin Laden without giving any evidence that they are aware of what the U.S. government knew before the 2001 invasion about bin Laden and his wide-ranging ability to operate along the Afghanistan-Pakistan border. Killing bin Laden once he was cornered in the mountains of Tora Bora was necessary not only to punish the author of 9/11 but to prevent him from escaping into an area he knows extremely well. Based on information gathered since the late 1980s, U.S. leaders should have been aware that on arriving in Pakistan in 1979–80, bin Laden established close working relationships with Afghan Islamist leader Gulbuddin Hekmatyar's Hizbi Islami Insurgent group[30] and with the Pakistani Islamist leader Qazi Hussein Ahmed and his Jamaat-e Islami political party. Both of those organizations were then and are now active in the tribal regions. In those first Afghan-jihad years, bin Laden—probably with the help of the Saudi intelligence service under Prince Turki—also developed a relationship with Pakistan's Inter-Services Intelligence Directorate (ISID) and the Pakistani army, both of which facilitated his access to the border regions during the Afghan jihad. Bin Laden also had a basis for finding sanctuary in the Pashtun tribal lands straddling the Pakistan-Afghanistan border through the activities of an Islamist NGO called the Makhtab al-Khidimat, or Services Bureau, which he and Shaykh Abdullah Azzam founded in the early 1980s to assist the Afghan mujahedin. Since the 1980s the Makhtab and tens of other Muslim NGOs have been active in the tribal areas in both humanitarian and military affairs. Overall, bin Laden spent almost a decade before al-Qaeda was formed in 1988 developing working relationships with Pashtun tribal leaders on the Pakistani side of the border and with the galaxy of Islamic NGOs (most sponsored by Saudi Arabia or other states on the Arabian Peninsula) that first set up shop in Peshawar, then spread into Afghanistan, and over time established offices across Pakistan. Most of the latter remain active today, contributing to the ongoing Islamization of Pakistani society.

On the Afghan side of the border, bin Laden began in about 1985 to cultivate ties with Yunis Khalis's Hizbi Islami faction, which had earlier split with Hekmatyar, and this gave him access to Nangarhar province and the adjacent areas in Pakistan; like Hekmatyar, Khalis and his commanders would be instrumental in facilitating bin Laden's escape from Tora Bora in 2001. At the same time bin Laden built a durable relationship with Khalis's top commander, Jalaluddin Haqqani, in the area around Khowst in Paktia province and the adjacent areas of Waziristan controlled by Haqqani's Zadrani tribe. Indeed, bin Laden appears to have gained his first combat experience by leading a team of combat engineers in support of Haqqani's fighters. The team used construction equipment brought to Afghanistan from the bin Laden family's company in Saudi Arabia. It also appears that bin Laden made some of his first contacts with Kashmiri insurgents— fighters who later formed the Harakat ul-Ansar and Lashkar-e Tayba—at the Khowst-area training camps run by Haqqani. In addition, by the mid-1980s bin Laden enjoyed a strong relationship with the Islamic Union party of Abdur Rasul Sayyaf, who currently is a member of the Afghan parliament. Bin Laden first trained some of his Arab fighters at Sayyaf's Sada Military Academy in northern Waziristan on the Pakistani side of the border, and he later built a camp of his own in an area controlled by Sayyaf's group in the Jaji area of Paktia province.

Finally, throughout the Afghan jihad bin Laden worked to ingratiate himself in Konar province and the area known as Nurestan, the northernmost Afghan sections of the Pakistan-Afghanistan border. Toward this end, he took advantage of Hekmatyar's presence in the area and of the close ties Shaykh Azzam had with Ahmed Shah Masood's forces and the Afghan Jamiat Islami party, to which Masood belonged. Bin Laden built on the latter by sending funding and military trainers and advisers to Masood; al-Qaeda's first military commander would use the nom de guerre Abu Ubayda al-Panshjeri, a name he earned while serving with Masood and operating out of the Panshjer Valley. Bin Laden also took advantage of the work Saudi Salafi NGOs and missionary organizations had long been doing on both sides of the border in the Nurestan-

Konar-Chitral (Pakistan) area, efforts that have made the area the most thoroughly Salafist-oriented region in Afghanistan. Bin Laden has said that he would have preferred to move in May 1997 from the Jalalabad area to Konar because of its remoteness and the prominence of Salafism there but decided that it was politically necessary to accept the Taliban's invitation to move to Khandahar.

Bin Laden and al-Qaeda, therefore, had plenty of friendly contacts and allies along most of the length of the Pakistan-Afghanistan border at the time of the U.S.-led invasion in 2001. And the Taliban, of course, is dominated by men drawn from the Pashtun tribes that live on both sides of the border and so had an even easier time securing assistance for their escape. This information was available to the U.S. government well before the invasion and shaped the analysis that the Intelligence Community provided at the time. The core of that assessment was simply that bin Laden's al-Qaeda had a wide variety of exit points along the border, stretching from Konar to Baluchistan, and would find no shortage of tribes, political groups, and insurgent organizations on both sides of the border that would be ready to assist their evacuation from Afghanistan. In addition, al-Qaeda could count on the networks of Islamic NGOs in Karachi, Peshawar, Quetta, and Lahore to assist those cadres leaving Pakistan once they exited the tribal regions on the border. The assessment also stressed that Pakistan's border forces were lightly armed militias that were drawn from the local tribes and were beholden to and took their orders from tribal leaders, not from political or military authorities in Islamabad. Because the Pashtun tribes along the border were pro-Taliban and pro–al-Qaeda, Pakistan's border forces would pose no obstacle to the Islamists' evacuation. Finally, the assessment stressed that the Pakistani military and intelligence services would be very inclined to assist Taliban forces evacuating Afghanistan and that it would be naïve to believe they would not likewise assist al-Qaeda fighters, notwithstanding President Musharraf's pledge to the contrary. In this regard, leading Saudi figures probably pressed Musharraf not to place too much emphasis on border control. Some support for this conclusion can be found in the fact that the Pakistani military did not stop Qazi Hussein Ahmed's Jamaat-e Islami and the Kashmiri Lashkhar-e Tayba—both supported by wealthy Saudi donors—from moving cadres from eastern Pakistan into the western border areas to assist fleeing Taliban and al-Qaeda fighters.

Faced with this well-documented reality, the U.S. government proceeded to ignore the clear and absolute necessity of deploying sufficient U.S. and coalition forces to close the Pakistan-Afghanistan border and instead relied on Pakistan to do so.[31] By seeking proxies to do its dirty work and by putting an unconscionably small number of troops in Afghanistan, Washington ensured that most al-Qaeda and Taliban fighters would escape with their arms to fight another day. And then things got much worse.

After bin Laden's escape and a spasm of inconclusive U.S. military operations concluding at Shahi Kowt in March 2002,[32] Washington's Afghan policy, which had bipartisan support, was dominated by policies that could only have come from unreformed Cold War thinkers. Washington's fixation on nation-states focused U.S. efforts in Afghanistan on trying to build a secular, pluralistic polity just as it did in Germany and Japan after World War II and the countries of Eastern Europe after the Soviet collapse. Washington installed Masood's minority-groups-dominated Northern Alliance in Kabul as the governing regime and put at its head Hamid Karzai, a detribalized Pashtun who had spent most of the war against the USSR abroad. In so doing U.S. officials did not seem aware that they were undoing by force of infidel arms a three-plus-century tradition of Pashtun rule in Afghanistan; if they knew of this tradition, they ahistorically and foolishly concluded that the Afghan world started anew on the day of the U.S.-led invasion. The subsequent elections for parliament and president put more Pashtuns into the central government, but the Pashtun tribes perceived that the United States was keeping both the levers of military power and the revenue coffers firmly in the hands of the Afghan minorities—their historic ethnic enemies—and the Westernized Pashtun elite. The upshot was, ironically, that because Washington decided to remake Afghan society in America's image rather than a two-millennia-old Afghan image, it ensured that not even a nominally effective nation-state—which is the best that has ever existed in Afghan history—would be created during the U.S. occupation. For the Pashtuns, the advent of elections and democracy in Afghanistan simply meant that their enemies would hold power and that therefore their only sensible option was to support the return of the Taliban and al-Qaeda to power and with them seek the reestablishment of their traditional political primacy by military means.

Concluding the War, Learning the Lessons of Defeat

For the United States, the war in Afghanistan has been lost. By failing to recognize that the only achievable U.S. mission in Afghanistan was to destroy the Taliban and al-Qaeda and their leaders and get out, Washington is now faced with fighting a protracted and growing insurgency. The only upside of this coming defeat is that it is a debacle of our own making. We are not being defeated by our enemies; we are in the midst of defeating ourselves. It makes one believe, or at least hope, that there is still some validity to Winston Churchill's maxim that God always protects drunks and the United States of America.

How did we manufacture this defeat? By deciding not to continue the military campaign to the point that the Taliban and al-Qaeda were annihilated. By incorrectly assuming that a six-month demonstration of our massive military power had permanently cowed the enemy and that we safely could move on to reconstruction activities aimed at bringing pluralistic democracy and secularism to an ethnically divided and intensely tribal Islamic land. By removing the tough but effective law-and-order regime the Taliban had established over most of Afghanistan and then failing utterly to replace it with a regime as good, causing increasing numbers of Afghans to yearn for the Taliban's harsh but effective security system. Most especially, by believing that the lessons of history did not apply to the United States. We let the enemy escape across open borders; we concluded that winning the Afghan cities equated to winning the war; we believed that Afghans wanted representative government more than security for their families; we stayed six-plus years in a country where a foreigner's welcome begins to decay the day he arrives; we believed we could do with a small, multinational force of 50,000 troops and civility what the Red Army could not do with 120,000 troops and the utmost barbarity; and we thought that by establishing a minority-dominated semisecular, pro-Indian government, we would neither threaten the identity nor raise the ire of the Pashtun tribes nor endanger Pakistan's national security.[33]

In view of the willful historical ignorance apparent in Washington's Afghan strategy and operations, it is important that, after the U.S.-led coalition is defeated in Afghanistan, Americans not let their political and military leaders off the hook of responsibility. These leaders are already beginning to claim—and the claims will grow shriller over time—that the coming U.S. defeat is the result of the unexpected consequences flowing from well-intended U.S. actions. Charity demands that we give U.S. leaders the benefit of the doubt when they claim that they did not intend the consequences that are causing us to lose the war. But we must not allow them to evade culpability for their historical ignorance. Unintended consequences are not always unpredictable consequences, and in Afghanistan (as well as in Iraq) the disasters that have befallen America since 2001 were predictable in the context of historical experience. For the continuing utility of learning history and the predictability of what the United States is now experiencing in Afghanistan, reflect on the following passage from the eminent classicist Frank L. Holt. Such reflection surely will discredit the official alibi of unintended consequences. "Alexander's reputation as a military genius, though richly deserved," Holt writes of a time two millennia past,

> cannot mask some of the miscalculations he pioneered in Bactria [the Greek name for Afghanistan] . . . Alexander's soldiers had been trained to wage and win major battles, but the king now shifted them into new and uncomfortable roles. One minute they were asked to kill with ruthless and indiscriminate intensity, the next they were expected to show deference to survivors . . .
>
> The mythical Hydra provides a defining image of Afghan warfare through the years. The ability of the foe to regenerate itself demoralizes even the most self-assured invaders. This kind of hydra-like warfare exacts a heavy toll on everyone, and its effects are psychological as well as physical. The smashing victories of Alexander's troops against the armies of Darius had occurred years earlier, closer to home . . . In those campaigns the veterans with Alexander had grown accustomed to a comforting expectation: when they fought someone, they absolutely prevailed, and the defeated enemy always stayed defeated. This arrogance of power, as so often since, lost its punch in Afghanistan. The place and its people took no heed of recent history, ignored the strength and sophisticated modernity of the invaders, and cared little for the time-honored conventions of treaties and truces. They fled like bandits if confronted with overwhelming force, then attacked whenever the odds were better. You could never tell if you were winning the war or not.[34]

CHAPTER 4

Iraq—America Bled White
by History Unlearned

A too great inattention to past occurrences retards and bewilders our judgment in every thing; while on the contrary, by comparing what is past with what is present, we frequently hit on the true character of both, and become wise with very little trouble.

Thomas Paine, 1777

He who is the author of war lets loose the whole contagion of hell and opens a vein that bleeds a nation to death.

Thomas Paine, 1777

The hen is the wisest of all the animal creation, because she never cackles until after the egg is laid.

Abraham Lincoln, 1863

As Thomas Paine noted in his more lucid moment above, history is important. This lesson was drilled into me as an undergraduate by Jesuit and lay professors in the department of history at Canisius College in Buffalo, New York. Those good men taught, and I accepted, that we get wisdom and an ability to realistically analyze our lives and our world from studying history. When I began researching my first book on bin Laden, my hold on the general history of the Islamic world was pretty superficial and needed to be greatly expanded. I hope it has improved, although some would argue it has regressed. Be that as it may, I initially turned to the works of Bernard Lewis, a scholar regularly ranked as the West's finest interpreter and analyst of the Muslim world. And indeed Dr. Lewis did not disappoint; his

117

work is voluminous, imaginative, detailed, and provocative. In an article he published in November 1998, for example, I learned a fact about which I was theretofore at best dimly aware. I was educated in an era that left many Americans believing that Jerusalem was the most important holy site for both Muslims and Jews, but Dr. Lewis corrected that perception, writing that while Arabia, Iraq, and Jerusalem were the most sacred sites in Islam, Westerners were not familiar with "the sequence and emphasis" Muslims attached to the three sites. "For Muslims, as we in the West sometimes tend to forget but those familiar with Islamic history and literature know," Dr. Lewis explained,

> the holy land par excellence is Arabia—Mecca, where the Prophet was born; Medina, where he established the new Muslim state; and the Hijaz, whose people were the first to rally to the new faith and become its standard bearers. Muhammad lived and died in Arabia, as did the Rashidun caliphs, his immediate successors at the head of the Islamic community. Thereafter, except for a brief interlude in Syria, the center of the Islamic world and the scene of its major achievements was Iraq, the seat of the caliphate for half a millennium. For Muslims, no piece of land once added to the realm of Islam can ever be finally renounced, but none compares in significance with Arabia and Iraq.[1]

I thus learned from Dr. Lewis the overwhelming historical and religious importance of Iraq in the Islamic worldview. Later, the ever-reliable guide Osama bin Laden buttressed my understanding through his many statements and interviews on the subject of Iraq's vital importance to Islam.[2] In an indirect way, Americans and Westerners also were warned about the dangers of occupying Iraq by the intensely negative Muslim reaction to the 1990 introduction of U.S.-led military forces into the Arabian Peninsula. That event was the last straw for bin Laden and to this day is a red flag for Islamists worldwide.[3] If the West's perceived violation of what Lewis called Arabia—now the multiple nation-states on the Arabian Peninsula— caused a state of war between the United States and the Islamist forces led by bin Laden, was it not reasonable to assume that the invasion and occupation of Iraq—second in importance only to Arabia—might well also cause a bloody fracas?

Nearly five years after the 2003 invasion of Iraq, it seems clear that not only did U.S. political and military leaders fail to read and understand Islamic history before they decided to invade Iraq, but also may not yet have done so. Writing in *The New York Times* on October 18, 2006, the *Congressional Quarterly*'s Jeff Stein discussed his several-month examination of U.S. counterterrorism capabilities and the extent to which official Washington understands America's Islamist enemies. One of Mr. Stein's basic questions for U.S. officials was "Do you know the difference between a Sunni and a Shiite?" Why was he asking? Explaining that this was not a "gotcha question" meant to embarrass the official being interviewed, and that he was not seeking detailed descriptions of the sects' theological differences, Stein said he was only looking for an answer that provided the basics: "Who's on what side today and what does each want?" Stein thought the following statement of reality justified an expectation that U.S. officialdom ought to know the rudiments of an enemy that currently is beating America in two insurgencies.

> The 1,400-year Shia-Shiite rivalry playing out in Baghdad's streets raises the specter of a breakup of Iraq into antagonistic states, one backed by Shiite Iran and the other by Saudi Arabia and other Sunni states. A complete collapse in Iraq could provide a haven for al-Qaeda operatives within striking distance of Israel, even Europe. And the nature of the threat from Iran, a potential nuclear power with protégés in the Gulf States, northern Saudi Arabia, Lebanon and the Palestinian territories, is entirely different from that of al-Qaeda.[4]

Certainly this was a fair enough reason to ask the Shia-or-Sunni question. And what were the results? Per Mr. Stein, "So far most Americans I have interviewed don't have a clue. That includes not only intelligence and law-enforcement officials, but also members of Congress who have important roles overseeing U.S. spy agencies."[5] Stein relates that the FBI is a hub of ignorance about Islam (no surprise there—senior FBI officers have long been resolutely proud of being clueless about all things Muslim), but the breadth of ignorance found by Stein betrays several factors that are more troubling than simple ignorance. First, the thousands of volumes about Islamic history, theology, and politics that the federal government bought after 9/11 appear to have not been cracked open and studied by many of America's civil servants. The saying "That's history, why waste time on it?" still seems to hold sway across the bureaucracy. Worse, the fact that these volumes lay unread suggests that U.S. officialdom still does not take the threat posed by nonstate actors—like al-Qaeda, its allies, and the Iraqi resistance—as seriously as it does the threat from nation-states. From my own experience, I never heard a senior U.S. official say that "I deal with the Soviet Union, but I do not need to know anything about Marx, Engels, Lenin, the Soviet order-of-battle, or Communist ideology." The USSR was a traditional nation-state, and officials, academics, and pundits were eager to learn all they could about its lineage, philosophy, motivations, armaments, and methods of operation. That Stein has found such enduring, post-9/11 ignorance augurs a continued series of bleedings and lethal surprises for America at the hands of Islamist nonstate actors. And in another irony for Americans, their leaders have abandoned one of the few Cold War behaviors that should have been properly retained—the ethos of knowing your enemy.

The reality is that if U.S. leaders had done their Islamic homework prior to invading Iraq, they would have known what a huge hornet's nest they were ordering the U.S. military to kick over. Perhaps the Bush team might even have decided not to invade once it had digested the stark, near-certainty of disaster that such a review of history would have exposed. "What ifs," of course, are fascinating to debate, but ultimately we have to deal with reality as it is, not as it might have been. That fact does not, however, diminish the importance of a government knowing the historical context in which its actions are about to be taken. Representative Terry Everett (R-Alabama), the vice chairman of the House intelligence subcommittee on technical and tactical intelligence, eloquently noted the importance of historical context after Mr. Stein explained to him the differences between Shiites and Sunnis. "Now that you've explained it to me," Mr. Everett told Stein with a truly disarming candidness, "what occurs to me is that it makes what we're doing out there extremely difficult, not only in Iraq but in the whole area."[6]

Stein's experience certainly was shared by many intelligence officers over the past several decades. In my own experience, I encountered U.S. senators who were surprised to learn that Muslims were going to govern Afghanistan after the Soviets withdrew in 1989, and we all saw and heard leading neoconservatives, like Richard Perle and R. James Woolsey, argue that so deep was the hatred of Sunnis and Shias for America that they had set aside sectarian differences and were cooperating in attacks against the United States. One wonders if those gentlemen and their jejune neoconservative colleagues have noticed how closely Shias and Sunnis are cooperating in the wake of the Iraq war that the neocons wanted and that their country is now losing. Taken together, the experiences that Mr. Stein and many U.S. intelligence officers have had with Islam-ignorant U.S. officials underscore the validity of the judgment of the *Atlantic*'s Robert D. Kaplan that "the greater the disregard of history, the greater the delusions regarding the future."[7] Such is not the stuff from which an effective U.S. national security policy can be made.

Going to War

In discussing America's war in Iraq, I must make two personal points. First, I am not an expert on Saddam Hussein, his regime, or the nation of Iraq and its people. My knowledge of Saddam and Iraq derives from having worked on identifying the Iraqi Intelligence Service's responsibility for trying to murder the first president Bush in 1993 and a much longer stint (1986–2004) watching how Saddam reacted to and dealt with Sunni extremist leaders and groups. I am therefore not an expert on the threat that Saddam's Iraq posed to the United States in the spring of 2003, but I am absolutely confident that there was a near-zero threat from the terrorism subset of the overall Iraqi threat. Most of the public's perception of a terrorist threat from Iraq came from a tendency among U.S. officials and media to conflate terrorist threats to Israel and those to America, and the prolonged and fortunately unsuccessful attempt by neoconservatives and their echoes at *The Weekly Standard*—especially Stephen Hayes[8]—to persuade Americans that there was a close working relationship between Saddam's Iraq and bin Laden's al-Qaeda.

The second point is that it has always seemed unfair to me to accuse the George W. Bush administration of "lying" about the existence of a WMD arsenal in Iraq at the time of the 2003 invasion. In 2002–3 most of the world's countries, not just the United States, believed that Saddam had WMD; the disagreement was over what should be done about them—more inspections or direct military action. The Bush team's mistake, it seems to me, is that it waited far too long before confessing that there were no mass-destruction weapons in Iraq; but again, the entire world anticipated finding such weapons there. Had I been asked about the threat from Iraq, I would have argued that even if Saddam had such weapons, he had no means of getting them to North America; again, Saddam's potential WMD threat to his Arab neighbors and Israel was equated—with the indispensable and deceitful neoconservative assistance—with a WMD threat to America. It also is a near certainty that Saddam never would have used WMD against Israel or Saudi Arabia, knowing that he would earn a catastrophic nuclear response from the former and devastating retaliation from the U.S. protectors of the latter. Saddam, moreover, would never have given WMD—weapons or technology—to al-Qaeda or other Islamists because he knew that the Islamists hated him nearly as much as they did Washington and Tel Aviv. In short, Washington failed to use the one Cold War strategy that was perfectly applicable to Iraq: it was a nation-state that could be neutered by continuing to apply the Cold War doctrine of containment. The Bush administration now has a second chance to use containment vis-à-vis the more dangerous but still eminently containable Iran, another state that may pose a threat to Israel while posing none to the United States, unless provoked.[9] We will see if they are smart enough to do so.

The real criticism of the Iraq war, it seems to me, should focus on the Bush administration's decision to start a second war before it had come anywhere close to annihilating the Taliban and al-Qaeda in Afghanistan. By the spring of 2002 the CIA's Counterterrorist Center (CTC) realized that the administration had decided to go to war with Iraq. There was no announcement to that effect, of course, but the intent was evident as the flow of officers sent to beef up the post-9/11 war against al-Qaeda ended and experienced Arabic-speaking officers were reassigned from CTC to Middle East posts and to the task forces at CIA headquarters charged with preparing for the Iraq war. While this shift was occurring, the pace of operations against al-Qaeda continued to accelerate, and successful captures of senior al-Qaeda leaders and their associates kept accumulating. Those involved with attacking al-Qaeda—unlike the White House, the Joint Chiefs, and both parties in Congress—recognized that the war in Afghanistan was just beginning and that it was premature to draw human resources away from the effort against al-Qaeda. The White House and Congress should also have recognized that it was daft to start a second infidels-attack-Islam war that would ensure that the first would be irretrievably lost, and that would speed the transformation of bin Laden and al-Qaeda from a man and an organization into a philosophy and a world-wide movement.

Intelligence officers who had been working against Sunni extremism since the early 1990s understood that the looming Iraq war was certain to destroy two of our most important and reliable de facto allies in that anti-Islamist struggle, Iraq and Syria. And they were the best kind of allies, in that Washington did not have to arm, coerce, bribe, or cajole them into acting in the most murderous manner against most Islamists. While our purportedly dear and loyal friends in Saudi Arabia, Kuwait, Qatar, and the United Arab Emirates cared little about what Islamist militants did in the world beyond the Arabian Peninsula—letting aid and would-be fighters flow to them, and funding the education of young Muslims worldwide in the jihadists' creed Saddam's Iraq and Hafez and then Bashir al-Assad's Syria were on a permanent war footing against them.

This is not to say that Saddam and the al-Assads were good guys—far from it. Yes, it is true that both Baghdad and Damascus did fund and train some Palestinian terrorists, secular and Islamic, who then attacked Israel. And Saddam did make cash payments to the families of successful Palestinian suicide bombers. Yes, Syria facilitated the flow of Iranian arms to Lebanese Hezbollah, which in turn used them to drive the Israel Defense Forces out of southern Lebanon. And yes, both regimes were willing to allow some Sunni extremists from groups like al-Qaeda, the Egyptian Gama'at al-Islamiyah, and the Egyptian Islamic Jihad to transit their territories, at times in a leisurely fashion. But what is even truer is that these Syrian and Iraqi actions primarily were meant to hurt Israel, not the United States, and that both the Baghdad and Damascus regimes viewed the Islamists as a significant threat to their hold on power. Neither state allowed Islamist groups bent on attacking the United States to establish permanent training camps or safe havens on their territory, and their security services dealt summarily with Islamists who overstayed their welcome or became involved in inappropriate activities while visiting. Each state tended to deal even more harshly with its domestic Islamist militants. In short, Saddam's Iraq and al-Assad's Syria were inherently helping the United States by standing as very effective bulwarks against any easy and secure westward movement of the Sunni jihad's main base in South Asia toward the Levant, Israel, and Europe.

Although it is not often mentioned, Saddam's Iraq also stood as a bulwark protecting Turkey and the Arabian Peninsula from al-Qaeda insurgents. One of bin Laden's worst nightmares has always been a Turkey that succeeds on its present course: an overwhelmingly Sunni Muslim state with the potential for proving that Islam is compatible with a semblance of Western democratic institutions. And of course, Saudi Arabia and the other oil-producing states on the Arabian Peninsula have been al-Qaeda's primary targets because Riyadh allowed U.S. and Western forces to deploy there starting in 1991 and because Kuwait, Qatar, Bahrain, and the United Arab Emirates have helped Washington maintain and, as needed, expand the U.S. military presence in the region since that year. As long as Saddam ruled Iraq, al-Qaeda and its allies had to content themselves with infiltrating Turkey from Europe and Iran, and the Arabian Peninsula through its ports and airports. Such infiltration could occur only in small numbers, giving local security regimes a sporting chance to suppress the activity. Without Saddam's effective police state, Islamist infiltration into Turkey and the Arabian Peninsula stands a far better chance of larger and more regular success.

Thus, after 9/11, as U.S. forces launched the war against al-Qaeda, Iraq and to a somewhat lesser extent Syria[10] stood in two ways as extremely important assets for Washington. In the short term the two countries were unwilling to host al-Qaeda fighters evacuating Afghanistan, thereby preventing an even greater westward dispersal than occurred. In the medium-to-long term, the existence and strength of the two regimes denied what bin Laden most needed to expand al-Qaeda's organizational and paramilitary operations into the Levant, Turkey, and states of the Arabian Peninsula; that is, contiguous safe haven. Bin Laden and his fighters had learned their insurgent trade during the Afghans' jihad against the Soviets. One of the major lessons bin Laden took from that war was the vital importance of contiguous safe haven for the survival, durability, succoring, and growth of the Afghan insurgency. The ability of the Afghan mujahedin and their Arab allies to establish facilities in Pakistan for refugees, to care for their wounded, and to train, rest, and store weapons and ordnance ensured that no matter how severe a drubbing they received at the hands of the Red Army and their Afghan Communist allies, the insurgents would never face a situation where they would have to fight to the death. Relatively safe areas inside Pakistan meant that Islamist fighters coming from outside South Asia were often able to relocate their families in the general vicinity of the war zone and visit them from time to time. The impression that the Pakistani safe haven made on bin Laden's thinking is clear. On several occasions he publicly described his inability to send a substantial number of fighters to Bosnia because there was no Pakistan-like entity in the Balkans; al-Qaeda could not stage out of or escape to Catholic Croatia or Orthodox Serbia. Likewise, bin Laden has railed against Jordan, Syria, Egypt, and Lebanon for refusing to allow non-Palestinian mujahedin to use their territory as a safe haven from which to attack Israel.[11]

So even as U.S. and NATO military and intelligence services continued to pursue and bomb al-Qaeda and Taliban fighters in the spring of 2003, bin Laden could see that the pending U.S.-led invasion of Iraq was going to present new opportunities for al-Qaeda and its allies to project force westward and into the Arabian Peninsula. After temporarily closing the Afghan window, Allah was, in effect, preparing to open the Iraqi door. The Bush administration's invasion of Iraq, therefore, yielded positive consequences for al-Qaeda from its first day, and while these consequences may have been unintended by Washington, they could certainly have been predicted. Absent the brutal but effective bulwark of Saddam's regime, al-Qaeda and the Islamists had an open field for acquiring contiguous safe haven on the borders of the Levant, Turkey, Saudi Arabia, Kuwait, and Iran and with it the ability to project power toward all points of the compass. By destroying the regime of America's de facto ally in Baghdad and weakening the helpful regime in Syria, Washington facilitated the relocation of the center of the Sunni jihad from Afghanistan to Iraq, in the middle of the Arab heartland, a thousand kilometers westward. The Bush administration's Cold War trait of preferring to fight and defeat nation-states immeasurably strengthened the much more dangerous transnational threat posed by the Sunni Islamists.

In the year preceding the U.S.-led invasion of Iraq, moreover, the continuing dominance of Cold War thinking among senior U.S. government councils was apparent in the case of Abu Musab al-Zarqawi. The al-Qaeda–associated al-Zarqawi had established a small presence in the Kurdish area of northern Iraq in the years prior to the 9/11 attack and reinforced it by moving fighters there from Afghanistan in late 2001. U.S. intelligence had followed al-Zarqawi's move to Iraq and managed to keep a good handle on his movements and activities there. By the spring of 2002, the intelligence showed that al-Zarqawi had established his headquarters in a camp in the Kurdish zone called Khurma or Khurmal. Physical and paramilitary training was being conducted in the camp, and there were credible reports that some members of al-Zarqawi's group were conducting rudimentary chemical-weapons experiments in the camp. The experiments focused on producing anthrax and ricin, and those toxins were used on horses and other farm animals to determine their effectiveness.[12]

Beyond knowing the location of the camp and having a good approximation of what was going on there, the information also showed that al-Zarqawi was in the camp. The flow of intelligence was steady, and thus the CIA's targeting officers' data quickly demonstrated the patterns of al-Zarqawi's activities, putting well within the realm of possibility the ability to fix him at a given place and time for an attack. Over the summer and fall of 2002 the quality of the intelligence on al-Zarqawi remained high, and the targeters came to the point of being routinely and reliably able to fix al-Zarqawi's location. Between March 2002 and the Iraq invasion, the White House had a chance to order an attack by the U.S. military on al-Zarqawi, his camp, and its chemical-weapons operations on at least a weekly basis. Reporting on such a high-priority target obviously was of high interest to the president, the NSC, and the Joint Chiefs of Staff, and data about al-Zarqawi's location and activities were delivered to them on an almost daily basis. To be frank, the officers on the team targeting al-Zarqawi believed his days were numbered: he was located in an area outside of Saddam's control, so an attack could not be viewed as an attack on Iraq; he was in Iraq preparing mujahedin forces to attack the U.S. military if an invasion occurred; his fighters were conducting experiments with chemical weapons; and all of this was occurring in a paramilitary training camp so there were no legitimate concerns about the collateral killing of civilians. Reinforcing this perception was the braying that senior administration and intelligence officials were doing about America having taken the gloves off its power after 9/11. They had betrayed these words by letting bin Laden escape from Tora Bora, so we were confident they would put their money where their mouths were in the case of al-Zarqawi. In the intelligence business there are very few dream targets, but we thought al-Zarqawi was one of those few.

We had to think again. Day after day, week after week, and month after month, complete target packages for al-Zarqawi were sent to those senior U.S. officials who could order an attack, but the order never came. Why? In the first instance, I think, the quality and steadiness of the intelligence gave policymakers the sense that they could kill al-Zarqawi when they pleased and so there was no hurry to make the decision. As during the Cold War, Washington believed the al-Zarqawi problem could be addressed at a time that fit its schedule. The more important reasons for not attacking, however, lay in three other Cold War attitudes: coalition-love, public-opinion currying, and fixation on nation-state threats. When the al-Zarqawi target packages were sent to policymakers, the reason consistently given to CIA targeters for not attacking was that the White House and the State Department were still working to convince the French and German governments to join the U.S.-led coalition for the invasion of Iraq. The policymakers feared that if they attacked and killed al-Zarqawi, European public opinion would judge the United States to be a trigger-happy gunslinger and thus reinforce the determination of Paris and Berlin to abstain from the war. In other words, Washington saw the threat from a traditional nation-state like Iraq as more dangerous than the threat from a less quantifiable transnational group, and so first things first: get the French and Germans on board against Saddam, and let al-Zarqawi live. A fairly irrefutable indictment of the failure of U.S. policymakers to wean themselves from Cold War thought-processes surely lies in the fact that al-Zarqawi was instrumental in killing more U.S. soldiers, civil servants, and civilian contractors, between the 2003 invasion and his own demise, than was Saddam Hussein's regime in the first and second Gulf Wars combined.

Conducting the War

The U.S.-led invasion and occupation of Iraq is another example of Washington's specialty: projecting immense military power without achieving lasting positive results for U.S. interests. U.S. soldiers and Marines, as always, displayed speed, innovativeness, and courage in quickly defeating Saddam's regular military forces. Encountering more resistance than anticipated from dispersed Iraqi regulars, armed Ba'ath party members, Iraqi irregulars (the Fedayeen Saddam[13]), and the first-arriving elements of non-Iraqi Islamist fighters, U.S. forces nonetheless prevailed in each battle in which they were engaged. Baghdad fell, Saddam's statue was pulled to the ground, and the media broadcast live scenes of Iraqis rejoicing in the capital and other major cities. Apparently unaware of Mr. Lincoln's advice about always being henlike and not cackling prematurely, President Bush, with some staged drama, declared that the U.S. mission in Iraq had been accomplished. Sadly, Mr. Bush, his lieutenants, and the American people did not recognize at the time that the mission that U.S. military forces had accomplished belonged to Osama bin Laden and the worldwide Islamist movement.

In those first heady days after the statue fell and while Saddam was staying a step ahead of his pursuers, U.S. generals, meeting in the Iraqi president's opulent palaces as befits imperial proconsuls, repeated their Afghan mistake of believing that to capture the cities of Iraq was to win the war. Like Ms. Rice viewing the scenes of rejoicing in Kabul after Taliban forces evacuated, the generals and the Bush administration extrapolated the celebrations in Baghdad and other cities into a country-wide assessment. In so doing, they misinterpreted relief over Saddam's departure as a durable and heartfelt welcome for an invading non-Muslim army of occupation. That this massive error occurred twice in eighteen months demonstrates the historical ignorance of our political leaders and seniormost generals. Generally speaking, history shows that most nation-state populations, with the possible exception of the French, do not like to be invaded and occupied, even if the invaders hand out MREs to families, candy to children, and fistfuls of greenbacks to all and sundry. History's list of unwelcomed and ultimately vanquished occupiers is far lengthier than the list of successful occupations. Iraq and Afghanistan were not Panama and Grenada.

As in the case of Afghanistan, Americans must not let their political leaders and generals off the hook of culpability by claiming that what happened in Iraq is a series of unfortunate but unintended consequences. Let us again be more than fair and accept that the bipartisan political leadership that took America to war in Iraq really did not intend to create the reality that now exists—the great intensification of the Islamists' power, motivation, manpower, and funding in Iraq and across the Muslim world. This surely is the major unintended consequence of the Iraq war, but it was an entirely predictable consequence. During the six years preceding the U.S.-led invasion, Osama bin Laden and Ayman al-Zawahiri conducted an education program that taught Muslims what to expect in terms of future

U.S. actions in the Islamic world. The United States would, they predicted, seek to destroy strong Muslim governments and replace them with "U.S. agent regimes." It would forbid or replace Islamic law and put man-made law, elections, and parliaments in its place, as well as destroy any Muslim regime deemed threatening to Israel, seek to control Muslim oil resources, and occupy or destroy Islamic holy sites. Briefly sketched, this was the perception trap that bin Laden and al-Zawahiri set for the Clinton and George W. Bush administrations; the former never understood it, and the latter walked unavoidably into it in Afghanistan and capriciously ensnared itself in it in Iraq. What most Muslims perceived in the U.S. invasion of Iraq was the confirmation of bin Laden's predictions about the malignant intent of America toward Islam and its followers. Victory in Iraq belonged to al-Qaeda and the Islamists from the moment the war began because Washington reliably and eagerly played the part assigned to it by al-Qaeda: the infidel invader of a Muslim country, against whom the Koran requires a defensive jihad. There must have been times when bin Laden and his lieutenants thought it was all just too easy.

Again, let us give the Bush team the benefit of the doubt and say they did not intend to provide the religious predicate for a worldwide defensive jihad against the United States, but they should be cut no slack whatsoever on the issue of predictability. Not a lick of classified intelligence information was needed to know what repercussions the invasion of Iraq would cause; all that was needed was to read the words of our Islamist enemies, know a bit about Islam and its history, and ignore the advice of politically motivated experts like Bernard Lewis, Charles Krauthammer, Fareed Zakaria, Max Boot, Fawaz Gerges, Reuel Marc Gerecht, and the rest of that prowar media lobby that helped sink U.S. interests in the sands of Iraq. And it is important to note that the damage done to the United States was done when the invasion's first air strike hit and the first armored unit crossed the start line in Kuwait. The looting of Baghdad, the disbanding of the Iraqi military, the complete de-Ba'athification of the bureaucracy, and L. Paul Bremer's reign of ruin and easygoing corruption all worsened the situation, but even without these factors the Islamists would have won. Once U.S. and Western forces set foot in Iraq, bin Laden's predictions were validated, and not even the tens of thousands of Islamic scholars and jurists who are fully owned and operated by Hosni Mubarak, Bashir al-Assad, the Algerian junta, and the Jordanian and Saudi kings could craft a credible theological argument to deny that the Koran's conditions for launching a defensive jihad had been met and then some. The Bush administration lost the war in Iraq, as in Afghanistan, because it did not know history and believed that, in any event, history held no lessons for the United States.

And regarding the chances of a Sunni-Shia civil war in Iraq? Again, this was and is a no-brainer for anyone with a nodding acquaintance with Islamic and Iraqi history. Most Americans bought the White House's denial that a civil war was occurring in Iraq for far too long primarily because of the absurd debate the administration generated with the media and academia over the definition of a civil war. Animosities between Sunnis and Shiites are deep, theologically substantive, a thousand years old, and always potentially lethal. No matter how dire the Afghan insurgents' prospects were against the Red Army or how intense and bloody the Taliban's campaign against Ahmed Shah Masood's Northern Alliance, for example, they always had time and resources to take a break and slaughter Afghan Shias or Iranian diplomats and intelligence officers. Sunni organizations in Pakistan have long made murdering Pakistani Shia and their leading clerics a top priority. The Sunni regimes on the Arabian Peninsula worry about Iran getting a nuclear weapon not because of the weapon itself (Sunni Pakistan has the bomb, and only a fool would be confident that the Saudis do not have nuclear warheads nestled on the top of their China-provided CSS-2 ICBMs) but because the finger on the trigger would belong to a Shia hard-liner in Tehran. For most Sunnis, Shias are heretics of the deepest hue, and while the Islamic world is replete with examples of Sunnis and Shias living amiably side by side, both sides are well aware that at some point the two sects will have a violent final reckoning. Indeed, there are those on each side of the sectarian divide who long for such a cataclysmic reckoning; the late Abu Musab al-Zarqawi was one of them.

Within the context of this latent and millennium-old intracivilizational conflict, the twentieth-century history of Iraq left a legacy that would have made it shocking if a civil war had not ensued after the destruction of Saddam's regime. For more than eighty years the Sunni minority had held the Shia majority, as well as the Kurds, in their murderous thrall. In the last thirty years Saddam held power by brutally instilling fear in all Iraqis and by delivering most of the necessities of life, while using his own

Sunni sect as the instrument for oppressing Shiites and Kurds. Enter George W. Bush, his team of reality-defying Wilsonians, and the bipartisan support of Congress. Besides handing a victory to the worldwide, bin Laden-led Sunni Islamist movement, Washington knowingly destroyed the governmental mechanisms that ensured Sunni supremacy and then expected to put in their place a secular, power-sharing government made up of Sunni, Shia, and Kurd leaders that would, with the rest of the Iraqi people, live happily and democratically ever after. After eliminating Saddam, the Bush administration and the bipartisan Congress appear to have believed that democracy could be quickly installed and that that event would cause Shiites and Kurds to forget the murders, gassings, rapes, tor-turing, and other injustices that were routinely doled out by Saddam and the Sunnis. And the American governing elite did not live alone in this fantasy world. Prime Minister Tony Blair's Britain, a country that experienced a very similar disaster in Iraq just after the Great War,[14] joined up, as did other NATO members and some U.S. allies from Asia and Latin America. As the radio host Don Imus often says when he is confronted by events or statements that seem singularly stupid: "You couldn't make this stuff up." But perhaps Machiavelli said it better: "And he deceives himself who believes that the great, recent benefits cause old wrongs to be forgotten."[15]

The U.S. governing elite's patent ignorance of the bitter Sunni-Shia schism also is visible in their belief that Iraq's Muslim neighbors would pitch in to make the post-Saddam nation a happy, multicultural, and secular place, a Switzerland on the Tigris, perhaps. It is best to ignore the prewar assertions by the above-mentioned political pundits that the Muslim regimes surrounding Iraq opposed the American invasion because they knew Washington would successfully establish a secular democracy there that would eventually spread across the region and destroy their tyrannies and police states. From the beginning these regimes knew that the U.S. government would fail in Iraq. How did they know? Well, for two reasons. First, the nearly inevitable post-Saddam Shia-Sunni civil war ruled out any chance of secular, democratic pluralism, even leaving aside the affront to Islam that the very idea of such a system presented. The Sunni-Shia face-off in Iraq would also be intensified by drawing popular support from the surrounding countries, with Iran and perhaps Syria backing Iraqi Shiites and the entire Sunni world backing their Iraqi brethren.

The second reason the region's Muslim regimes knew that the American plan for Iraq was going to fail was that they were going to make sure it failed. In a global sense, of course, the Sunni oil-producing states saw the end of the Cold War as greatly lessening their need to defer to the United States; they no longer needed U.S. military protection against the armed threat of Soviet Communism. From a regional geopolitical and national-interests perspective, moreover, Iraq's Sunni neighbors found the idea of creating a second large-population, oil-rich Shia state in the Sunni heart-land simply intolerable. For the Sunnis, Iran alone was enough of a prob-lem and threat, but at least the power of Iran was steadily being eliminated by its rapidly dwindling energy reserves. Sunni governments knew that in fifteen years, more or less, Iran would be home to a huge Shiite population but would lack the oil revenues to provide the economic wherewithal to threaten offensive actions against its Sunni neighbors. The creation of an oil-rich Shiite state in Iraq that would be allied with Iran against the Sunni world, however, would right the balance that was otherwise shifting in favor of the Sunnis.

For reasons of both sectarian hatred and national security, therefore, Iraq's Sunni neighbors would clandestinely intervene to whatever extent was necessary to defeat the U.S. effort. They were confident also that coalition-obsessed Washington would do nothing about their interference because it had long misled Americans by telling them that the Sunni states that would do most of the interfering in Iraq—Saudi Arabia, the other Gulf States, Egypt, Jordan, Algeria, and Yemen—were indispensable partners in the "Global War on Terrorism." In addition, the possibility of a strong U.S. response to this Sunni interference, which was designed to kill as many U.S. military personnel in Iraq as possible, was ruled out because the U.S. economy and the U.S. troops deployed in Iraq and Afghanistan were dependent on energy supplies delivered by the Sunni states of the Arabian Peninsula. The U.S. governing elite's failure to heed the warning sign attached to Saudi king Faisal's 1973 oil embargo ensured that the king's heirs could act with impunity to protect their national, as well as Sunni, interests in Iraq.

When it came to defeating U.S. efforts in Iraq, the Sunni states and Iran found their task almost ridiculously easy. They simply did nothing to con-tradict the jihad-is-the-road-to-paradise education that they had long deliv-ered to their young; through their clerical establishments they identified the

U.S. invasion of Iraq as proper Islamic justification for a defensive jihad; and they left open all or parts of their land borders with Iraq. By doing nothing out of the ordinary, therefore, these regimes acquiesced in the start of the flow of non-Iraqi Islamist insurgents to Iraq.[16] Here a piece of historical information is useful. During the Afghan jihad against the Soviet Union (1979–89), the Afghans played the most vital role in defeating the Red Army. Nonindigenous Muslims did, of course, travel to Afghanistan to assist the Afghans. How did the nonindigenous Muslim fighters get to the battlefield during the Afghan jihad? Well, their travel to the battlefield was certainly facilitated by the Muslim Brotherhood and other Islamist organizations—and some members of those groups, like bin Laden's close associates Shaykh Abdullah Azzam and the Saudi Wael Juliedan, actually joined the fight—as well as by some wealthy Muslim individuals and Arab governments. It is well known, for example, that Osama bin Laden's family business helped to get would-be mujahedin from across the Middle East to Afghanistan, and that Riyadh ordered Saudia, its international airline, to offer reduced-fare "jihad-fare" tickets to young men on their way to Afghanistan.[17]

While many of these non-Afghan Islamist fighters came to the anti-Soviet jihad on their own or were sponsored by wealthy individuals or private groups, many others came to Afghanistan out of the prisons of Arab states. The West often forgets that Arab prisons are built not only to house criminals but also to confine religious opponents of the regimes. Thus the prisons are generally full to overflowing with Islamist militants who, for example, oppose the brutality of Mubarak's Egyptian regime or the al-Sauds' greed, corruption, and opulence. Incarcerating these militants helps the regimes maintain societal control. Their detention, however, also has proved to increase their Islamic militancy because the extremist inmates tend to congregate and to be easy targets for instruction by jailed Islamist scholars and clerics, both of which breed a sense of fraternity. Al-Qaeda deputy leader Ayman al-Zawahiri emerged more militant and vicious after his incarceration and torture in post-Sadat Egypt, as did Abu Musab al-Zarqawi after his imprisonment in Jordan, during which he received extensive religious instruction by the renowned Salafi scholar Abu Muhammad al-Maqdisis.[18]

Faced with a large population of young Islamists during the Afghan jihad, governments across the Muslim world found a release valve for the radical religious pressures in their societies by freeing religious prisoners on condition that they go to fight the atheist-Soviet invader in Afghanistan. Many such prisoners agreed and were released by regimes that hoped they would go to Afghanistan, kill some infidels, and be killed in the process. Many of these men fought and were killed, but some survived and returned home to bedevil their governments—even to this day. Currently, for example, Afghan jihad veterans lead several antigovernment political-military groups in Thailand, and in Bangladesh five or more Afghan veterans will run as candidates when the next parliamentary election occurs.[19]

And today? It is hard to know for certain whether history is repeating itself. We do know three things for sure, however: (a) every Arab government faces a domestic Islamist movement that is broader and more militant, though not always more violent, than those in the 1980s; (b) the insurgency in Iraq, because the country is the former seat of the caliphate and is located in the Arab heartland, is an attraction for would-be Islamist fighters far more powerful than was Afghanistan in 1979; and (c) the flow of foreign fighters into Iraq and post-2001 Afghanistan seems to be more than sufficient to cause a steady combat tempo in each insurgency. Thus the situation seems ideal for Arab governments to try a reprise of the process that lessened their problems of domestic instability during the Afghan jihad.

This circumstantial argument—that the current situation in Iraq is an almost irresistible opportunity for Arab regimes to export their Islamic firebrands to kill members of the U.S-led infidel coalition and hopefully be killed in turn—is strengthened, if not fully validated, by the large numbers of Islamist militants that have been released by Arab governments since the 2003 invasion of Iraq. Following are several pertinent examples drawn from the period November 2003–February 2007:

- November 2003: The government of Yemen freed more than 1,500 inmates, including 92 suspected al-Qaeda members, in an amnesty to mark the holy month of Ramadan.[20]
- January 2005: The Algerian government pardoned 5,065 prisoners to commemorate the feast of Eid al-Adha.[21]
- September 2005: The new Mauritanian military government ordered "a sweeping amnesty for political crimes, freeing scores of prisoners . . . including a band of coup plotters and alleged Islamic extremists."[22]

- November 2005: Morocco released 164 Islamist prisoners to mark the end of the holy month of Ramadan.[23]
- November 2005: Morocco released 5,000 prisoners in honor of the fiftieth anniversary of the country's independence. The sentences of 5,000 other prisoners were reduced.[24]
- November–December 2005: Saudi Arabia released 400 "reformed" Islamist prisoners.[25]
- February–March 2006: In February, Algeria pardoned or reduced sentences for "3,000 convicted or suspected terrorists" as part of a national reconciliation plan.[26] In March, 2,000 additional prisoners were released.[27]
- February 2006: Tunisian president Zine el Abidine Ben Ali released 1,600 prisoners, including Islamic radicals.[28]
- March 2006: Yemen released more than 600 Islamist fighters who were imprisoned after a rebellion led by a radical cleric named Hussein Badr Eddin al-Huthi.[29]
- March 2006: The Libyan government released 132 Islamist political prisoners; 86 of the freed prisoners are members of the Muslim Brotherhood in Libya.[30]
- March–April 2006: The Egyptian government released 900 members of the Gama' at al-Islamiyah organization.[31]
- May 2006: Kuwait authorities freed five of their nationals who had been held in Guantanamo Bay for raising money for al-Qaeda.[32]
- July 2006, Yemeni courts released 19 men linked to al-Qaeda, claiming a lack of evidence to justify their continued incarceration.[33]
- July 2006: Saudi authorities announced seven Islamist prisoners were missing from a Riyadh prison. "Somehow they left the prison, they ran away," explained the interior ministry spokesman.[34]
- July 2006: The Mauritanian government released eight men linked to al-Qaeda and ten others linked to Algeria's Salafi Group for Call and Combat, an al-Qaeda ally. Three other al-Qaeda fighters had "escaped" from a Mauritanian jail in the preceding April.[35]
- February 2007: The Moroccan government pardoned more than 9,000 prisoners—including twelve under death sentences—to celebrate the birth of a new daughter to King Mohammed VI and his wife. The releases came after Moroccan authorities had, in 2006, identified eleven

networks moving would-be Moroccan mujahedin from Morocco to Iraq.[36]

Just this incomplete sample provides a pool of released Sunni and Shiite prisoners numbering nearly thirty thousand, 137 of whom are identified as al-Qaeda or al-Qaeda–related fighters. The justifications offered by Arab governments for these releases vary. Some claim they are to commemorate religious holidays or political anniversaries, others describe them as part of national-reconciliation plans, and some are chalked up as simple "escapes."[37] In some of the official statements announcing prisoner releases, Islamists are said to be excluded from the prisoners being freed; in others they are specifically included. In all cases, the releasing governments are Muslim police states worried about their internal stability in the face of rising Islamic militancy across the Muslim world, the animosities of populations angry at Arab regimes for assisting the U.S.-led invasions of Iraq and Afghanistan, and the powerful showings Islamist parties have made in elections across the region.[38] While the motivation of Arab governments in releasing large numbers of prisoners is not now possible to definitively document, those regimes are likely aware of the attraction the U.S. occupations of Iraq and Afghanistan will have on newly freed Islamists, and that it might take no more than a slight incentive to dispatch some of the former prisoners to the war zones. It may well be that the West is seeing but not recognizing a replay in Iraq of the process that supplied a steady stream of manpower to the Afghan mujahedin two decades ago.[39]

None of the foregoing should be attributed to hindsight. It is the result of conducting a war that is dominated by the policies formulated and actions taken by the history-challenged men and women of the U.S. governing elite. These individuals appear to have known nothing of the Sunni-Shia schism; failed to review the U.K.'s 1920s-experience in Iraq; lacked the common sense to know that decades of persecution and likely civil war would follow the overthrow of a brutal and long-dominant minority regime; and were ignorant of the from-prison-to-jihad policies of many Muslim states, and especially our Arab allies. Thus, today's Iraq disaster and its strong anti-U.S. repercussions around the Islamic world may have been unintended, but they were anything but unpredictable. Our leaders lacked not clairvoyance but humility and a basic knowledge of history.

The Cold War Hangover Bedevils Iraq

Because U.S. leaders had good, snappy slogans—democracy! elections! women's rights! etc.—but no achievable war aims in Iraq, the U.S. military was fated to be defeated in Iraq no matter how well it performed. The victory of the Islamists, as noted, was complete when the first U.S. military boot hit Iraqi soil. That said, however, the Cold War–era assumptions that U.S. political leaders, senior bureaucrats, and generals brought to the war might well have defeated America even if our war aims fell within the scope of reason possessed by those with a high school education.

First, Washington's preparations for war clearly progressed on Cold War time. The war in Iraq was going to be a cakewalk, and so U.S. leaders spent a year leisurely and publicly getting ready to attack. They thereby gave Saddam time to disperse his irregulars and their ordnance and to cultivate animosity and hatred of America among Muslims because of the increase of U.S. forces on the Arabian Peninsula and Washington's manifest, licking-its-chops eagerness to invade Iraq. The year also allowed domestic Iraqi Islamist groups like Ansar al-Islam, later renamed Ansar al-Sunnah, and Abu Musab al-Zarqawi's organization to build bases, acquire arms, and ready reinforcements. The year-long run-up to the war likewise allowed external groups like al-Qaeda to map out secure travel routes to Iraq and to build a reserve of recruits and funding for use there. When the U.S. invasion came, the Islamist forces that would be the core around which the Iraqi insurgency formed were on the ground, and they were well positioned, armed, prepared, and rested.

Together with this glacial pace, Secretary Rusmfeld and his so-called military transformers, aka the RMA'ers, handicapped the U.S. military by giving it a total of 140,000 men and women to conquer and control a nation-state the size of California. As in Afghanistan, the Rumsfeldian plan of spare human forces and plentiful precision weaponry allowed U.S. forces to quickly destroy a brittle regime but did not permit the consolidation of U.S. control, the annihilation of all enemy forces, or the flexibility to adapt to changing circumstances, especially the manpower-heavy requirements of fighting a steadily growing insurgency. Had Iraq been an isolated and difficult-to-access country, Rumsfeld's mix of forces might have prevailed, but given that each of Iraq's contiguous Muslim neighbors was eager to defeat U.S. democracy-building efforts in the country (and there is no excuse for the Bush administration and Congress's failure to factor this certainty into prewar planning), the force was and is entirely inadequate to contest a war against insurgents armed with AK-47s, RPGs, IEDs, and all the other weapons that the RMA'ers deemed hopelessly obsolete and nonthreatening to U.S. forces.

Once ensconced in Iraq, the U.S. military found itself set up for defeat by a peculiar weakness of the American governing elite's mind: the inability to perceive even dimly the role that land borders play in achieving security either at home or overseas. Faced with a situation where some of the fighters, ordnance, and funds to support the Iraqi insurgents were moving into Iraq across the country's borders with Jordan, Syria, Iran, Saudi Arabia, and Kuwait, a decision to close the borders did not require a rocket scientist's brain, only common sense. To have done so would have slowed the pace at which foreign fighters and externally acquired materials of war could join the fray. Likewise, closed borders would have made insurgent field commanders inside Iraq unsure about the dependability of the inward flow of replacement fighters and suicide bombers for their units and therefore probably would have limited their willingness to undertake operations likely to result in heavy casualties. From the U.S.-led coalition's perspective, closed borders would have isolated our enemies in Iraq, allowed a more systematic approach to eliminating them, and facilitated an ability to measure the damage being inflicted—and therefore progress made—by avoiding a situation where insurgent manpower grew daily via open borders. Clearly, closing Iraq's land borders would have been all-win for America and all-loss for its enemies. Naturally, the borders remained open; indeed, the Bush team's only real concern with Iraq's borders was whether it could work up the issue of the unclosed Syria-Iraq border into a *casus belli* with Bashir al-Assad's regime.

Closing the borders could have been accomplished by one of three paths. First, a massive effort by the Saudis, Jordanians, Syrians, Kuwaitis, and Iranians could have done the trick, but they were not going to act because they wanted a U.S. failure in Iraq and were improving their internal security by unloading their Islamist firebrands across the borders. Second, the U.S. military and its coalition allies could have massively reinforced their armies of occupation and done the job themselves. This was a nonstarter, however, as it would have made clear that Secretary Rumsfeld's transformed and massively expensive, light, fast, and precision-weapon-armed military could not do what hordes of old-fashioned ground-pounding infantry could do to ensure a U.S. victory. Third, Washington could have tried some combination of the two, if it had been able to extensively use a tool that is very effective in closing borders—the land mine. Alas, the land mine is the mortal enemy of many of the Cold War's antinational groups—NGOs, UN components, human rights organizations, etc.—and their large-scale deployment apparently was never seriously considered. Washington was content to lose Iraq and Afghanistan by allowing insurgents easy and reliable cross-border access because they were fearful of offending the antinational groups, and they were even more afraid of the frenzy those groups loved to whip up among their media and academic supporters.

Several other Cold War leftovers helped to defeat America in Iraq. The Bush administration's goal of creating a secular, pluralistic, and multicultural post-Saddam Iraqi society could have been imagined only if even the most conservative Republicans, neoconservatives, and just plain war hawks fully bought into the multiculturalists' bankrupt notion that all cultures are equal and able to live together peacefully. While the vote-chasers in both houses of Congress, especially on the Democratic side, naturally endorsed the sham war aim of multiculturalism, one would have hoped for more historical awareness from the reputedly hard-headed Republican "realists." But such was not the case, and so America's initial goal was unachievable, not to say laughable. That U.S. leaders thought such an outcome possible in Iraq can be seen only as confirming the immense insularity, ill education, and willful mental isolation of the bipartisan U.S. governing elite. History gives no reason to assume that different cultures can easily coexist, the noted historian Elizabeth Fox-Genovese has written, and "[w]hat makes less sense is the pretense that relations among the embodiments of different cultures should be harmonious."[40] Any American tourist, business person, intelligence officer, or soldier who has spent any time overseas, particularly in the Muslim world, knows unashamedly from first-hand experience that (a) in terms of fairness, legal equity, broad opportunities for improvement in life, and basic security, American society is superior in every way to anything they encounter abroad, and (b) be that as it may, most Muslims are immensely proud of their religion and history, have no wish to become just like Americans, and regard anything that smacks of secularism as inherently inferior to their way of life and an affront to their faith, indeed, as fighting words. Only among the U.S. governing elite is multiculturalism an attainable goal, and it has that status only because our elite, while extraordinarily well traveled (usually at the taxpayers' expense), is crewed by common-sense-immune, history-ignorant, mental isolationists who are eager to shove politically divisive and tolerance-fraying multiculturalism down the throats of U.S. voters and are able to see but unable to understand anything overseas that does not mesh with their preconceived notions. "Yet our mastery, our very knowledge of the world remains spotty in the extreme," Fouad Ajami wrote of U.S. leaders in October 2000. "We have traffic with the rulers of Arab and Muslim states, but it gives us precious little insight into these lands."[41] To this day, truer words were never spoken.

Other Cold War assumptions have also happily fallen by the wayside in Iraq. Obviously, amid the mounds of severed heads, disfigured, headshot, and blindfolded corpses, destroyed holy sites, and random murders, the Cold War's limits on violence are long gone, and the rules of engagement imposed by U.S. politicians and leaders who listen to the just-war theorists have made America's military children targets rather than the killers they should be.[42] And although Joseph Nye continues to lament that Washington has not used sufficient amounts of our "soft power" in the war against Islamists,[43] events in Iraq have proven that soft power without definitive military victory is impotent. We have conducted repeated elections, built roads, dug wells, provided prenatal and most other kinds of health care, created employment opportunities, handed out U.S. cash by the unaccountable boxload, established schools, sung the praises of democracy loud, long, and multilingually, and generally exploited soft power to a substantial extent. And it has failed for two reasons. First, no matter how many of these soft-power components we bring to bear, we still run up hard against the fact that Muslims hate U.S. foreign policies. Most Iraqi Muslims appreciate better schools, health care, and water, but they still hate U.S. foreign policy in the Islamic world—as in "Thanks for the dental work, but why did you stand by and watch Israel gut Lebanon in the summer of 2006?"—and it is arrogance to assume that potable water will make Muslims forget that they hate us for what they perceive as the infidel occupation of Iraq, the demeaning of their faith, and the killing of their brethren. Second, soft power will not work unless the enemy is first defeated to the extent that there is no doubt in his mind, or that of the local populace that supports him, that they have been well, truly, and conclusively whipped. William T. Sherman had the sequence exactly right when he said in 1864 that he would defeat his armed foe and "make old and young, rich and poor, feel the hard hand of war," and only then, after such a persuasive defeat, would he become "the advocate of mercy and restoration to home, and peace, and happiness of all who have lost them to my acts."[44] In later years the U.S. experience in Vietnam and its current situations in Iraq and Afghanistan have served to revalidate a conclusion made by a U.S. soldier fighting to suppress the Philippine Muslim insurrection more than a hundred years ago. "This business of fighting and civilizing and educating at the same time doesn't mix very well," the soldier noted.[45]

The Iraq war also has proven that the usefulness of advice and guidance from expatriates, exiles, and ethnic experts has not transferred well from the era of the Cold War. At a time when al-Qaeda and its allies are defeating the U.S. armed forces in the Iraqi insurgency—and other Islamist groups are making significant headway in places like Thailand, Bangladesh, Somalia, and the North Caucasus—the message from these advisers is invariably upbeat. Take Fareed Zakaria, for example. In 2002, Mr. Zakaria expected a "massive benefit" from the Iraq invasion because "[d]one right, an invasion would be the single best path to reform in the Arab world."[46] Two years later, when the tide was turning against the U.S. led coalition, Mr. Zakaria was still confident. "[T]he bad guys are losing," he wrote. "Unable to launch major terrorist attacks in the West, unable to attract political support in the Middle East, militant Islam is searching for enemies and causes . . . By now surely it is clear that al-Qaeda can produce videotapes but not terrorism."[47] And then there is the analysis of the Sarah Lawrence College professor Fawaz Gerges: "We are in the throes of the beginning of a new wave [in the Muslim world]," Gerges has claimed, while also dismissing al-Qaeda as a deadly nuisance, "—the freedom generation—in which civil society is asserting itself. Its vanguard is the generation under 30 years old, which represents more than 60 percent of the Muslim population."[48] Oddly, a good deal of scholarship suggests that the educated, under-thirty generation increasingly belongs to bin Laden and the Islamists.[49] And again Zakaria, this time telling Americans not to worry but be happy because U.S. foreign policy and its actions in Iraq have not motivated Muslims to wage war against America; rather Muslims are just so dumb and gullible that "militant, political Islam has brainwashed young Muslims around the world who believe it is their duty to fight against the modern world."[50] Mansoor Ijaz takes Zakaria's point about masses of retarded Muslim automatons and lays it on even thicker, thereby introducing a few shadowy Muslim wizards of Oz hiding behind Bedouin robes. "[A]l-Qaeda and its affiliate terrorist networks have evolved their global operating system," Ijaz prates, "into an airborne virus capable of infecting concentrated cells of disaffected followers to carry out by proxy the orders of their hidden masters."[51] Taken together, the mostly inaccurate advice and guidance of these individuals and others of their ilk will ensure that America never gets back to Kansas.[52]

Taking the Right Lessons from Defeat

When the U.S. defeat in Iraq becomes clear and unquestionable, it will be very important, as it is in Afghanistan, that Americans do not permit the Republicans and Democrats, and the punditry aligned with each, to effectively sell the idea that all would have been well in Iraq if Washington had had an extravagantly expensive and ready-to-roll reconstruction plan to implement after Saddam's regime was destroyed. As defeat becomes obvious, some in high places will step up this already loud assertion. They will say, if only we had stopped the looting; if only we had a plan for restoring and expanding electricity production, if only we had not disbanded the army; if only we had quickly modernized the energy infrastructure; and on and on, and louder and louder it will get. Most of this blather will emanate from the Democratic Party, which will argue that the use of military force against the Islamists has been unsuccessful and then urge the spending of untold billions of U.S. dollars on a "New Deal" for the Middle East. This, they will contend, will deradicalize Muslims and make them peaceful, moderate, prosperous democrats; in short, al-Qaeda and its allies will be made into a slightly more aggressive version of the Rotary Club. Armed with the irrelevant Marshall Plan analogy, officials from Mr. Clinton's administration are already beating the drum for vast increases in U.S. aid to the Muslim world. "If we are to be serious about promoting fundamental reform in pivotal [Islamic countries]," Daniel Benjamin and Steven Simon have written,

142

We need to do more than hector them and sprinkle money on small-scale initiatives. We must engage the societies deeply and dramatically. We have done this before. Decisive American action along these lines helped preserve democracy in Western Europe during the years after World War II, thereby laying the groundwork for the NATO alliance and eventually victory in the Cold War. Our tools then were the economic assistance of the Marshall Plan and, of course, military resolve in the face of a massive Soviet presence in Eastern Europe. The differences between Europe in 1945 and the Middle East today are huge, as are the differences between America then and now. Nevertheless, we did engage in a profound degree in other societies whose political development was crucial to our national security, and we were successful. Democracy in Western Europe flowered as voters rejected the future offered by the Soviet Union.[53]

Beyond the always pervasive Democratic itch to spend the taxes of Americans on things and people that do not benefit them, this passage brings to mind Machiavelli's warning that history should be used creatively, not in a cookie-cutter fashion; history provides lessons to be learned and adapted, not opportunities for past experiences to be exactly duplicated. The Marshall Plan analogy is often used as a staple bipartisan justification for U.S. involvement in Iraq and across the Middle East. It provides a road map to disaster. Europe in 1945 was economically devastated and convinced that fascism was untenable; the enemy states and their militaries were annihilated; and the continent as a whole was, after witnessing the Red Army rape eastern Germany, afraid to death of the USSR. Perhaps more important, the United States shared a common heritage with Europe; both sides of the Atlantic were grounded in the Classical experience, Christianity, the Renaissance, the Reformation, the several Enlightenments, and the Industrial Revolution. Utter defeat, fear of Moscow, and broad underlying cultural and religious commonalities made the Marshall Plan work as much as did dollars. In the Pacific, the annihilation of Imperial Japan's armed forces and the Japanese will-to-war were complemented by a culture willing to submit to its U.S. conqueror, as well as by President Truman's wisdom in sending the self-imagined divinity General Douglas MacArthur to deal with Emperor Hirohito. Here truly was an instance when the god America sent was bigger than the god sitting on Japan's throne.

None of the conditions that allowed the Marshall Plan and its Pacific counterpart to succeed are present in the Muslim world. That world is not defeated; it is America that is being beaten by that world's youth in two locations. In cultural terms, we share almost nothing with the Islamic world. There are no historical commonalities on which to build; indeed, the historical experiences that the West shares with the Islamic world are crusades, colonialism, imperialism, and military intervention—not exactly the stuff from which happy-ever-aftering is made. In the area of religion, we could not be more dissimilar. Our faith is a barely tolerated, once-a-week duty; an as-needed and often cynical fillip to political rhetoric; and nothing worth fighting for. Their faith infuses all of life and is lived daily, treasured and taught as a proud history, and dutifully and even joyfully defended to the death. With this lack of positive cultural, historical, and religious commonalities, a Marshall Plan for the Muslim world would be as successful as pouring water on sand and hoping for a bumper crop of wheat. Indeed, it would be just as successful as has been the many billions of dollars in aid that the West has poured into the Muslim world since 1945.

Americans also must reject any claim by their leaders that does not acknowledge the most important reason for U.S. defeat in Iraq—Washington's attempt to build a secular democratic polity there. We failed to replace Saddam's regime with a functioning, durable government precisely because we tried to export our political model to Iraq. Our subsequent bipartisan effort to blame the Iraqis for their failure to build the secular democracy we wanted reveals a staggering level of ignorance and dishonesty. The Iraqis had no appreciable experience with a democratic system, are deeply torn by sectarian differences, and are divided among three major ethnic groups, none of which had more than a modicum of interest in sharing power with the others, each fearing it would become the target of Saddam-like abuse if one group finagled a way to come out on top. Moreover, the great majority of Iraqis saw secular democracy as anathema to their Islamic faith. To a people whose religion rejects as apostasy the concept of deliberately separating church and state, American advice suggesting that Iraqis govern themselves on the basis of such a separation is tantamount to telling the advisees to turn their backs on God. This reality was easily knowable before we invaded Iraq; it is one of the first lessons drawn from even a cursory reading of Islamic theology and history. "If the Iraqi government," write the Iraq Study Group's geriatric Cold Warriors to fix blame on Iraqis for the catastrophe wrought by the elite to which the group belongs, "does not make substantial progress toward the achievement of milestones on national reconciliation, security, and governance, the United States should reduce its political, military, or economic support for the Iraqi government."[54] In other words: "You ungrateful little brown brothers better shape up or the Yanks are going to ship out."

The most important lesson for Americans to draw from defeat, however, is that our failure to install democracy in Iraq, as well as in Afghanistan, shows beyond question that our current governing elite is either ignorant of U.S. history (what Paine called "a too great inattention to the past") or holds that history and the people who have made it in contempt. The bedrock ethos, political philosophy, and religious principles on which the American republic and its democracy are based go back many centuries, with contributions dating as far back as Aristotle and the republics of Rome and Sparta. A plausible starting point for the political evolution that would lead to the American polity lies eight centuries back at the time of the drafting and signing of the Magna Carta in 1215, which circumscribed the arbitrary powers of England's King John. Then Americans, as Americans, had 150 years of self-governing experience and reliable political stability in North America before the signing of the Declaration of Independence. Since the Declaration, Americans have battled through bitter politics and elections; westward expansion; economic depressions; slavery and civil war; industrial strife; segregation, Jim Crow, and lynch mobs; two world wars; and the Cold War in an ongoing communal effort to bring our society as close as possible to the always unachievable targets of perfect equity and equal opportunity for all citizens and peace at home and with foreign nations. The length, the difficulty, and the many miles still to go in this process are starkly apparent in recalling that the Voting Rights Act is only a bit more than forty years old, and we remain engaged in wars, large and small, all around the world.

U.S. political leaders with any knowledge of, pride in, or respect for the political and social hardships and achievements of the American people could not possibly have expected to build anything even faintly resembling it in Iraq. The building blocks of the American republic—Runnymede, the Glorious Revolution of 1688, Calvinist Christianity, Jefferson's Declaration, Madison's Constitution, Hamilton's *Federalist,* the New Deal, the Voting Rights Act, etc.—are simply absent from the Iraqi experience and that of Muslims generally. The Iraqis and their Islamic brethren have their own set of founding documents—the Koran, the Hadith, and the Sunnah—but U.S. leaders want no truck with the sort of society and country that would be built on them. The American governing elite's effort to blame the Iraqis for failing to achieve in four years what America has not fully achieved in eight hundred years is the act of ill-informed, cynical, and utterly despicable villains. This is surely a vital lesson about their bipartisan leaders that Americans must keep foremost in their minds when deciding if they believe any current U.S. leader of note has any genuine desire to protect their families and their country's interests.

CHAPTER 5

And the Islamists' Fire
Quietly Spreads

A fatal mistake in war is to underrate the strength of feeling and
resources of an enemy.

William T. Sherman

He [Jefferson Davis] would accept nothing short of severance of the
Union—precisely what we will not and cannot give. His declarations
to this effect are explicit and oft-repeated. He does not attempt to
deceive us. He affords us no excuse to deceive ourselves.

Abraham Lincoln, 1864

Eventually, the call of freedom comes to every mind and every soul.

George W. Bush, 2005

While the U.S. government, the media, and Americans generally have
focused on Iraq and to a lesser extent Afghanistan, Osama bin Laden
and his allies have continued on their course of trying to instigate anti-
American animosities and hostility across the Islamic world. The Iraq
and Afghan insurgencies are important to al-Qaeda's goals, but bin Laden
et al. now regard them as self-sustaining, appropriately led by Iraqis and
Afghans, abundantly funded, supported by al-Qaeda and non–al-Qaeda
foreign volunteers, and largely won. For these reasons al-Qaeda has been
free to use much of its resources to develop the jihad elsewhere, either
through the dispatch of cadre or, as noted, by providing training in its
reestablished camps in South Asia. The U.S. government seems largely to
have missed this reality; indeed, Washington's steadfast refusal to take seri-

ously and analyze the words of bin Laden and Ayman al-Zawahiri[1] has yielded a situation in which few U.S. officials seem cognizant of al-Qaeda's long-standing number-one goal: to instigate an ever-increasing number of Muslims in an ever-increasing number of places to join the jihad against America and its allies. Bin Laden and his lieutenants are preeminently incendiaries, and while America is bore-sighted on Afghanistan and Iraq, they have been setting fires—through words, deeds, and personal example—across the Muslim world.

The Ability to Set Fires

The Islamists' post-9/11 fire-setting successes have much to do with the animosities sparked in the Muslim world by the U.S.-led invasions of Iraq and Afghanistan. It would, however, be a great mistake and somewhat egotistical for Americans to attribute the international growth of Islamist sentiment to those conflicts alone. More important has been bin Laden's steady avoidance of becoming engaged in what can be described as a civilization-based slanging match with America and the West. The Islamists' extreme distaste for the West's secular societies is beyond question; the countries they eventually conquer will not be ruled so as to resemble Canada. Still, the my-civilization-is better-than-yours-and-must-destroy-your-civilization theme has been at most a subtext of bin Laden's rhetoric. On the other hand, the message of irrefutable civilizational superiority has been at the core of the rhetoric of Mr. Bush, the prime ministers of Britain, Australia, Canada, Israel, and other Western states.

The words of the main Islamist leaders have been a rhetoric of insularity directed at America and the West; they amount to an argument that you have your civilizations and lands, stay in yours, stay out of ours, and leave us alone. This reality has been deliberately obscured by U.S. neoconservatives who, after every aspect of their blood-soaked, imperialist, win-one-for-Israel campaign in the Middle East had come a-cropper, raised the wild-eyed bogeyman of the imminent success of the Islamists' plan to establish a worldwide Islamic Caliphate.[2] And good Cold Warriors that they are, many U.S. and Western leaders have, in an almost default manner, purposely given the Islamists' agenda a Bolshevik or even a Hitlerite today-Iraq-tomorrow-the-world cast. Their term of choice—*Islamo-*

148

fascist—does the trick nicely, although several prominent scholars, including the neoconservatives' patron saint, Bernard Lewis, have argued that Islam and fascism are incompatible and implicitly that if there are "Islamo-fascist" entities in the Arab world today, they are the nation-states that are the allies of the United States.[3] Nonetheless the aching post–Cold War discomfort of U.S. leaders over the lack of a universal threat to replace the USSR has given the imminent-caliphate argument a much more receptive hearing than it merits. The term has the added benefit, for the pro-Israel U.S. governing elite, of cynically evoking the memory of the Holocaust conducted by genuine fascists, thereby making criticism of U.S. policy toward Israel by Americans appear pro-Nazi, pro-Holocaust, and anti-Semitic. But using the Nazi analogy is "usually false," as Ian Buruma has correctly noted, "although [it is] highly effective as a way to denounce people with whom one disagrees." Behind this neoconservative smoke-screen, however, the story of Islamic history and aspirations is often told with a very insular voice,[4] and so the Islamists' insular rhetoric resonates loudly and positively in Muslim minds. On the contrary, the West's rhetoric of imposing elections, parliaments, and women's rights is perceived as a universal and immense threat to Islamic insularity, and as such it is an oral recruiting poster for al-Qaeda.

Bin Laden and his ilk have been able to light more fires since 9/11 because they have found tangible issues that appeal to all Muslims, issues that are visceral, need little analysis, and easily lend themselves to those great and more or less unstoppable and globalizing engines of militancy— al-Jazirah, al-Arabiyah, the BBC, and the Internet. Al-Qaeda's sharp, remorseless focus on the substance and impact of U.S. foreign policy in the Muslim world, reinforced graphically and endlessly by the just-mentioned media, is the always reliable dry kindling for jihad instigation. Holding an umbrella over this tinder, moreover, is the U.S. governing elite's maintenance of a foreign-policy status quo and its refusal to even consider the possibility that those policies motivate America's Muslim foes and thus undermine U.S. national security. The Islamists' indictment sheet against the United States has been precise, limited, and consistent for more than a decade.

1. The U.S. military and civilian presence in the Arab Peninsula
2. Unqualified U.S. support for Israel[5]

3. U.S. support for states oppressing Muslims, especially China, India, and Russia
4. U.S. exploitation of Muslim oil and suppression of its price
5. U.S. military presence in the Islamic world—Arabian Peninsula, Afghanistan, Iraq, etc.
6. U.S. support, protection, and funding of Arab police states.[6]

By keeping this list squarely in view, it is simple to see how events since 9/11 have strengthened bin Laden's argument in the minds of hundreds of millions of Muslims. Beyond their much-strengthened bases on the Arabian Peninsula, U.S. military forces are now in Afghanistan, Iraq, the Philippines, and more than a dozen countries in eastern and western Africa. In addition, the summer of 2006 saw the United States and the other G-8 nations dutifully hold Israel's coat while the Israel Defense Forces gutted Lebanon's economic infrastructure, and Washington very publicly announced an urgent operation to replenish the arsenal of precision weapons that Israel had expended in dismantling Lebanon's economy. In the same period and since, the massive run-up in oil prices—from $30 to above $90 per barrel—drove home to Muslims worldwide the validity of bin Laden's message about how much revenue they are losing because of the West's traditional ability to persuade Muslim oil-producers to keep prices acceptable to Western and especially U.S. consumers. While American motorists winced and railed against a gallon of gas costing more than three dollars, many Muslims entertained visions of what might be possible vis-à-vis their standard of living if a barrel of oil was pegged at bin Laden's goal of at least $100 and the titanic thieving of their governments could be reduced to the merely gross.[7]

Post-9/11 events have seen the United States expand its support for powers that are perceived across the Islamic world as oppressing Muslims. Washington has continued to identify Russia's war in Chechnya as identical to the U.S. war against al-Qaeda; U.S. diplomats continue to describe China's Uighur Muslims as terrorists, abetting Beijing's Tibet-modeled, genocide-by-inundation policy against them; and President Bush inaugurated a strategic relationship with India—complete with potential U.S. assistance for New Delhi's nuclear program—that supports Indian military operations in Muslim Kashmir and that appears to threaten Muslim Pakistan. In what increasingly seems to be the single most damaging bin

Laden indictment of the United States among Muslims, Washington continues to back and protect Arab tyrannies to the hilt. Since 9/11 Saudi Arabia has held rigged municipal elections that ensured little or no criticism of the al-Sauds' dictatorship;[8] Jordan has rolled back the ability of Islamic parties to operate, causing the Islamic Action Front—the largest opposition party—to withdraw from municipal leadership elections;[9] and Egypt has cracked down on the Muslim Brotherhood after it had gained an unexpected number of seats in parliamentary elections and plans to outlaw religion-based political parties.[10] As in the case of the Israeli nation-state, I accept and support the idea that Muslim nation-states must do what they need to do to survive, but the discrepancy between Washington's syrupy we-want-democracy-for-Muslims rhetoric and its hard-line, unquestioning support for brutal Arab tyrannies negates even the theoretical impact of America's soft power and amounts to nothing less than a total and durable U.S. strategic defeat in the battle for Muslim hearts and minds, a defeat that has been steadily deepening for more than thirty years.

As important as is the substance of these issues, and the ease with which the media keep them in front of the Muslim masses on a daily basis, they are perhaps more important as the glue of unity they apply across the Muslim ummah. Bin Laden and his lieutenants were in their late teens and early twenties during the heyday of Iran's Ayatollah Khomeini, and they saw how Khomeini utterly failed to stimulate a durable anti-American jihad by relentlessly attacking the decadence and debauchery of U.S. and Western civilization. It is clear, in retrospect, that virtually no Muslims were willing to kill themselves by attacking Americans because they drank beer, voted in elections, and attempted to ensure that women and men are treated equally. Even the Lebanese Hezbollah fighters who killed themselves in attacks against U.S. and French targets in Beirut in 1982–83 did so under the umbrella of the ayatollah's rhetoric, but they were in fact executing nationalist operations aimed at driving what they perceived as occupying Westerners out of Lebanon.[11] Indeed, the still-dominant belief of U.S. leaders that these attacks were manifestations of Muslim hatred for Western civilization is a major reason they have incorrectly assumed that bin Laden is using the same arguments as Khomeini to inspire today's jihadis.

Remembering the ayatollah's fizzled Western-degeneracy-based jihad, bin Laden and other Islamist leaders have stressed the negative impact of what Muslims perceive as anti-Islamic U.S. foreign policies. In doing so, they have given Muslims around the world a focus that is based on issues that mean something to them no matter where they live in the world: the killing of Muslims by infidels and the occupation of Muslim lands and holy sites.[12] Now, the use of the term *Muslims* is often criticized as a stereotyping mechanism that demeans Muslims through its implicit assumption that every Muslim thinks alike. Such criticism usually comes from the staunchest multiculturalists, a powerful subset of our governing elite whose members more often than not know next to nothing about any foreign cultures and even less about their own. Well, those with more than a tenth-grade education know that almost all societies lack homogeneity, but they also know it is almost impossible to have a substantive conversation or debate if generalizations cannot be used. In this case, however, the multiculturalists have a point, and no one recognized its validity more than Osama bin Laden.

Contemporary Islamic civilization is as diverse as any of the world's other great civilizations, perhaps more so. Dispersed geographically across five continents, Islam, especially its Sunni variant, is further riven by ethnic, linguistic, and sectarian differences. Muslims also live under a variety of political systems (although most live under authoritarian regimes of one sort or another) and in places where their faith has roots as old as the Prophet Muhammad or as new and fragile as those formed in late-twentieth-century America. Likewise, the availability to Muslims of education, health care, employment, public services, and the rule of law varies wildly around the globe. Given this vast array of differences, the idea of asking Muslims to forgo their daily effort to work, care for their families, and avoid persecution by security services and instead risk their lives to fight to deprive Americans of their right to vote is ludicrous on its face. It brings into question the basic brainpower and common sense of those who argue that hatred of U.S. lifestyles and electoral processes motivates our Islamist enemies. So idiotic is this contention that any U.S. leader who asserts the point—that legion includes George W. Bush and most of his would-be successors, including Hillary Clinton, John McCain, John Edwards, Barack Obama, and Rudolph Giuliani—is either sadly stupid or a studied liar, because it is impossible to know anything about the Islamist enemy we are fighting and come to that conclusion. Whichever descriptor fits, any U.S. political leader who mouths this concept is a politically correct threat to

America's national security. Such men or women ought to be sent packing by the voters at the earliest possible moment so Americans can continue their search for someone who can see the world as it is and prevent America's defeat.

So great is the diversity of the Islamic world that any kind of unity—anti-American, anti-Christian, anti-Jew, or otherwise—would be almost impossible to achieve if it were not for the one universal motivating factor that U.S. leaders refuse to acknowledge and talk about: the Islamic faith. From Chechnya to Chile, from Nigeria to North Carolina, and from Saudi Arabia to Sulawesi, Muslims share the same faith, one that is more pervasive and durable in its influence on individuals, personal relationships, community affairs, and international relations than any of the current iterations of the world's other great religions. Now, before the multiculturalists go berserk, it must be recognized that Muslims are not an unthinking monolith acting on a single theological script as a 1.3 billion-person automaton. Yes, the practice of Islam varies in different regions of the earth, mixing, for example, with millennia-old local traditions and mores in the Far East and Africa. And yes, there are numbers of Muslims who have fallen away from their faith or are at best sporadic participants in its rituals. But at day's end, each Muslim's identity is grounded in his faith, its requirements, and the culture it has produced, and this grounding is about the only basis upon which any kind of Muslim unity, any sense of the Muslim ummah, could be constructed. And it is precisely on this grounding that Osama bin Laden has built.

As *Indiana Jones*'s Holy Grail–guarding knight said, bin Laden "chose wisely" by discarding Khomeini's debauchery-degeneracy message; instead, he based his appeal to Muslims on the idea that they and Islam are under attack by the policies of the United States and the West. The photos of Israeli soldiers killing Muhammad Dura as his father sought to shield him and those of the aftermath of the U.S. Air Force mistakenly bombing an Afghan wedding party are irrefutably more likely to motivate Muslims than is a call to kill Americans because of their excessive Budweiser consumption. A Russian-speaking Chechen, an Arabic-speaking Yemeni, and a Malay-speaking Thai—Muslims all—will find the glue of Islam-defending unity in the anti-Americanism inspired by such photos, as will many Muslims born and bred in the United States and Europe. Bin Laden has thus found what perhaps is the only means with which to bridge the diversity of a highly fragmented Islamic civilization and unite an increasingly large portion of that worldwide community in attitude, outrage, and sympathies, if not yet in action.

In conceiving how to produce a glue of unity, bin Laden's focus on the impact of U.S. foreign policies in the Muslim world suggests either genius or extraordinary good luck on his part. As a former intelligence officer, I am not a big believer in coincidence; more often than not events occur because someone intends them to occur. Even at the risk of being accused of fawning over the man U.S. leaders refer to as a monster, therefore, I think it is best to give America's most dangerous enemy the benefit of the doubt and judge bin Laden to be near a political genius. In no other area of U.S. foreign affairs are policies so completely enmeshed with domestic politics as those that are directed toward the Islamic world. Energy supply and prices, support for Israel, and the championship of democracy are all issues that have been fully integrated into U.S. political contests. At least at the level of federal elections, a candidate who demands major changes in these policies—or in the case of Israel, even minor ones—knowingly takes the risk of fatally handicapping his or her chances of victory. Urging the necessity of higher prices and taxes to promote energy self-sufficiency, for example, is not a likely way to positively influence voters. And for nearly twenty years, since William F. Buckley and the Israel-firsters joyously diced up Patrick J. Buchanan as an anti-Semite, urging any change in U.S. policy toward Israel amounts to a martyrdom operation for any American politician.[13] This reality was driven home again in the summer of 2006 and fall of 2007, when the noted scholars Stephen Walt and John Mearsheimer published a paper and then a book outlining their view of the negative impact of pro-Israel influence groups on the conduct of U.S. foreign policy in the Islamic world. Walt and Mearsheimer were mercilessly attacked by the Israel-firsters, including some scholars and pundits whose contempt for the intelligence of Americans is so great that they denied the existence of anything that could be called an "Israeli lobby."[14] As I wrote in Anti-War.com at the time, the vicious attacks on the two scholars by leading Americans in the media, politics, and academics—in effect, Americans savaging other Americans in favor of a foreign country—smacks of nothing so much, at least for a former intelligence officer, as a superbly executed and very successful Israeli covert political action campaign.[15]

In sum, bin Laden has identified a set of U.S. policies, which are the daily focus of Western and Muslim media, that can be steadily and effectively used to persuade Muslims that the U.S. government is attacking Islam and that, at the same time, are the one set of U.S. government policies that is least liable to substantively change at any point in the foreseeable future. As I have written on previous occasions, U.S. foreign policy in the Muslim world is the only indispensable ally of bin Laden and the Islamists, and at this time they have no cause whatsoever to worry that their ally will leave them high and dry by changing policy. Parenthetically, the current wartime situation faced by American taxpayers must be a unique one in their history; because of the policies and actions of our governing elite, Americans today fund the enemy's war effort via their consumption of Arab oil and provide the basis for their enemies' motivation. For U.S. leaders, this must be seen as a negative and self-destructive achievement of truly epic proportions.

While the Islamists' ally in the form of U.S. policy appears entirely reliable, bin Laden and his lieutenants—good, forward-looking strategists that they are—have been looking for some redundancy in allies, and they may have found another that again is being provided by the United States and Europe. Polls taken in the Islamic world by reliable Western firms, Pew, Gallup, BBC, Zogby, etc., over the past fifteen-plus years invariably find two consistent realities. First, enormous majorities in Muslim countries, usually in the 60 to 90 percent range, express hatred for the same set of U.S. and Western foreign policies that Osama bin Laden and other Islamist leaders have identified as mortal attacks on Islam. Overall, the University of Maryland's spring 2007 poll showed 80 percent of Muslims worldwide agree with bin Laden in seeing America as hostile to or an enemy of Islam.[16] Second, majorities (sometimes sizable ones) in the same Muslim countries express admiration for the striving of Americans for political and social equity for all citizens, for American generosity after natural disasters, and for the ability of American parents to find work and housing, education, and health care for their children. Taken together, these poll results strongly suggest that U.S. leaders are lying when they tell Americans that they are being attacked for how they think and live and not for what their government does overseas.

Beyond that leadership's lie, however, Americans have cause to worry about how long these two sets of poll results will show the same level of dichotomy. While the high percentages showing hatred for U.S. policies are rock solid as long as the policies are constant, those showing that Muslims do not hate Americans as Americans may prove softer and less durable. Since 9/11, Washington's prosecution of the war on terror has produced a series of subsidiary events that have deeply dented the reputation of Americans for evenhandedness and decency. The handling of prisoners in Guantanamo Bay and the Abu Ghraib prison; the CIA's rendition program—which I helped author and then ran for nearly four years; the burning of the bodies of dead Taliban fighters; the awarding and subsequent withdrawal of the Dubai ports deal; the publication in Europe of caricatures of the Prophet Muhammad; the remarks of Pope Benedict XVI regarding Islam; Britain's knighting of author Salman Rushdie; and the killing of civilians in Iraq and Afghanistan often have been handled in the U.S. and European media as instances of Bush administration lawlessness and Western Islamophobia, or as mistakes made in the confusion of war evidencing the U.S. military's lack of respect for human rights and by Christendom's history toward Muslims. The Muslim and Islamist media have portrayed them as interrelated parts of a comprehensive U.S. and Western attack on Islam.

It seems necessary these days to follow a recitation of such events by saying that one is not trying to shame, embarrass, or denigrate America by raising these issues. Indeed, as a principal architect of the CIA's rendition program, I have been outspoken in identifying and defending its successes and urging its continuation.[17] But I am also fully aware that the U.S. government is both too fearful and too politically correct to even publicly admit that the United States has a problem with Islam, let alone build a focused, multifaceted attack on the faith.[18] Still perception is always reality, and across the Islamic world—and in parts of the U.S. media, Europe, and the Democratic party—the litany of these events is seen as part of an anti-Muslim campaign that is based on the West's hatred for the Islamic faith and its followers, a hatred that both denigrates the Islamic religion and Muslim society as medieval, imperialistic, and barbarous and that assigns a far higher worth to non-Muslim lives than Muslim. The latter is a point on which al-Qaeda has focused for more than a decade and that was driven home in the summer of 2006 for Muslims when they perceived the West to be standing aside and allowing Israel to inflict casualties in Lebanon at a rate of more than ten Lebanese for one Israeli. "O My Muslim nation," Ayman al-Zawahiri said at the time, "it has become known to you without doubt that the governments of the Arab and Muslim states are not only helpless, but also involved in collusions [against you]. The institutions are paralyzed and you are left in the field alone."[19]

While these events have yet to cause a precipitate decline in Muslims' positive views of Americans (as opposed to the U.S. government), it behooves U.S. officials and citizens to think about how to handle the unavoidable negative repercussions of these events and similar others that are bound to occur in the confusion and emergencies of war. To date, Washington has tended to regard the events as public relations problems that can be handled by a fuller public explanation of U.S. intent, a public apology, or the payment of cash to aggrieved parties, such as those individuals who lost family members in mistaken U.S. attacks on several wedding parties in Afghanistan. Such measures provide a temporary moderation of anger, but the Cold War is long over, and America today does not have the bottomless we-are-the-good-guys account that it had to draw on when confronting the Soviet Union. Over time these events have a cumulative negative impact and leave a wide and broadening perception across the Islamic world that Washington regards Muslim life as cheap and inconsequential. Once lodged in the Islamic culture's collective perception, any U.S. public diplomacy argument to the contrary is likely to meet an impervious wall of made-up minds. At that point, polls would likely begin to show that Muslims are beginning to regard Americans in a less favorable light. Given that Washington is being overwhelmed by an Islamist opponent whose hatred for U.S. foreign policy is shared nearly unanimously among Muslims, anything that advances the tendency of Muslims to hate Americans simply because they are Americans would greatly complicate already-failing U.S. efforts to protect American interests at home and abroad.

An Islamic Reformation That Brings Not Peace But the Sword?

Beyond Iraq and Afghanistan, the growth of Islamist power, popularity, and violence has been strengthened by bin Laden's success in defining resistance to the United States as a Koran-justified defensive jihad that requires the obligatory participation of all Muslims. Bin Laden's success in this regard is vitally important not only because it has pushed the anti-U.S.

jihad from words to deeds and provided the glue of unity for the diverse Muslim world, but also because it has demonstrated to Muslims around the world that the Afghans' defeat of the Soviet superpower was not a fluke, and that the United States, its allies, and their own local governments can be successfully challenged by the relatively lightly armed mujahedin. The actions of al-Qaeda and bin Laden's rhetoric have inspired Muslims worldwide to jihad, but this inspiration has been magnified in such places as Thailand, Nigeria, and Bangladesh by local grievances that have few or no direct links to the United States or its foreign policy, unless Washington, in its wisdom, chooses to make someone else's fight America's. The combination of bin Laden's leadership, Muslim hatred for U.S. foreign policy, and long-festering localized Muslim grievances, usually against oppressive regimes, has yielded a Muslim world awash in inflammable materials and potential.

Another important but less quantifiable factor that is facilitating bin Laden's success in incitement is the declining influence of Islamic clerics, scholars, and jurists who work with and are employed by Muslim governments, especially those in the Arab world. When comparing Islam to Christianity's many sects, it has long been a commonplace to claim that the former does not have the centralized, hierarchical leadership that the latter have established in Rome, Canterbury, and elsewhere. While this claim remains true, each Muslim country has long had a hierarchy of senior Islamic clerics to whom the population looks for religious guidance on issues ranging from the pedestrian to the earthshaking. Again, this is especially true in the Arab world. For most of the post-1945 period, these clerics had tremendous power over the decisions and actions of their national populations, as well as the manner in which those populations interpreted and understood domestic and international events. The clerics, in other words, have been the Arab regimes' most important, nay indispensable, spinmeisters. That power is ebbing, however, and as it does, the Islamists' campaign to win people to a more conservative brand of Islam and to jihad will become easier.

Why the ebbing? Part of the answer lies in the success that Arab governments in Saudi Arabia, Jordan, Kuwait, Egypt, and the United Arab Emirates have had in coopting a large number of their country's leading Islamic clerics, scholars, and jurists. Through their control of the state's financial resources, censoring apparatus, and security services, these regimes have used carrots and sticks to control and influence their religious establishments. Clerics who reliably find Koranic justifications to validate the regime's policies and actions, especially those that allow the immense corruption of various royal families, find themselves well paid and housed, comfortably ensconced in the pulpits of large and ornate mosques, as distinguished members of university faculties, and even as advisory members of their government's ruling clique. Those clerics who have trouble finding immediate, on-demand religious validation for regime actions, however, tend to lose their pay, pulpits, professorships, and oft-times their freedom.

Today the evolution of such cooption has created an environment in which Muslim citizens or subjects perceive the senior levels of the religious establishment as an arm of the government, not as independent clerics fulfilling their role of ensuring that the regimes govern according to Islamic law—preventing vice and promoting virtue, as it were. Again, this has been a slowly evolving popular perception, but the breaking point, after which clerical establishments were no longer given the benefit of the doubt, can be found after Iraq's 1990 invasion of Kuwait, when the senior Saudi council of clerics endorsed King Fahd's religiously invalid decision to allow U.S. and Western military forces to have bases on the Arabian Peninsula. This decision was clearly a case of claiming black is white, because nothing is clearer to Muslims than that their Prophet, on his deathbed, forbade such an infidel presence in Islam's birthplace, and he pledged to remove it if he lived. In the years since 1990 Arab governments have persuaded their senior clerics to sanction the expansion of the Western military presence on the Arabian Peninsula; negotiations and agreements with Israel; support for non-Muslim invasions of Muslim states and the provision of bases and other assistance to facilitate those actions; almost unimaginable governmental corruption; and the apprehension and incarceration of mujahedin fighting to protect Muslim lands. To even illiterate Muslims, these actions are un-Islamic and have validated the clerics as the mere paid mouthpieces of corrupt, apostate regimes.

This negative popular attitude toward the clerical establishment certainly would have been present with or without Osama bin Ladin. However, bin Laden has given Muslims a loud, persistent, passionate, and credible voice that invariably attacks the un-Islamic decisions and lifestyles of those he terms "the king's clerics." His public criticism has been a consistent theme of his rhetoric since he began speaking publicly in 1996, but the ferocity of his commentary has increased over the years. Initially bin Laden was reminding the religious establishment of its duty to enforce Islamic law, treading carefully around the traditional propensity of Muslims to respect and obey Islamic scholars, a tendency he fully shared before 1990. Bin Laden's rhetoric gradually took on a much more condemnatory, adversarial, and finally dismissive tone. In late 2001, for example, he warned young Muslims "not to fall victim to the words of some scholars who are misleading the ummah" by denying that a defensive jihad is obligatory for all.[20] Still shy of declaring war on those he described as "the authority's scholars and ruler's clerics," bin Laden in late 2002 harshly reminded them that they were failing in their duty to God as "the inheritors of the Prophet."[21] Calling on young and independent clerics to put themselves at the "head of the ranks [of the mujahedin], and lead the action, and direct the march," bin Laden said that much of the ulema had sided with the regimes and were practicing "deception and misguidance" of the people. They had, he said, "sold their faith for temporal gain."[22] By mid-2003 bin Laden essentially declared war on the ulema of the rulers. "Great evil is spreading throughout the Islamic world," he argued,

> The imams calling people to hell are those who appear more than others at the sides of the rulers of the region, the rulers of the Arab and Islamic world . . . [F]rom morning to evening, they call people to the gates of hell. They all, except for those upon whom Allah had mercy, are busy handing out praise and words of glory to the despotic rulers who disbelieved Allah and His Prophet . . . The true danger [to Muslims and their faith] is when the falsehood comes from the imams of religion who bear false witness every morning and evening and lead the nation [ummah] astray.[23]

The confluence of decisions by the ulema that many Muslims thought theologically invalid and bin Laden's pointed attacks on these invalid judgments has drastically undercut the authority of senior ulema in many Muslim countries. In both Afghanistan and Iraq, for example, assemblies of senior clerics have repeatedly called for the cessation of the violence pitting Muslim against Muslim, which all have been ignored by those doing the fighting. The eroding credibility of the religious establishments across the Arab world is producing an environment in which the Muslim leaders that Washington counts as allies will be able to do less and less to shape by religious fiat their peoples' understanding of U.S. policies and actions in the Islamic world. And they will, in turn, be even less able to control the actions their subjects take in response to U.S. activities.

The cynical use of Islam by Muslim rulers, the clerics' hypocrisy and corruption, and the constant urging of Muslims by bin Laden and Ayman al-Zawahiri to ignore the "rulers' ulema"[24] and to think and decide for themselves about how to best protect their religion seems to be reinvigorating Islam's original status as a literal, everyman's religion—a faith that is between God and an individual who has no need for clerics either to interpret God's word or to mediate and manage the relationship. "Muslims do not consider the Messenger of Islam [the Prophet Muhammad] a mediator between God and people," the noted scholar of Islam Tariq Ramadan has written. "Each individual is invited to address God directly, and although the Messenger sometimes did pray to God on behalf of his community, he often insisted on each believer's responsibility in his or her own relationship with the One [Allah]."[25]

The al-Qaeda chief's success in reducing the impact of establishment clerics on individuals appears to be substantial.[26] "Bin Laden hijacked Islam from the jurisprudence scholars," argues the distinguished Saudi academic Dr. Madawi al-Rashid, "and broke their monopoly of jurisprudence, which was established under the umbrella of the state."[27] Here Dr. Madawi argues not that bin Laden has hijacked the religion of Islam, as do so many in the West, but that he has worked to return Islam to Muslims, thereby destroying much of the power of each Muslim regime's ulema to control their populations. "Bin Laden," Dr. Madawi continues in her brilliant, ground-breaking essay,

> has been able to transfer Islam from the local to the international arena in an era that has its own peculiarities. The most important of these peculiarities are information, media, intellectual [activities], and economic communication. He also has been able to transfer Islam from the hands of the jurisprudence scholars and their monopoly to those of the simple ordinary Muslim.

> Bin Ladin's address[es] is [sic] popular in the Islamic world, even the Western experts themselves testify to this, because he transferred from the jurisprudence assembly to two domains: the first domain is the en-

tire world, and the second domain is the private individual. The inter-
actions of the Somali in Somalia, the Pakistani in Leeds, the Egyptian in
Germany, and the so-called Saudi in Mecca with these address[es] indicate
clear privatization. With bin Ladin, Islam has become an individual project
beyond the restrictions of the jurisprudence scholars or of political authority; a project that this individual could carry with him to the port of Aden
or Mombassa, or to the noise of Bangkok or New York. The individual
could also travel with this project through the Al-Nafudh Desert [in Saudi
Arabia], and settle down with it in the mountains of Mecca, or take it with
him to the cold land of Chechnya, and the jungles of the Philippines and
Bali.

This privatization and individualization [of Islam] has broken the shackles of the local identities, be they sectarian, tribal, or regional. Despite the
fact that the followers of bin Ladin insist on their local aliases and titles that
indicate their roots, they are people who rebelled against the local tribal,
sectarian, and even geographical aspects. They represent the traveling and
immigrating Muslim running away from the homeland, the shackles and
improvisations of the jurisprudence scholars, and the oppression of [nation-
state] authority and its men.[28]

Dr. Madawi's contention that bin Laden has initiated the return of
Islam to each individual Muslim must be seen as extremely worrying
both for the United States and for its Western allies, and for all Muslim
regimes that have counted on their population's respect for and obedience
to the judgments and guidance of their ulema. If Dr. Madawi is correct, and
I believe she is, the West may well be witnessing the Islamic reformation
it has long predicted and yearned for, and which it has been sure would
yield a pacifist, liberalized, and emasculated Islamic faith. In a century, the
noted commentator on Islam Reza Aslan wrote in early 2006, "we may
look back at bin Laden not only as a murderous criminal but also as one of
the principal figures of an era that scholars are increasingly referring to as
an Islamic reformation." Clear in Mr. Aslan's prediction is his belief that
the eagerly awaited reformation will be in the direction of moderation preferred by the West and hoped for by Westernized Muslims, the sort of full
eradication of religion from the public square that is now enforced by law
in Europe and championed by the Democratic Party and the multiculturalists in the United States.[29]

Let us say that Mr. Aslan and others are correct and there is a reformation under way, but let us also pose the question: "What if they are wrong about the direction that the reformation is going to take?" What if the direction suggested by Dr. Madawi, the direction agitated for by bin Laden and other Islamists, toward the individualization and personalization of Islam is where the reformation is headed? What if, to paraphrase the American historian Carl Becker, we are headed toward an environment in which "every Muslim is his own imam"? This reality would negate the rosy expectations of Mr. Aslan et al., which are largely shared by America's governing elite and its ethnic, exiled, and expatriate advisers, all of whom seem to have forgotten that the hundred-years-of-war-producing Protestant Reformation of Messrs. Luther and Calvin was precisely an effort to restore the direct relationship between man and God and to eliminate the intermediary role played by the corrupt priesthood of the Roman Catholic Church. Bin Laden, by slowly negating the ability of regime scholars to put a brake on popular enthusiasm for jihad, has ensured the continuing growth of the worldwide Sunni insurgency he is inciting.

A final factor belongs in an analysis of the sort of Islamic reformation that is occurring, and that is the notion of liberation from tyranny, a subject that above all ought to be understandable to Americans with an awareness of their own history. I must admit that this is an issue to which I failed to give enough attention in either of my other books, especially in the second. Having documented bin Laden's aim of inciting Muslims to overthrow Muslim regimes that do not rule by Islamic law, I left the emphasis on the replacement of the rule of apostates by the rule of the Koran. This surely remains the Islamists' central goal in Egypt, Saudi Arabia, Jordan, Yemen, and elsewhere.

Also in bin Laden's rhetoric of urging the defeat of these governments, however, is a central theme that damns the regimes for their denial of basic natural rights, their corruption, their persecutions and tortures, their nepotism, and the cruelty they widely and liberally apply through security and police services. In some ways these claims, as I have previously said, are not entirely unlike those which Jefferson wrote into the Declaration of Independence in the long litanylike indictment of Britain's George III contained in the "He has done this" and "He has done that" section of the Declaration.[30] Consider, for a moment, bin Laden writing in the late summer of 1996:

Today we begin to talk, work, and discuss ways of rectifying what has befallen the Islamic world in general and the land of the two holy mosques [Saudi Arabia] in particular. We want to study the ways which could be used to rectify matters and restore rights to their owners as people have been subjected to grave danger and harm to their religion and their lives . . .

The same thing has befallen the people in industry and agriculture, the cities and the villages, and the people in the desert and the rural areas. Everyone is complaining about almost everything. The situation in the land of the two holy mosques is like a giant volcano about to erupt and destroy heresy and corruption, whatever their sources. The explosions of Riyadh [November 1995] and Khobar [June 1996] were only a small indication of that torrential flood resulting from the bitter suffering, repression, coercion, great injustice, disgraceful debauchery, and poverty [imposed by the al-Saud family].

They [the people] feel that God is tormenting them because they kept quiet about the regime's injustice and illegitimate actions, especially its failure to have recourse to the Shariah, its confiscation of the people's legitimate rights, the opening of the land of the two holy mosques to the American occupiers, and the arbitrary jailing of the true ulema, heirs of the Prophet.[31]

If I am correct that bin Laden is appealing to Muslims to seek what George W. Bush has correctly called the earnest desire of all people to live freer lives,[32] then the reality is that the al-Qaeda chief is tapping not only into hatred of U.S. foreign policy and its impact and an almost genetic eagerness to defend Islam against infidel attack, but also into the desire of Muslims to attain what Jefferson called the "inalienable rights" that the Founders believed to be hard-wired into human beings simply because they are human beings. That is, bin Laden is urging Muslims to liberate themselves from tyranny in order to attain life, liberty, and the pursuit of happiness in terms that are compatible with their Islamic faith and not dictated by effete but brutal and corrupt tyrannies like the al-Sauds. And while it is true that the record of Islamists after gaining power is a sorry and frequently bloody one that does not reflect the ideals of the American Enlightenment,[33] that does not alter the mobilizing and motivating power of the idea of striving to create an environment where Muslims can exercise their natural rights—however they believe Allah has defined those rights—

in place of the screw, the rack, and the electric cattle prod; unimaginable royal corruption that impoverishes them; imprisonment without charge; and a religion distorted to protect tyranny. If a component in bin Laden's rhetoric of incitement urges Muslims to liberate themselves from those attributes of coercion common to all police states, Muslim or Western, then his appeal will be considerably wider and more durable than we—or at least I—had previously estimated. He will strike a resonant chord not only with those who share his piety, but also with those who are nationalists and those who are enraged by the seemingly permanent and arbitrary denial of the natural rights that our Founders believed came from God and on which they predicated the American Revolution and then entrenched in the U.S. Constitution.

Dealing with a World Aflame

The world, six years after 9/11, is increasingly awash with Muslims angry and hateful about the impact of U.S. and Western policies and actions on the Islamic world, and the U.S. government and its allies seem oblivious to the enemies they are making. Preoccupied with Iraq and Afghanistan, Washington and the NATO states only sporadically focus on the growth of Islamic militancy in other areas of the world, and when they do, they tend to look at each as an isolated problem; for example, "the Somalia problem" or the "Thai insurgency problem." Underappreciated is the reality that there is a rising tide of anger against Western actions across the Islamic world, and that thanks to those actions—and to bin Laden's leadership, al-Qaeda's military attacks, Arabic satellite television, and the omnipresent Internet—the Muslim world is increasingly beginning to think of itself as not a collection of individual nation-states but as a unity—the ummah or community of believers demanded by Allah, launched by the Prophet Muhammad, defended by Saladin, and championed by bin Laden and other Islamist leaders. This rising sense of community is nowhere near to producing the homogenous Islamofascist caliphate so dear to the hearts of scare-mongering neoconservatives, Israeli politicians, and the media shills of each, but a worldwide Muslim anger is taking shape in different ways in different parts of the world. Some of this anger is dangerous, even potentially fatal to the United States, but much of it is not; some of it can be neutralized or defeated by America, but most of it cannot. That which cannot be blunted by America, however, either will fall or can be shifted to fall on others and need not be a national-security concern for us. One case, Europe, will be of deep and abiding concern to Americans, but it may be the one area of the world where we can do the least to help against Islamist forces.

For the foreseeable future, Iraq, Afghanistan, and Pakistan will be the three major producers of Islamist fighters to be confronted by the United States, its allies, and the incumbent governments of the Muslim world. Afghanistan was in that category before 9/11, but Pakistan and Iraq are there only because of U.S. actions after 9/11. The relevant actions here were not the U.S. invasions of Afghanistan and Iraq, but rather that we failed to win and get out of either place and instead stayed on until we were defeated. Afghanistan will return to Taliban-like rule, and Iraq will be ruled by Islamist Shias or Sunnis, and both will remain unstable. Pakistan's ability to avoid Islamist rule weakens with each passing month and now largely depends on how much longer the U.S.-led coalition occupies Afghanistan, which in turn depends only on how long it takes U.S. forces to find and kill bin Laden and his lieutenants. Minus the U.S. and its allies, Musharraf would be able to fully support the Taliban and its allies, destroy Karzai's government, and reestablish Pashtun rule in Afghanistan. This process would yield a Pakistan-friendly, insular Islamist government in Kabul, the chance of gradually quieting the fierce anti-Islamabad discontent in the Pashtun tribal areas, and the recreation of a balance of power between Pakistan and India. Thus the possibility of avoiding an Islamist-run, nuclear-armed Pakistan remains, but it is a wasting chance and one that almost entirely depends on Musharraf being able to hold the Pakistani polity together under the Bhutto-caused imposition of emergency rule and the United States doing what it should have done before the year 2002 was out—kill bin Laden, al-Zawahiri, and as many of their followers as possible and then leave immediately.[34]

Common sense and quick action may limit the damage done by U.S. policies and actions in Afghanistan and Pakistan, but it is hard to see the end of the damage flowing out of Iraq. Whether Shias or Sunnis emerge on top, Iraq will remain unstable, unreconstructed economically, and a cauldron in which neighboring countries will intervene clandestinely to protect and pursue their national and sectarian interests. This in itself is not necessarily a bad thing for the United States—Muslims killing Muslims instead of Americans is a goal to be aggressively sought—but we will have to put up with some losses. Saudi Arabia and the other Arabian Peninsula states probably will remain stable by promoting, funding, and facilitating civil war in Iraq and posing as the protectors of Sunnis there and everywhere. These actions will add another strong element contributing to the containment of Iran, as they will force Tehran to bleed itself in blood and treasure to support Iraqi Shias even as the clock ticks out the final decade of its reliable oil reserves and its return to Third World impoverishment.[35]

For Jordan and Syria, however, the jig is up. Jordanians do not strongly support King Abdullah II's Hashemite monarchy, which has earned a substantial dollop of additional hatred by supporting the U.S.-led invasion of Iraq and recently cracking down yet again on domestic Islamist political parties. The long-suppressed Jordanian Islamist community is large and restive—witness its support and admiration for the late Abu Musab al-Zarqawi—and an unstable Iraq will serve as the base from which al-Qaeda and other groups will infiltrate and stage attacks in Jordan. It is difficult to see Jordan surviving in its present form or with its present level of stability after the U.S.-led occupation of Iraq ends, without a drastic change in the regime's authoritarianism in which Washington acquiesces.[36] In Syria, Bashir al-Assad has never had the iron grip on the country that his father did, and so the Islamist fervor created in Syria by the U.S. occupation of Iraq and Washington's humiliation of the young al-Assad by forcing Syria's withdrawal from Lebanon has emboldened domestic Islamists. Because of the strength of Syria's military and security services, the Islamists will not have an easy time carrying the day, but they will be accommodated. Thus, Syria can no longer be counted on as a bulwark against Islamist militancy. As noted earlier, the U.S. invasion of Iraq destroyed the bulwarks provided by Saddam and al-Assad.[37] What does all of this mean for Lebanon and Israel? Who knows, but very often two and two does sum to four.[38] Lebanon is already dealing with renewed civil strife, and what appears to be the growing al-Qaeda presence in the country's north suggests that bin Laden's organization is already projecting its forces and influences westward from Iraq. And needless to say, Israel's long-term strategic outlook—thanks mainly to its "friends" among America's neoconservatives—has seldom looked dimmer or grimmer.

Pakistan, Afghanistan, Iraq, Syria, and Jordan are all potential disasters, but only in Pakistan is there a chance for the United States to protect its interests and then only if it can wind up its Afghan calamity both with rapidity and with the corpses of bin Laden and al-Zawahiri. The other four states are likely to become involved in an intracivilization conflict in the Muslim world. That conflict need not involve the United States in warfare, so long as oil supplies are not disrupted and Washington is wise enough to avoid allowing the Israelis to ensnare us into fighting their fight. That, alas, is a very long shot.

The United States will have many other countries of concern as the tide of Islamic anger rises, but few will either require or allow direct military intervention. I will look briefly at what I believe are the six most worrisome sites for America: the North Caucasus, because of the adjacent Caspian Sea oil reserves and the base it provides Islamists for proselytizing and nuclear procurement in Russia; Bangladesh, because it has the potential to be the East Asian hub for jihadism and a threat to India's stability; Nigeria, where Christian-vs.-Muslim violence is rife and the U.S. economy's interests are hostage to an increasingly unstable situation in the country's oil fields; Thailand, because of U.S. military commitments to the Thai regime; and Somalia, where the United States has no genuine national-security interests but where Washington's involvement might help trigger the spread of jihad across much of sub-Saharan Africa. The sixth site is Europe, which is many ways the most important to the United States and, at the same time, the place where we can—and should—do the least to help.

The North Caucasus: Russia's military has fought two wars in Chechnya since 1994, losing more than 6,600 soldiers. Moscow lost the first, but in the second it has slowed the pace of fighting there; although the Chechen rebel leader, Dokku Dumarov, recently declared the North Caucasus an "Islamic emirate" and declared war on Britain, Israel, and the United States. At this writing, the Russians maintain close to 100,000 military, security, and police personnel in Chechnya.[39] As the Russians made some progress in Chechnya, however, the Islamists' ideology and fighters have spread and are taking root in several other of the former Soviet republics in the North Caucasus, including Dagestan, Kabardino-Balkaria, North Ossetia, and Ingushetia.[40] Particularly worrying for Moscow is the increasing Islamist presence in Dagestan; it is historically an "ancient Muslim region," is the largest and most populous North Caucasus republic, and controls a large part of the Caspian Sea coast, giving Moscow access to the world's largest untapped oil reserves in the Caspian Basin. In Ingushetia, too, Moscow is faced with a Muslim population that has long supplied Islamist fighters to the Chechen insurgents and in recent years has developed what C. J. Chivers of *The New York Times* has called "a potent anti-Moscow insurgency of its own." Indeed, Moscow sent two thousand Interior Ministry troops there in July 2007, but the fighting continues and is "threatening to ignite a full-fledged guerilla war there."[41]

The overall security situation in the Caucasus is deteriorating.[42] This reality and the region's historically porous borders allow the entry of Arab mujahedin into the region; Georgia's Pankisi Gorge, for example, has long been a hub for Arab fighters, and Moscow puts heavy culpability on Saudi Arabia and other Arabian Peninsula states for funding Islamist insurgent organizations, allowing their nationals to fight alongside the Chechens and others in the region, and sending Islamist NGOs to the North Caucasus to inculcate Wahhabism among the inhabitants. The smuggling-friendly borders also facilitate the ability of Islamist missionaries to enmesh themselves among Russia's current Muslim population of between twenty and twenty-five million, which could grow to a minimum of 20 percent of Russia's population by 2020,[43] and for al-Qaeda and other Islamists to attempt to purchase or steal nuclear components or devices from the Former Soviet Union's (FSU) still-unsecured nuclear-weapons arsenal. In the summer of 2006, for example, Georgian authorities arrested a Russian national who was in the country to sell what the Georgians described as 100 grams of bomb-grade uranium (U-235) "to a Muslim man from 'a serious organization' " for one million dollars. That arrest followed a similar apprehension in 2003. In both cases, the quantities of uranium seized were too small to make a bomb but had been enriched to nearly the 90 percent level, which is ideal for bomb-making.[44]

For the United States, growing domestic insecurity and Islamist militancy in the North Caucasus poses several significant problems. First, the continuing failure of Washington and Moscow to fully secure the FSU's nuclear arsenal encourages al-Qaeda and other Islamist organizations to keep trying to purchase or steal components for a weapon or a complete device. With porous borders, smuggling abounding, and rife corruption, the North Caucasus is an ideal base from which to reach into Russia for acquisition purposes. This instability also has the potential of disrupting the development of energy resources in the Caspian Basin, at a time when U.S. energy requirements continue to grow. Finally, the flow of Islamist missionaries into Russia—one expert estimates that in 2007 there were more than one thousand—promises to quicken the radicalization of the country's already large Muslim population and accelerate the pace at which Russians are converting to Islam. Together these factors will increase the political power of Russian Muslims at a time when the country's population is rapidly declining—148 million in 1982 to an expected 130 million in 2015. Russia's Muslim population, moreover, far outpaces the population-maintaining fertility rate of 2.1 live births per woman, while the overall Russian population's fertility rate is 1.14.[45] As in European countries, the United States will one day have to deal with a Russia whose diplomatic positions and national interests are defined in increasing measure by the demands of its Muslim peoples.

Bangladesh: A country known in the West largely for its poverty and its recurrent, massive natural disasters, Bangladesh is the world's third most populous Muslim country, with a population of 152 million, 88 percent of which is Muslim.[46] After gaining independence from Pakistan in 1971, the first Bangladesh government declared the country a secular state, and Islam there remained "more relaxed" than in the Arab world and "overwhelmingly moderate" for most of the rest of the century. Even today, for example, the leaders of the two major political parties are women.[47] In 2001, however, Prime Minister Begum Khaleda Zia tempered secularism by inserting in the constitution that Bangladesh would be ruled according to "the sovereignty of Allah."[48] This switch occurred after Zia had formed an electoral alliance between her Bangladesh National Party and two Saudi-backed Islamist political parties (Jamaat-e Islami and Islamic Oika Jote) and defeated the rival Awami League. Like other such cooptation attempts in the Muslim world, Zia's successful 2001 effort provided her coalition with the margin of victory but created a postelection environment in which Islamists have made significant organizational and political advances across the country. By mid-2005, for example, at least fifty-eight militant Islamic networks had been identified in Bangladesh.[49]

Zia's admission of the Islamists into her government helped to accelerate the gains they had been making since the end of the Afghan-Soviet war in 1989. The significant number of Bangladeshis who fought in that jihad brought back and spread a more militant and militaristic brand of Islam, and they brought in their trail Islamist NGOs and Salafi and Wahhabi missionaries from the Arabian Peninsula, especially from Saudi Arabia, Dubai, and Kuwait. Some Bangladeshis, including the recently executed insurgent leader Bangla Bhai, trained in al-Qaeda and Taliban training camps in the late 1990s. Bin Laden and al-Qaeda, moreover, have been assisting the Bangladeshi Islamists with their domestic organizational efforts for more than a decade.[50] Adding to the proselytizing power of these Islamist entities have been Bangladeshis who returned home after serving a "tour of duty" as workers in the states of the Arabian Peninsula, during which they worshipped according to Wahhabi or Salafi doctrine. This large two-way flow of workers—at any given time nearly a million Bangladeshis work in Saudi Arabia—has accelerated the shift of moderate Bangladeshi Islam toward the militancy common across the Arab world.[51] Pakistani and Saudi charities have emerged as major benefactors for education in Bangladesh, offering scholarships for universities in their countries and providing funding for the building and staffing of religious schools and madrassas in Bangladesh. Islamist NGOs such as Kuwait's Society for the Revival of the Islamic Heritage and others based in the Arabian Peninsula and Pakistan, for example, have funded the creation of thousands of Salafist- and Wahhabist-oriented madrassas for primary and secondary students across Bangladesh.[52]

The pace of Islamist militancy and violence in Bangladesh has increased significantly during the past five years, and while Prime Minister Zia pledged to "crush" it, she has not and her political future depends on Islamist support.[53] In addition, the Islamists may already have struck such deep roots that they are now a permanent player in the country's politics. Native Islamists and foreign Islamist missionaries have focused on rural Bangladesh and have made great strides there by providing social services and education.[54] The militarization of Bangladeshi Islamists also appears to be increasing as a consequence of the Taliban fighters who arrived after the 2001 U.S. invasion of Afghanistan and the Bangladeshi Islamists' longstanding ties to Burma's Islamist Rohingya and Arakan organizations of Islamist insurgents.[55] The growth of Islamist strength in Bangladesh and the enormous corruption of the society suggest that the country has the potential to serve as a hub from which Islamist groups can base and operate. Media reports claim that Islamist military training camps already are operating in the rough terrain of the Chittagong Hills. The Indian government, moreover, claims that Pakistan's Inter-Services Intelligence Directorate (ISID) trains Indian Islamists and other secular Indian insurgent groups, such as the United Liberation Front of Assam, in Bangladeshi camps. The country's porous 4,100-kilometer border with India also provides easy entry for Arab missionaries seeking to radicalize India's huge Muslim population.[56]

For the United States and its war against Islamist insurgency, Bangladesh is a disaster in the making, and one that Washington can do little about. In 2007, an unelected caretaker government—supported by the military—took over at the end of Zia's term; regularly scheduled elections in Bangladesh have been delayed; violence has flared repeatedly in Dhaka's streets; and the opposition Awami League has recruited six Islamists to run for parliament and has formed an alliance with the Bangladesh Khelefat party, an Islamist party headed by two Bangladeshi veterans of the Afghan-Soviet war. With both major national parties now cooperating with the Islamists; a level of corruption that makes the country an ideal base for illicit commercial and financial activities that facilitate Islamist military operations; porous land and sea borders; a rapidly Islamicizing educational system; and the steady flow of funding for Islamists from Saudi Arabia and other Arab states, Bangladesh is set to become a regional hub for Islamist activities and a geographical link between groups in South Asia and those in the Far East.[57]

Nigeria: Nigeria is home to more Muslims than Egypt. With a population of about 140 million people—divided nearly equally between Muslims and Christians—Nigeria has seen a steady growth in Islamist militancy since its Muslim-dominated northern provinces began in 1999–2000 to rule according to sharia law.[58] With this growth has come a steady increase in sectarian strife and violence between militant Christians, mostly Anglicans, and Muslims; the violence has been vicious on both sides, including the burning of mosques and churches, the killing of women and children, and the disfiguring, dismembering, and burning of corpses.[59] As in Bangladesh, moreover, Islamist NGOs and missionaries supported by Saudi Arabia and other Muslim states have been very active in Nigeria and most of West Africa since the early 1990s, and Nigeria's Islam is taking on the militant tones of the theology that the NGOs preach. "You go there [to

Nigeria]," according to a human rights organization, "and you'll find the Saudis, and you'll find the Sudanese there, you find the Libyans there, you find Syrians there, Pakistanis there, and it's all part of worldwide Islamization."[60] In 2003, bin Laden declared Nigeria to be ready for an Islamic takeover, and since then UN investigators have claimed that al-Qaeda has recruiting and training bases in the country.[61] In late November 2007, Nigerian authorities arrested an al-Qaeda-related cell that had trained in Algerian Salafist camps and intended to bomb government buildings.

For the United States, Nigeria's deepening Christian-vs.-Muslim conflict is an issue of escalating importance because Nigeria is home to the largest energy industry in Africa. Estimates show that the country has an oil reserve of about 36 billion barrels and natural gas reserves of 184 trillion cubic feet, all of it located in the Niger Delta, a 27,000-square-mile area of swamp and mangrove forest.[62] In 2006, Nigeria was the fifth largest exporter of oil to the United States, and it and the other oil fields in the Gulf of Guinea are expected to provide the United States with 25 percent of its oil by 2012 or 2013.[63] Washington has recognized the importance of Nigerian oil to the U.S. economy and in 2002 declared oil reserves there and across Africa to be a "strategic national interest" that would be secured by the U.S. military if necessary. To date, Washington has supplied the Nigerian military with radars, communications gear, and boats for coastal defense, and U.S. forces, with the British military, have trained Nigerian naval personnel in maritime warfare operations.[64] In 2005, President George W. Bush met with the Nigerian president and assured him of America's commitment to maintaining political stability in the country, but so far Washington has refused Nigeria's late-2006 request for the deployment of U.S. Marines to the Niger Delta to counter insurgent activities.[65]

The oil-producing Niger Delta is located in Nigeria's Christian-dominated south, but over the past decade a shadowy and quasi-Islamist group known as the Movement for the Emancipation of the Niger Delta (MEND) has undertaken violent activities aimed at destroying the Nigerian government's ability to export crude oil. In an e-mail message sent to Reuters in midsummer 2006 MEND declared, "We are resuming an all-out war on the eastern sector [of the Niger Delta] with an aim to wiping out fields there and the export terminals."[66] Although operating in an overwhelmingly Christian population, MEND fighters have taken advantage of local resentment toward the central government for its failure to use oil revenues to develop the area and relieve its intense poverty.[67] In an area where rivalry between rebel factions has traditionally been intense—there are up to 120 militant groups operating in the Niger Delta—a degree of cooperation is now emerging under MEND's leadership. Armed with such Afghan-jihad-type weapons as AK-47s, heavy machine guns, and RPGs (this seems to be another set of potential U.S. enemies who are not abiding by the rules of the Revolution in Military Affairs) and conducting kidnappings for ransom, attacks on energy infrastructure, ambushes, and a few car bombings, MEND has proven itself able to severely disrupt oil production and export. In the first eight months of 2006, for example, the activities of MEND and its associates reduced Nigerian oil exports by approximately a half-million barrels per day. And in the year between April 2006 and April 2007, Nigeria lost an estimated 12 billion dollars in oil sales due to the actions of MEND and other groups.[68]

Although the Islamist presence and influence in the Niger Delta seems now to be quite limited,[69] MEND and other insurgent groups have had a major impact on Nigeria's oil production. The emerging Islamist tone of MEND's rhetoric, the escalating violence of the overall Christian-Muslim relationship in Nigeria, and bin Laden's placing of Nigeria on al-Qaeda's target list all portend a threat to reliable U.S. access to the Niger Delta's energy resources. Of the many locations where U.S. forces may have to intervene to secure oil supplies, the prospect of doing so in the Niger Delta may be the most appallingly difficult and bloody. Why? Because of the topography, the dispersed condition of the energy industry's infrastructure, and diversity of the local population.

- One of the most obvious military obstacles in the Niger Delta is terrain. According to the Niger Delta Development Commission, the delta is the world's largest wetland and is composed of 27,000 square kilometers of dense mangrove swamps and waterways, making it an ideal location for guerilla operations.[70]
- The sheer number of oil installations also makes protection of the infrastructure difficult. Shell, which is the largest foreign oil company in Nigeria, has more than 1,000 oil wells, 90 oil fields, and 73 flow stations in the delta region, and these wells are linked to a 6,000-kilometer pipeline network.[71]
- Some 20 million Nigerians, from 50 different ethnic groups, speaking

250 dialects, across 3,000 communities live in the Niger Delta. 70 percent of these people live on less than one dollar per day.[72]

Thailand: For most of the post-1945 period, the peoples of Thailand's Muslim-dominated southern provinces have resented what they believe is discrimination against their region's economy and society by the Buddhist-dominated government in Bangkok, leaving the south as the country's most impoverished area. Other sources of resentment lie in Bangkok's refusal to officially recognize the Thai Muslims' language, culture, and Malay ethnicity, its failure to ever appoint a Muslim provincial governor in the south, and its stationing of Buddhist military units in the south to maintain order and coerce assimilation. The behavior of these units toward the population, particularly women, has not always been exemplary.[73] And as in Nigeria and Bangladesh, Saudi Arabia and other Arab states have been active in sending Islamist NGOs and missionaries to proselytize among the Muslims in the south and have likewise funded local Islamist organizations. Similar support for Thai Muslims also appears to be flowing in from donors in Indonesia and Malaysia.[74]

Since the late 1960s, armed Muslim resistance has flared sporadically in the southern provinces of Pattani, Yala, and Narathiwat; in the 1990s this violence was in part the responsibility of Thai Muslims returning from the Afghans' war against the USSR. This violence took a broader and more sustained turn in late 2003 and early 2004. As violence escalated, then-Thai prime minister Thaksin's government took a hard line against the Islamists, reinforcing Thai forces in the south and giving them a free and brutal hand in dealing with both insurgents and civilians; declaring what amounted to martial law in much of the south in July 2005; and ruling out talks with Thai Muslims about the possibility of autonomy for the southern provinces, which for the five hundred years prior to 1909 formed an independent Islamic sultanate.[75]

With Thaksin's hard-line policies, the military's aggressiveness, and a casualty total approaching two thousand dead, several Thai generals deposed Thaksin in a coup in September 2006. Thaksin was replaced by General Sonthi Boonyaratglin, a Muslim, who immediately launched a policy-oriented effort to defuse Muslim animosities and stop the insurgency. Sonthi visited the region twice, offered an "unqualified apology" for the Thai military's excesses, offered the southern provinces increased autonomy, and expressed a willingness to allow sharia law to be used there. Sonthi has been so forthcoming, in fact, that some Buddhist politicians have criticized him for appeasing the Islamist militants. So far, however, the Thai insurgents have responded with continuing violence— claiming five more years of war are needed before talks can begin— suggesting that their goal may have escalated from autonomy within Thailand to independence for the southern provinces. The insurgents have created large areas in the south where they operate with impunity and are also in the midst of moving attacks into Buddhist-dominated areas of Thailand; they may have, for example, detonated eight bombs in Bangkok on New Year's Eve 2006, killing 8 and wounding 36, which caused General Sonthi to return early from making the Hajj pilgrimage in Saudi Arabia. And over the course of 2007, General Boonyaratglin gradually backed away from his carrot-and-stick policy and by midyear had ordered the resumption of large-scale military operations against insurgent networks.[76]

For the United States, the Thai insurgency could ultimately require the provision of military assistance if the stability of the Bangkok regime is threatened. Under Cold War–era multilateral and bilateral agreements— the Manila Pact of 1954 and the Thanat-Rusk Communiqué of 1962— Washington appears committed to assisting the Thai government to prevent its defeat. U.S. policymakers added a much greater commitment of American prestige and credibility to those agreements when they designated Thailand a "Major Non-NATO Ally" in December 2003. In a less quantifiable category, Washington's support for the Thai also is predicated on memories of Thai forces fighting alongside the U.S. military in the Vietnam War. Under the noted accords, the U.S. military has used Thai airbases, worked with Thai forces on Thai territory to stem the narcotics flow from the Golden Triangle, and established stockpiles of prepositioned, war-reserve munitions in the country. In addition, U.S. forces have equipped and trained Thai forces and regularly perform exercises with them.[77]

With a bilateral military cooperation agreement based on dated Cold War requirements, Washington may be committed to respond positively to a Thai request for military help against the Islamist insurgency. While this is clearly a worst-case scenario, even the bare possibility of U.S. involvement in Vietnam-like jungle combat—which would in turn draw other regional Islamist fighters to Thailand like a magnet—ought to give U.S.

policymakers pause to reconsider its leftover Cold War commitments not only in Thailand but also across the international board.

Somalia: Somalia is an overwhelmingly Muslim East African country of no particular strategic importance to the United States. Without a government since Prime Minister Muhammad Barre was overthrown in 1991, the country has been the scene of unending anarchy, tribal warfare, and starvation.[78] President George H. W. Bush's ill-considered, New World Order–building decision to lead a UN humanitarian intervention there in 1992 ended with a few dozen U.S. military casualties and an ignominious Clinton-ordered retreat in March 1994. The evacuation of U.S.-led intervention forces was followed by a decade of intra-Somali warfare between and among ruthless, well-armed warlords, as well as by an influx of Arabs and their money—especially Saudis and Saudi money—which together worked to move Somali Muslims toward a greater adherence to Salafism and Wahhabism and some of their leaders to aspire to form an Islamic state.[79]

The patient and bloody effort of Somali Islamists and their Arab supporters seemed to be helping Somalia to right itself in June 2006, when Islamist leaders, working together under the umbrella of the Islamic Courts Union (ICU), took control of Mogadishu from more secular Somali warlords. Over the following months the ICU imposed a harsh sharia-based rule that brought some stability to Somalia for the first time since 1991.[80] Turning its back on a useful measure of stability in the Horn of Africa, which is home to more than 90 million Muslims, Washington backed the December 24, 2006, invasion of Somalia by the Ethiopian military. U.S. officials argued that Addis Ababa's action was based on its "genuine security concerns," but at least as important in Washington's decision was its still dominant Cold War–era lust for finding proxies to do America's dirty work. The Ethiopians quickly overthrew the ICU and installed Prime Minsiter Ali Mohamed Gedi's secular, UN-backed Somali Transitional Federal Government that had been based in Baidoa. At this writing, Gedi has resigned and the regime—now led by President Abdullahi Yusuf— seems destined to become dependent, after the Ethiopians withdraw, on the same Somali warlords that the ICU defeated in 2006.[81] The Somali Islamists' anger over Washington's public support for the Christian

Ethiopians' invasion, moreover, was sharpened by the simultaneous U.S. air strikes aimed at three al-Qaeda leaders reported to be near Hayo, in southernmost Somalia near the Kenyan border.[82] Taken together, the invasion and the air strikes have strengthened the Somali Islamist leaders' belief that the United States intends to destroy their faith, and the likely result seems to be that the ICU chiefs (whose forces and ordnance were dispersed not destroyed) will start an insurgency against the UN-supported Somali regime and perhaps launch terrorist operations inside Ethiopia and Kenya and against the U.S. Special Forces base at Camp Lemonier in Djibouti.[83]

Leaving aside the social and humanitarian mayhem that the Ethiopian invasion will cause in Somalia, that invasion and the U.S. military action have put America at a turning point in the Horn of Africa. In a locale not of pivotal importance to the worldwide Sunni Islamist insurgency, U.S. policy and actions have quickly brought it close to that status. This evolution is due not only—or even mainly—to the air raids and the invasion, but also to the fact that U.S. leaders again walked into a trap laid by bin Laden over the past decade. Since the withdrawal of the U.S.-led UN mission in 1994, bin Laden and Ayman al-Zawahiri have warned Muslims that the United States would return to Somalia, Sudan, and all of the Horn for three reasons: (a) to control oil reserves in Sudan and elsewhere in the Horn; (b) to stop the spread of Islam in the Horn; and (c) to acquire ports on the coast of East Africa to give the U.S. military bases from which to strike at Yemen and the holy places in Saudi Arabia.[84] None of these three points, of course, may genuinely be part of the U.S. strategy in the Horn of Africa; indeed, one doubts that U.S. strategy there amounts to anything more than knee-jerk anti-Islamism. As always, though, perception is reality, and the Bush administration has taken a thoroughly necessary military action—trying to kill Somali-based al-Qaeda leaders when the chance arose—and turned it into another *casus belli* for jihadists by endorsing the Christian Ethiopians' destruction of an Islamist government and subsequent stationing of troops in the country to fight Somali Islamists.[85]

Europe: While the Islamist fire burning in Europe, particularly in Western Europe, is neither as bright nor always as obvious as the fires burning elsewhere in the world, it may be burning more deeply and damagingly than most anywhere else.[86] For the United States, this reality is worrisome and poignant; worrisome because America is Europe's child and natural international partner, and poignant because Europe's Islamist problem underscores just how close to irretrievably America and Europe have parted ways and how very little America can do to help. Indeed, given demographic realties, there is strong reason to doubt that the Europeans can even help themselves.

Like Americans, Europeans are bedeviled by a failed governing generation that has few contact points with reality and virtually no knowledge of or respect for either history or the power of religion. Unlike Americans, however, Europeans appear to lack the courage—may one say the manliness?—to refute their weakling, utopia-purveying European Community leaders and reassert the national identities that once made Europe the world's center of material, social, educational, artistic, and economic progress. On the basis of the cringing, cowardly, and fantastical assertion that European nations' amalgamation into the European Community was mandatory because they could not otherwise prevent themselves from going to war—has man not free will?—European leaders have turned their backs on nationalism, the tool that has, despite savage interstate wars, brought more good to more people than any other instrument in the toolkit of human organization. In its place they have erected a banal, bureaucrat-ridden, and economically bankrupting supranational authority that combines the French Enlightenment's goal of perfecting man and society, a hysterical animosity toward Christianity (without which of course there be would no entity identifiable as Europe and no reminder in men's minds that only God is perfect), and a pacifism that reeks not of conviction and humanity but of cowardice, sloth, and an insatiable desire for ease. In place of self-respect, tradition, nation, and faith, the Europeans have adopted an appeasing, guilt-ridden multiculturalism, the euro and the Common Agricultural Policy, an unrelenting presentism, and a ferocious appetite for atheism and for ignoring history. The governing philosophy of today's European leaders, as then-cardinal Joseph Ratzinger wrote accurately in 2005, "consciously severs its own historical roots depriving itself of the regenerating forces from which it sprang, from the fundamental memory of humanity, so to speak, without which reason loses its orientation."[87]

Most Americans and Europeans are simply not on the same wavelength. While a few of America's elite are still representative of their harder-working, tougher-minded, more nationalistic, and far more religious countrymen, the tie between Europe's leaders and people seems to be much closer. This is especially and most fatally true in the area of religion's role in shaping individual lives and civil society. "[C]ontemporary Europe is the closest to a godless civilization the world has ever known," Mark Lilla wrote in early 2006.

> Since World War II, Europeans have stared in blank amazement across the Atlantic at a new global power whose citizens and even leaders seem to believe myths about the old bearded man in the sky. They call that American "exceptionalism" on the assumption that living without God is the ultimate destiny of the human race. . . . The Europeans find it hard to believe that people can still take God seriously and want to shape their society according to his dictates.[88]

While a person's or a people's religious beliefs or nonbeliefs are no one else's business, Europeans, (like much of the American elite, and especially Democratic leaders) seem unable intellectually to credit the importance and dangerous ramifications of the religious resurgence in today's world. Inside Europe the EC bureaucracy and its emasculated national governments continue to attribute the growth in Islamism's appeal and in the number of jihad-oriented young Muslims to economic inequality, a failure to eradicate the last Muslim-offending remnants of Christianity from the public square, and evanescent racism among those they regard as the few retrograde Europeans with archaic attachments to their own nations and histories. Increase the dole, annihilate Christianity, coerce the perfection of the thinking of all Europeans by enforcing stringent anti–hate speech legislation, and maybe throw in a Europe-wide Islamic holiday, goes the EC's recipe, and the Islamist fire will be smothered and out will pop peaceful, cowardly Euro-Muslims ready to have no children, spurn God, and like all good Europeans, quietly obey their nonelected bureaucratic masters in Brussels.

Well, no. These steps certainly will not solve Europe's Islamist problem, but they may blind the Europeans to the problem until it defeats them. Why will they fail? What makes it almost impossible for Americans to help Europe control or defeat its Islamist foes? It is simply another case of what John Adams called "stubborn facts," this time demographic facts. I cannot improve on the excellent descriptions and analyses of Europe's pending demographic calamity already provided by Niall Ferguson, Tony Blankley, George Weigel, and Mark Steyn.

Ferguson: The greatest of all the strengths of radical Islam . . . is that it has demography on its side. The Western culture against which it has declared holy war cannot possibly match the capacity of traditional Muslim societies when it comes to reproduction . . . While European fertility had fallen below the natural replacement level in the 1970s, the decline in the Muslim world has been much slower. By the late 1990s the fertility rate in the eight Muslim countries to the south and east of the European Union was two and a half times higher than the European figure.[89]

Blankley: The replacement rate for a population is an average of 2.1 babies per woman. Western Europe is currently at approximately 1.4. Russia is about 1.1 . . . As birthrates slip below the replacement rate, two things happen. First, the average age of the population goes up. This becomes important for funding retirement benefits, with ever fewer working and tax-paying younger people supporting ever more non-working and benefit-collecting older people. It is also significant for the overall productivity of an economy. There is no example in history of a nation becoming more prosperous when it doesn't have an expanding population.[90]

Weigel: Above all, and most urgently, why is Europe committing demographic suicide, systematically depopulating itself . . . Why do 18 European countries report "negative natural increase" (i.e., more deaths than births)? Why does no western European country have a replacement-level birthrate? . . . Why will Europe's retired population increase by 55 percent in the next 25 years, while its working population will shrink by 8 percent—and, to repeat, why can't Europeans, either populations or the public, draw the obvious conclusions from these figures about the impending bankruptcy of their social welfare, health care, and pension systems?[91]

Steyn: For a stable population—i.e., no growth, no decline, just a million folks in 1950, a million in 1980, a million in 2010—you need a fertility rate of 2.1 live births per woman. That's what America has: 2.1, give or take. Canada has 1.48, an all-time low . . . Europe as a whole has 1.38; Japan, 1.32; Russia, 1.14. These countries—or, more precisely, these people—are going out of business . . . Europe, like Japan, has catastrophic birthrates and a swollen pampered elderly class determined to live in defiance of economic reality. But the difference is that on the Continent the successor [Muslim] population is already in place and the only question is how bloody the transfer of real estate will be.[92]

So that is Europe's problem in a nutshell—or time bomb?—made of cold, hard demographic statistics. Today Europe is faced with a shrinking and aging native population that will require an ever increasing flow of immigrants to maintain a workforce to keep its social-welfare system from bankruptcy for a bit longer. Where will the new workers come from? "[A] talented ambitious Chinese or Indian," Mark Steyn has correctly argued, "has zero reason to immigrate to France, unless he is consumed by a perverse fantasy of living in a segregated society that artificially constrains his economic opportunities yet imposes confiscatory taxation on him in order to support an ancient regime of indolent geriatrics."[93] Europe's thirst for young workers therefore will be quenched by the high birthrates of its already on-hand Muslim citizens and increasing numbers of Muslim immigrants from the Islamic world, especially North Africa.

This number-driven coming reality seems to have so far escaped the notice of Europeans—leaders and led—who continue to speak and behave as if increased funding for national-level and EC-wide social-welfare programs will satisfy Muslim discontent and buy them away from the faith. In many ways European leaders have come to resemble Saudi rulers, by attempting to fix all problems with the checkbook, the difference being that the Europeans are edging toward bankruptcy and have neither the Saudis' oil-based cash cow nor their jugular-cutting instinct for survival. There are no duplicates of Riyadh's execution square in any European capital. So bribery will not work for the Europeans. Indeed, the more social programs are used to bribe Muslims, the more taxpayers will be needed to pay for them, the more Muslim immigrants will be needed to become taxpayers, and the larger will become the mass of Muslims still confronted and angered by Europe's racism and aggressive war on religion.[94] And so the cycle will begin over again and continue until the euro is replaced by the riyal.

Europe is determined not to pay the piper for having governed for the last thirty years by the philosophy of the French Enlightenment; that is, for trying to mandate through universal laws and coercive regulations the perfection of that absolutely nonperfectible entity, man. The EC elite's decades-long effort to legislate the end of class, public debate, religion, nationalism, and history in Europe will come to its unintended but predictable end by producing a passive, homogenous, self-centered, noncompetitive, bureaucrat-ruled, militantly secular, and antimilitary society that is consuming itself and heading toward extinction. The contemporary EC's elites are much like the French philosophes, of whom the brilliant Gertrude Himmelfarb has written: "[T]hey could aspire to bold and imaginative thinking, unconstrained by such practical considerations as how their ideas might be translated into reality . . . [They] believed that the function of reason was to produce universal principles independent of history, circumstance, and national spirit." [95] As things stand, Europe seems destined to leave its decaying and bankrupt hulk in the hands of a vibrantly religious, semimartial, youthful, and hardworking Muslim population.

But hold on. What is of interest to the United States will be to see if Europe goes quietly into its Islamic good night. The end of French Enlightenment thought, the end of all efforts to produce the perfect European man, has been massive human destruction. From the French Revolution and the Napoleonic Wars through the eras of fascism, Communism, and Nazism, totalitarianism and mass murder have been the end-state of political systems aimed at perfecting humanity. Total warfare and genocide, moreover, are European inventions and thus reside in the history locker that contemporary Europeans have kept double-padlocked and tried to ignore. Who is to say that Europe, in extremis, will not try to save itself by taking recourse to that at which it has traditionally excelled: chauvinistic nationalism, government-sponsored persecution of minorities, and unlimited warfare? And because history suppressed has a way of roaring back to life, might not a last-ditch European survival effort wage its battles under the banner of a revived Christianity? EC leaders already have fully absorbed the attitude Walter Bagehot attributed to the French philosophes—"everything for the people, nothing by them . . . they wished to do everything by fiat of the sovereign" [96]—and might well turn into supernationalists in order to save their own skins. Whether Europe seeks to save itself or simply begins studying Arabic and the lunar calendar, the United States can do little to affect events as they unfold, save perhaps stopping our idiotic insistence that the EC leaders commit demographic suicide even more quickly by allowing Turkey and 70 million more Muslims into the EC.

What Does It Mean for the United States?

Although geographically dispersed, the locations just discussed have several commonalities. None of the six, for example, is a direct nation-state threat to the United States. Rather it is the internal instability and rising Islamist militancy in each that poses concerns for Washington, challenging its traditional fixation on threats from nation-states.

How to cope with these problems? First, Washington must look at each with the narrow and more accurate definition of *national interest* captured in the idea of life-and-death issues. From this perspective, it is clear that of the six locales only two, the North Caucasus and Nigeria, meet the life-and-death standard; the former because it provides access to the FSU for Islamists seeking to procure WMD, and the latter because of the fast-growing importance of its energy resources to the U.S. economy.

Three of the locations, Thailand, Bangladesh, and Somalia, present no obvious threat to U.S. national security. That said, the risk that Washington will become involved in each is significant and already under way on a small scale in Somalia. In Thailand, Cold War–era commitments leave open a possible requirement for U.S. military support for the Bangkok regime against the growing Thai Muslim insurgency. Such a U.S. involvement would dramatically increase the anti-U.S. focus of Islamists across the Far East and would provide further validation for bin Laden's claim that Washington intends to keep Muslims under the control of oppressive governments. U.S. interests therefore would be best served by revisiting and abrogating any commitments that could lead to U.S. military involvement in Thailand.

Washington has no treaty obligations in Bangladesh or Somalia, but antinationalist groups are certain to press for U.S. intervention, and it will be at risk of involvement to the extent that it lacks the will to resist their entreaties. As political instability and the Islamists' ascendancy increases in each place, NGOs, human rights groups, and women's rights groups will demand that the United States "do something." But in neither country would U.S. involvement be wise, let alone necessary. Violent human tragedies seem certain to unfold in each place, but none of that violence will be directed against America or its interests unless we intervene. Washington should turn back the pressure from the antinationalists. If Amnesty International, or an NGO, or Franklin Graham's Samaritan's Purse organization wants to ride to the rescue in Bangladesh or Somalia, the U.S. government should advise them of the dangers in each and likewise warn them that if they do go into such dangerous environments they will be on their own—no U.S. military units will be coming to their aid. This must be made especially clear regarding Somalia, as antinationalist groups tend to couple Somalia, Sudan, and Darfur into a single "cause" and already have the support of Senator John McCain and several of his colleagues for sending some sort of U.S.-U.K. military force to Darfur, where no conceivable U.S. national interest is at stake.

Europe is a quandary for Americans and their government. There is nothing that the United States can do to slow or halt Europe's demographic free-fall and the inevitable reshaping of societies and foreign policies there in a more Islamic direction. Only the Europeans can save themselves, but it seems too late for them to do so simply by having more babies. Their only other option is to take a draconian approach to limiting Muslim immigration and apprehending and deporting all Muslims who are in Europe illegally. But given Europe's need for ever more workers to fund their pensions and other social programs, and the impervious-to-reality nature of EC institutions and member-state governments, such draconian measures are likely to be put off until their implementation is futile. The choice at that point would be a turn toward authoritarianism or get fitted for a burqa. For the United States, the beginning of wisdom seems to be to plan deliberately for a troublesome future for NATO and overall transatlantic relations due to the demographic realities of Europe.

Two final points are pertinent for the still-mentally-in-the-Cold War U.S. elite when examining these six locations. First, five of the six are hosting Islamist militants armed with weapons that the RMA advocates have deemed obsolete and for which, as the Afghan and Iraq wars have shown, U.S. ground forces are neither armed correctly nor numerous enough to defeat. While never losing sight of potential nation-state threats, Washington must act to ensure that it has enough appropriately armed and trained U.S. ground forces to avoid defeat in the next Islamist insurgency that America confronts.

Second, the Islamist unrest and violence in all six locations is being driven by entities in Saudi Arabia and, to a lesser extent, the other states of the Arabian Peninsula. Through Saudi-government-sponsored educational, religious, and social programs; the work of Islamist NGOs based in or supported by the kingdom; and the steady and large donations from wealthy Saudi individuals and families, Salafisim and Wahhabism are spreading in all six locales and in all but Europe appear to be supporting armed groups. In Europe the Saudis spread their militant doctrines from their embassies or through individuals or groups associated with their diplomatic and cultural facilities. Though both Democrats and Republicans regularly praise Saudi Arabia as an important ally in the war on terror, the truth is that these assertions are untrue and that outside the kingdom the goals of al-Qaeda and the al-Saud regime are similar, although of the two Riyadh is much more imperialistic, anti-Christian, fascist-like, and oriented toward the creation of a caliphate.

PART III

WHERE STANDS THE WAR?

There are no accidents in my philosophy. Every effect must have its cause. The past is the cause of the present and the present will be the cause of the future. All these are links in the endless chain from the finite to the infinite.

Abraham Lincoln, quoted by W. H. Herndon, 1889

Whoever wishes to foresee the future must consult the past; for human events ever resemble those of preceding times. This arises from the fact that they are produced by men who have ever been, and ever shall be, animated by the same passions, and thus they necessarily have the same results.

Niccolò Machiavelli, 1517

A country without a memory is a country of madmen.

George Santayana, 1906

It is no accident that, in early 2008, the United States is losing the war against al-Qaeda and Sunni Islamist militancy. U.S. leaders have ignored their own country's history and that of Muslims; they have lied to Americans about their enemies' motivation, size, and capabilities; and they have used the military forces for which Americans pay so dearly in such a sparing manner that our Islamist enemies not only have survived but also are flourishing and hold U.S. soldiers and Marines in contempt. Washington has no credible public diplomacy campaign to win Muslim hearts and minds (because it ignores the enemy's claims about its motivations and maintains the status quo in U.S. foreign policy), and it continues to falsely claim that the many tactical victories scored by U.S. forces have moved the strategic situation in America's favor. Not surprisingly, this litany of failures speaks directly to this governing generation's lack of talent, worldliness, historical knowledge, and sadly, concern for genuine national interests. The leadership desert that exists in American politics mirrors the one that bin Laden has taken full advantage of in the Muslim world. Alas, America's bin Laden has yet to emerge from its political-leadership desert.

In early 2008, the worldwide Sunni Islamist insurgency led, inspired, and symbolized by Osama bin Laden and al-Qaeda are gradually accomplishing the war aims defined by bin Laden: bleed America to bankruptcy, and spread out U.S. military and intelligence forces. The former is being pushed toward realization because of the wars won by the mujahedin in Iraq and Afghanistan, and the latter by U.S. spending on those wars, on homeland security, and on bountiful bribes to keep U.S. allies in the war on terror. Bin Laden's ability to send two mujahedin with an al-Qaeda banner to multiple spots on the earth, then sit back and watch U.S. forces deploy and spend money, most recently in Somalia, pushes forward the latter goal and assists in accomplishing the former.

CHAPTER 6

"The bottom is out of the tub"

Taking Stock for America in 2008

The greatest lie told in the last fifty years is that the world has changed so that victory is no longer possible. Victory is *always* possible. But it does not come to the irresolute . . . Time and again . . . the valor of our troops was undone by the cowardice of our political leaders . . . If we do not mean to fight to win, we should not fight at all.

Ralph Peters, 2006

I hold the maxim no less applicable to public than to private affairs, that honesty is always the best policy.

George Washington, 1796

I consider knowledge to be the soul of the republic, and as the weak and wicked are generally in alliance, as much care should be taken to diminish the number of the former as of the latter. Education is the way to do this.

John Jay, 1785

In the first days of 1862 a weary and worried Abraham Lincoln surveyed the Union's failing war effort against the Confederacy. In the face of defeat at First Manassas the previous July, General George McClellan's idling away of the fall 1861 campaign season, and a deeply troubling economic situation, Lincoln said that "it is exceedingly discouraging . . . nothing can be done." The disconsolate president enumerated the problems America confronted to his splendid quartermaster general, Brigadier General Montgomery C. Meigs, on January 10, 1862. "The people are impatient," Lincoln said. "[Treasury Secretary Salmon P.] Chase has no money and he tells me he can raise no more; the General of the Army [McClellan] has typhoid fever. The bottom is out of the tub."[1]

In early 2008 Americans again find that "the bottom is out of the tub." The United States has been defeated, stalemated, or frustrated on every front on which it has chosen to engage al-Qaeda and the forces it leads and inspires. And despite this unfolding disaster, neither U.S. party in the 2006 midterm election campaign gave any hint that it saw defeat ahead: one urged Americans to stay the course, the other called for course corrections, and after the elections nothing changed. The hard reality is that the U.S. government and, more especially, the American governing elite have bitten off far more than the country can chew. At the most elemental level, that of population base, the Muslim world outnumbers America by nearly five to one, roughly 1.4 billion to roughly 300 million. A nation the size of America would be hard put to defend itself against such odds, and the United States today is operating under a doctrine that calls for offensive operations without limit. A counterinsurgency is said to require ten counterinsurgents for every insurgent to have a fair chance of prevailing. Even with the reintroduction of conscription, America could not field the number of military personnel needed to fight an offensive war in every place in the world troubled by Islamist fighters. In addition, the blind devotion of the Pentagon to an ever-increasing reliance on precision weapons and high-tech gadgetry spurs a coordinate growth in number of support personnel; a heavy tail coupled to a few sharp teeth is a certain prescription for defeat in an insurgency.

The geographic dispersal of our Islamist enemies also poses a daunting and nearly insurmountable obstacle to U.S. victory. The Sunni Islamic world circles the globe, and Sunni militants can strike U.S. interests and personnel almost anywhere on earth. As important, the presence of Sunni communities in virtually every country creates a milieu in which the fighters of al-Qaeda and like-minded groups can safely reside, work, transit, and plan. Many U.S. and Western leaders have declared that al-Qaeda's attack on September 11, 2001, was a failure because the Muslim masses, the much-vaunted Arab street, did not rise up in support of bin Laden, overthrow their governments, and drive every last vestige of the U.S. presence from their world. This assertion misses the mark twice. First, there is no evidence in the pre- or post-9/11 rhetoric and writings of bin Laden, al-Zawahiri, or their lieutenants that they believed the attacks would prompt such a reaction. Western leaders are rightfully relieved that a civilizationwide rebellion did not occur, but they can identify this nonrevolt as a defeat for al-Qaeda and the Islamists only by falsely claiming that the 9/11 plan meant to spur such an uprising. Indeed, no one knows better than al-Qaeda's leaders and their allies the absurdity of attempting to motivate the largely unarmed Muslim masses to man the barricades against murderous police states backed unequivocally by the planet's only superpower.

The second miss is more dangerous for U.S. security. Whatever the immediate post-9/11 reaction was in the Muslim world, Western polling firms, as noted, have since detected only increases in the level of hatred for the same U.S. foreign policies that al-Qaeda has identified as constituting attacks on Islam and its followers. As noted earlier, nearly 80 percent of Muslims worldwide deem the United States Islam's foe.[2] Thus the countries dominated by or hosting Sunni communities, within which Islamist fighters can live and move, are at least indifferent to their presence and activities and at worst more than willing to shelter and assist these defenders of the faith. At base, al-Qaeda at this stage of its activities does not expect or require (though it surely would not oppose) a popular, multistate Muslim uprising. It simply needs the broad acquiescence of its brethren. And while the current status quo of U.S. foreign policy continues, they will have it.

Numbers and a globe-straddling dispersal are major advantages for al-Qaeda and its allies in their contest with the United States, and given the growth rates of the world's Muslim population compared to that of America, both of the Islamists' strategic pluses will only grow with the passage of time. Unfortunately, these two issues are only the tip of the iceberg toward which the good ship America is blithely sailing. Other problems fall into the military, Western unity, public diplomacy, and leadership categories.

The Cost of Our Military Burlesque

While it does not yet seem to be sinking into the minds of Americans, our al-Qaeda-led enemies have become confident that the main characteristic of the U.S. military—the strongest that the earth has ever hosted—is that it never wins any war it fights, whether against a strong or a weak enemy. Among Islamist fighters, the appropriate motto for the U.S. military probably is a wordy paraphrase of Caesar's: "We came, we saw, we claimed to conquer, and we left defeated with the enemy intact and reinvigorated." Haiti, Somalia, and the Balkans are all places where this motto can be accurately applied, although the Balkans are now hovering in a holding pattern until we and the Europeans leave and that religiously motivated war of all against all can resume.

As bad as these examples of past mediocre military performances are, the coming defeats of U.S. forces in Iraq and Afghanistan will be much worse. The pride and specialty of post–Cold War U.S. military power has been the projection of that power to even the most remote locales on the planet. Our military's exercises with NATO members, with India, Israel, the Philippines, and Latin American states, and with a host of other nations are designed to perfect the projection of power and to familiarize all military personnel, from the general to the foot soldier to the logistician, with foreign militaries we may one day have to fight with or against, as well as with often barely known topographies. All told, we have learned to project military power with breathtaking speed—and yet we never win. Getting there, as the saying goes, may be half the fun, but in war there is really no point in going if you do not intend to do whatever it takes to win an unambiguous victory after you get there. And what is winning? Three things: first, setting out with clear and achievable goals; second, using whatever force is necessary on arrival; and third, leaving immediately when the job is done.

In projecting U.S. military power into Iraq and Afghanistan, we have proven once again that America's stunning ability to rapidly deploy military force abroad is an expensive and self-defeating exercise because U.S. political leaders have neither achievable war aims nor an intention to win. Most U.S. general officers, moreover, are unwilling to object to that reality, preferring safe routes to promotion that are paved with the waste of their soldiers' lives and their nation's resources. We have taught the Islamists that if they can ride out the initial U.S. air campaign—the childish shock-and-awe part—they have little to fear from the U.S. military.[3] By 2008, the Taliban, al-Qaeda, and the host of Islamist insurgent groups in Iraq have rightly concluded that they have survived the best shot U.S. leaders decided to deliver (though certainly far from the best they could have delivered) and that they are now well along in the process of sending the U.S. military home with its tail tucked between its legs. To paraphrase Alexander Hamilton writing in *Federalist 15,* when our Islamist foes look on the post-Iraq U.S. military, they see not a genuine and irresistible military power but a mere pageant of mimicked military power neutered "by the imbecility of our government."[4]

Why is this the case? Again, there are two answers, both of which emanate from the extended duration of Washington's Cold War hangover. In the Cold War world peace was maintained because the Soviet Union's leaders not only knew the strength and survivability of our nuclear arsenal but also truly believed that Washington would use those forces to annihilate the USSR if Moscow launched a first strike on the United States. In large measure the U.S. deterrent consisted not only of its land-sea-air nuclear triad but also, as important, the Bolshevik chiefs' conviction that U.S. nuclear weapons would be used if a situation warranted their use. Moscow projected the same nuclear reality and demeanor in response and thereby happily locked the world into the peaceful era of Mutually Assured Destruction. So strong was the Soviets' belief that U.S. leaders would complete Armageddon if it was initiated by Moscow that even Washington's abject failure to use the full force of U.S. military might to prevail in Vietnam (a crystalline reality in Moscow, notwithstanding the efforts of Nixon, Kissinger, and many U.S. generals to disguise their sell-out of the U.S. military) did not fatally shake Moscow's faith in Washington's willingness to use nuclear weapons.

This happy era of deterrence crumbled simultaneously with the Berlin Wall. Soon thereafter America began to encounter Islamist enemies who were unafraid of the U.S. nuclear and conventional deterrents and unconvinced that we would use them with definitive effect. Our current Islamist enemies used the 1990s as a decade-long educational exercise in which they kept pushing the envelope to see how much pain they could inflict on the United States without triggering an annihilating U.S. military response. Al-Qaeda's attacks on U.S. targets in Yemen (1992), Somalia (1993–94), Saudi Arabia (1995–96), East Africa (1998), and Yemen again (2000) proved what bin Laden had anticipated: America was a paper tiger that could be attacked with impunity and declared war upon repeatedly (1996 and 1998) and whose response would be "proportional" (another word for ineffective) and designed to please international opinion, antinational organizations, and the just-war theorists. Bin Laden was right. The net U.S. military response over the 1992–2000 period was the August 20, 1998, launching of seventy-five cruise missiles against training camps around Khowst, Afghanistan, which cost the Islamists fewer than forty dead and at most a few weeks' delay in training cycles.[5]

It was, then, in this context that al-Qaeda launched the 9/11 attack. Bin Laden had not—as then-DCI George Tenet and other senior Bush administration officials claimed—underestimated the ferocity of the U.S. military reaction to the attack but rather had gambled, on the basis of a decade's worth of feckless U.S. military responses, that the odds were in his favor, that America would respond in a way that would leave al-Qaeda and the Taliban intact to fight another day. The gamble paid off: President Bush, senior officials in the administration and Intelligence Community, the neoconservative clique and their media acolytes, and Democratic Party chieftains swaggered as if simply possessing a huge nuclear arsenal and the world's most powerful conventional military would so frighten the Islamists that a relatively mild application of lethal force in Afghanistan would destroy the enemy physically and induce an abandonment of their jihad. Clearly this conclusion merited at least one more serious think-through before being implemented, but no careful second review occurred, and the same losing modus operandi was applied in Iraq.

U.S. political leaders, policymakers, and generals must now face up to the fact that as far as America's Islamist enemies are concerned, the United States has no credible military deterrent. Al-Qaeda and its allies believe that the attacks of 9/11, in and of themselves, destroyed the concept of deterrence. This conclusion is only partially accurate. The 9/11 attacks pushed the already weakening believability of the U.S. deterrent to the edge of a deep abyss, but it was the anemic and ineffective military invasions and occupations of Afghanistan and Iraq that put deterrence flat on its back at the pit's bottom. Too few troops, too little boldness, far too few enemy corpses, too tight rules of engagement for U.S. soldiers and Marines—all these have proven that America's bark is loud and its bite virtually toothless. Today America possesses no deterrent in the minds of al-Qaeda and its allies and at this late date must seek to reestablish one.[6]

And precisely here a second impact of the Cold War hangover kicks in as a major obstacle to recasting a credible deterrent. This obstacle is the amalgam of antinationalist groups that have survived and proliferated since 1991: human rights organizations, NGOs, disarmament groups, environmental organizations, and the school of just-war theorists. Even though the United States and its allies are clearly losing the war against al-Qaeda-ism, these organizations are trying to limit in every way possible America's ability to capture or kill the enemy in sufficient numbers to give us a chance at victory. Truculent, sensationalist, and media-abetted campaigns by these organizations are in full swing to halt the CIA's anti-al-Qaeda rendition program, ban depleted-uranium ordnance, maintain rules of engagement that make U.S. military personnel targets not killers, close prisoner camps, and allege war crimes against as many American military personnel as possible. President Bush and his administration are slowly buckling to the demands of these groups, and Senator John McCain (R-Arizona) and most Democrats appear eager to have the opportunity to outbuckle Mr. Bush in the name of protecting the rights of those endeavoring to kill Americans. Overall the political influence of the antinationalist groups is undermining the already tepid U.S. military and intelligence response to the attacks of 9/11.[7]

Ironically, the antinationalist organizations also are the victims of the Cold War hangover. During that era the issues they fought for and the goals they achieved were played out under the peace-inducing nuclear umbrella. Their largely theoretical and unrealistic world flourished because, on balance, U.S. and Western leaders valued them as useful symbols of Western freedom to dissent without censorship, harassment, or imprisonment. These leaders dealt politely with the groups but never for a moment let them cast doubt on their willingness to use the U.S. nuclear deterrent. Like pacifists and conscientious objectors, the antinationalist groups are able to aggressively champion their views because most Americans were willing to risk their lives to defend the society that allows them to do so. Now, however, these groups significantly damage U.S. security, especially the human rights advocates and the just-war theorists, by constraining America's ability to wage war aggressively and ruthlessly.

Oddly, the ascendancy of these organizations comes at a moment when they have proven themselves to be driven, not by any real ethical or moral considerations, both of which require a religious grounding that most do not have, but by anti-Americanism. While human rights groups and others describe Washington's half-hearted and ineffective war-making as unjust and overly bloody, none of them seem to have the least interest in bringing

Vladimir Putin and his colleagues to justice. These men were participants in and are the direct legatees of a system of government that killed more than forty million innocent people over its history. It is, of course, much easier and more fun to make cowardly U.S. politicians squirm and to criticize the intelligence officers who did their bidding than to take on a man who was a proud and distinguished member of a regime that out-Hitlered Hitler seven times over.

Once the dust settles from America's military debacles in Iraq and Afghanistan, U.S. leaders will have to find a way to reestablish a deterrent that is credible in the eyes of the world and our Islamist enemies. Sadly, proclaiming the existence of such a deterrent will not make it believable; the only way to achieve credibility will be to build a deterrent and use it. Al-Qaeda and its Sunni militant allies come from an Islamic civilization in which force remains a lingua franca, an environment in which the weak are exploited and the strong who are afraid to use their power are destroyed. Bin Laden and his allies place the United States in the latter category, and frankly we have fully earned the top spot on that list since 1996. They will continue to do so until we prove that we do not belong there. Most emphatically, the onus is on the United States. What this means, of course, is that the next time that Washington concludes that it must project military power somewhere in the world to defeat Islamist fighters, it must do so with an intensity the world has not seen from the United States since 1945. Whether the theater of operations is South Asia, the Horn of Africa, or some unexpected arena in the Middle East or elsewhere, U.S. forces must be sent to score a definitive victory, one that is clear to the world and irrefutable in the minds of the defeated Islamists and their supporters. And because we are fighting an enemy who wears no uniforms and is supported by local populations, such a victory necessarily will mean massive and unavoidable noncombatant casualties and damage to civilian infrastructure; indeed, the object lesson delivered for the world, friend and foe, will be the sheer breadth and totality of the destructiveness attendant to the projection of American military power. This course of action will have to be undertaken if America is to survive, and the longer we wait to do so, the more destructive the action will have to be when it is finally taken. We had the opportunity to establish such a baseline reputation for ruthlessness in Afghanistan—a window for savagery was open for six months or more after 9/11—but we chose to use minimal force in order to keep our European allies on board and appease Muslim oil producers and their populations. We thereby allowed the enemy to escape and reconfirmed in the Islamists' minds that Washington's threats to annihilate them are hollow, even when they attack in the continental United States.

To reestablish a credible perception that the United States has a military deterrent and will use it—just as Hiroshima and Nagasaki were the essential predicates for the U.S. Cold War deterrent—U.S. leaders will have to accept the reality that while suicide attackers cannot be deterred, the populations that aid and abet them may well be persuaded to reduce such support if they are punished with sufficient vigor. When U.S. power is projected after the next attack by al-Qaeda inside the United States, the best way to honor the attack's casualties will be a military response that obliterates something that is prized by the enemy—not an improvised bier of flowers, silly placards, whining prayers, and flickering candles. America today would be a far more credible military power and a far safer place if, instead of endless, puerile bickering over what sort of monument should be built at the site of the World Trade Center, we had fire-bombed Kabul and Khandahar, demolished whatever ruins were left, and sown salt over the length and width of both sites. That would have been a proper monument to the dead of 9/11, and one that would have made their surviving countrymen safer.

Withering Western Unity

Even a brief review of the media shows that the Western unity engendered by the 9/11 attacks on the United States is ebbing. The reason for this is that the U.S. government should have seen the death and destruction of 9/11 for what it was: an attack solely directed at the United States, its people, and its economy. Nothing could have been more incorrect than, for example, Secretary of State Powell's September 14, 2001, claim, "This is not just an attack against America, this is an attack against civilization and an attack against democracy."[8] Echoed in one form or another by President Bush, National Security Adviser Rice, Secretary of Defense Rumsfeld, Vice President Cheney, former president Clinton, all members of Congress, and most NATO leaders, such words were simply those of Cold Warriors defaulting to comfortably familiar rhetoric. Any untoward action by the

USSR against the West was always labeled a "threat to the Free World," and after 9/11 the phrase "Free World" was simply replaced by "Western civilization" or another synonymous phrase. Powell's words also sharply underscored several other Cold War assumptions that are still deeply and debilitatingly embedded in official Washington's mind: proxies would be needed, a coalition was necessary, and the traditional ballet of international politics had to be managed, each of which subsumed that old Cold War standby, time is on our side. As Powell said, "We are engaging with the world. We want to make this a long-standing coalition."[9]

Well, we engaged the world, and most of it came along. But that unity was ephemeral from the first. Once the emotions spurred by 9/11 faded, our coalition partners began to recognize that they are, at most, secondary targets for al-Qaeda and its allies. Bin Laden and his lieutenants knew this from the start—they are not mad, apocalyptic men, eager to take on the whole world at once—and began to target Western unity. A core tenet in al-Qaeda's grand strategy is that the United States and its allies, Western and others, cannot stand martial pain over prolonged periods. The examples the Islamists use as evidence are familiar to all: the U.S. and French withdrawal from Beirut after being attacked by Hezbollah in 1982 and the collapse of the U.S.-led multinational UN humanitarian intervention in Somalia in 1993–94. Iraq and Afghanistan will provide weightier examples in the years ahead. Both the 1990s interventions were in areas and about matters that were at best peripheral to genuine U.S. and Western national-security interests, and once the troops were bloodied, Western leaders quickly concluded that which was obvious before the interventions began: the game was not remotely worth the candle. After 9/11 bin Laden operated on the assumption that while the United States probably would not disengage after minor casualties—the attack, after all, had struck the continental United States—most U.S. allies were unlikely to stay the course after suffering even minor damage. He was right.

Bin Laden has long seen the need to conduct political warfare that is tied closely to Islamist military activities, and he has laid out a doctrine for al-Qaeda and its associates to follow. This political-warfare policy is designed to be delivered over the heads of U.S. and Western leaders to opposition political leaders and the mass of voters in non-Muslim countries. It is meant to do two things: change the policies of countries allied with the United States by eroding popular support for assisting America to fight a war against Islamist militancy, and second, by so doing, slowly strip allies away from America and leave it increasingly isolated. Bin Laden laid out this political-warfare doctrine after the 9/11 attacks and the subsequent U.S. invasion of Afghanistan. In a November 2002 speech he explained to the populations of America's European allies that the United States was attacked because "[America] is killing our sons in Iraq [through UN economic sanctions], and [because of] what America's ally Israel is doing, using American airplanes to bomb houses in Palestine with old men, women, and children in them." These are "crimes" that were conducted by the United States, said bin Laden, adding that al-Qaeda thought such U.S. actions would cause "the sane leaders among you to distance themselves from this criminal gang [the Bush administration.]"[10] Because no distancing occurred, bin Laden told the peoples of U.S. allies that the status quo between the Islamist movement and their governments was not sustainable. "The road to safety begins by lifting the aggression," bin Laden concluded. "Reciprocity is only fair."[11]

Bin Laden then explained that the cost of supporting the United States would be attacks by al-Qaeda and its allies on the interests of countries providing such support. Citing al-Qaeda's 2002 attacks on German tourists in Tunisia and on Australian and British tourists in Bali as examples of al-Qaeda's ability to apply reciprocal violence, bin Laden warned the Europeans: "Just as you kill, so you shall be killed."[12] Bin Laden suggested that the peoples of states allied to America ask themselves the following questions:

> Why are your governments allying themselves against the Muslims with the criminal gang in the White House? Don't they know that this gang is the biggest murderer of our age?
>
> Why are your governments, especially those of Britain, France, Italy, Canada, Germany, and Australia, allying themselves with the Americans in its attacks on us in Afghanistan?
>
> How long will fear, killing, destruction, displacement, orphaning, and widowing be our [the Muslims'] sole destiny, while security, stability, and happiness are yours? . . . The road to safety begins with the cessation of hostilities, and reciprocal treatment is part of justice.[13]

In subsequent speeches bin Laden and al-Zawahiri reiterated this message, and over time they designated twenty-three countries by name as allies of the United States in Afghanistan, Iraq, or both. They pledged each would be attacked. At this writing all twenty-three have been attacked, either domestically or in the geographic theaters in which their military forces are deployed with the U.S. military. Of course not all of these attacks can be linked to fighters directly under bin Laden's command-and-control, but it cannot be a coincidence that al-Qaeda and its allies have exhausted the target list. In determining whether these attacks can be accurately described as complements to al-Qaeda political-warfare strategy, it is worth noting that the attacks were carefully modulated in their destructiveness. In their aftermath European populations, in particular, tended to blame their political leaders for stimulating the attacks by maintaining pro-U.S. policies in Iraq and/or Afghanistan. After the July 2005 subway attacks in London, for example, much of media commentary immediately linked the attacks directly to Prime Minister Blair's resolute commitment to the U.S.-led invasion and occupation of Iraq. Thus, the attacks were sufficiently painful to incite anger among European publics toward their leaders, but they were not damaging enough to inspire widespread fear and vengefulness and thereby drive the Europeans to closer counterterrorism cooperation with the United States.

In April 2004, bin Laden had also spoken to the populations of America's allies, warning them that the previous month's attack on the Atocha train station in Madrid was an example of what al-Qaeda has in store for them. He went on to claim that the European peoples and those of other U.S. allies were being lethally exploited by their leaders and multinational corporations, and he suggested a possible peaceful resolution of the situation.

> If one looks at the murders that are still going on in our countries and yours, an important truth becomes clear, which is that we are both suffering at the hands of your leaders, who send your sons to our countries, despite their objections, to kill and be killed. So it is in the interests of both sides to stop those who shed their own peoples' blood, both on behalf of narrow personal interests and on behalf of the White House gang . . . It is all too clear, then, who benefits most from stirring up this war and bloodshed: the merchants of war, the blood suckers who direct world policy from behind the scenes.
>
> So I present to them [Europe's peoples] this peace proposal, which is essentially a commitment to cease [al-Qaeda] operations against any

[nation-]state that pledges not to attack Muslims or intervene in their affairs, including the American conspiracy against the great Islamic world. The peace can be renewed at the end of a government's term and the beginning of a new one, with the consent of both sides. It will come into effect on the departure of its last soldier from our lands, and is available for a period of three months from the day this statement is broadcast.[14]

Bin Laden closed his speech offering a truce by reminding Europeans that al-Qaeda and its allies attack non-Muslims only if Islamic lands are attacked, and that therefore "the solution to this equation . . . lies in your own hands."[15] The governments of Europe contemptuously rejected bin Laden's truce offer, and al-Qaeda made its chief's words good by attacking the London subway system on July 7, 2005.

Since 2002, then, bin Laden has carefully delineated a doctrine of international political warfare that combines the promise of reciprocal violence—if you attack us, we will attack you—and a pledge not to attack if assistance from U.S. allies for Washington's terrorism war is halted. Declaring such a doctrine is well and good, but the question is, "Has it worked?" Has al-Qaeda's policy resulted in any decease in the will of U.S. allies to support American military operations against the group and its allies? The following suggests that the answer to both may well be: Yes, it is beginning to have some impact.

- The conservative, pro-U.S. government of Spanish prime minister José María Aznar was defeated in an election soon after the March 11, 2004, attack on Madrid's Atocha train station. The victorious socialist regime of Prime Minister José Zapatero is much less pro-American and has withdrawn Spanish troops from Iraq.[16]
- In summer 2006, Italian prime minister Silvio Berlusconi's conservative, pro-U.S. government was defeated by a narrow margin, much of which appears to have consisted of those voters opposed to Rome's military support for the U.S.-led war in Iraq. The new Italian government of Prime Minister Romano Prodi kept its campaign pledge and completed the withdrawal of Italian troops from Iraq in 2006.[17]
- After facing a near revolt in his Labor Party in summer 2006, British prime minister Tony Blair was compelled to appease the dissenters by announcing, well before he intended to, a date for stepping down from

201

the premiership. The Labour Party's anger, backed by many public opinion polls, stemmed from Blair's hardy military backing for Washington's war on terror.[18]

- In October 2006, a group of Thai military officers staged a coup that removed Prime Minister Thaksin from office. Allegations of corruption have since been made against Thaksin, but the generals appear to have acted in large part to stop Thaksin's harsh military and law-enforcement operations against Islamist separatists in the country's three Muslim-dominated southern provinces. The coup leaders named a Muslim Thai general as the new prime minister, and he immediately announced his willingness to slow military operations and consider increased autonomy for the southern provinces, each of which Thaksin had refused to do.[19]

- In the fall of 2006, Iraqi prime minister Nouri al-Maliki and Afghan president Hamid Karzai repeatedly tried to distance themselves from the "excessive" military focus of U.S. operations in their countries.[20]

- In December 2006, President Jacques Chirac's government, in the face of rising violence in Afghanistan and public condemnation of the Iraq war, decided to withdraw France's entire contingent of Special Forces from Afghanistan.[21]

- In February 2007, U.K. prime minister Tony Blair announced plans to withdraw about 25 percent of Britain's military contingent in Iraq; Denmark announced that it would withdraw its 460-man force that had been serving under British command. Blair's action was taken in the context of polling results that showed strong majorities opposing a continued U.K. military presence in Iraq and Afghanistan.[22]

- Also in February 2007, Italian prime minister Prodi's government was defeated in parliament on Italy's support for the U.S. war on terrorism. The specific issues were the maintenance of a two-thousand-person Italian military force in Afghanistan and permission for the U.S. military to expand its base at Vicenza, Italy.[23]

- In October–November 2007, the parties of Polish Prime Minister Jaroslaw Kaczynski and Australian Prime Minister John Howard were defeated in their respective general elections. Both men were strong supporters of U.S. policy in Iraq; that support contributed to their defeat. The new Polish and Australian prime ministers quickly announced they would withdraw their troops from Iraq in 2008.[24]

- By November 2007, the rising lethality of the Taliban insurgency in

Afghanistan and/or domestic political dissatisfaction had caused Japan to end its naval support for U.S.-led operations in Afghanistan; South Korea had begun the withdrawal of its troops from the country; Germany, France, and Denmark were leaning toward ending the military component of their Afghan commitment; and politicians and media outlets in several NATO countries were urging Afghan Prime Minister Karzai to negotiate with the Taliban for an end to the insurgency.[25]

All the foregoing have weakened the Western coalition that initially supported the United States after 9/11, and the impact of each was sharpened in that it occurred in tandem with the gradual post-9/11 resurgence of ingrained anti-Americanism in Europe. Moreover, each clearly advances the goals of the doctrine for international political warfare that bin Laden established for al-Qaeda: the erosion of popular support for the war on terrorism among the populations of America's allies, and the gradual isolation of the United States. Al-Qaeda's leaders, and those of the groups allied to or inspired by it, clearly see this doctrine as making an effective contribution to their war effort, one that is even having an impact in the United States. The Islamists interpreted the 2006 U.S. midterm congressional elections that overturned Republican majorities in the Senate and House of Representatives as demonstrating that the Americans, like the French, British, and Italians, did not have the stomach for the casualties and expenses they are suffering in Iraq and Afghanistan. For the Islamists, the midterm election results confirmed that Allah's victory was edging closer.

Not Even in the Race for Hearts and Minds

Since 9/11 Americans have been bombarded by categorical assertions from Democratic and Republican leaders, academics, U.S. generals, and the media that the United States and its allies are in a race with the Islamists to win the hearts and minds of Muslims. The politicians and the generals' claims are cynically grounded in the fact that they have used the nation's military power too sparingly and are afraid to urge its more abundant use; thus we have too-little-too-late half-measures like President Bush sending five more brigades to Iraq when fifty would be too few to assure victory. These individuals are trying to convince the citizenry, and perhaps themselves, that they have not failed in Iraq and Afghanistan, and that military might has completed its part in the struggle and now victory hinges on a successful hearts-and-minds campaign. From academia and the media come claims that are grounded in abhorrence of the U.S. military and any use of martial force, a desire to pull out all the stops to prevent its further use, and career-focused ambitions to play the leading role in a gigantic, federally funded hearts-and-minds campaign; after all, is that not the proper role for sensitive, multicultural social scientists and kum-bayahing journalists? Starting from different points, the two groups arrive at the same conclusion: we must win the war against al-Qaeda with a hearts-and-minds campaign. If honesty were in their toolkits, however, both would have to admit that they have nothing with which to win or even purchase Muslim hearts and minds, and that in that arena America will be drubbed to death for as long as the status quo in U.S. foreign policy exists.

To date, much of the U.S. public diplomacy effort has been conducted so as to avoid the issue of the Islamists' motivation. For example, U.S. officials have placed great emphasis on the bin Laden-has-hijacked-and-distorted-Islam gambit. We have therefore tried to win Muslim hearts and minds by debating theological points, citing hadiths and passages in the Koran, or by backing one Islamic scholar's interpretations over those of another. None of these tacks, however, address the main issue, which is the Muslim perception that U.S. foreign policy is an attack on Islam. Our hearts-and-minds voices claim that the renowned Salafist scholar Abu Muhammad al-Maqdisi has disavowed the late Abu Musab al-Zarqawi's justification for killing civilians, and Muslims respond, that is interesting, but why are you giving $3 billion a year to that butcher Mubarak? We say that Ayman al-Zawahiri is not a trained Islamic scholar so he cannot legitimately call for a jihad, and Muslims say, interesting point, but why are you helping Catholic Filipinos kill Moro Muslims in Mindanao? Theological challenges do not get at the main motivation of anti-U.S. Muslims, we cannot out-Islam the Islamists. The concept itself is, at best, rickety; it is like arguing we could have won hearts and minds in the Soviet Bloc by claiming that Moscow's understanding of Marx and Lenin was way off target and that Washington had a better take on what Karl and Vladimir Ilyich really meant. Or, from the other side, for Brezhnev or Gorbachev to tell Americans that the Soviet Academy of Political Science had a better handle than Thomas Jefferson on the natural-law theory that informs the Declaration of Independence.

Ten years into the war declared by bin Laden, then, official Washington resolutely refuses to address the Islamists' true motivation; only a single member of America's governing elite—representative Ron Paul (R-Texas)—has publicly indicated that he has caught on to the reality that our enemies are motivated by U.S. foreign policy. Instead, U.S. government officials, and the leaders of both political parties, simply and reflexively repeat that the Islamists hate America and are waging war against it because of our freedoms, liberty, and gender equality, not because of what the U.S. government does in the Islamic world. This claim is a blatant lie, bad for that reason alone but worse because it keeps Americans from clearly gauging the enemy's motivations and intentions, or bin Laden's enormous potential appeal among the world's 1.4 billion Muslims. Frankly, persisting in this lie amounts to a death wish.

Not that bin Laden and his ilk are admirers of American freedoms; they are not, and no society they govern, be it Saudi Arabia, Jordan, or Afghanistan, will even remotely resemble ours, although each is likely to be a more efficient and less corrupt government than the one they replace. But it is a lethal mistake for Americans to assume that because the Islamists would not adopt our society lock, stock, and barrel, they must surely be fighting to destroy it. Though incorrect in every conceivable way, this assumption is the one on which our governing elite is operating, and it is one, when boiled down to its essence, that concludes that the Islamists and their supporters are warring against the United States because they hate Americans as Americans, as well as everything they stand for in the political and social spheres, and in the end intend to eradicate our society from the planet.

Now, if this assumption were true, there would be no point in considering how best to conduct a public diplomacy campaign to change the hearts and minds of Muslims. If Americans are hated because they are Americans, the choice is black and white simple: we can completely abandon our beliefs, our lifestyles, and how we behave in the domestic, political, and social arenas to appease our enemies, or we can undertake the task of killing every last Muslim because that is what they intend to do to us. This is an unpalatable choice between ingesting strychnine and ingesting arsenic, but there it is.

Fortunately, there is a third option open to Americans, notwithstanding the seemingly permanent obtuseness of their elite. A careful review of the speeches, statements, and interviews that flow like a torrent from bin Laden, al-Zawahiri, and other Islamist leaders shows that they pay no more than lip service to what might politely be called our civilization's failings. That we have such failings they leave no doubt, but they are never the focus of attention. These men, however, are all children of the era of Iran's Ayatollah Khomeini, and they all saw how the dour old Iranian failed utterly to initiate a global jihad based on the supposed threat from what he described as the debauched and degenerate society of the American Great Satan. Having witnessed that almost no Muslim was motivated to become a suicide bomber because American women compete with men in every field or because we have presidential primaries, bin Laden and his colleagues focused on what the U.S. government does in the Islamic world.[26] By doing so, they have produced a motivational message that appeals to and, to a gradually increasing extent, unites the extraordinarily diverse and fragmented Islamic world. It also is producing a steadily growing flow of volunteers for jihadi activities, suicide and otherwise. The success of bin Laden et al. in this regard would have made the late Ayatollah salivate with envy.

If U.S. leaders would recognize that bin Laden has much more effectually defined Great Satan–ness as U.S. actions overseas and not as the lifestyle of Americans at home, they would be able to begin constructing a hearts-and-minds strategy that would slowly start to narrow the commanding lead that Islamists now enjoy among Muslims worldwide. Such a grasp of reality and common sense, however, would be out of character for our elite. It also would require senior members of the last three presidential administrations to recant most of what they have sworn to be true about our Islamist enemies' motivations, to take on the politically powerful Saudi and Israeli lobbies, and to begin to destroy the energy-policy status quo that works so much in favor of the U.S. oil industry and against American interests. It is a tall order indeed, and as is typical in the post–Cold War world, the U.S. government does not have a lot of time in which to recognize reality and begin to make these changes. Time is running out for the United States if it wants to start clawing back some of the vast amount of ground it has lost to the Islamists in the hearts-and-minds competition.[27]

How to proceed? First, we have to admit to ourselves that we have been trumped and cornered by Osama bin Laden, who as the years pass increasingly emerges as a genius in waging the war of ideas and setting its parameters. While paying lip service to damning the decadence and ungodliness of U.S. and Western societies and regularly raising the banner of the new and blessed caliphate, bin Laden has shown relentless consistency in keeping the Muslim world tightly focused on U.S. foreign policies and their impact on Islam and its believers. With the aid of al-Jazirah, al-Arabiyah, and the Internet, bin Laden has kept these policies and their visible impacts before Muslims on a daily basis.

In this environment, the United States is almost never given the benefit of the doubt in what is, to be sure, a very limited public square in the Islamic world. Because this battle of ideas is not like that of the Cold War, "free society" versus "non-free society," our efforts to sell the freedom-liberty-democracy product that worked against the Soviets are feckless. Polls by Pew, Gallup, BBC, and Zogby all show that in most Muslim countries polled our way of life is admired; this finding is validated by the seemingly endless numbers of Muslim families who want to immigrate to the United States. Thus, when our hearts-and-minds voices say that American society allows parents to feed, educate, and provide health care for their children, Muslims say, that is great, we admire that and applaud you, but why the hell are you protecting those corrupt, apostate criminals who rule Saudi Arabia? When our voices say, Americans are generous, look how much we helped after the tsunami and the Pakistani earthquake, Muslims say, thanks and God bless you for that, but why have you supported, armed, and protected Arab police states that have oppressed and tortured us and our children for the last half-century?[28]

Americans frankly have no hearts-and-minds product to sell that will get us a hearing or the benefit of the doubt in Islam's public square. As noted, the positive beneficial aspects of U.S. society are not being contested. Because bin Laden has successfully made U.S. foreign policies the center of the war of ideas, any Muslim who publicly argues that America should be given the benefit of the doubt is implicitly acquiescing in U.S. support for Israel, manipulation of oil prices, and support for Russia in Chechnya. This is the reason why Americans hear so few "moderate Muslim voices" opposing bin Laden and the Islamists; the moderates are out there and often do not approve of the Islamists' military actions, but they hate U.S. policies with just as much venom and passion as the Islamists, per the polls by Pew, Gallup, BBC, and Zogby.

The need to correct American misperceptions of what motivates our Islamist foes is obvious, mandatory, and easy to carry out: our elites simply must stop lying and tell the truth. The hatred being generated by Guantanamo Bay, rendition, and killing Iraqi and Afghan civilians, moreover, is an unavoidable price of fighting a war against a nonuniformed, nonstate actor under the terms of international agreements, treaties, and traditions that can accommodate only nation-state-vs.-nation-state conflicts. But we need to be mindful that their cost is more than mere public relations fallout; that hatred for Americans as well as for their government is growing in the Muslim world, and the solution to this problem lies in winning—and winning soon.

A final handicap problem for the United States in the hearts-and-minds arena emanates from Bernard Lewis's book *What Went Wrong? Western Impact and Middle Eastern Response.*[29] My own view is that Dr. Lewis did not intend the book to be a final, definitive, and unreserved condemnation of the worthlessness of Muslim civilization. For many Americans and Westerners, however, the book has been portrayed as making that case, and many appear to have adopted that view as their own. To serve their own war-mongering purposes, for example, the neoconservatives most strongly broadcast this description of the book, but President Bush and his colleagues, Democratic Party leaders, media commentators, academics, generals, and many everyday Americans have stated much the same view in one form or another. Protestant evangelicals and Israeli leaders and pundits have given the argument the added and powerfully offensive negative twist of describing Islam as a religion of evil and wickedness, the Prophet as a murderer and a pedophile,[30] and those who believe themselves to be defending Islam—and implicitly tens of millions of Muslims—as mad, nihilistic, and apocalyptic gangsters. Through this interpretation of Dr. Lewis's book, be it merited or a bit exaggerated, we now have an increasingly widespread, common-wisdom type of criticism of Muslims and Islam as evil, warlike, medieval, antimodern, woman-hating, archaic, and inhuman.

Standing against these negative assumptions and judgments is a reality that seems contradictory. Today Islam is the fastest-growing[31] religion in the world, a fact that suggests that the best answer to Dr. Lewis's "What went wrong?" question is that the evolution of Islam is not working out the way elite Westerners wanted it to work out. "The constant media refrain about 'what went wrong' with Islam—to paraphrase Bernard Lewis," William Dalrymple has commented in *The New Statesman,* "ignores its self-evident success and its increasing popularity."[32] Much of this growth clearly is due to the much higher fertility rates of Islamic countries, but as Dalrymple notes in Britain, France, and the United States it has "as much to do with conversion as immigration."[33] In Britain, for example, it has been estimated that by 2025 the number of converts in the British Muslim population will overtake the number of immigrants.[34] Islam, it seems, is attractive to an increasing number of non-Muslims, who, we must assume, find in it spiritual solace, a means of understanding the world, and guidance for how a decent life should be lived by individuals, families, societies, and nations. Now, some analysts will contend that Western converts to Islam are the dregs of Western society, and no doubt U.S. and European prisons are places where such conversions occur at a brisk pace. Nonetheless, the rapid, natural, and by-conversion growth of the world's Islamic population must be the result of something more than a sudden willingness to adopt a war-mongering, medieval, and inhuman religion. Common sense would suggest, I think, that most people are unlikely to seek solace and direction from that sort of faith.

My point here is not that the neoconservatives, and many others who echo what may be an extreme interpretation Dr. Lewis's book, are wrong (though I think they are) but that the deliberately added portion of denigration they inject into the Western-vs.-Muslim debate is a further obstacle to any successful hearts-and-minds campaign by the United States and its allies. Already faced by a difficult-to-overcome substantive issue—the near-unanimous belief of Muslims that U.S. foreign policy is meant to humiliate Muslims and attack Islam, and that Washington regards Muslim lives as cheap and expendable—Washington's would-be hearts-and-minds warriors must overcome a blanket and scabrous Western condemnation of an increasingly popular religion. This condemnation can be expected to enrage Muslims who both love their faith and oppose violence against the United States and the West, and thereby contribute to their silent acquiescence in the face of the Islamists' arguments and military actions.

Every American, of course, is and must remain free to think and speak as they will, but Americans would do well to review their own history for lessons about how such consistently denigrating language can greatly worsen deep divisions over substantive political issues. Politics in antebellum America, for example, confronted such divisive issues as the protective tariff, states-rights issues, banking, slavery, the addition of new states, and the extension of slavery into the western territories. These issues generally took on the form of a North-vs.-South sectional confrontation that led to civil war. Complicating any chance of ameliorating this substantive confrontation, moreover, was a northern view of the South that, over the course of the antebellum years, took on the character of a wholesale denigration not only of the institution of slavery and southern political views but of the character, faith, lifestyle, and culture of southerners. "Northerners believed that southern society was basically degenerate," the noted historian Kenneth M. Stampp has written. "The want of national spirit, the rejection of political democracy, and the preference for slave labor were only a few of the many signs of social decadence." Most of all northerners believed their southern countrymen were antimodern and determined to oppose and block societal progress. Northerners believed, Stampp writes, that "secession itself was a 'revolution against civilization,' a southern attempt to take revenge on the nineteenth century."[35]

Adding to the vitriol and hatred of this general sentiment was a group of northerners who behaved in the same manner as those who have used Dr. Lewis's book as a comprehensive condemnation of Islam and Muslims. The ardent abolitionist William Lloyd Garrison and his supporters chose the wholesale denigration of southerners and their society as the means for defining the antislavery cause as a confrontation between goodness and enlightenment on one side, and wickedness and medieval obscurantism on the other. While Garrison's strategy did not cause the Civil War, it contributed mightily to the hardening of southern attitudes toward the North and the ultimate termination of debate on sectional compromise in favor of war. "But if Garrisonian abolitionism was not the original cause of sectional conflict over slavery," the eminent U.S. historian Don E. Fehrenbacher has tellingly argued, "it nevertheless had a critical influence on the temper and shape of the conflict."

Out of passionate conviction, but also as a deliberate choice of strategy, the new [Garrisonian] abolitionists set out to destroy slavery by direct, personal attack upon everyone associated with the institution and everyone acquiescing in its existence. Their campaign of denunciation lacerated southern feelings as never before. The primary target, of course, was the slaveholder, whom they convicted of criminality, atrocity, and so on. The language had the effect of degrading and dehumanizing the slaveholder, even as he was said to be degrading and dehumanizing his slaves.[36]

And the cumulative negative impact of this constant denigration? Well, perhaps it was the production of a significant contribution to the coming of the war—the U.S. Supreme Court's 1857 *Dred Scott* decision. In his recent study of President Abraham Lincoln and Roger B. Taney, the Maryland-born chief justice of the Supreme Court, the distinguished legal scholar James F. Simon details Taney's rising anger and resentment over the North's constant antebellum denigration of southerners as inferior both as human beings and in their culture and way of life. Simon assesses Taney's pre–*Dred Scott* career on the Court as one of sound, well documented, and Union-preserving constitutional reasoning and decisions. But Simon notes that even years before the *Dred Scott* case, Taney had begun to resent "northern humiliation" of the South and to worry that its continuation would push the South toward secession, a tragedy that was being made more likely by "the condescending attitude of northern politicians toward the south and their assumptions of moral superiority." By 1857 Taney apparently had had enough. In drafting the Court's majority opinion in the *Dred Scott* case, Simon argues, Taney was "influenced by his southern heritage," and in the decision's substance it "seemed as if the deep reservoir of southern resentment over the slavery issue suddenly poured out." Chief Justice Taney "was a proud member of his region's aristocracy," Simon writes, "and when his class was attacked, he vehemently defended it. He bristled at the charge that slavery made the South morally inferior to the North."[37]

In the *Dred Scott* case, Taney's "bristling" not only overpowered the steady and talented mind that produced a career of prudence, good sense, and sound decisions, but also helped to bring on a civil war in which more than 600,000 Americans died. And several of the themes of the North's denigration of the South are heard today in what is verging on a blanket Western condemnation of Muslim society: the Prophet Muhammad and Islamic society are "degenerate"; Muslims are in revolt against modernity and progress; secular Westerners are "morally superior" to pious Muslims; and Muslims are inferior because they oppose the separation of church and state. At bottom, the impact of such denigration is hard to quantify, but like Taney sharing and defending the proud southerner's view, all Muslims share the heritage of Islam, tend to spring to the defense of their faith, society, and brethren, and bristle at the "humiliation" they perceive in Western criticism. Today, in fact, many millions of Muslims likely share the conclusion reached by the antebellum senator Judah P. Benjamin (D-Louisiana)—who later was a Confederate cabinet secretary—that "the heart of the matter was not so much what the abolitionists and Republicans had *done* or might *do* to the South, as it was the things they *said* about the South—and the moral arrogance with which they said them."[38] Thus, the shaping of Western thought and rhetoric toward wholesale denigration by the popularization and perhaps distortion of Dr. Lewis's what-went-wrong thesis further reduces the already slim chance that any U.S. hearts-and-minds arguments will get a fair hearing among Muslims, radical, conservative, moderate, liberal, or otherwise.

A Leadership Desert

Successful political leadership is about consistently telling the hard, cold, and very often unwelcome and disturbing truth. In post-Reagan America we seem to have deliberately bred this trait out of our leaders and increasingly out of the students in our university system. As John Adams, perhaps the most perceptive of the Founders on the subject of human nature's foibles, told a jury, "Facts are stubborn things." Adams was right of course, but in contemporary America we have solved the problem by collectively deciding to ignore inconvenient facts. Blatant bribery and payoffs in the funding of election campaigns becomes a form of First Amendment–protected "free speech," and historically unacceptable and destructive behavior in civil society is abetted by claims that America must encourage the growth of a "diverse and multicultural society." The astounding zest of contemporary Americans for disguising stark facts can be seen in the attribution of the term *music* to much of what is heard today on the radio. In the domestic sphere, U.S. political leadership today consists mostly in building a vocabulary that will allow our elite to disguise as modern, sophisticated, and humane the "stubborn facts" that are eating away the core of America's civil and political society.

In foreign affairs, leadership also is about telling the truth, and it is also about discernment. In the war that bin Laden declared in 1996, we have had neither from our leaders. Not once in that decade has any U.S. political leader stood up and talked to Americans about what our foes are claiming this war is about from their perspective. They have taken no steps to ensure that words of our Islamist enemies are available for Americans to read, study, and consider; ten years on, the only verbatim text of a bin Laden speech easily accessible to Americans is the one he delivered on the eve of the 2004 presidential election.[39] The goal of making this material available would not be to cultivate empathy or sympathy for the Islamist perspective—it would not be to propagate an "Oh, poor Muslims!" syndrome, as some of the conservative media claims[40]—but to help Americans understand the threat their country faces, their enemies' motivation, and the debilitating lies about both that their bipartisan political leaders have foisted on them for the last decade. As always, for America to function and survive as a republic—and protect itself from what John Jay called the "weak and the wicked"—its population must be educated in ways that permit an understanding of the world and, perhaps more important, that allow them to assess the arguments, reasoning, and justifications presented to them by their elected leaders.

So here is the dilemma that Americans face in the leadership realm in as unvarnished a form as I can present it: Americans are not being led, they are being lied to. The lies are causing them to (a) underestimate the threat posed by bin Laden and his allies; (b) not recognize that the current U.S. foreign policies in the Muslim world are pushing toward Samuel Huntington's clash of civilizations; and (c) realize that our governing elites will never adequately protect America unless they are forced to do so by their countrymen. On the latter point, Americans will have to decide whether these men and women are illiterate fools or cynical self-servers who value office over U.S. security—these are the only two options in explaining their behavior.

In this context, there is room in America for a leader who cares about his country more than his office; who is willing to do the hard work of protecting Americans over the easy task of perpetuating failed policies; and most of all who is willing to tell the truth that the price of America's defeat by the Islamists will be that Americans, for the first time, would have to live as they must and not as they aspire to. What America needs, in a sense, is an Osama bin Laden of its own. Our Saudi foe's appeal comes not only from his eloquence, strategic vision, patience, combat record, and managerial skills, though he has all of those in ample measure. The astounding breadth and durable appeal of bin Laden and his message also owe much to the near-absolute lack of popular and credible leaders in the Muslim world, from Morocco to Malaysia. In a crowd of dictators, absolute monarchs, effete princes, and coup-installed generals, bin Laden was like the unexpected cream that gradually but inevitably rose to the top of Islam's bottle of fat-free milk.

Sadly, there is a similar opportunity for the rise of a bin Laden–like leader in the United States. In an American polity dominated by the uninspiring Harry Reid, the flip-flopping Hillary Clinton, the quick-tempered bully-boy John McCain, the ambulance-chasing John Edwards, and a raft of other no-discernible-talent politicians, the dire need for truthful, credible leadership is obvious. In just five presidential terms America's political elite has squandered the opportunities left for them by Ronald Reagan's annihilation of the Evil Empire. The political pygmies who inherited that amazing gift simply dragged it to the edge of the abyss. At this point it seems far more likely that the path ahead will lead over the edge and not, as in the past, to safety by the almost providential emergence of a leader of the caliber of Washington, Lincoln, Theodore Roosevelt, Franklin Roosevelt, or Ronald Reagan. Self-inflicted defeat by the befuddled vacuity and moral cowardice of our leaders, and not victory, appears today as America's most likely fate.

CHAPTER 7

"O enemy of God,
I will give thee no respite"

Al-Qaeda and Its Allies Take Stock

The important fact remains demonstrated, that we now have more men than we had when the war began; that we are not exhausted, nor in the process of exhaustion; that we are gaining strength, and may, if need be, maintain the contest indefinitely.

Abraham Lincoln, 1864

The better rule is to judge our adversaries from their standpoint, not from our own.

Robert E. Lee, c.1870

Over and over again this individualism of theirs [the Arabs] . . . has gravely weakened them; yet over and over again they have suddenly united under a leader and accomplished the greatest things. Now it is probable enough that on these lines—unity under a leader—the return of Islam may arrive.

Hilaire Belloc, 1938

In all of America's wars, the enemy has had a viewpoint that is based on his cultural and historical perspective, and through this lens he sees wartime events and assesses the state of his war effort. This, of course, is a truism. But in contemporary America that truism is accepted intellectually but spurned in reality and viciously attacked if it is spoken in public. When, for example, Congressman Ron Paul (R-Texas) said in a May 2007 debate in

South Carolina among Republican presidential candidates that the Islamists' motivation for attacking us on 9/11 was our foreign policy and its impact in the Muslim world, he was immediately smashed verbally by Rudy Giuliani (speaking for the obsessive U.S. interventionism that is dogma in both parties) for even suggesting such a thing.

> **Rep. Paul:** Have you ever read the reasons why they attacked us? They attacked us because we've been over there; we've been bombing Iraq for ten years. They don't come here to attack us because we are rich and free. They come here to attack us because we are over there.

> **Mr. Giuliani:** That is an extraordinary statement, as someone who lived through 9/11, that we invited the attack because we were bombing Iraq. I don't think I have heard that before, and I have heard some pretty absurd explanations for September 11. And I would ask the congressman to withdraw that comment and tell us that he really didn't mean that.[1]

Notice that Giuliani focused on Rep. Paul's phrase "we've been bombing Iraq for ten years" and ignored the Texan's core argument that America is being attacked by Islamists because "we are over there." The tough but ignorant cop Giuliani simply denounced Paul and, in essence, warned him never to say such an "absurd" and—implicitly—un-American thing again. After the debate Michael Steele, the Republican Party's spokesman, said that Paul should probably be excluded from future debates because of what he said about U.S. foreign policy.[2] Rep. Paul, to his credit and in America's interests, did not retract anything, and continues to publicly oppose unnecessary U.S. intervention abroad.

Mr. Giuliani's reaction to Rep. Paul's remarks reflects the U.S. governing elite's reliable, knee-jerk rejection to the idea that the enemy has a different perspective from our own and that, to win, Americans need to understand it. To take on that threat to understanding, the tone and voice of this chapter is more in the first person than its predecessors and successors. The change is deliberate and is meant to underscore the difficulty any American faces when trying to present a Rep. Paul–like, nonmainstream analysis of how Osama bin Laden, al-Qaeda, and their allies assess the progress of their war against the United States. It is easy to present an assessment of al-Qaeda's estimate if an author uses—Giuliani-like—

216

prevailing mainstream assumptions: Islamists hate Americans for how they live, think, and vote, not for what their government does; al-Qaeda et al. are the Muslim's world lunatic fringe; the U.S.-Israel relationship is not a severe handicap for U.S. national security; America's dependence on foreign oil is not a danger; and U.S. support for Muslim police states—Saudi Arabia, Kuwait, Egypt, etc.—does not foment universal Muslim anger. Analysis based on these assumptions finds that America and its allies are winning the war.

When an American disagrees with or dismisses these assumptions as analytically unsound and dangerous for U.S. national security, however, the epithets begin to fly. Suggest, for example, that hundreds of millions of Muslims support or sympathize with the Islamists' goal or that unqualified U.S. support for Israel is costing American blood and treasure—and will cost much more of each—and an author is defamed as a defeatist, an appeaser, an America-hater, or that most powerful and debate-silencing epithet, an anti-Semite.

In this chapter my intention is to defy the epithet-slingers, especially the pro-Israel American citizens—the Israel-firsters—who for too long have hurled the anti-Semite slur and successfully suppressed a frank and comprehensive debate on the content and conduct of U.S. national security policy in the Islamic world.

The chapter is divided into two parts. The first deals with my own experience with the Israel-firsters. I do not intend to defend myself in this section; my past work and its pretty consistent accuracy speak for themselves. I do, however, welcome the animosities the Israel-firsters have expressed for the chance they give to display their speech-limiting intentions and to argue the importance for Americans to ignore childish name-calling and begin voicing their views in a national debate that keeps no foreign policy issue—Israel, energy, or Arab tyranny—off the table. A good day for Americans, and for their families' safety, will be the day when the Israel-firsters hear nothing in response to their slanders except the perfectly appropriate childhood chant: "Sticks and stones may break my bones, but names will never hurt me."

The chapter's second part bends to the limits on public discourse about U.S. foreign policy displayed in the exchange between Rep. Paul and Mr. Giuliani. It offers an estimate of how al-Qaeda and its allies assess the status of their war against the United States, and it underlines the justifiable confidence they now have in the progress they have made as well as in ultimate victory. This section is seen through our enemy's eyes and is written from his cultural and historical perspective. It is an assessment that I believe is both authentic and compelling, one that should be mulled over by Americans. Our Islamist enemies are more lethal, numerous, pious, sophisticated, patient, and modern than most of us have thought. They are motivated by what the U.S. government does—as Rep. Paul said, "because we are over there"—and not by how Americans think, vote, or live. This reality comes through clearly in the voice I have given al-Qaeda, a voice which is necessary only because of the debate-suppressing power of the Israel-firsters and those others—like Mr. Giuliani, his coterie of neoconservative advisers, and the bulk of both parties' presidential candidates—who see no need for changing the U.S. foreign-policy status quo that is pushing America toward military defeat and economic disaster.

When I resigned from the Central Intelligence Agency in November 2004, my intention was to speak and write about the failure of the U.S. government and the American people to understand the nature and severity of the threat posed to the United States by Osama bin Laden, al-Qaeda, and their other Islamist allies. I thought then—and believe more strongly now—that America's governing elite had almost completely underestimated the threat and, indeed, had done so deliberately for the sake of domestic political ease. This deliberate misunderstanding has disguised a situation where, in early 2008, al-Qaeda and its allies stand just as Mr. Lincoln saw the political strength and military forces of the Union in 1864— stronger, more vigorous, and increasingly numerous as compared to the start of the war. "We judge," the U.S. Intelligence Community concluded just before the sixth anniversary of the 9/11 attacks, "[that] the U.S. Homeland will face a persistent and evolving terrorist threat over the next three years. The main threat comes from Islamic terrorist groups and cells, especially al-Qaeda."[3]

My post-CIA intention was simply to stick to the facts as they were presented in the words of bin Laden, Ayman al-Zawahiri, and the essays published by al-Qaeda's theologians, commentators, strategists, and allies. For me, these words presented a compelling and consistent story of a growing group of Islamist militants bent on driving the United States from the Middle East and the Islamic world generally in order to remove U.S. protection—military, economic, and political-diplomatic—from Israel and incumbent Muslim regimes so that they can be destroyed. On review, those words also left the strong impression that these men were intelligent, patient, calculating, ruthless, hard-working, and driven by genuine religious motivation, an always dangerous combination of attributes in any enemy. Their multiple successful attacks against the interests of the United States and its allies between 1992 and 2004, moreover, tended to confirm both their intent and their ability to wage a destructive and geographically widespread war against America.

By sticking to these facts, I thought it would be a fairly straightforward task to accurately explain the nature of the Islamist threat and the motivation of those prosecuting it. I likewise believed that Americans would be relieved to learn that the Islamist threat was not the nihilistic and apocalyptic one described by their leaders—the annihilation of American society, all Christians and Jews, Western civilization, etc.—but rather a much more limited one that focused not on U.S. culture and society but almost exclusively on what the U.S. government did in the Islamic world. Better for Americans to know, I thought, that they faced a smart, thinking enemy, with limited war aims, and not the irrational, inchoate foe President Bush described: "They hate Christianity. They hate Judaism. They hate everything that's not them."[4] My message, then, had nothing whatsoever to do with promoting empathy or sympathy for America's Islamist enemies. My goal was to more precisely define how the enemy thought, his motivation and war aims, and the nature of the threat he posed. Having a solid handle on these issues is the indispensable grounding that is necessary before we can do what we must do—utterly destroy America's Islamist foe.

Well, it did not turn out to be as easy a task as I thought. Republicans and their media advocates decided that, by explaining what bin Laden and al-Qaeda were up to and motivated by, and why U.S. efforts to defeat them were not yet nearly adequate to the job, I was a Bush-basher, an America-hater, a liberal-appeaser, and a mole who worked for the 2004 Kerry-Edwards campaign from inside the CIA. From the Democratic side, I was identified as a war-monger, a strident nationalist (apparently American nationalism is hate speech for Democrats), an isolationist, and an unreconstructed Reaganite. (They had me cold on the last one.) The one thing that both sides agreed on was that I was indisputably a rank anti-Semite who wanted to abandon Israel. On this issue, American-citizen Israel-firsters led the charge, and their work was given a certain gravitas by *Commentary*'s senior editor, Gabriel Schoenfeld. The latter wrote an article that would have been lawsuit-worthy except that the anti–hate speech laws are written to exempt from protection any individuals the Israel-firsters target for public scourging as anti-Semites, which is their long-standing and only real talent. A small sampling of this reasoned and mature criticism of my work follows, none of which, of course, contained a single point that demonstrated any substantive value America derives from its relationship with Israel.

> Writing as if he stole [Patrick] Buchanan's playbook, Scheuer's chapter head on this topic [Israel] is called "The Burden of an Eternal Dependent." He blasts what he calls America's "overwhelmingly one-way alliance with Israel" and, like Buchanan and other sniveling weasels of the far right, complains that any criticism of the alliance is branded anti-Semitism . . . Maybe the problem was the CIA. Because if an idiot like Scheuer could be entrusted with U.S. intelligence, then the people running the CIA weren't as smart as we were led to believe. When former CIA officials wind up on the same page as Michael Moore and Pat Buchanan, you know something was very wrong at Langley. It's high time these fools were turned out on their ears. [Jonathan Tobin, December 16, 2004][5]

> Sentiments like these [criticisms of Israel] mark the author of *Imperial Hubris* [Scheuer] as something of a political hybrid—a cross, not to put too fine a point on it, between an overwrought Buchanan and a raving Chomskyite. This alone, one might think, should have unfitted him for a high position within the CIA . . . All of which leaves only the question: How did a person of such demonstrable mediocrity of mind and unhinged views achieve the rank he did in the CIA, and how could so manifestly wayward and damaging a work have been publicized by someone in the Agency's employ. [Gabriel Schoenfeld, March 2005.][6]

> Not to be outdone by mere academics, a former head of the CIA's "Bin Laden Unit" at its Counterterrorism Center, Michael Scheuer, reacted to "The Lobby" [the paper by Walt and Mearsheimer] with his own claim that "U.S. citizens have been the subject of a political action campaign designed and executed by Israel" . . . With people like Scheuer in charge at Langley, *Mein Kampf* could well become required reading. [Morris J. Amitay, April 20, 2006.][7]

"O enemy of God, I will give thee no respite"

What the foregoing texts by Americans clearly say is that their fellow Americans cannot be patriots if they use their right to free speech to question any aspect of the U.S.-Israeli relationship; that U.S. citizens should not be allowed to work at CIA—or presumably elsewhere in the U.S. government—if they are not Israel-firsters and a pogrom is needed to remove critics of Israel from federal employment; and that any American who claims that the impact of unqualified U.S. support for Israel in the Muslim world is unreservedly damaging to U.S. interests is a "sniveling weasel," an "idiot," a person with "demonstrable mediocrity of mind and unhinged views," and that old-reliable epithet of the Israel-firsters' scourge-machine, a *Mein Kampf*–reading Nazi.

Besides the authors listed above, other distinguished U.S. citizens are reliable Israel-firsters. These men, for example, fairly swarmed to attack Stephen Walt and John Mearsheimer when they published an article critical of the influence that pro-Israel groups are allowed to have on U.S. policies.[8] On this occasion, the list of U.S. citizens acting as Israel's thought police was impressive: James Carroll, Max Boot, Steven Simon, Alan Dershowitz, David Gergen, Christopher Hitchens, Marvin Kalb, and Eliot Cohen.[9] These authors claim or imply that criticism of Israel by U.S. citizens is anti-Semitism, and some have such contempt for their fellow citizens that they practice the Big Lie by asserting definitively that there is no such thing as an "Israeli lobby."[10] Among these writers are found the *takfiris* of contemporary American politics, men who, with delicious irony, mirror Muslim *takfiris* in taking it upon themselves to decide who is and who is not a "good American," then mete out punishment to those of their countrymen who do not make the grade.[11]

These are all dangerous men who, in my judgment, are seeking to place de facto limitations on the First Amendment to protect the nation of their primary attachment. They are the type of individuals about whom General Washington warned his countrymen, noting that the success of such men in limiting free speech would cause disaster for America. "For if men are to be precluded from offering their Sentiments on a matter which may involve the most serious and alarming consequences, that can invite the consideration of mankind," General Washington told his officers in 1783, "reason is of no use to us; the freedom of Speech may be taken away, and, dumb and silent, we may be led, like sheep, to the Slaughter."[12]

Let me pause here to say, first, that the Israel-firsters' attempts to silence criticism by Americans of the manner in which their government conducts the U.S. relationship with Israel are now leading the U.S. lamb to the slaughter; and second, that I have never accepted and will forever reject the idea that to intensely dislike the nature of the relationship the U.S. government has fabricated with Israel, and to believe that that relationship is not only a burden but a cancer on America's ability to protect its genuine national interests—which I do believe—equates to either anti-Semitism or a lack of American patriotism. Indeed, my own view would be that those Americans who are quickest to wield the debate-silencing anti-Semitism sword are either the most suspect in the realm of loyalty or are simply resolute liars who champion the fantasy of identical U.S. and Israeli national interests.

Let me be clear: the only country I care about is the United States. I care not a whit whether or not Israel survives. I likewise do not care if Zambia, Saudi Arabia, Bolivia, Papua-New Guinea, Spain, or most any other nation survives. Foreign nations are important only insofar as they can benefit America, and our relations with them should be predicated on that consideration and not on emotion, irrational guilt, Pollyanna-ish ideas about democracy, or the political influence bought by corrupt and corrupting lobbies, be they supporting Israel, Saudi Arabia, Armenia, Greece, or Lebanon. America should associate with those nation-states that benefit America, steer clear of those that do not, and run as fast and as far as possible from those that seek to involve us in fights in which we have no stake, particularly fights between religions. The only exceptions to this general rule should be Great Britain, Canada, Australia, and New Zealand, to each of which we owe a debt of honor due to our collective, bloody, and successful efforts to prevent the triumph of tyranny in the twentieth century. In sum, let me bluntly say to the Israel-firsters, in the words Franklin Roosevelt used to defy the New Deal opponents he called Economic Royalists: "They are unanimous in their hatred for me—and I welcome their hatred." [13]

Now back to the business at hand. The lesson I learned after resigning from the CIA was that sticking to the facts was not going to do the trick, and if I wanted to get a hearing and give Americans a chance to discern the prevarications of their governing elite, I would need to find a vehicle that did not raise hackles and cause vitriol to spurt the minute the message began playing. Then over the summer of 2005, I happened to be listening to a course on CD-ROM called *Tocqueville and the American Experiment*,[14] presented by William R. Cook, a historian from the State University of New York at Geneseo. The entire course was excellent, but specifically Dr. Cook's lectures on Tocqueville suggested the reason why my arguments had so angered virtually the entire American political spectrum. Writing after his tour of America in the 1830s, Tocqueville said that he had found,

> There is nothing more annoying in the habits of life [in America] than this irritable patriotism of the Americans. A foreigner would indeed consent to praise much in their country; but he would want to be permitted to blame something, and this he is absolutely refused. America is therefore a country of freedom where, in order not to wound anyone, a foreigner must not speak freely.[15]

Well, okay. Tocqueville, I think, was right, thus validating Walter A. McDougall's witty but starkly perceptive contention that "complete objectivity about America is a characteristic only of God and Alexis de Tocqueville."[16] Americans do not like to be criticized by foreigners, and so perhaps it is not unnatural that Americans do not want to be taken to task and are irritated by the words of a foreigner named Osama bin Laden. I share this feeling whenever I hear criticisms of America from bin Laden, Jacques Chirac, Hugo Chavez, or some of the American politicians who seem endlessly foreign to me. But here I am, an American by birth, talking to other Americans about a life-and-death threat to our common country. Why should that effort draw such vitriol? Not surprisingly, Tocqueville has an answer for that too. As much as Americans hate hearing foreigners criticize their country, the Frenchman writes, they hate the same sort of criticism coming from American mouths even more. In America, Tocqueville explained, "as long as the majority is doubtful, one speaks;

> but when it [the majority] has irrevocably pronounced [a consensus belief], everyone becomes silent and friends and enemies alike then seem to hitch themselves together to its wagon . . . I do not know any country where, in general, less genuine independence of mind and genuine freedom of discussion reign than in America . . . In America the majority draws a formi-

dable circle around thought. Inside those limits, the writer is free; but unhappiness awaits him if he leaves them . . . But the power that dominates in the United States [that is, a consensus opinion] does not intend to be made sport of like this. The slightest reproach wounds it, the least prickly truth alarms it; and one must praise it from the forms of its language to its most solid virtues. No writer, whatever his renown may be, can escape the obligation of singing the praises of his fellow citizens. The majority, there-fore, lives in perpetual adoration of itself, only foreigners or experience can make certain truths reach the ears of Americans.[17]

Right, that explains it. President George H. W. Bush, President Clinton, and President George W. Bush, their political lieutenants, and their media and academic supporters drew and then retraced and blackened what Tocqueville called the "formidable circle" around the current consensus view of America's war with al-Qaeda and other Islamists. That consensus? Simple: America is being attacked because of its liberties, freedoms, elec-tions, and gender equality, and not for what the U.S. government does in the Muslim world. Like the issues of Social Security and Israel, this mantra has become another, increasingly venerable third rail in American politics, one that fits perfectly into the Cold War paradigm of defending the "Free World" against tyranny, this time the tyranny being Islamofascism. To ques-tion the mantra, therefore, reliably earns epithets but not a fair hearing.

Since resigning from the CIA, I have had the enormous good for-tune and honor to teach a short course on al-Qaeda to U.S. military person-nel, mostly junior officers and NCOs working on the collection and analy-sis of human intelligence. For this class, it is not appropriate to criticize serving political leaders, and so I decided to play the role of al-Qaeda's intelligence chief in the United States. In this guise I present to the class an assessment—addressed to Osama bin Laden and Ayman al-Zawahiri—of the status of al-Qaeda's war against the United States based on what I believe would likely be al-Qaeda's perspective. I chose this means of instruction for two reasons. First, bin Laden, Ayman al-Zawahiri, and their lieutenants have produced an enormous corpus of statements, speeches, and interviews. These materials provide a clear understanding of how our enemies see and think about their world, and highlight their goals, priorities, and motivations; they allow the construction of an analy-sis grounded in primary sources that display our foe's most intensely held convictions. Second, the bipartisan criticisms I outlined above came after I spent twenty-plus years attending briefings for intelligence and military officers presented by senior Democratic and Republican administration officials and their media and academic associates. I felt certain, therefore, that many men and women in my little audiences would have heard such speakers extol U.S. strategy and discuss the weapons systems, manpower, allied countries, and propaganda plans that would be used to utterly defeat an enemy. I was also sure that they had heard little or no hint from such speakers that a living, breathing, thinking, talented, pious, and adaptable Islamist foe sits across the table from America. I therefore designed my talk to try to remedy that shortcoming.

What follows then is an assessment of the war written from al-Qaeda's perspective. The format roughly follows a reporting format that is used by CIA station chiefs overseas to provide senior officials in Washington with an overall assessment of where things stand in their country or region. They are designed to give Washington a frank and realistic view of how things look to the senior U.S. intelligence officer on the ground, and—sometimes implicitly, sometimes explicitly—how likely U.S. interests are to be impacted either positively or negatively. These reports are generally closely held, initially going to the DCI and his senior lieutenants for both reading and a decision about further distribution. Many of these reports are sent to the president, cabinet-level officers, and their deputies.

Here, then, is what I believe to be a reasonable estimate of how al-Qaeda's intelligence chief in the United States—and we can be sure there is one—would assess the status of the Islamists' war against America eleven years-plus after his boss declared war on the United States. That is, it shows al-Qaeda talking to al-Qaeda about al-Qaeda problems, failures, and successes; it is an effort, in other words, to follow General Lee's rule of judging the enemy from his standpoint, not our own. I would add that the assessment is without the justifying citations from the Koran and the Prophet's sayings and traditions that an Islamist would surely use but that are beyond the ken of a mackerel-snapping Catholic like me. Unlike U.S. intelligence officers, the al-Qaeda chief here had the distinct advantage of drafting his assessment in the context of the clear and plausibly attainable war aims that bin Laden has established. Those aims are captured in two terse phrases: "Bleed America to bankruptcy" and "Spread out American forces."[18] Finally, American readers will notice that Al-Qaeda's chief

writes in a very personal and informal manner that reflects Islam's enduring egalitarianism. The outside-CIA readers of the same kind of CIA
reporting format, of course, would expect—nay, demand—significantly
more forelock-tugging.

TO: Al-Qaeda/Headquarters
FROM: Al-Qaeda/Washington
SUBJECT: Assessing the Jihad Against America

1. In the name of God, the most merciful, the most compassionate.
2. Brothers Osama and Ayman: First, I give all praise and thanks to Allah for His
grace and mercies, and then to our Prophet, peace be upon him, for the soundest
advice and truest guidance. Next, Brothers, I give thanks for your messages this
past year to the American people, especially Brother Osama's recent speeches
offering Americans another chance to embrace Islam.[19] Your statements are clear
and practical; you spoke directly to Americans and not to their arrogant leaders.
You warned them that our al-Qaeda brothers are nearly ready to again attack
inside the United States, and that they will do so unless U.S. policies in the
Islamic world are changed. And you have clarified your words of warning in their
own language through the English speeches of our mujahid American brother,
Azzam al-Amriki.[20]
3. Brothers, all Muslims now know that you have gone many extra miles to warn
the American people, and thereby you have fully obeyed the traditions of the
Prophet Muhammad, peace be upon him, and followed the honorable practices of
Saladin, Islam's first great defender against the medieval Christian Crusaders.[21]
But sadly, dear Brothers, I do not believe the Americans will heed your words.
Though you spoke directly to them, they have heard President Bush and Vice
President Cheney describe your warning as "words of desperation" and contemptuously reject your truce offer by flippantly proclaiming: "We don't negotiate
with terrorists, we put them out of business." And amazingly, after Brother
Osama's recent speech, President Bush's homeland security advisor told the
media al-Qaeda is "all but impotent," apparently forgetting she was responding
to our challenge and that America is losing two wars to the "impotent" mujahedin.[22] Brothers, many Americans are going to die because of their leaders' arrogance and, while regrettable, this arrogance is, all thanks to Allah, good news for
al-Qaeda and its allies. It means the government of the world's richest and most

powerful nation still does not understand the motivation of the mujahedin, the goals for which we fight, or God's promise of victory that makes us steadfast.

4. Because of your speeches, Brothers, and because it is eleven years since you sent me to America as al-Qaeda's intelligence chief, and more than six years after the blessed September raids, I thought I should send you my appraisal of where al-Qaeda and its allies stand in regard to America's understanding of what motivates our movement and what it is trying to do. I also write because the results of the November 2006 U.S. congressional elections and their aftermath have shown—as you predicted, Brother Osama—that the Americans have neither the will, patience, political cohesion, nor ruthlessness to continue their war against us. Their will is cracking, Brother, and even President Bush's father's friends—the Iraq Study Group—told him that the mujahedin are beating America in Iraq.[23] Brothers, Bush has rejected the group's conclusion and disregarded its advice. He has now sent five more brigades to Iraq. Fifty brigades would have been a problem for the mujahedin, but five will make no difference; the Americans will fight more, bleed more, but still will have to leave Iraq in defeat. For this all thanks are due to Allah. And thanks also are due to the Almighty for the surge of support and confidence our victory in Iraq will earn from the Muslim masses. That support will be as great as and perhaps greater than that which arose when Allah imposed defeat on the Red Army in Afghanistan through the rifles of the mujahedin. And when the Americans leave Iraq, many of our brothers will go to Afghanistan again to drive the American-led infidels to their doom as they did the atheist Russians.

5. To begin, Brothers, let me first say that I have rigorously followed your directions. As a white American Muslim convert, I and my family have lived an ordinary life here in the suburbs outside Washington. I have been employed in the same well-paid engineering position for these eleven years and was just promoted to a management position. As you told me, I have not associated with anyone who the Americans could remotely identify as an "Islamic extremist." I have, as you ordered, told no one—not even my American wife—that I had the honor to serve God by fighting the Communists in Afghanistan. As you directed, I have closely observed everyday life, read widely in the American media and scholarly and scientific journals, and listened to and studied the words of major U.S. political leaders. After more than a decade, and on the eve of al-Qaeda's next raid on America, therefore, I thought it best to send you my assessment of what I see as the downside and the upside of our fighting the United States, and on which side the balance of advantages currently stands in the war brother Osama calls the bleed-America-to-bankruptcy struggle.

227

The Downside: An Unimaginably Powerful Country

6. Brothers, we must always keep focused on the huge downside of this war: we are being hunted and attacked by the most powerful nation in history. And despite the heavy personnel losses al-Qaeda and its allies have suffered, may God accept them as martyrs, the United States has not yet made its full power felt. The American leaders appear to believe that we are afraid of and intimidated by their military power, may God help them cultivate this delusion. Even more, they are afraid of what the world will think of them if they use their military might in its full measure. Praise to God, Brothers, these are not the Americans who annihilated their enemies in Germany and Japan; these are the Americans of Vietnam, but even weaker in terms of resolve and ferocity. Still, the American people hate us intensely for the September raid of the blessed nineteen,[24] may God reward them, and their efforts against us are powered by an amazingly productive economy that has recovered much of what was lost from that blow. With this in mind, Brothers, we should rejoice over the 2006 U.S. election results and falling public support for the war in Iraq, but we should not deceive ourselves into believing that the American people hate us with any less venom. Indeed, it is my view that the American people are far more bloody minded than their leaders, and would have supported and applauded a far more aggressive and destructive war against us than Washington has waged.

7. Another problem for us, Brothers, is that American society, although far from perfectly equitable, is on the whole tolerant, including toward its Muslim citizens. At this time, Brothers, we do not have in America the advantage provided by the racist and anti-Islamic policies followed by the European Union countries. We therefore have hard and dangerous organizational work to do in the United States because we cannot wait for the demographic victory that will occur, God willing, in Europe where, as Brother Ayman has said, Allah is ensuring that the cradles of Muslim homes will ultimately return Spain and all of Europe to the Muslim ummah. And as you know, however, we do have a sound foundation of young men on which to build al-Qaeda in America as a mid-2007 poll showed. Among Muslim youth here under thirty years of age, 26 percent believe martyrdom operations are sometimes justified.[25] I must also stress again that the military, emotional, patriotic, and economic power of the United States has been neither harnessed nor focused; the latent power of this country is enormous, and we have yet to feel its impact. God willing, the Americans will continue to accept their leader's half-measures.

The Upside: God Has Given His Enemy Incompetent Leaders

8. Brothers, we must acknowledge and be thankful for the bounty of advantages God has given us: Brothers, believe me, the Americans' leaders are either soundly asleep, unwilling to face reality, or fundamentally stupid. Based on my experiences, observations, discussions, and studies, U.S. leaders do not have a clue as to what their war with us is about. This is, thanks to God, our greatest advantage. As examples, I cite the following for your consideration:

A.) They do not understand our motivation; as Brother al-Amriki would put it, "they have not figured out what makes us tick." Their political leaders of both parties, as well as their media, military, economic, and academic elites, continue to claim al-Qaeda hates America for "what it believes and how it lives" and not "for what the United States does in the Islamic world." And you have seen for yourselves, brothers, how Bush and Blair responded to our 2005 attacks in London: Like trained parrots they exclaimed: "The terrorists hate us for our freedoms not for what we do."[26] And in 2006, after Canadian police arrested a group of young mujahedin, Canada's prime minister described our brothers' activities as an "attack on Canadian values."[27] Then in summer 2007 the Australian prime minister said that the blessed operation by the mujahid Muslim doctors in London and Glasgow was conducted by those "who hate our way of life" and "oppose the way we live."[28] Thanks to God, Brothers, human ignorance and self-deception know no borders, but only God's love for Muslim believers could have kept our enemies deceiving themselves for so long. It is worth thinking about how long this self-imposed ignorance can endure, but on that score there is good news.

B.) The Americans are hamstrung by what some here call political correctness, which is a refusal to discuss matters of serious danger to their country because such debate might upset domestic politics. In some ways, Brothers, the U.S. press does not have the freedom permitted by the apostate Jordanian tyrant Abdullah. And even if our fears are realized, and Americans begin to understand that tens of millions of Muslims hate their government's foreign policies and not their society, it would take a near-revolution in their public discourse to allow frank debate about the issue of the mujahedin's motivation. Brothers, the indictment of the U.S. policy in the Muslim world that you have so clearly outlined has put them at a disadvantage, for to publicly debate the policies you have identified as attacks on Islam would be to ignite a firestorm in U.S. politics, for each policy is a political poison. Let me review the status of these policies.

<u>U.S. Support for Israel:</u> To criticize, let alone condemn, this policy would be a martyrdom operation for any U.S. politician. Our claims that Israel leads America around by the nose are true. As you can see, dear Brothers, the Americans slavishly followed Israel's lead and rejected the fair election of Hamas in Palestine, and they have now moved to support the apostate Palestinian president Mahmoud Abbas after the lions of Hamas drove Fatah from Gaza. And all Muslims are now watching the Americans and Israelis starve Palestinian children in Gaza, while they and their European friends pour tens of millions of dollars into the accounts of their corrupt agent Abbas. This proves for Muslims the validity of Brother Osama's warning that the Americans want to dominate not democratize the Muslim world. Currently, the Israelis and their agents in the U.S. Congress, media, and administration are leading the Americans toward war with Iran by promoting such absurdities as the existence of an alliance between our Taliban brothers and Tehran. And last winter the Israeli butcher Netanyahu told an American audience in Los Angeles that this is 1938 again and Iran is Nazi Germany; war is unavoidable he said, and Israel will not wait to be attacked. The American audience cheered, and not long afterward the Zionist Senator Lieberman said "that the Iranian government, by its actions, has declared war on us [the United States]."[29] Last summer we all watched Lebanon, where the obedient American lackeys held the country tight, like a just-caught fish, while their Israeli masters gutted it. And as I write, Washington is supporting Israeli air strikes in Gaza, and American generals are building walls to divide Muslims in Baghdad. They are apparently blind to the Iraqis' belief that they are importing Israel's apartheid methods to Iraq. If I was not living here, Brothers, I would not accept this contention, but in this country, thanks to God, criticism of Israel is not allowed. Men are called anti-Semitic and their careers are ruined if they criticize Israel. By God, even former American presidents like Carter are viciously attacked in public if they make negative comments about Israel, and it seems that the apostate Mubarak is criticized more openly in Egypt than is Israel in America. And, Brothers, the influential members of Bush's Iraq Study Group report should put your minds at ease regarding the durability of America's Israel policy. They wrote: "No American administration—Democratic or Republican—will ever abandon Israel."[30] Truly, God is great!

<u>U.S. Support for Nations That Oppress Muslims:</u> For U.S. leaders to alter this policy would mean losing face with other, rival Great Powers. Wash-

ington does not seem to know how much its support for the genocides by Russia's Putin against Chechen Muslims, and Beijing's against Uighur Muslims, hurts them in the Islamic world. And practically speaking, the Americans must continue to fawn over Czar Putin because, more than sixteen years after God's beloved mujahedin destroyed the Soviet Union, and all glory is God's for that victory, the U.S. and Russian governments cannot account for all of the Former Soviet Union's nuclear weapons. Only last summer the FBI director held an emergency meeting in Miami that stressed American fears—and, as you know, Brothers, with good reason—that al Qaeda will find several and deliver them to their rightful owners. More recently, the British media published a U.K. government report describing al-Qaeda's readiness to conduct "Hiroshima-style" attacks on Britain and America.[31] Brothers, only the Lord of the Universe could have put Bush so squarely on the side of Butcher Putin and force him to abide by the Russian dictator's will.

U.S. Energy Policy: It is incredible, Brothers, but three decades after King Faisal's blessed 1973 oil embargo, U.S. leaders are unwilling to install an energy policy that would remove Arab domination of their economy and those of its allies. One must earnestly and humbly thank God for the great good fortune he has given us in this regard. And Brothers, when the apostate Saudi king Abdullah agreed to expand the kingdom's oil production by the end of the decade, President Bush unbelievably welcomed this move, which can only increase America's dependence on Muslim oil, keep demand high, and make prices rise. Imagine, Brothers, with the steady increase in the price of a barrel of oil from $30 to above $90, our blessed financial benefactors have increased their support for the mujahedin to unprecedented levels. And what irony, Brothers Osama and Ayman, American parents are now paying exorbitant prices at the pump, and we are receiving a portion of the resulting profits to help us kill their soldier-children in Iraq, Afghanistan, and elsewhere. All praise to God for this wonder.

U.S. Support for Muslim Tyrannies: We can be confident that this policy will continue, Brothers. U.S. energy dependence means that Washington's talk of democracy-building in the Islamic world will remain mostly talk. Indeed, pictures of President Bush's hand-holding with the Saudi tyrant Abdullah, his economic strangling of Hamas, his befriending of the Libyan despot Qaddafi, his use of the Christian Ethiopians to invade Islamic Somalia, and his failure to condemn Mubarak for jailing candidates

231

whose only crime is to profess "There is no God but God and Muhammed is his messenger" tell Muslims all they need to know about U.S. intentions regarding democracy for Muslims. This damaging reality is not widely recognized in America because U.S. leaders call these tyrants "allies against terrorism," and so people here do not see the mockery of America's heritage of freedom—which so much of the Muslim world admires—by Washington's support for Arab tyrannies and police states in Egypt, Kuwait, the UAE, Saudi Arabia, Algeria, and elsewhere. This point will be underscored by Washington's recent decision to give the tyrants in Cairo and Riyadh $60 billion worth of weapons to help them suppress and torture Muslims. And Brothers, while the Israeli lobby has a powerful and corrupting influence on the American Congress and media, the Saudi lobby—thanks to God, for whom all things are possible—is less publicly known but just as powerful, successful, and malignant. The apostate al-Sauds send their smiling English-speaking princes, like Bandar and Turki, and now the U.S.-educated al-Jubeir to be their ambassadors in America with orders to buy the U.S. Congress. Our infidel enemies naïvely believe they are dealing with the true leaders of the Arabian Peninsula. And even more, Brothers, the al-Sauds buy the loyalty of retired U.S. ambassadors, senators, congressmen, generals, and senior intelligence officers to lobby the Congress and White House on their behalf, as well as to keep the *Wall Street Journal*'s editorial pages full of pro–al-Saud essays to mislead Americans. And all the while, and for this all praise is due to the Lord of the Universe, the blessed Ulema in the Land of the Prophet, may God's peace and blessings be upon him, are using funds from the al-Sauds to finance the spread of God's word around the globe, and nowhere more aggressively than under the nose of the Bush and Brown governments in the United States and Britain. Praise to God, Islam's huge coming generation of youth is being educated by our Ulema in what the Americans call "Wahhabism." As this gift from God proceeds, the American elites take the al-Sauds' word as they would take a hallucinogenic drug. It denies them contact with reality and they believe—truly they do, Brothers—that Saudi Arabia is their ally, and all the while Saudi clerics are lighting a worldwide anti-American fire. God is great.

U.S. Military Presence in the Arabian Peninsula and Other Muslim Countries: Brothers, we also can rely on this U.S. policy. As the Pentagon builds bases in the Islamic world, the U.S. government does not see that it is voluntarily donning the cloak of nineteenth-century European colonialism and imperialism, thereby energizing a new generation of Mujahedin to fight in God's path. U.S. leaders have no conception of how taking over this Sykes-Picot role from the Europeans hurts America, and rallies Muslims to Brother Osama's views. To prove this, Bush's Iraq Study Group has suggested that when U.S. troops are withdrawn from Iraq, some of them should be based on its periphery, perhaps in the Levant and the Arabian Peninsula. Then, in support of the Group's call for broader occupation of Muslim lands, the Zionist U.S. Senator Lieberman also called for stationing U.S. forces in the Land of the Two Holy Mosques. And in late 2006 the Americans began a military intervention in Muslim Somalia, intent—as you predicted years ago, Brother Osama—on destroying Islam there, stealing oil from the Horn of Africa, and building military bases across the Red Sea from blessed Yemen and the Land of the Two Holy Mosques.[32] Brothers, the Americans and their proxies now occupy four Islamic capitals: Kabul, Jerusalem, Baghdad, and Mogadishu, and this colonial reality will not be lost on the minds of Muslims. May God keep the Americans believing that they must broaden their occupation of the Arab heartland and the Muslim world, and ignorant of each Muslim's extremely long historical memory of European imperialism's long record of crimes against Islam.

9. Brothers, I must make one more point about American policy. As I have already said, God has made America blind to the hatred that the impact of their policies in the Islamic world is earning them. But Brothers, they also seem blind to the impact on Muslims of their behavior at Guantanamo Bay, Abu Ghraib prison, toward the holy Koran, their decision to burn the bodies of martyred Taliban mujahedin, and their killing of Afghan and Iraqi civilians.

U.S. leaders treat these issues as manageable public relations problems and do not see, thanks to God for their blindness, that their behavior is causing some Muslims to hate Americans simply because they are Americans. Brother Osama has said that many Americans are "good people" and "wise people" and are therefore hard to hate. But now, may God be praised, their actions at Guantanamo, Abu Ghraib, and toward God's holy book are beginning to make them hated as a people. Brothers, only the Lord of both worlds could have made the Americans take leave of their senses and dress captive mujahedin in hoods, manacles, and orange prison suits; put them in cages and at the end of dog leashes; and then make them watch the desecration of God's book. Brothers, with these acts the Americans as peo-

233

ple have become major inspirers of Muslims to join our jihad. God is truly great!

And, Brothers, Washington's European allies have added to their woes by publishing blasphemous caricatures of our beloved Prophet, may God's peace and blessings be upon him. Also adding to America's woes is Britain's decision, and praise to the Almighty for it, to honor the apostate writer Salman Rushdie with a knighthood for his lust to denigrate God's messenger, may peace be upon him.[33] And all the while, much of the U.S. media approved the publication of the cartoons and Rushdie's vile blasphemies as examples of the freedom of the press that they want Muslims to adopt. Thanks to God for their honesty. Brothers, the Americans are unknowingly sacrificing a precious asset: their reputation for fairness, decency, and as champions of freedom for all peoples. With God's grace many more believers will come to jihad when they learn to hate Americans as well as American policy.

10. To go on, and by God Brothers brace yourselves, I tell you that U.S. leaders in both political parties continue to tell their people that al-Qaeda and its allies have nothing to do with our blessed religion, nothing to do with Great Islam. Indeed, they seem deathly afraid of the word *Islam*; for example, the word only appears in the Iraq Study Group's report as an adjective, as in "Islamic world."[34] And they do not listen even when the Catholic pope—may God punish this formidable opponent of Islam for saying our beloved Prophet is "evil and inhuman"[35]—truthfully warns Western leaders that Muslims see their secularism "as an attack on their most profound convictions." Instead, thanks to God, they viciously rebuke the pope for fomenting discord between Christianity and Islam.[36] Again, only the truly great God could keep Western leaders and peoples from recognizing the plain truth spoken by that accursed Christian preacher.

11. The American leaders also call us criminals, gangsters, deviants, psychopaths, murderers—they tell their people that we represent only "the lunatic fringe of the lunatic fringe of the Muslim world." And so important people like President Bush, Mayor Giuliani, Mrs. Clinton, and hundreds of others within their elite group claim "we will hunt them down one at a time and bring them to justice." Just last spring, for example, the Americans celebrated the death of our valiant Taliban brother Mullah Dadullah—may God accept him as a martyr—as if it would badly hurt the jihad in Afghanistan. U.S. and NATO leaders cited the death as proof that their goal of killing or capturing those they call "terrorists" one at a time is working, ignoring that they have pursued this policy since 1995 and

that there are many more mujahedin now than then.[37] And on this point, reality never interferes with their beliefs and claims. Amazingly, Brothers, even after the British chief of internal security publicly explained that her service was surveilling two hundred al-Qaeda–related organizations in the U.K., with more than sixteen hundred known members—and that there are many more not yet identified—then-Prime Minister Blair reiterated the goal of bringing each of them to justice.[38]

12. Pray God this continues, for it ensures they will not recognize that our movement is large and growing; that your description of U.S. foreign policy as an attack on Islam resonates with hundreds of millions of Muslims, even if they disagree with al-Qaeda's military operations; and that you, Brothers Osama and Ayman, are heroes and leaders in the Islamic world, especially among the youth. U.S. leaders do not know that their identification of you as "gangsters" will offend all those who see you as good and credible leaders in an Islamic world which is held tight by dictators and tyrants using U.S.-made chains.

13. U.S. leaders also refuse to recognize that al-Qaeda's twenty-year campaign to instigate Muslims to jihad across the world is succeeding, with attacks in Madrid and London, the growth of Islamist networks in Europe, North America, Southeast Asia, and Central Asia, and—all praise to God—an increasing flow of Muslim men from around the world to fight as mujahedin in Iraq and Afghanistan. Those fighters who survive—and may God accept those who fall as martyrs—will return to their native lands with military skill to impart to others, and, most important, an ardent faith in God and His promise of victory. For all this, pray God let the Americans continue to believe and loudly preach that we are just "gangsters."

14. And, Brothers, the Americans have not found serious men to lead them—God has blessed us with this reality for nearly twenty years. Six years after the 9/11 raids, U.S leaders have not closed their borders or found out who is in their country. Our brothers working here are as safe as they were on the Tuesday of God's glory. Truly only God could have provided our movement with such a miracle. Astoundingly, Brothers, the American politicians lack the wisdom and moral courage to enforce the immigration laws they have passed. God is great! They refuse to stop illegal immigration because, they loudly assert, "America is a beacon of liberty to the world that we do not want to dim."[39] As you know from al-Qaeda's extensive experience, Brothers, there is nothing more beneficial to the mujahedin than U.S. politicians who prefer that the United States be seen as the "glowing beacon of liberty" rather than a country of enforced laws. Our brothers

now move unnoticed here in a pool of illegal immigrants that exceeds eleven million. Pray God that America long maintains this glow of liberty, which provides a light that warms, guides, and shelters al-Qaeda fighters and the many members of other jihad groups based in the United States.

15. Because the incompetence I have just described is difficult to credit, let me tell you, Brothers, several items that the media are reporting about what America's nonserious leaders have said and done during the year past.

Notwithstanding the raids by the heroic nineteen, may God be pleased with them, the U.S. Department of Homeland Security has for the past two years significantly underfunded the defense of New York City and Washington; only God could have inflicted this blind stupidity on them. And other reports say virtually no U.S. city is prepared to cope with another attack. Indeed, so confused are U.S. officials that the media are reporting that locations in rural America like Kansas, where al-Qaeda has no targets, are far better protected than the country's urban centers. Praise to God, Brothers, the Americans are still at the drawing board.[40]

More than a decade after al-Qaeda's declaration of war, senior FBI officials have said their institution and officers do not need expertise about Muslims, Islam, and the Middle East. This view was supported by the FBI director, may God keep him at his post, a man who also, like his predecessor, has failed to equip his organization with modern computers and communications systems. Truly Brothers, we will derive comfort, safety, and, if God so wills, victory from the arrogant refusal of these men to learn that it is the most essential part of their war against al-Qaeda and its allies to understand Islam, just as we, with God's help, have labored long and hard to understand America and its history. Yet again the Americans' self-defeating contempt for Islam's motivating power is starkly highlighted. Is it not strange, Brothers, that U.S. leaders try to humiliate Muslims as uneducated and medieval, but it is al-Qaeda and its allies that have studied and learned from Sun Tzu and Machiavelli. Clearly, Brothers, the infidels' police forces in Britain, Canada, and even Australia are gaining knowledge about al-Qaeda's activities, and they threaten our operations. We have no such worries in the United States, where the FBI revels in its ignorance of Islam and spends its time digging up farms looking for a man named Hoffa who has been dead more than thirty years and also finds its claim of having found "no evidence" of our brothers in America publicly contradicted by the U.S. director of national intelligence, who says, "There are sleeper cells directly tied to al-Qaeda inside the United States."[41] And more good news for us, Brothers, Bush's Iraq Study Group has recommended that the FBI send more officers to help the Iraqi police. Forgive my sarcasm, Brothers, but one would have thought that the Iraqi apostates have enough trouble already.[42] In addition, the FBI's willful ignorance of Islam and Muslims also seems rife across the U.S. government; recent media stories show that many senior U.S. officials cannot even distinguish between Sunnis and Shias.[43] Brothers we must thank the Almighty God, for only He could have created this situation in a country that brags about the excellence of its education system.

Since 2004, two U.S. intelligence chiefs, Mr. Goss and his successor, Mr. Negroponte, have said they have knowledge of the location of al-Qaeda's leaders, and even of Brother Osama's location.[44] They said all are based in Pakistan, but that the U.S. military would not hunt and attack them there because of respect for the country's sovereignty. Then in December 2004 Mr. Goss proved himself a liar by ordering an attack inside Pakistan on Brother Ayman. In other words, Brothers, U.S. leaders first said they were willing to let us kill Americans rather than upset, anger, and endanger the reign of their agent Musharraf. Then, they changed their minds, tried to kill Brother Ayman, and almost wrecked their ties to the apostate Musharraf; who, as you have written, Brother Ayman, is the most important U.S. ally in the war against us and the only one who has hurt al-Qaeda and impeded its operations.[45] Inexplicably, President Bush followed this blow to Musharraf by traveling to India and agreeing to give U.S. assistance to India's nuclear program, thereby strengthening Pakistan's mortal enemy and shaming Musharraf in front of the Pakistani general officer corps that put him in power and keep him there.[46] Brothers, it is with some embarrassment that I tell you that I cannot explain these counterproductive U.S. actions, but we must thank Him for whom all things are possible for them. To continue, Mr. Negroponte, in early 2007, and his successor, Admiral McConnell, later in the year, publicly implied that Musharraf is a liar by refuting Islamabad's claim of having broken al-Qaeda's back and driven "al-Qaeda remnants" into Afghanistan by asserting that you, Brothers, and a reinvigorated al-Qaeda are operating safely in Pakistani territory.[47] And now, Bush, other U.S. leaders, and their stooge in Kabul, Hamid Karzai, are promoting the downfall of their proxy Musharraf by calling for the restoration of the idolatrous practice of democracy in Pakistan and trying to force the triumph of that brazen female miscreant Benazir Bhutto—and God knows nothing could be more helpful to the mujahedin.[48] Truly, Brothers, the U.S. leaders seem confused, indecisive, and perhaps desperate regarding Pakistan; as the proverb says, Brothers, the Americans "wander around in a daze like a duck hit in the head." By God, Brothers, I tell you only the Lord of the Universe could give us an enemy led by such incompetent men.

Finally, Brothers, and as important to our movement as the foregoing, President Bush, former secretary Rumsfeld, and their gang gave the mujahedin in Iraq a historic and invaluable victory. That victory was over the only American fighters who, as Brother Osama has said, merit our respect—the U.S. Marines. On the brink of success, Bush foolishly ended the Marines' first attack on Fallujah to please their cowardly European friends, people who stupidly believe the mujahedin will respect powerful foes who do not use all the power at their command. In so doing, Bush not only wasted the lives of his best fighters, and all thanks to God for that, but also showed all Muslims that the Sunni mujahedin in Iraq could defeat Marine assaults, and, thereby, that Sunni fighters could match Shia Hezbollah's legendary defeat of the Marines in Beirut. Brothers, the Lord of the Universe has made sure that henceforth all Sunnis will see their mujahedin brothers as the "Victors of First Fallujah," who, with light weapons, bared chests, and the Prophet's banner, stopped and threw back the infidel's best fighters, before being driven away by the enemies' hugely more powerful forces.[49] Almost as if to underscore that victory, Bush's Iraq Study Group clearly told all Muslims that "there is no action the American military can take that . . . can bring success in Iraq."[50] God is truly great!

16. Brothers, there is one more great advantage al-Qaeda enjoys through God's grace, and that is the practice of all U.S. leaders to publicly define the status of our war against America only in terms of the detonation of explosives. There has been much proud crowing and preening among these leaders that al-Qaeda has not attacked in America since the blessed 9/11 raid, and a belief that therefore the United States is winning the war against al-Qaeda. May the almighty God keep them mired in this dream. Brothers, as those who read history know, war is much more than detonating explosives, and the mujahedin's nonexplosive attacks on America, with God's help, have continued with telling effect every day since 9/11. In this regard, I have learned the following in conversations with work colleagues and social acquaintances, and by reading the media and listening to radio

call-in programs. I readily admit these stories are anecdotal, but I believe they faithfully reflect the apprehensive mood of many everyday Americans.

We are slowly changing their way of life. People here are upset and angry with the difficulties of air travel, may God smile on the blessed nineteen for this happy reality, as well as the Pakistani mujahedin in London who made our enemies quiver in fear over the threat to airliners posed by toothpaste tubes.[51] People here also are appalled by security that requires the children of grammar-school classes to empty their pockets and clear metal detectors before entering an art museum.

In the area where I live, near Washington, people worry about the under-siege look of the city. One man said to me in wonder: "Roosevelt did not have this much protection in all of World War II." I also have heard people express anger over what are at times invasive and militarized security procedures in the capital of the world's most powerful nation, often citing the 2004 presidential inauguration as a graphic example. "We behave as if we are scared to death," they said.

Americans are worried, thanks to God, by the spiraling federal budget deficit. Brothers, it is impossible to imagine the amount of money the U.S. government is spending on what it calls "homeland security" and on the wars it is waging to kill Muslims in Afghanistan, Iraq, Palestine, Somalia, and elsewhere. In 2006, for example, the Congress raised the debt ceiling to $9 trillion to accommodate the expenses of the U.S. war on Islam.[52] The Iraq Study Group's report, moreover, helpfully told al-Qaeda and its allies that Brother Osama's bleed-America-to-bankruptcy strategy is working in Iraq, that Washington is spending $8 billion per month there and that it cannot sustain that rate. More recently, the U.S. media have reported that the strain is increasing and spending in Iraq and Afghanistan is now approaching $12 billion per month. And a famous American economist and financier recently published a book saying "the U.S. Government is in a weakened financial position to respond to another terrorist attack."[53] And so when al-Qaeda next strikes the United States, with God's permission, Americans will know that all this spending has been for naught, and that immense additional amounts will be required. We will then, if God permits, tear the heart out of their economy and their morale as well. As an indication of the future, the warning of more attacks issued by Brother Osama in January 2006 drove up the price of oil and gold and caused U.S. stocks to drop by 200 points.[54] Imagine, Brothers, the damage that the mujahedin will cause when, if God wills it, our words are again replaced by bullets and bombs inside the United States.

Americans are frightened. I have heard much discussion about their worries of more al-Qaeda attacks—perhaps with nuclear weapons—and recent polling here shows more than half of those questioned believe that another al-Qaeda attack is inevitable and that it will be more damaging than that of our nineteen brothers, may God reward them in paradise. Moreover, Americans are both angry and fearful that the erosion of their civil liberties is worsening, because of President Bush's eavesdropping on telephone conversations inside the United States, secretly accessing private bank records, and profiling each American air traveler. May God worsen these fears.[55] It is as you have said, Brothers: Because Americans have not experienced war on their soil since the 1860s, they regard necessary war measures as evidence of incipient dictatorship. Brother Osama's 2001 judgment has proven to be accurate: al-Qaeda needs to do nothing to terrorize Americans because their leaders and the media will reliably perform that task. And nothing clarifies that reality more than the enhanced fears caused, not by a new al-Qaeda attack, but by the mid-2007 publication of the National Intelligence Estimate on our presence in the United States and the media's reporting about it.[56]

Iraq: God's Gift to His Mujahedin

17. Before ending this message, Brothers, I want to specifically focus on Iraq, where the great and happy news is that God seems to have rendered U.S. leaders ignorant of the wondrous opportunities they have opened for all mujahedin by invading and occupying the country. And just as clearly, these men have yet to fathom the dimensions of the victory, and the surge of confidence they will hand to those fighting in God's cause when they decide to leave Iraq, and later Afghanistan, pray God, without success.

Let us first praise God for a miracle that only He could have delivered. The Americans are now occupying the three most holy places in Islam: the Arabian Peninsula, Iraq, and Jerusalem.[57] Regarding Jerusalem, U.S. leaders know but shield from Americans the fact that they are viewed by Muslims as interchangeable with Israelis. Muslim hatred for Israelis, praise be to God, also accrues to Americans, and will be increased by Washington's recent gift of $30 billion worth of U.S. arms to Israel to help it murder Muslims. And by invading and occupying Iraq, the U.S. government has created a magnet for mujahedin even more powerful than that which Moscow created in Afghanistan, the first blessed land of jihad.

And, Brother Osama, by occupying Iraq, U.S. leaders, through their disregard or ignorance of your words, have made your predictions come true in the eyes of the Muslim ummah. You said: America will destroy strong Muslim states, and it did. You said: America will destroy Muslim regimes that threaten Israel, and it did. You said: America will seize Muslim oil, and it did. You said: America will try to destroy our religion and occupy our holy places, and it did. You said: America will replace God's law with blasphemous, man-made laws and secular governments, and it did. Praise to the Almighty God for showing you the truth, Brother Osama.

And, Brothers, God has now properly validated your call for a defensive jihad in accordance with the terms of His blessed religion. In their intensely legalistic way, the Americans always took delusional solace from the fact that neither of you is a trained Islamic scholar. They convinced themselves that, because you lacked diplomas, no Muslim could legitimately answer your call to jihad; apparently they have never heard of another non-scholar mujahid named Saladin. But now the U.S. invasion of Iraq has called forth fatwas from many well-credentialed Islamic scholars. These decrees declare a defensive jihad in exactly the terms you used.[58] Praise to God, the Sustainer of both worlds.

Most important for our movement, U.S. leaders do not appear to see that in Iraq they have opened a door for us to infiltrate our message and mujahedin into Turkey, Kuwait, Saudi Arabia, Syria, and Jordan and through the latter two to Lebanon and Israel. The late mujahid Abu Musab al-Zarqawi, may God reward him, attacked Jordan and Israel from Iraq, and the leaders of al-Qaeda in Lebanon, Palestine, and Syria have broadcast their readiness to attack Israel. Indeed, in the summer of 2007 our brothers in Lebanon stubbornly fought the Christian Lebanese army for more than a month.[59] Brothers, the Americans see Iraq as honey to attract the mujahedin so they can be killed there; and President Bush and his administration teach the American people that if the U.S. military fights our brothers in Iraq, they will not have to be fought in the United States. Do they not know there are 1.4 billion Muslims? The Americans will understand this is nonsense when they find themselves fighting, if God wills it, the mujahedin in both places, and many others as well. Washington, thanks to God, fails to see that the U.S. military presence in Iraq not only gives the mujahedin U.S.

targets there but also helps satisfy al-Qaeda's goal of securing contiguous safe haven from which to infiltrate fighters into the Levant, Turkey, and the birthplace of our Prophet, may God's peace and blessings be upon him. Even at this late date, Brothers, American leaders have still failed to recognize—and all thanks be to the Lord of both worlds for their blindness—that they have built a west-bound highway for the mujahedin that leads from Afghanistan through Iraq to the Levant and beyond. It will be too late, God willing, when Washington discovers that the flow of non-Iraqi mujahedin through Iraq into the Levant, Turkey, and the Arabian Peninsula is far more dangerous to their interests than the mujahedin entering Iraq from Syria, Jordan, and Saudi Arabia.

What Next?: With God's Grace, Press On

18. For now, Brothers, and all thanks to God for this, the good news for the mujahedin outweighs the bad by a large measure. But we must remember that the United States is a powerful enemy, and historically one terrible in war when it is ably led and its people are roused to united and focused anger. Based on my own decade of experience living and working here, Brothers, I believe the American people are much tougher and more willing to kill than are their leaders. We must always keep this reality in mind to prevent us becoming arrogant and overconfident, characteristics which recent U.S. administrations have shown through their constantly expressed contempt for the mujahedin as mere criminals: this, praise to God, is a devastating vulnerability for them. Our main advantage now lies in the failure of U.S. leaders to understand their Islamist enemy. Part of this failure is due to their woeful lack of historical knowledge, both ours and, most surprisingly, their own. The rest is due to the moral cowardice that prevents U.S. leaders from enforcing immigration laws and frankly debating their foreign policies because of the potential for negative domestic political consequences.

19. We also greatly benefit from the paralyzing and contemptible fear U.S. leaders have of fully employing America's overwhelming military power, a fear shown by President Bush, his top political and military officials, and Democratic Party leaders when they repeatedly say the U.S. government intends to wage what they call a "Long War" against the mujahedin.[60] By God, Brothers, this seems to mean that the mujahedin, with God's permission, have driven the Americans crazy. They appear ready to sacrifice all of the advantages that a focused, unlimited application of military power would afford, and instead fight

us in insurgency situations all around the world, a scenario where the patient and dedicated mujahedin will surely bleed America to death in terms of money, lives, and political unity. Truly, Brothers, these Americans are astounding; history suggests that only fools would reinforce failure by sending five more brigades to engage the mujahedin in house-to-house fighting in Baghdad. If God permits, Vice President Cheney will soon find it is the mujahedin, not the Americans, who have the "stomach" for such a fight.[61]

20. Also, Brothers, the futility of the "Long War" approach by America was underscored by Bush's Iraq Study Group, which said, "U.S. ground forces have been stretched to the breaking point," and that Washington has "little reserve force to call on if it needs ground forces elsewhere in the world," which presumably also dooms to failure their intervention in Somalia.[62] The Group's report also said that the God-loving mujahedin had so worn out the U.S. military that it will take at least five years and massive but undetermined funding to restore it to pre–Iraq-war readiness.[63] Praise to God, Brothers, al-Qaeda's aim to spread American forces as thinly as possible to dilute their ability to focus their unprecedented military power appears to be succeeding. While it is hard to believe, God has validated Brother Osama's prediction that al-Qaeda needs only to send two men carrying an al-Qaeda banner to any spot on earth, and the U.S. military will rush there.[64]

21. Overall, Brothers, it is my assessment, and God knows best, that the U.S. leaders' combination of historical ignorance and moral cowardice is, with God's support, a potential war-winner for the mujahedin. No U.S. administration can develop a strategy for victory over al-Qaeda and its allies as long as they refuse to listen to and understand what we tell them about our motivation. However, Brothers, it is necessary to continue waging war against them aggressively, ruthlessly, and globally; we must resist the arrogance which would cause us to rely on the Americans remaining ignorant forever. U.S. leaders may someday, and may God make it far in the future, recognize that their country's destiny is in their hands; they alone can change the foreign policies that are helping the mujahedin's drive toward God's victory. Indeed, last year a Republican presidential candidate truthfully said that al-Qaeda attacked Washington and New York because of U.S. intervention in the Muslim world. But, and all thanks to God for this, his fellow candidates and most of the media ridiculed him and demanded he retract his words. This episode, however, points out that only the Americans can change the policies that are powering our campaign for God's glory, and that fact, for

al-Qaeda, is a constant threat to the effectiveness and durability of our effort to keep Muslims focused on the far American enemy, and not those so much closer to home.[65]

As you know, Brothers, God told our beloved Prophet, may God's peace and blessings be upon him, that He will only help those who do everything possible to help themselves, and so we must continue to carry this war to the Americans while they remain asleep. Our strategy must continue to be, as the Prophet, God's peace and blessings be upon him, said to Satan, "I will give thee no respite."[66]

22. And my final prayer is that all praise is due Allah, Lord of the worlds, and may His peace and blessings be on our master Muhammad and upon his family and companions. And, Brothers, may Allah's peace and blessing be upon you.

PART IV

WHERE TO FROM HERE?

It is natural to man to indulge in the illusions of hope. We are apt to
shut our eyes against a painful truth—and listen to the song of the
syren, till she transforms us into beasts. Is this the part of wise men,
engaged in a great and arduous struggle for liberty? Are we disposed
to be of the number of those, who having eyes, see not, and having
ears, hear not, the things which so nearly concern their temporal sal-
vation? For my part, whatever anguish of spirit it might cost, I am
willing to know the whole truth; to know the worst and provide for it.

Patrick Henry, 1775

Americans should take Patrick Henry's advice and accept the anguish of
seeing that the United States stands at a uniquely dire moment in its history; indeed, America stands at a moment that may be unique in terms of
the history of any Great Power that has ever existed. If tomorrow the
fighters of al-Qaeda or another Islamist insurgent group detonate a nuclear
device in an American city—or cities, given al-Qaeda's predilection for
multiple, simultaneous attacks—the U.S. government would find itself
with an unprecedented national emergency, stunning numbers of dead,
besieged by a population rabid for revenge, and having no meaningful military or political target against which to unleash the earth's most powerful
military. Washington might temporarily dodge this reality by pulverizing
Iran, which would have had nothing to do with the attack, or by destroying
a Muslim holy site, such as Mecca or Medina. The sole U.S. option of irrational military retaliation, in itself, speaks eloquently about the effective

245

strategy of our Islamist foes and the degree to which American leaders have played into their hands. But when the smoke from those retaliatory attacks cleared, the American governing elite would have rallied even more of the Muslim world to the support of the nuclear attackers and would find itself detested and untrusted by American citizens. On that day U.S. political leaders would be as bankrupt in terms of domestic support and empathy as they are today in terms of intellectual capacity and common sense.

While there has been an abundance of recommendations about how to service this uniquely dangerous moment in U.S. history, most have been predictable—and useless—manifestations of a continuing Cold War–era worldview. Politicians, pundits, and generals of all persuasions, as discussed throughout this book, stick to the good-vs.-evil scenario: "The Islamists hate us for our liberties and freedoms, not for what we do, and we will bring them to justice one man at a time." From academics and think-tank denizens come such gems as: we "must work with moderate and liberal Muslims to prevent extremists from taking over mosques"[1]; "it is necessary to establish an anti-defamation league to monitor such [Islamist] hate speech . . . Anti-American or anti-Western hate speech is unacceptable"[2] and "we must divorce the Islamist mujahedin from their faith by calling them proponents of 'Arab Fascism.' "[3] From the same sources come such enemy-intimidating ideas as "stigmatize the extremists and their war" by changing the war on terror to " 'the war on jihadis' and 'the war on jihadism' "[4] "demonstrate our commitment to the rule of law"[5] and, "replace the language of warfare . . . with the language of development and construction and the patience that goes along with it."[6]

Having prepared America to triumph semantically, most policy recommendations then default to the Cold War gold standard: American intervention everywhere. The U.S. government "will resist any and all efforts to establish governments on these [Islamist] principles anywhere in the world," and while doing this, Washington and its allies must "find ways to promote orderly and peaceful development."[7] How do we do the latter? With money from U.S. taxpayers of course! Washington's contributions after an Arab-Israeli settlement must be a "substantial, conspicuous, and inspiring sum,"[8] and U.S. government funds should be used "to support the development [in the Muslim world] of a resilient civil society and moderate opposition political parties."[9] Also needed, naturally, are more U.S. funds for participation in "global governance," new multilateral institutions, the "restructuring and reform of the UN," and America's role as the "guarantor" of "human dignity." [10]

And finally the crowning touch, one that surely demonstrates the homogeneity of the U.S. governing elite from far right to far left. For all the hatred that most academic and think tankers direct at the neoconservatives, their post-9/11 policy recommendations reflect just as great a willingness to intervene and go democracy-crusading, albeit with dollars and do-gooders rather than guns. "Only democratization," wrote one academic who would surely be appalled to be put in the neoconservative camp, "will directly attack the jihadist ideology while creating governments that are more responsive to their citizens." [11] Another writes that the "U.S. government must show strong support for such a [anti–hate speech] program to support universal tolerance and peace." [12] And yet another, a just-war scholar apparently intent on involving her countrymen in just about every war possible, writes, "As the world's superpower, America bears the responsibility to help guarantee that international stability, whether much of the world wants it or not." [13]

Generally absent from most of these recommendations is any notion that there should be substantive changes in U.S. foreign policy; that America should start looking out for itself first and foremost; or that, heaven forbid, the level of U.S. military power applied against our Islamist enemies must be massively increased. To be sure, very few of America's elite have signed on to the timeless wisdom of the motto of the *National Review*'s John Derbyshire: "Rubble Doesn't Cause Trouble." [14] Indeed, the whole elite seems to hold a sneaking suspicion that it really does not have a clue about how to defeat bin Laden et al. "We are going to have to learn to live with it [terrorism]," concludes one academic musing from Radcliffe and Harvard, "as the price of living in a complex world." [15] Which only goes to show that, sadly, the Cold War's devotees of nuance, as well as its masters of the international political ballet, are still with us and are prepared to see untold numbers of Americans die rather than consider anything so gauche as using Reagan's we win–they lose formula to bring victory over the Islamists.

Given the quality of the foregoing advice—it is what Patrick Henry called "the song of the syren"—there clearly is no certainty that a nuclear calamity can be prevented. Americans must begin to do the thinking that their elites have proved themselves incapable of doing. Foreign policy must be changed to focus only on genuine national-security interests; nonessential political, diplomatic, and military intervention abroad must be stopped; and when the use of military force is mandatory, it must be applied with more ferocity and less discrimination. Domestically, homeland security must become a reality and not just a catchphrase used to justify enormous, nonproductive federal expenditures. And finally, a beginning must be made to return the American political system to the framework of responsible republican government crafted by the Founders. The people themselves must become the engines of their own and their country's survival. And time is running short for them to do so. They must examine their history afresh; relearn its lessons to know where they came from, where they are, and where they are going; and prepare to confront and defeat some of the most dangerous foes their republic has faced. "To see what others have done in important junctures, and to have both their merits and mistakes analyzed by a competent critic," wrote a talented citizen-soldier in Mr. Lincoln's armies in words pertinent to the need of today's Americans to act in their country's defense,

> rouses one's mind to grapple with the problem before it, and begets a generous determination to rival in one own's sphere of action the brilliant deeds of soldiers who have made a name in other times. Then, the example of the vigorous way in which history will at last deal with those who fail when the pinch comes, tends to keep a man up to his work and make him avoid the rock on which so many have split, the disposition to take refuge in doing nothing when he finds it difficult to decide what should be done.[16]

CHAPTER 8

A Humble Suggestion–
America First

The advice nearest to my heart and deepest in my convictions is that the Union of the States be cherished and perpetuated. Let the open enemy to it be regarded as Pandora with her box open; and the disguised one as the serpent creeping with his deadly wiles into paradise.

James Madison, 1834

We have not journeyed all the way across the centuries, across the oceans, across the mountains, across the prairies, because we are made of sugar candy . . . If anybody likes to play rough, we can play rough too.

Winston Churchill, 1941

Writing in the 1780s, Great Britain's King George III squarely faced up to the fact that the British military had been defeated by George Washington's army and that Britain's thirteen English-speaking North American colonies were irretrievably lost to his realm. "America is lost," George III wrote, then went on to survey what was to come next. "Must we fall beneath the blow? Or have we resources that may repair the mischief? What are those resources? Should they be sought in distant Regiouns [sic] held by precarious tenure, or should we seek them at home in exertions of a new policy?"[1] Ironically, the leaders of the nation established by General Washington's victory today find themselves in much the same position as George III. They have lost the wars in Iraq and Afghanistan and must now disengage from them with as much decorum as possible. The longer they wait, the more difficult it will be to prevent a Saigon-like exit. For Americans generally, the unavoidable conclusion is that their political leaders have bitten off overseas far more than the country can ever reasonably hope to chew. Americans and their leaders will henceforth have to decide, as did George III and his ministers, whether to continue adventuring about "in distant Regiouns," or seek to find national security "at home in exertions of a new policy."

The bottom line for America is that the war against bin Laden, al-Qaeda, and their allies was and is one that we must fight. As Abdel Bari Atwan has written, "We ignore al-Qaeda at our own risk. It is not going to go away."[2] We are, however, in the entirely enviable position of being able to decide how big a war we need to fight, and we can choose, once we evacuate Iraq and Afghanistan, where we need to fight it. As I have written previously, the United States is not the main enemy of bin Laden and other Islamists, and while this reality may dent our collective sense of self-importance, it is the beginning of wisdom. America is simply in the way of Islamist forces and so prevents the attainment of their goals in the Islamic world; that is, to destroy the family-owned and U.S.-supported Muslim tyrannies that have ruled the region since 1945 and to destroy Israel. This is, of course, serious business, but it is America's business only to the extent that Washington allows it to be, and that extent will be determined by whether or not the U.S. government maintains the status quo of its policies toward the Muslim world, energy supplies, and Israel. Since 9/11 the Bush administration, all of Congress, and the country's bipartisan governing elite have behaved as if the threats to the Muslim tyrannies and Israel were equally threats to the United States and its citizens. What this means is that U.S. leaders have decided to forgo fighting a necessary but limited war in favor of fighting a worldwide and very likely unending war, one that holds every possibility of causing Americans to live a lifestyle shaped by war and their enemies' actions, and not by their traditions, preferences, and aspirations.

What Is in Pandora's Box?

To use James Madison's metaphor, Osama bin Laden and the forces he leads and inspires have long held Pandora's box open so U.S. leaders could examine its contents. They do not like what they see, however, because from the box are flowing woes for America that derive from the cumulative impact of thirty years of their counterproductive foreign policies. The U.S. governing elite has allowed—indeed, it has promoted—the steady development of a situation in which the energy resources upon which the U.S. economy depends are controlled by foreigners, among whom are Muslim leaders and regimes that regard our culture, political system, and dominant faith with contempt; work actively to spread a violent, anti-American brand of Islam in the United States and the societies of our European allies; and no longer believe that U.S. military power merits respect. Our immense and growing federal deficit is increasingly held by China and Saudi Arabia, the first a nation that appears headed to become America's main economic rival, and the latter, already our energy master, a nation that funds the worldwide spread of a faith that encourages the acceptance of bin Laden's message and therefore runs directly counter to U.S. national-security interests. In addition, our elite has put the United States in the addle-brained position of backing both sides in a vicious religious war between Israelis and Arabs, thereby making us part of an endless war in which we have nothing at stake but the emotions, religious affiliation, and divided loyalties of two small segments of our population.

Because of our governing elites' willful blindness to this reality, the most important decision that can be made by an independent people, the decision of peace or war, is drifting ever further from American hands. Unexpected and disruptive fighting in Saudi Arabia's oil-rich Eastern Province or in the Niger Delta would, for example, prompt the large-scale deployment of U.S. military forces to restore reliable pumping, processing, and export in one or both locations. The U.S. president and Congress of the day would publicly go through a set of rushed "high-level deliberations," quickly "consult with allies," and then would roll out full-blown Cold War rhetoric and lie to Americans that "freedom is threatened" and "aggression must be crushed." It will sound like that old-time religion and might temporarily rally Americans. But it all will be play-acting: America would be on the way to war because of Washington's decades-old, near-criminal negligence regarding energy policy.

Likewise, U.S. participation in future Middle East wars is now virtually automatic; as the bipartisan Iraq Study Group Report recently declared: "No American administration—Democratic or Republican—will ever abandon Israel."[3] Written by a group of unelected Cold Warriors, the report thereby definitively formulated the long-unstated reality that Washington has surrendered control over the decision for war or peace in the Middle East to Israel's government of the day or any Muslim regime that chooses to attack Israel. In sum, the U.S. governing elite's longtime use of blithe, best-case-scenario operating assumptions—i.e., the market will ensure adequate supplies of inexpensive oil, and the Arab-Israeli peace process will succeed—has vitiated the Founders' careful, checks-and-balances-laden delineation of the process by which the United States would go to war, a process meant to leave that decision in the hands of the elected members of the U.S. Congress, not to the president, and certainly not to foreigners seeking our wealth and military protection. But in many cases it is foreigners who will decide when the United States goes to war, and to add insult to injury, today's political environment tends to label Americans who object to this reality as less than loyal.

This situation also highlights what today may be the most important and potentially destructive class division existing in U.S. society. U.S. politicians, the media, and our governing elite generally spend a great deal of time, talk, and ink describing black-vs.-white, rich-vs.-poor, educated-vs.-less-educated, old-vs.-young, and English-speaking-vs.-non-English-speaking divisions in American society. Such divisions undeniably exist and need focused, consistent, and sustained remedial attention, especially in the current environment in which Washington's refusal to enforce federal immigration and border-control laws sharpens many of the just-noted societal divisions. But the greatest and most dangerous divide in American society is between our governing elites—political, economic, military, and media—and the great bulk of workaday Americans on the issues of foreign policy and war. Nonelite Americans are slowly coming to confront a reality in which those who govern them are eager to be "citizens of the world" and are more concerned with affairs outside the United States then they are with fixing such daunting domestic problems as illegal immigration and funding for Social Security. Even leading private-sector Americans do not seem immune from this aspiration. With so much to do in furthering equity, health care, and basic infrastructure rehabilitation, our leading and richest citizens prefer to donate their excess funds to foreign endeavors. Bill Gates, Ted Turner, Warren Buffett, and others have adopted an America-second attitude and are engaged in large, high-profile, and

Davos-pleasing donations outside the country that nurtures, protects, and awards them breathtaking tax deductions. And now Bill Clinton, the ultimate European-wannabe ringmaster for this circus of aspiring world citizens, is strutting about the world seeking donations for humanitarian activities outside America. Even President Bush's multibillion-dollar plan to combat HIV-AIDS in Africa seems an oddly ranked priority when the District of Columbia has an AIDS problem worse than some countries in sub-Saharan Africa.

The most dangerous aspect of the division between the domestic focus of Americans and the international fixation of their elite, however, lies in the elite's casy willingness to sacrifice the lives of the former's sons and daughters in wars meant to install freedom and democracy in the Islamic world. These men and women have consciously made the decision that they will steadily spend the lives of our children to bring democracy, women's rights, parliamentary government, human rights, and secularism to those who want no part of any of them in the Westernized form that is offered. And even if they did want them, it is no part of the U.S. government's responsibility or constitutional writ to spend the lives and treasure of Americans to satisfy the desires of foreigners.

What we are seeing today in Afghanistan is a perfect example of the willingness of U.S. leaders to spend the lives of America's young for patently unobtainable goals, and why it is our elite—and not the Islamists—who can be accurately characterized as Madison's disguised serpent creeping into our paradise in North America. The U.S. mission in Afghanistan was to kill Osama bin Laden, Ayman al-Zawahiri, and as many of their lieutenants, foot soldiers, and Mullah Omar's Taliban as possible. Our mission was strictly military in nature, accomplishable given the immense power of thc U.S. military, and needing to be done quickly and in a way that would leave behind enough smoldering physical wreckage and high enough piles of corpses to (a) make future Afghan regimes think twice about hosting America's enemies and (b) leave the clear idea in the minds of all Muslims that they can think and say what they will of the United States, but the cost of actually killing or helping to kill Americans is horrendous.

This limited and doable task was never given a thought, however, as our bipartisan governing elite blithely ignored the absolute need for a thorough, north-to-south military flaying of our Islamist enemies in Afghanistan and instead undertook a project to build an America-like democracy in the mountains of the Hindu Kush and the deserts of Khandahar. Instead of our soldiers and Marines fighting, being maimed, and dying to eliminate the threat to America, they are doing so to make sure Afghans can vote—whether they want to or not, or even understand what they are doing—and so that a defined portion of the Afghan parliament is reserved for female Afghan parliamentarians. In other words, the lives of our military-children are being sacrificed so that U.S. leaders can bleat and preen in international conferences about the pride they take in bringing democracy and freedom to Afghanistan's unwashed Muslim masses. In the era of the all-volunteer military, of course, precious few U.S. leaders have any children serving in the military. It is at least a point of curiosity to wonder how today's gold-star mothers can bear to have lost a son or daughter to sate the democracy-mongering of the U.S. governing elite. Knowing, in years past, that a son or daughter perished to help protect America from the genuine national security threats posed by Nazism, Japanese barbarism, or Bolshevism would have been difficult enough. It would take an odd mindset indeed for any parent to be able to take comfort in knowing their child was killed so Mrs. Muhammad can vote, vamp, and abort.

Iraq is another case of the U.S. governing elite embarking on a look-how-great-we-are exercise designed to bring secular democracy to Muslims, the blood-and-treasure bill to be paid, as always, by Americans whose leaders care not a whit about protecting them or their children. As noted in Chapter 4, Saddam Hussein and Bashir al-Assad were strong, ruthless, and reliable de facto U.S. allies in the war against Sunni Islamist militancy. They were the cork in the bottle's neck that prevented the easy westward flow of Islamist fighters from South Asia to the Levant, Turkey, Europe, and the Arabian Peninsula. Neither regime needed convincing, arms, or funding from the United States to resist and persecute the Islamists; as is almost always the case, regimes that are scared to death for their survival—as were those of Saddam and al-Assad—make the best allies. Faced with the chance to use this cost-free bulwark, the Bush administration and Congress destroyed it in the name of trying to outdo Woodrow Wilson, a human scourge who is not often enough ranked with the twentieth century's top bloodletters. Unsatisfied with simply annihilating al-Qaeda, the one foe who could attack in the United States, the Bush team embarked on a second, democracy-crusading mission that showed them to be ignorant not only of the Muslim world but of how long it has taken to develop a functioning, equitable republican society in their own country. They scored what may well be a singular historical achievement: they were strangers in a strange land both at home and abroad. And now the American people are paying for it, and their children face a decade or more of fighting the current and, most assuredly, future wars that the Bush administration and Congress are destined to leave behind.

Time to Play Rough

Recommendations for how to conduct the U.S. struggle against the Islamist threat have ranged, as we saw at the start of this section, from the Cold War standard (America must intervene abroad so "that democratic civil society can be built or rebuilt"[4]) to the simply insipid (America must "isolate the terrorists and inoculate their potential recruits from them"[5]). Is there a doctor in the house? Clearly, such thinking lines each side of the road to perdition. But give the devil his due—to resurrect the durable manliness that Churchill claimed brought us safely through the travail of centuries will not be easy. Everything that needs to be done at home and abroad is hard, painful, and fraught with danger, but thanks to God—as our Islamist enemies would say—all that needs doing is in our own hands to do. We need no other country's indulgence or resources to rectify the dilemmas of our own manufacturing, but we do need what we have sorely lacked for the last three presidencies, leaders with courage, determination, common sense, bloodymindedness, and a fiercely America-first orientation. When these leaders emerge, and American history gives us hope they can, they must make the home front job one. Until the continental United States is secured to the greatest extent possible in the three areas discussed below, it can do nothing overseas beyond the current and bloody attempt to avoid defeats that are too obvious.

At a moment when the United States is fighting two losing wars and also supporting other peoples' wars, it seems counterintuitive to claim that U.S. defense priorities should be at home. But that is the case. Indeed, there is no better advice for Americans and their leaders, in conducting their necessary war against al-Qaeda–led Islamist forces, than that which is dispensed to each airline passenger before every takeoff: in the event of losing air pressure in the cabin, be sure to put on your own oxygen mask first before trying to help others. Washington's failure to heed this advice is most apparent in the areas of immigration and border control, securing the Former Soviet Union's (FSU) nuclear arsenal, and energy policy.

Since the United States figuratively lost cabin pressure on 9/11, Washington has been gadding about the world trying to put oxygen masks on foreigners. Our military results to date show the validity of the airlines' advice against creating a lose-lose situation: we have not affixed the foreigners' masks and so are losing overseas, while at home we are gasping because we have not put the needed flow of oxygen and common sense to the design of domestic security. Why in the world are U.S. leaders and elites so border-challenged? In Afghanistan, Washington refused to close the border with Pakistan, and as we are seeing today, the Taliban and al-Qaeda escaped to regroup, rearm, train, and fight another day. In Iraq, the president did not order the U.S. military to close the borders, and so the country's Islamist insurgents, Sunni and Shia, have had a constant and reliable flow of fighters, ordnance, and funding, provided by the private and public sectors of neighboring countries, with which to kill U.S. service personnel. In the continental United States, the majority of U.S. politicians, academics, new-age Christian do-gooders, and antinational organizations—be they human rights, refugee rights, or women's rights groups—have prevented the lawful and effective control of U.S. borders with Mexico and Canada.

A pox on all of them. In America's war with Islamists the only place to start is with the physical security of the United States. Because our bipartisan elite has refused to control either our borders or illegal immigration, law enforcement agencies at all levels of government—local, state, and federal—have been left without even a fighting chance to defeat our U.S.-based Islamist enemies or those who are coming in from abroad. As long as the immigration-and-borders status quo remains, police agencies will be working against an undocumented pool of aliens that grows by the hour. In this context, the billions of dollars that Washington has spent to install electronic- and biodetection gear at official border crossings, ports, and airports is of use only if the Islamists are stupid enough to walk through an official entry point—whether at Tijuana or Detroit-Windsor—wearing I-love-Osama T-shirts and carrying AK-47s, explosives, al-Qaeda identification cards, or WMD components. Unfortunately for America, al-Qaeda's fighters have proven to be anything but stupid, and they are most unlikely to help us defend the United States by exposing themselves to the world's most sophisticated detection equipment. In essence, we have, since 2001, spent untold billions beefing up security at official border-crossing points—which still allowed more than 21,000 illegal aliens to enter America since October 2005—and are now equipped to reliably interdict only the unimaginably careless or certifiably idiotic Islamist fighters. This failure also undercuts the unavoidably limited impact of the many admirable tactical victories that U.S. military and intelligence personnel have scored overseas. These men and women are executing Washington's clearly inadequate policy of killing or arresting the Islamist fighters "one man at a time"—which has minimal negative impact on an extremely numerous enemy—only to find that their leaders have done nothing to prevent the fighters they do not apprehend or kill from getting into the United States and scoring a strategic victory.

How to proceed? Well, the best answer would be to deploy the U.S. Army and Marines along U.S. land borders to prevent the entry of illegals until an effective network of fences, trenches, watch towers, radars, and—if necessary—minefields can be built in a crash program along the Canadian and Mexican borders. But the world's best and most expensive military is fully deployed overseas in losing Wilsonian wars meant to install the secular democracies that Muslims are resisting to the death. And even if U.S. forces were not stretched so thin, those elected to run the federal government have, for decades, failed completely, knowingly, and deliberately to ensure the physical security of U.S. borders. On this issue, Americans today find themselves in what Thomas Paine described as the "intolerable state" of being "exposed to the same miseries by a government, which we might expect in a country without government."[6]

Currently, it is best to let federal officials babble lies about "greatly improved Homeland Security" and act instead at the state and local levels to protect Americans by taking hold of the responsibility for domestic security that Washington long ago abdicated. This means that state and local governments must effectively defy the federal government by working together; this is the only means by which U.S. domestic security can begin to be protected. At times this defiance will take the form of state governors using the same state-government powers they invoke when manmade or natural disasters occur; at other times, defiance will require blatantly refusing to obey Washington's edicts. But in either case state governors must for now be the leading agents of this defiance. If America is to be protected, the governors must work across party lines and focus solely on the security of their citizens and nation.

The governors should exert their control over the military reserve units that fall under state jurisdiction and refuse to transfer control of them to the federal government. The governors should then mobilize and deploy these units to staff and administer state-mandated, border-control regimes to stop the flow of illegal immigration. Of course all governors do not have a border-control problem, but all governors do suffer from the adverse consequences derived from those who do. If extra military manpower is needed by the governors on the front lines of this federally mandated and protected immigration debacle—such as those in California, Arizona, Washington, Texas, New York, Michigan, and New Mexico—the governors of interior states who do not have contiguous borders with negligent, apathetic, or ill-intentioned foreign powers should provide it. If federal authorities threaten legal or physical action against the states, the governors must defy them. Washington will quickly find that the electorate, in time of war, will rally to governors who act to protect them when the federal government will not. At this point Washington also would find itself impotent: can any American imagine a U.S. soldier shooting a fellow citizen for defying the federal government in an effort to protect all citizens?

The governors can also use their control over military reserves to begin to rein in the president's unilateral and unconstitutional war-making ability. Nothing in our Constitution is clearer than the requirement for Congress to declare war. In *Federalist 69* Alexander Hamilton stressed that the U.S. Constitution ensured that the president's ability to make war would not equal that of the British king. The president's power to make war "would be nominally the same with that of Great Britain," Hamilton wrote, "but in substance much inferior to it" because the powers to declare war and raise and regulate military forces "all which by the constitution . . . appertain to the Legislature."[7] Our first and greatest president respected this limit on his power. "The constitution vests the power of declaring war in the Congress," George Washington wrote, "[and] therefore no offensive expedition of importance can be undertaken until after they shall have deliberated upon the subject and authorized such a measure."[8] The U.S. military's reserve forces, including those commanded by state governors, are key components of America's war-making ability; without them large, long-duration wars overseas are not possible. Because the federal legislature since 1941 has allowed the president to effectively abrogate the constitutional requirement that Congress declare war, the governors must begin to deny the federal government this vital military manpower for use overseas unless Congress has formally declared war, thereby negating the ability of a president to take America to war simply because he or she is so inclined. There are, after all, few better definitions of a tyranny than a state where the decision to go to war rests with one individual. By retaining state military units under their command, the governors will provoke a long-needed constitutional confrontation between the electorate and the federal government that may at last return constitutional sanity to the issue of making war. Such actions would not, of course, be meant to make America vulnerable or render it unable to wage war abroad. Rather, they are meant to help destroy an unconstitutional power that has been assumed by presidents and to make domestic security certain and reliable, without which winning victory over our enemies overseas is, in any event, an illusion.

Unfortunately for Americans, the state governors cannot do all that must be done. Although it does not at first blush appear to be a matter of domestic-security policy, the securing of the Former Soviet Union's (FSU) nuclear arsenal must be a top homeland-security goal if the continental United States is to be protected. As noted, sixteen years after the fall of the USSR, the Cooperative Threat Reduction Program (1991) for securing the FSU's nuclear weapons is less than half complete and has been reduced in personnel and funding during the tenures of presidents Bill Clinton and George W. Bush. This is horrifying and unconscionable. A nuclear attack in the United States by our Islamist foes would cause untold human casualties, catastrophic economic and environmental damage, and requirements for rescue, quarantining, martial law, and reconstruction on a scale that could be addressed only by the resources of the U.S. military, thereby constraining the ability of those forces to operate overseas. Harvard's Graham Allison has desribed such an attack in the United States as "the ultimate preventable catastrophe," but so far Washington has not even done the minimum to reduce the chance of such a calamity to as near to zero as possible.

Additionally, only the federal government can lead the Manhattan

Project–like effort that is required to release the United States from energy dependence on governments who are our enemies, who cannot control their own territory and ensure reliable energy production and export, or who would be tempted to disrupt our economy for religious reasons—such as, respectively, Venezuela, Nigeria, and Saudi Arabia. That we are in this dependent state is a fact; that we must stay in that condition is not. Energy policy must become a priority national-security issue because it is quite clearly a life-and-death issue for our economy and lifestyle at home, as well as for our ability to conduct a foreign policy of our choosing—one that gives us options—and not one ultimately controlled by foreigners. The exploitation of oil and natural gas reserves in the Arctic and coastal waters, higher miles-per-gallon requirements for automobiles, the greatly increased use of nuclear power, the development of alternative and renewable energy sources, and conservation programs at all levels of government will need to be included in the drive for as large a measure of energy self-sufficiency as it is possible to attain.

The exact provisions of a national energy policy are beyond my writ—and wit—but the urgent need for such a policy is starkly apparent to all who see energy as a national-security issue and not just an aspect of economic policy. Those, like Daniel Yergin, who argue for letting the free market, increasing global integration, and the "great bubbling all along the innovation frontier" work out energy supply problems[9] miss the point that the United States, in terms of ensuring its national security, is no longer operating in the nation-state-dominated Cold War era. If the threat came only from nation-states like Venezuela and Saudi Arabia, it would be manageable. To a great extent, self-interest will drive the activities of nation-state oil-producers, and presumably none would want to create a situation where the United States would simply have to take control of their oil resources and production facilities. But that is not the whole picture. Today al-Qaeda and other Islamist organizations are focused on disrupting the supply of oil to the United States as a means of achieving their war aim of driving America from the Muslim world by bleeding it to bankruptcy. "This [energy] vulnerability isn't lost on Islamic terrorists," the incisive energy analyst Gal Luft has explained. "They have identified the world energy situation as the Achilles heel of the West and have made attacking it a central part of their plan."[10] The ability of these groups to significantly disrupt U.S. oil supplies has not been proven, but their failed attacks have caused prices to spike. It would be short-sighted and negligent in the extreme to plan U.S. energy policy on the basis of a best-case scenario that assumes the Islamists cannot do so. Energy self-sufficiency, like border and immigration-control and securing FSU nuclear devices, is a measure of self-defense against a nonnation-state enemy whom we cannot deter by the prospect of military retaliation, who has no qualms about using any weapon he can acquire and exploit, and against whom our military power cannot always be delivered in an annihilating manner.

And Abroad—Hold Tight, Then Disengage

After the process of securing the home front has become irreversible, Washington can, over time, begin unshackling the United States from its failed policies in the Muslim world. In this context, achieving energy self-sufficiency is again pivotal. In the conduct of foreign policy, the degree of energy self-sufficiency America attains will be the degree to which it can begin to aggressively disengage from the problems, hatreds, and wars of the Muslim world in which it has a stake only as long as U.S. energy supplies are insecure. Put bluntly, as progress is made toward U.S. energy self-sufficiency, it will become obvious that there is no U.S. national interest in the Arabian Peninsula that is worth the life of a single U.S. Marine.

Disengagement clearly will take a number of years and again is not possible without progress toward energy self-sufficiency. But by gradually breaking the energy shackle, Washington will reacquire the option of making policy changes aimed at redirecting—deflecting, if you will—the anger and violence of the al-Qaeda–led Islamist movement back against its primary enemy: the Muslim tyrannies that rule much of the Islamic world and Israel. Currently, the activities that Washington undertakes to facilitate the success of its current foreign policies in the Muslim world succeed only in digging a deeper hole for the United States. U.S. intelligence operations, for example, that help the Mubarak and al-Saud regimes survive and continue oppressing their domestic populations validate the claims of bin Laden and his ilk that Washington's championship of democracy is rank hypocrisy and that America prefers that Muslims be ruled by tyrants. For the Islamists, the visible, often-televised impact of a U.S. policy that protects and prolongs the existence of Muslim dictatorships is an invaluable asset. This point is often very hard for Americans to see because U.S. policy does help to maintain a superficially stable and orderly, if brutally authoritarian, political environment in much of the Muslim world, and because U.S. leaders never deign to tell them how much danger Washington's life-support program for Arab tyrannies has caused for U.S. security, and how much more pain for Americans is stored up for the future.

Thus, the reality is that the United States is becoming, and in some cases is now, identified by Muslims as the cosponsor of the tyrannical systems of government they live under. It is a common belief in many Muslim countries that U.S. financial, military, political, and diplomatic aid ensures that tyrannies remain in power. This belief in turn assists bin Laden in persuading Muslims that the key to overthrowing their rulers is to drive the United States from the region and thereby weaken the ruling regimes to the point where they can be destroyed by the mujahedin. Whether bin Laden is correct in this strategic assumption is an open question, but the fact is that his argument has won the agreement of millions of Muslims over the past decade. More important, it has won significant support among Sunni militants, as best exemplified by al-Zawahiri's fundamental shift of focus from trying to destroy Mubarak's regime to working to bankrupt Mubarak's U.S. government financiers. And from a justifiably narrow U.S. national-security perspective, what price are Americans going to pay for their government's unqualified support for Israel when the day arrives—and it surely will—when the Palestinians conclude that Israel cannot be driven from Palestine until its soft and indulgent U.S. patron is hurt badly at home? We fail to see this trend at our own peril, especially given the size of the Palestinian diaspora in the United States. If there is one hard-and-fast rule in U.S. national security, it should be that U.S. leaders must never adopt policies that tend to bring other peoples' conflicts, especially religious wars, inside the United States. Washington's current policies in the Muslim world are open invitations to others to bring their religious wars—Arab-vs.-Israeli and Sunni-vs.-Shia—to America.

I want to stress that the foregoing is not a purist's argument against any U.S. support at any time for an authoritarian or tyrannical government. Because human beings are hard-wired for war and lesser conflicts, the United States will inevitably and repeatedly find itself in wartime situations where our interests will mandate such an association. We should have no moral qualms about working with any regime that can further U.S. security; these kinds of relationships, however, should be kept to the necessary minimum and the ties should be transitory, with disengagement becoming a priority once the wartime situation has ended. Most of our current relationships with Muslim tyrannies do not meet that criterion. The billions of dollars we annually pay to the Egyptian regime to pretend it does not hate Israel, for example, earn America nothing but a diplomatic mercenary in a peace process that will never come to fruition, and the hatred of common Egyptians who daily feel the wrathful whip of Mubarak's U.S.-funded security services. I will leave it for the American people to decide whether they believe the Founders would have, for even a moment, endorsed the federal government taking money from its citizens' pockets to pay a massive annual bribe to a Muslim dictatorship to pretend to be friends with the near-theocracy in Israel that American taxpayers also are lavishly funding.

So the first step toward American security after Iraq and the drive toward energy self-sufficiency is a thoroughgoing revision of U.S. policy in the Islamic world in the direction the Founders intended: noninterventionist, commerce-oriented, nonideological, focused on genuine life-and-death national interests, and undergirded by an inflexible bias toward neutrality in other peoples' wars. Now, before the hyperventilating begins, let us hand out oxygen supplies to the any-change-in-U.S.-foreign-policy-is-appeasement-or-surrender-to-the-terrorists crowd. And bring lots of oxygen because this crowd includes most of the U.S. governing elite. So pervasive is this no-change sentiment that at times you would swear that U.S. foreign policy was not drafted by fallible humans but rather arrived in the Rotunda, hand-etched by the Deity on stone tablets. It did not. The first thing most military and intelligence officers learn is to never, ever reinforce defeat; if a plan on execution lands you in a no-win situation, get out of the mess as cleanly as possible and go back to the drawing board. Our elite, however, invariably and perversely shows resolve only when it defends and reinforces policies that have America being defeated on every front. For example, the Muslim world's anti-American hatred was raging in July 2006 because Washington and its G-8 partners were standing by and letting Israel gut Lebanon's economy and infrastructure. Okay, what do we do? Right, publicly announce that the U.S. military is urgently sending large shipments of precision weaponry to assist Israel in making the gutting more destructive. Where is the sense in that? Enough. America is the greatest economic and military power the world has ever seen. What on earth do we have to be afraid of if we change foreign policies that are palpable failures and detrimental to U.S. security? Foreigners will think we are weak? Our allies will doubt our constancy? Domestic lobbies will retaliate in the next election? Churchill would never surrender? So what. We are the superpower, the policies are ours for the changing, and if other peoples and countries do not like the changes—tough. We are in business as a country to please and protect ourselves, and it is truly stupid, not altruistic, to stubbornly stick to status quo policies and bleed blood and money because our self-image might suffer if we admit to being wrong and thereby earn the criticism of others.

U.S. foreign policies are not addenda to the Ten Commandments; changing our policies is a sign of common sense, not weakness; and protecting America is infinitely more important than seeking to avoid driving Europeans and Arab royals into a snit. Foreign policy success can be measured only by the extent to which it preserves and expands freedom and liberty domestically. As Walter Lippman wrote, foreign policy is the "shield of the republic"; it is not the agent of planting the republic or clones thereof outside North America. The right path for America, therefore, is nonintervention and a studied aloofness from affairs outside the United States that have no bearing on our national interests. Nonintervention is not isolationism; the former is a policy, the latter is a slur used by America's governing elite to quiet any voice that asks, for example, why are you dropping thousands of tons of bombs on Serbs who never attacked or even threatened the United States? To ask such a commonsense question is to be labeled by the elite and the media, right and left, as a Luddite isolationist who thinks America can hide behind its oceanic frontiers and have no truck with the outside world. Well, no, there is nothing explicit or implicit in the question "Why are you bombing the Serbs?" that suggests a desire to hermetically seal America. The question asks only what it asks: "Why are you intervening in the affairs of a people and a region who have done nothing to threaten or harm you and of whose politics, culture, and history you know next to nothing?" To respond by saying, "Be gone, you ignorant isolationist!" is not an answer, it is an arrogance that says, "We know so much more than you about the complexity of world affairs and—here it is again—the ballet of international politics and, in this case, the nuances of

Balkan politics, that you must accept our analysis and actions as correct. Please go home, be quiet, and watch television."

This modus operandi ought not to wash with Americans, but it does far too frequently, and our elites are today running a foreign policy in the Muslim world that has left the United States with no options in the ongoing war and that, if left as is, will ultimately destroy America. U.S. foreign policy neither protects Americans at home nor brings much benefit, let alone democracy to anyone abroad. Indeed, it is an absolute mystery as to why our elites believe that any American should give a tinker's damn, much less a son or daughter, about whether any foreigner ever has a chance to vote in a democratic election. Mimicking President Woodrow Wilson, President George W. Bush has implanted more of this nonsense in the American political lexicon. "We are led, by events and common sense to one conclusion," President Bush said in January 2005. "The survival of liberty in our land increasingly depends on the success of liberty in other lands. The best hope for peace in our world is the expansion of freedom in all the world."[11] Like Wilson's half-baked assertion of an American security requirement to install a League of Nations, facilitate universal self-determination, and fight wars to end wars, Mr. Bush's assertion is false and fatuous, and where applied as policy it can only lead to a grievous and unnecessary squandering of American lives and treasure.

Finally, it remains to say that the proper future use of the U.S. military against our Islamic enemies has been suggested repeatedly throughout this book. The force that we will have to employ will be far in excess of anything most Americans have seen in their lifetimes, as will the resulting casualties and physical damage. Writing in 2007, the peerless Israeli military historian Martin van Creveld explained that fighting Islamist insurgents can be done with a discriminate use of military power only if excellent intelligence is available about them. As this would not usually be the case, Dr. van Creveld went on to make the case for the indiscriminate and overwhelming force that America will have to employ in the future:

> The other method [the indiscriminate use of military power] will have to be used when good intelligence is not available and discrimination is therefore impossible and, in case things reach the point where they run completely

out of control. The first rule is to make your preparations in secret or, if that is not feasible, to use guile and deceit to disguise your plans. The second is to get your timing right; other things being equal, the sooner you act, the fewer people you must kill. The third is to strike as hard as possible in the shortest possible time; better to strike too hard than not hard enough. The fourth is to explain why your actions were absolutely necessary without, however, providing any apology for them. The fifth is to operate in such a way that, in case your blow fails to deliver the results you expect and need, you will still have some other cards up your sleeve.[12]

An Abiding Uniqueness

The liberties of our country, the freedom of our civil constitution are worth defending at all hazards; and it is our duty to defend them against all attacks. We have received them as a fair inheritance from our worthy ancestors; they purchased them for us with toil and danger and expense of treasure and blood, and transmitted them to us with care and diligence. It will bring an ever lasting mark of infamy on the present generation, as enlightened as it is, if we should suffer them to be wrested from us by violence without a struggle, or cheated out of them by the artifices of false and designing men.

Samuel Adams, 1771

The single most important lesson to be drawn from America's defeats in Afghanistan and Iraq is really an exercise in relearning a reality that has gradually become nearly opaque since 1945: American democracy and republicanism are unique and largely nonexportable. In saying that the American experience is unique, an idea often described and derided as "American exceptionalism," one is merely stating what should be obvious to all. While the Founders certainly drew on the workings and experiences of earlier republican polities—Sparta, Athens, Carthage, Rome, the Italian city-states, etc.—they studied republics not only to see how they functioned but also, more important, to understand why each one inevitably failed.

The package the Founders ultimately put together for their republic in the U.S. Constitution took what they thought was best from the history of republicanism and reinforced it with a bracing dose of Machiavellianism and a central focus on the most important point of the American Enlightenment, that man is deeply flawed and not a perfectible creature. Thus,

American constitutionalism to this day is infused with precepts drawn from the Bible, the history of other republics, the American Enlightenment, the Protestant Reformation, the hard-headed common sense of the philosophers of the Scottish Enlightenment, and the successes and tragedies of the now four-hundred-year-old American national experiment. Composed of these varied influences, the uniqueness of American constitutionalism became more prominent because it was tucked safely away in North America and for centuries developed with minimal influence from the outside world, save those entering due to the never-changing American lust and talent for business and commerce—a sort of profit-seeking insularity, but certainly nothing remotely akin to isolationism.

To be sure, America has prospered because of the Founders' design, and one must assume they would be pleased that others in the world are inspired to emulate the system they hoped would be imitated. But no set of men was ever more confident that they were creating a unique system than the Founders: they intended to produce a scheme of self-government applicable to Protestant, English-speaking America, not to all the world's cultures and religions. The American model is what it is, the American model. There is no boast or sense of superiority in that claim, but rather an estimate of the very real limitations on the applicability of the American model outside America and especially outside what has historically been called Christendom. So clear are these limits that only the willfully blind or the politically reckless can miss them—both of which strike me as excellent descriptors for the contemporary American governing elite.

At base, the United States has been defeated in Iraq and Afghanistan because U.S. leaders forgot or ignored the history of their country. The Founders clearly saw the undoing of their republic if its government became involved in efforts to install the American model abroad, even if such an endeavor was launched in response to requests for help from foreign champions of liberty and democracy. The memorization of John Quincy Adams's 1821 warning to Americans should be required as a condition of graduation from all American high schools and as a recitation from each presidential candidate preceding each presidential debate:

> She [America] well knows that by once enlisting herself under other banners than her own, were they even the banners of foreign independence, she would involve herself beyond the power of extrication, in all the wars of

interest and intrigue, of individual avarice, envy, and ambition, which assume the colors and usurp the standard of freedom.

The fundamental maxims of her policy would insensibly change from liberty to force. She might become dictatress of the world. She would no longer be the ruler of her own spirit.[1]

The results for America of "enlisting under banners other than her own" are now being played out in the mountains, deserts, and cities of Afghanistan and Iraq. In trying to install America's system in devoutly Islamic lands, U.S. leaders display an arrogance derived from an odd combination of ignorance and naïveté. Ignorance, in not recognizing America's uniqueness or accepting that our political experience is not reproducible in a society characterized by the powerful pervasiveness of the Islamic faith, a creed whose believers hear a recommendation that they adopt secular democracy as an urging that they turn their back on God. And naïveté, in not realizing that people like Afghanistan's Hamid Karzai and Iraq's Ahmed Chalabi are quintessential representatives of what Adams called men of "individual avarice, envy, and ambition" who can be counted on to "assume the colors and usurp the standard of freedom." As has so often been the case since 1945, Karzai and Chalabi used U.S. leaders who confidently assumed that their foreigner friends were in sync with American interests and ideals.

Adams and the Founders knew the power of religion and the uniqueness of what they were creating; they successfully accommodated the devout and pervasive Protestantism of their countrymen in a way that allowed religious dissent and freedom, and they warned against the dangers of allying the unique new nation with foreigners, even those who claimed to be championing the same ideas. Had Messrs. Bush, Powell, Cheney, and Rumsfeld and Ms. Rice spent a prewar weekend or two with Washington's Farewell Address, Alexis de Tocqueville's *Democracy in America,* and *The Federalist Papers,* they would have quickly recognized the utter impossibility and irresponsibility of what they were about to undertake as a political project in Iraq and Afghanistan and across the entire Islamic world. Or they might have simply recalled the late George Kennan's 1995 warning, based on Adams's 1821 argument, "that it is very difficult for one country to help another by intervening directly in its domestic affairs or in its conflicts with neighbors. It is particularly difficult to do this without creating new and unwelcome embarrassments for the country endeavoring to help. The best way for a larger country to help smaller ones is surely by the power of example."[2]

The George W. Bush administration's failure to learn and apply the Founders' wisdom is different only in degree, not in kind, from that of its two predecessors. Together the three administrations have left a legacy of disaster abroad and insecurity at home. Their behavior, ahistorical thinking, and lack of common sense have, alas, put the American experiment at risk. In 1936 Winston Churchill posed a question about whether the political and cultural inheritance of Britons was being protected; the same question can serve as an appropriate and hopefully haunting query for U.S. leaders who seem bent on squandering the heritage of Americans. "We must recognize," Churchill said in September 1936, in words echoing those of Samuel Adams in 1771,

> that we have a great treasure to guard; that the inheritance in our possession represents the prolonged achievement of the centuries; that there is not one of our simple uncounted rights today for which better men than we are have not died on the scaffold or the battlefield. We have not only a great treasure; we have a great cause. Are we taking every measure within our power to defend that cause?[3]

Are we? We clearly are not.

Notes

Introduction to the Paperback Edition: The More Things Change . . .

1. Marc Sageman, *Leaderless Jihad: Terror Networks in the Twenty-First Century* (Philadelphia: University of Pennsylvania Press, 2008), viii and 200. For a useful antidote to this social-science claptrap, see Bruce Hoffman, "The Myth of Grass Roots Terrorism," *Foreign Affairs,* May/June 2008.
2. See Peter Bergen and Paul Cruickshank, "The Unraveling," *New Republic,* June 11, 2008; Lawrence Wright, "The Rebellion Within. Al-Qaeda Mastermind Questions Terrorism," *New Yorker,* June 2, 2008; and "The Self-Destructive Gene," http://www.economist.com, July 18, 2008. For differing views see Stephen Ulph, "Can the Doctrinal Ambiguities in Jihadism Be Exploited?" http://www.jamestown.org, June 12, 2008, and M.F. Scheuer, "Rumors of al-Qaeda's Death May Be Highly Exaggerated," *Terrorism Focus,* vol. 5, no. 2, June 3, 2008, http://www.jamestown.org.
3. Frederick W. Kagan, Kimberley Kagan, and Jack Keane, "The New Reality," http://online.wsj.com, July 16, 2008. To assess how far U.S. neoconservatives will go to mislead their countrymen—and how deeply they believe Americans are stupid—the scholar Bernard Lewis provides suitable grist. "But what is important in Iraq is not that it's being ruled by the Shiites, but that it is being ruled by a democracy, by a free, elected government that faces a free opposition." For more from Lewis see "Seven Questions: Bernard Lewis on the Two Biggest Myths About Islam," http://www.foreignpolicy.com, August 2008. For a more realistic view of what is going on in Iraq see Immanuel Wallerstein, "Has the 'Surge' in Iraq Worked?" http://www.aljazeera.com, July 20, 2008.
4. Tom Leonard, "Al-Qaeda's Influence Is Spreading, Says CIA Chief," http://www.telegraph.co.uk, November 14, 2008, and Paul Schemm, "Ultraconservative Islam on Rise in Mideast," *Associated Press,* October 19, 2008.
5. Matt Korade, "Nuclear Threat Going Unheeded, Initiative Official Warns," http://www.cqpolitics.com, May 21, 2008; Jonathan Tirone, "Nuclear Terrorism Is No. 1 Threat, El Baradei Says," http://ww.bloomberg.com, September 30, 2008;

and Graham Allison, "Nuclear Deterrence in the Age of Nuclear Terrorism," *Technology Review* (Internet version), November/December 2008.

6. Jane Perlez and Pir Zubair Shah, "Pakistan May Have Underestimated the Militants," *New York Times* (Internet version), November 11, 2008, and Anthony Loyd, "Captured Battle Plan Shows Strength and Training of Taliban Forces," http://www.timesonline.co.uk, November 11, 2008. For a firsthand view of the U.S. Special Forces' fight against the more militarily proficient Taliban forces see "60 Minutes: Green Berets Recount Deadly Taliban Ambush," http://cbsnews.com, April 20, 2008. For NATO's faltering, see the admission of the British general commanding UK forces in Afghanistan that the war cannot be won, in "We're Not Going to Win This War," http://www.reuters.com, October 6, 2008, as well as Thomas Omestad, "NATO Struggles Over Who Will Send Additional Troops to Fight in Afghanistan," http://www.usnews.com, February 13, 2008.

7. "McCain, Obama Vow Afghan Troop Buildup," http://seattletimes.nwsource.com, July 16, 2008, and "Obama: Now Is the Time for Iraq Withdrawal," http://www.cbs news.com, July 20, 2006.

8. On this emerging threat to Pakistan's stability and a vital NATO resupply route into Afghanistan, see Jason Burke, "On the Front Line in War on Pakistan's Taliban," http://www.guardian.co.uk, November 16, 2008, and "Attacks Halt Truck Convoys into Afghanistan," http://www.latimes.com, November 17, 2008.

9. For a fuller analysis of how the U.S. polite elite continues to view the world and international events through the Cold War's now-distorting lens, see M.F. Scheuer, "Stuck in the Cold—McBama's Nostalgia for the 20th Century," http://wwww.takimag.com, October 12, 2008.

10. Sam Dagher, "Rift Threatens U.S. Antidote to Al-Qaeda in Iraq," http://www.csmon itor.com, February 13, 2008; Sabah al-Bazi, "Al-Qaeda Sows Fear in Iraq's North after Sunset," http://www.reuters.com, February 18, 2008; "Iraq: Police Say al-Qaeda Has Infiltrated Force," http://www.adnkronos.com, June 27, 2008; and Mark Kukis, "Dark Days for Iraq's Awakening," http://www.time.com, September 1, 2008.

11. Patrick Seale, "A Provisional Iraq War Balance Sheet," http://www.middle-east-online.com, September 1, 2008.

12. Tim Cocks, "Iraq's Sunni Anti-Qaeda Patrols Fear for Future," *Reuters* (Internet version), September 24, 2008.

13. Murad Batal al-Shishani, "Al-Qaeda 'Awakens' in Iraq," http://www.atimes.com, November 18, 2008.

14. For the CIA chief's view that there is a bleed-through problem from Iraq and Afghanistan, see Mark Mazetti, "CIA Chief Says Qaeda Is Extending Its Reach," http://www.nytimes.com, November 14, 2008. At http://www.jamestown.org, I have tried to offer a preliminary assessment of the mujahedin bleed-through from Iraq to the Levant in "A Mujahedin Bleed-Through from Iraq? A Look at Syria," *Terrorism Focus*, vol. 5, no. 36, October 22, 2008; "A Mujahedin Bleed-Through from Iraq? Part Two—A Look at Lebanon," *Terrorism Focus*, vol. 5, no. 38, November 5, 2008; "A Mujahedin Bleed-Through from Iraq? Part Three—The Case of Jordan," *Terrorism Focus*, vol. 5, no. 39, November 19, 2008; and "A Mujahedin Bleed-Through from Iraq? Part Four: A Look at Palestine and Israel," *Terrorism Focus*, vol. 5, no. 41, December 10, 2008.

15. That Senators McCain and Obama knew during the presidential campaign that anything more than a small-scale U.S. military withdrawal from Iraq would compromise

Israel's security—which both said is "sacrosanct"—see "Conversation with Sen. John McCain," http://www.jewishledger.com, April 12, 2008; "In Cleveland, Obama Speaks on Jewish Issues," http://www.nysun.com, February 25, 2008; and "Israel to Warn Obama Against Iraqi Withdrawal," http://www.ynetnews.com, July 20, 2008. General Petraeus seems to have laid down a marker regarding this no-withdrawal reality in mid-September 2008, when he said that the U.S. military exit from Iraq would be "slower and smaller than anticipated." See Mark Tran, "General Petraeus Warns of Long Struggle Ahead for U.S. in Iraq," http://www.guardian.co.uk, September 11, 2008.

16. See, for example, "Son of Israeli Immigrant Accepts Obama Offer to Serve as Chief of Staff," http://www.ynetnews.com, November 5, 2008; Orly Azoulay, "Obama's Israel Adviser: Next White House Chief of Staff," http://www.ynetnews.com, November 2, 2008; Natasha Mozgovaya, "U.S. Jews Laud Obama Pick of Rahm Emanuel for Chief of Staff," *Haaretz* (Internet version), November 9, 2008; Hillel Kuttler, "The View from the Top," *Jerusalem Post* (Internet version), July 1, 1997; and Philip Giraldi, "AIPAC's Man in the Obama Camp," http://www.antiwar.com, November 18, 2008. These facts are not mentioned in Rep. Emanuel's official biography, http://www.house.gov/emanuel/biography.pdf.

17. Hebah Saleh, "Islamist Militants Rise Again in Algeria," http://www.ft.com, September 1, 2008; Amir Tahei, "Al-Qaeda's Sinister Creep into North Africa," http://timesonline.co.uk, July 30, 2008; Andrew England, "Algeria Fears Tightening Grip of al-Qaeda," http://www.ft.com, August 22, 2008; "Al-Qaeda Leader Threatens France and Spain," http://www.adnkronos.com, September 22, 2008; and "Al-Qaeda Leader in Maghreb Denounces 'Occupation' of Ceuta, Meilla," http://www.elpais.com, September 23, 2008.

18. "Islamists Regain Control Over Much of Somalia," http://www.reuters.com, November 16, 2008; Shashank Bengali, "Islamist Rise in Somalia Is Latest Worry for U.S.," http://www.miamiherald.com, November 23, 2008; Peter Beaumont, "Somalia Sinks Deeper into a State of Total Disintegration," http://www.guardian.co.uk, November 23, 2008; "Kenya Issues Ultimatum to Somali Islamist Fighters," *KTN Television* [Nairobi], November 18, 2008; "Somalia: Roadside Bomb Kills Police Chief in Lower Shabella Region," *Agence France-Presse,* October 28, 2008; and "The World's Most Utterly Failed State," http://www.economist.com, October 2, 2008.

19. Gregory D. Johnsen, "Al-Qaeda in Yemen Reorganizes under Nasir al-Wahayshi," *Terrorism Focus* (http://www.jamestown.org), vol., 5, no. 11, March 18, 2008; Shihab al-Hijazi, "The Just Retribution of Rabish," *The Echo of Epic Battles* (Internet), November 9, 2008; and "The Indications of the Embassy Operation," *The Echo of Epic Battles* (Internet), November 9, 2008.

20. James T. Areddy, "In China's Far West, Violence Is Just the Eruption of Long-Pent Tension," http://www.wsj.com, August 8, 2008; Peter Navarro, "The 'Hanification' of Xinjiang," http://www.atimes.com, August 18, 2008; Edward Wong, Wary of Islam, China Tightens a Vise of Rules," http://www.nytimes.com, October 19, 2008; and Aryn Baker, "A Recurring Nightmare," http://www.time.com.time/asia, June 17, 2006.

21. Michael F. Scheuer, "Don't Do an America," *India Today* (Internet version), December 4, 2008. To get a sense of India's rising communal tensions and what they may portend for the country, in the context of what is now a multiyear terrorist campaign, see A.G. Noorani, "Merchants of Hate," *Frontline* (Internet version), June 21–July 4, 2008;

Ranjona Banjeri, "Are the Gujurat Blasts a Backlash?" http://www.dnaindia.com, August 5, 2008; Subir Bhaumik, "Who Is Behind the India Bombings?" http://www.newsvote.bbc.co.uk, May 14, 2008; R. Venkatesan Iyengar, "Serial Bomb Blasts: The Buck Stops Here," http://www.india.merinews.com, July 31, 2008; and Nitin Pai, "The New Jihadis," http://www.isn,ethz.ch, June 13, 2008.

22. M.F. Scheuer. *Marching Toward Hell: America and Islam After Iraq.* (New York: Free Press, 2008), 165–186.

23. Mohamed Olad Hassan and Elizabeth A. Kennedy, "Somali Islamists Emboldened, Set Sights on Capital," *Associated Press,* November 15, 2008, "Islamist Official Admits Foreign Jihadis Fighting Alongside al-Shabab," *Somaliaweyn* (Internet), October 28, 2008; and Mohamed Olad Hassan, "Ethiopia to Pull Its Troops Out of Somalia," http://www.sfgate.com, November 29, 2008. The quoted al-Shabab commander is Shaykh Mukhtar Robow Abu Mansur, who also told the media—probably with some exaggeration—that his group is "negotiating how we can unite [with al-Qaeda] into one. We will take our orders from Shaikh Osama because we are his students. Al-Qaeda is the mother of the holy war in Somalia. Most of our leaders were trained in al-Qaeda camps. We get our tactics and guidelines from them. Many have spent time with Osama bin Laden." The Shaykh also claimed mujahedin from Kenya, Sudan, Iraq, Afghanistan, Algeria, India, Chechnya, and the United States were fighting in Somalia with al-Shabab. See Edmund Sanders, "Conditions May Be Ripe for al-Qaeda in Somalia," http://www.latimes.com, August 25, 2008.

24. Mairbek Vatchagev, "From Derbent to Narzani: Rebels Step Up Attacks in North Caucasus," *North Caucasus Weekly* (http://jamestown.org), vol. 9, no. 36, August 1, 2008; "Fight Against Gangs in North Caucasus Is Priority for Security Bodies," *ITAR-TASS* (Internet version), September 30, 2008; "No Plans to Reduce Chechen Internal Troops So Far—Deputy Commander-in-Chief," http://www.istock analyst.com, July 30, 2008; Thomas de Waal, "Mysterious Shifts in Chechnya," http://www.themoscowtimes.com, May 22, 2008; Islam Tekushev, "It Is Time for the Kremlin to Show Some Responsibility," *Caucasus Times* (Internet version), September 24, 2008; Vitaly Proskurin, "A Test Range for Mercenaries: Who Supports the Terrorists and Separatists in the North Caucasus," *Voyenno-Promyshlenny* (Internet version), June 18, 2008; Mairbek Vatchagaev, "Political Chaos Rules in the North Caucasus," *North Caucasus Weekly* (http://jamestown.org), vol. 9, no. 29, July 24, 2008; and Richard Galpin, "Ingushetia in State of Civil War," http://news vote.bbc.co.uk, November 23, 2003.

25. "MEND Statements," *Threat and Claim Monitor, IntelCenter* (Internet), August 12 and September 1, 2008; Will Conners, "The Nigerian Rebel Who 'Taxes' Your Gasoline," http://www.time.com, May 28, 2006; and "Nigeria Beefs Up Oil Security," http://www.english.aljazeera.net, June 21, 2008.

26. Edmund Harris, "Nigeria Militants Renew Attacks," http://www.news24.com, April 22, 2008, and Edmund Harris, "Militants in Nigeria Oil Area Seek Mediation by Jimmy Carter," http://www.auburnpub.com, May 10, 2008.

27. Ian Story, "Thailand Cracks Down on Southern Militants," *Terrorism Monitor* (http://www.jamestown.org), vol. 5, no. 17, September 13, 2007; Zachary Abuza, "The Role of Foreign Trainers in Southern Thailand's Insurgency," *Terrorism Monitor* (http://www.jamestwon.org), vol. 5, no. 1, June 7, 2007; "Interview with Pattani Darussalam Mujahedin," *Khattab Publications for Media Releases* (Inter-

Notes

net), August 26, 2008; "Conflicting Parties in South Thailand Meet in Bogor," *Antara* (Internet version), September 20, 2008; "Violence Declines During Ramadan but Number of Fatalities Rises," *ISARA Institute* [Thailand] (Internet version), October 4 and 5, 2008; and Pricha Sathitruangsak, "Analytic Review of "Two-Pronged Strategy: Extinguishing the Southern Fires is Kindling the Flames of a Vendetta," *Siam Rat* (Internet version), November 3, 2008. Notably, the Thai insurgents—like those in Somalia—are seeking to strengthen their association with al-Qaeda. "[T]he Mujahedin Shura Council in South East Asia," a Thai mujahedin group, proclaimed in August 2008 that it "renews its allegiance and obedience to the commander of the mujahedin, Usama bin Laden, may God protect him and his companion, the mujahid Shaykh Ayman al-Zawahiri. By the will of God, we will fight under the banner he has put in place and raised." See "Statement by Mujahedin Shura Council in Pattani Darussalam," *Khattab Publications for Media Releases* (Internet), August 26, 2008.

28. "The Unnoticed Emergency," http://www.economist.com, July 2, 2008; Sumanta Ray Chaudhri, "ISI-BOR Joint Venture: 75 Terror Camps," *Daily News and Analysis* (Internet version), October 27, 2008; Samir Kumar Dey, "125 Extremist Outfits Active; Have Suicide Squads," *Shamokal* [Bangladesh], November 18, 2008; Selig Harrsion, "Get a Grip on Dhaka," http://www.latimes.com, July 2, 2008; and "U.S. Brands Bangladeshi Islamist Group 'Terrorist,'" http://www.reuters.com, March 7, 2008.

29. Duncan Gardham, "Terror Threat in UK 'Approaching Critical,'" http://www.telegraph.co.uk, October 3, 2008; Sean Rayment, "Report Identifies UK Terrorist Enclaves," http://www.telegraph.co.uk, November 9, 2008; and "Terrorism Threat in UK 'Growing,'" http://newsvote.bbc.co.uk, November 9, 2008.

30. See "Al-Qaeda-in-Islamic-Maghreb Claims to Avoiding Spilling Muslim Blood in Battle," http://www.alhesbahweb.net, November 6, 2008, and "Ingush Rebels Pledge More Blasts, Shootings Against Russians," Kavkaz-Tsentr News Agency (Internet), October 20, 2008.

31. Osama bin Laden, "A Message to Our People in Iraq," *Threat and Claim Monitor, IntelCenter* (Internet), October 23, 2007.

32. Osama bin Laden, "Declaration of War on the United States," *Al-Islah* (Internet), September 2, 1996.

33. See the results of the Gallup organization's multiyear polling effort in thirty-five Muslim countries: John L. Esposito and Dalia Mogahed, *Who Speaks for Islam?: What a Billion Muslims Really Think.* (New York: Gallup Press, 2007), xv and 204.

34. On the quality of American generalship in recent decades, see the interesting analysis in Andrew Bacevich, *The Limits of Power: The End of American Exceptionalism.* (New York: Metropolitan Books, 2008), 143–152.

35. Abraham Lincoln, quoted in *The Oxford Dictionary of Civil War Quotations,* John D. Wright, ed. (New York: Oxford University Press, 2006), 216.

Preface

1. Tim Russert, "Interview of Vice President Cheney," *Meet the Press,* NBC Television, September 10, 2006.

2. Francis Fukuyama, *The End of History and the Last Man* (New York: Free Press, 2006), 464.

Notes

Introduction

1. *The 9/11 Commission Report* provides numerous examples of this refusal to doubt the utter perfection of U.S. foreign policy in the Muslim world. "American [foreign] policy choices have consequences," the commissioners wrote. "Right or wrong it is simply a fact that American policy regarding the Israeli-Palestinian conflict and American actions in Iraq are dominant staples of popular commentary across the Arab and Muslim world." So far, so good, but this promising start fades into complete support for the foreign-policy status quo and the implication that Muslims are too stupid to understand what is best for them. "This does not mean U.S. policy choices have been wrong," the commissioners continue, cementing their places in the governing elite. "It means that those choices must be integrated with America's message of opportunity to the Arab and Muslim world . . . The United States must do more to communicate its message." See Thomas H. Kean et al., *The 9/11 Commission Report* (New York: W.W. Norton and Co., 2003), 376–77.

2. Walter A. McDougall, *Promised Land, Crusader State: The American Encounter with the World Since 1776* (New York: Mariner Books, 1997), 206, 218.

3. I spent nearly twenty years managing CIA covert-action operations, and when discussing whether or not to proceed with—or even to propose—a particular operation, the first question always asked by the Agency's seniormost managers was, "Will it pass the *Washington Post* giggle test?" That is, no operation aimed at protecting Americans or furthering U.S. interests abroad could be considered if the *Post* and other media would ridicule it if it failed and became public knowledge. Again, *The 9/11 Commission Report* is helpful on this issue. Quoting a cable I wrote on the instruction of DCI George Tenet explaining why a May 1998 operation to capture bin Laden was canceled, the commissioners note that the bottom line was that the Clinton administration preferred to let the killer of Americans remain free to plan additional attacks rather than risk bad press. At Mr. Tenet's direction I wrote that the Clinton cabinet had stopped the operation because "the purpose and nature of the operation would be subject to unavoidable misinterpretation—and probably recriminations—in the event that bin Laden, despite our best intentions and efforts, did not survive." See Kean et al., *9/11 Commission Report*, 114.

   Worries about what others would think seemed, at times, to be taken rather far. When planning the operation to capture bin Laden, for example, CIA engineers were required to produce an ergonomically correct chair for bin Laden to be seated in after he was captured. Likewise, well-padded restraint devices were manufactured to avoid chafing his skin, and a full medical suite was acquired in case he was wounded. The crowning glory of the Executive Branch's tender concern for this killer of Americans was a session held at the National Security Council's offices of lawyers from several Intelligence Community components. Their task? To examine rolls of masking, duct, and medical-adhesive tape and determine which had the right amount of stickiness to ensure that bin Laden's face and beard would not be excessively irritated if his mouth had to be taped shut after capture.

4. *Niccolò Machiavelli, The Prince*, trans. N.H. Thompson (New York: Barnes and Noble Books, 1999), 79.

Notes

Author's Note

1. *Through Our Enemies' Eyes: Osama bin Laden, Radical Islam, and the Future of America,* rev. ed. (Dulles, Va.: Potomac Books, 2005), and *Imperial Hubris: Why the West Is Losing the War on Terrorism* (Dulles, Va.: Potomac Books, 2004).
2. James A. Baker III and Lee H. Hamilton, co-chairs, *The Iraq Study Group Report: The Way Forward—A New Approach* (New York: Vintage Books, 2006), xvii.
3. Notwithstanding the urgent tone in which *The Iraq Study Group Report* is written— "The situation in Iraq is grave and deteriorating," for example—the authors present the Iraq debacle as mainly a Cold War–style problem produced by Washington's substandard planning and management.

> There is no magic formula to solve the problems of Iraq. However, there are actions that can be taken to improve the situation and protect American interests . . . Our [U.S.] political leaders must build a bipartisan approach to bring a responsible conclusion to what is now a lengthy and costly war . . . The United States has long-term relationships and interests at stake in the Middle East and needs to stay engaged . . . What we recommend in this report demands a tremendous amount of political will and cooperation by the executive and legislative branches of the U.S. government. It demands skillful implementation. It demands unity of effort by government agencies. And its success depends on the unity of the American people in a time of political polarization.

This policy prescription could have been applied to almost any issue during the Cold War. The resolution in Iraq needs the help of the Iraqi regime—the *Report* stresses this—but at bottom it is up to the United States to draft and implement better policies, improve U.S. interagency coordination, teach the Iraqis to adopt less corrupt and more Western-style policies in budget planning and taxes, and train them to build a law-enforcement system that mirrors America's. For the Baker-Hamilton commission, when Washington gets the bureaucratics right, success will be just around the corner, and it appears that the enemy will not have a voice in the outcome. Ibid., ix, x, xiii.

4. Kean et al., *9/11 Commission Report,* 108–43.
5. Ibid., xvi.
6. The members of each of the three investigatory panels were served by a large and competent staff. The staff of the Kean-Hamilton 9/11 Commission, however, stood head and shoulders above the others. The intellect, work ethic, determination, and integrity of that staff cannot be too highly praised. The many failings of the final 9/11 Commission report must therefore be ascribed to the political objectives of the commissioners and their most senior lieutenants—and most especially to the moral cowardice evident in their decision not to "point fingers"—and not to the work of the staffers. My impression is that the staffers found the truth but the commissioners balked at telling it.
7. All of us recalled, for example, that then-DCI George Tenet fired a young and just-married CIA contract employee after the U.S. Air Force mistakenly bombed the Chinese embassy in Belgrade on May 8, 1999. The discharged employee had provided information on the target but was unaware that it was the embassy. Mr. Tenet volunteered the CIA to take the blame for the bombing, but every IC officer knew that the

U.S. military was responsible for the mistake. In wartime situations the U.S. military routinely solicits target suggestions from several IC components. These suggestions are presented in files called target packages. U.S. military intelligence reviews and independently verifies them as legitimate targets, then forwards them to a senior U.S. commander for a decision on whether an attack is to be made. The Chinese embassy in Belgrade was attacked, therefore, either because military intelligence failed to do its job or because the demand for targets from senior commanders was too strong to permit a complete evaluation. No target is ever attacked simply because the CIA tells the U.S. military it should do so. In the same way, in early 2004, the 9/11 commissioners indicated that they were intending to name an even younger CIA officer as the only individual to be publicly identified for a pre-9/11 failure. A group of senior CIA officers, however, let it be known that if that officer was named, information about the pre-9/11 negligence of several very senior U.S. officials would find its way into the media. The commissioners dropped the issue. For the 1999 Belgrade attack, see Alva McNicol, "NATO hits Chinese Embassy," BBCNEWS.com, May 8, 1999.

It also should be noted that the commissioners mislead readers throughout their report by saying that the CIA withheld information from the FBI. A number of junior and senior FBI officers were assigned to the bin Laden unit after it was formed in 1996, and each had access to all of the information that came into the Agency. When I was the unit chief, the FBI officers who served there read all the mail I read, except for fitness reports for CIA officers overseas. The FBI officers were in the unit for two specific reasons: (a) so that they could cull incoming messages for information pertinent to U.S. domestic security, and (b) so that they could take action on such information because the CIA could not operate inside the United States.

In addition, one of the main reasons senior FBI officials assigned their officers to the bin Laden unit—and to the CIA's Counterterrorist Center generally—was to steal information from the CIA. On at least three occasions in which I was personally involved between 1992 and 2004, FBI officers were found to have stolen large numbers of classified CIA documents, removed them from CIA headquarters in an insecure manner, and distributed them to individuals at FBI headquarters and—at least—the FBI office in New York. On each occasion senior CIA officers refused to act to recover the documents.

8. I make this point so starkly because I have been told by several retired IC officers that after I resigned from the Agency, several of the young officers who worked for me were subjected to very adversarial polygraph examinations. These officers were accused of passing me classified information, were recalled several times for repolygraphing, and were delayed in taking new assignments because of the prolonged and hostile polygraph process. No serving officer has ever passed me classified information, but because the polygraph can always be used to discipline and harass employees, I want to make my sole responsibility for this book as clear as possible.

9. A few items in the latter category provide an interesting bit of context to *The 9/11 Commission Report*. The *Report* notes that in May 1998 the government of Saudi Arabia agreed to try to purchase Osama bin Laden from the Taliban but failed to do so. Oddly enough, the Clinton administration's decision to welcome and rely on the Saudis to do what they promised—which was criticized by some in the CIA who had seen Riyadh's post-1995 noncooperation vis. bin Laden—precisely coincided with both DCI George Tenet's memorandum advising Mr. Berger to let the Saudis take the

lead against bin Laden, and what the former DCI has described with the phrase "I made the decision not to go ahead with the plan" to capture bin Laden, an operation that had been a year in the making and was ready to launch. Some doubt must be cast on Mr. Tenet's assertion that he alone—not the White House—decided to terminate the operation. As related by the 9/11 Commissioners in chapter 4 of their report, Mr. Tenet told his officers that "cabinet-level officials" had turned down the plan. In addition, and at exactly the same moment, former Senator Wyche Fowler (D-Georgia), then the U.S. ambassador in Saudi Arabia, advised Clinton's National Security Adviser Sandy Berger to let the Saudis take the lead against bin Laden. Naturally, the Saudis did not keep their promise, and nine weeks later al-Qaeda destroyed two U.S. embassies in East Africa—killing 300 and wounding 5,100 Americans and Africans—proving both the sound advice "put not your trust in kings" and that, although the Cold War is over, U.S. governments are still desperately looking for proxies to do their dirty work. I have often wondered if the documents showing the real reason the May 1998 operation to capture bin Laden was cancelled were among the papers that Mr. Berger placed in his garments and ultimately destroyed with scissors, an act that saved Mr. Clinton's reputation and Mrs. Clinton's run at the presidency. See Kean and Hamilton, *9/11 Commission Report*, pp. 114–115; George Tenet, *Center of the Storm*, p. 114; "Complete 9/11 Timeline," http://www.cooperatiivereserach.org/timeline.jsp?timeline=complete_911_time line&before_911=huntforbinladen; James Risen, *State of War: The Secret History of the CIA and the Bush Administration* (New York: Free Press, 2006), p. 184; and Steve Coll, *Ghost Wars*, pp. 516–518.

10. The other two investigatory panels the CIA inspector general's and the Congress's Goss-Graham—had access to complete documents, whereas the 9/11 Commission did not. I decided to pass the binder to the commission after a session in which I answered questions for Phillip Zelikow, the commission's executive director. In the session Mr. Zelikow asked a question about a chance to eliminate bin Laden based on a CIA document he held in his hand. I could not understand the question, and when he showed me the document, the reason was clear. The CIA screeners had redacted the document in a way that made it almost incoherent. Having seen the document, I flipped through the pages in my binder and found the same but unredacted document, and we were able to compare the two and have a more cogent conversation.

11. See, most recently, Larry Margasak, "Clinton Aide Stashed Classified Documents under a Trailer," Associated Press, December 21, 2006; R. Jeffrey Smith, "Document-theft Probe Criticized," *Washington Post,* January 10, 2007, A-4; and "Berger Mystery Deepens," *Boston Herald,* January 21, 2007.

12. George Tenet, *At the Center of the Storm:My Years at the CIA* (New York: Harper-Collins, 2007), xviii.

13. Richard A. Clarke, *Against All Enemies: Inside America's War on Terror* (New York: Free Press, 2004), xiii.

14. Tenet, *Center of the Storm*, 249.

15. Ibid., esp. 123.

16. Ibid., xxii, 505.

17. Ibid., 499.

18. Ibid., 261.

Notes

19. Ibid.
20. Thomas Jefferson to John Adams, September 8, 1817, in Lester J. Cappon, ed., *The Adams-Jefferson Letters* (Chapel Hill: University of North Carolina Press, 1959), 519.
21. Andrew Bacevich, "Fighting a War in Name Only," *Los Angeles Times,* June 21, 2004.

Part I. Getting to 9/11

1. Lincoln is reported to have said this after learning of the army's disastrous defeat by Lee's Army of Northern Virginia at Fredericksburg in December 1862. Quoted in John D. Wright, ed., *The Oxford Dictionary of Civil War Quotations* (New York: Oxford University Press, 2006), 248.

Chapter 1. Readying bin Laden's Way: America and the Muslim World, 1973–1996

1. Machiavelli, *Prince,* 80.
2. Ibid., 81. Although jumping ahead a bit, it is worth noting that the leading neoconservatives, men like Paul Wolfowitz, William Kristol, and Richard Perle, clearly are among those most in need of advice from Machiavelli. The U.S. disasters in Afghanistan and Iraq, of course, demonstrate that the strictures of neoconservatism have nothing to do with Machiavellian common sense or foreign-policy realism but are rather the yield of an uncompromising ignorance of American and world history and a fantasy-based interpretation of how the world works. Interestingly, the man who is usually cited as the mentor of the leading neoconservatives, the American political philosopher Leo Strauss, believed Machiavelli to be a source of evil in the politics and life of the Western world. See Leo Strauss, *Thoughts on Machiavelli* (Chicago: University of Chicago Press, 1958).
3. On this issue see Michael F. Scheuer, "Does Israel Conduct Covert Action in America? You Bet It Does," www.antiwar.com, April 8, 2006. Let me say here, as I did in the article and in public venues, covert political action is a clandestine tool used by all nation-states to further their interests abroad. Only a negligent or Pollyanna-ish government would fail to use such a tool, and it ought to be a source of pride for Israeli citizens that their intelligence services have been so demonstrably successful. Israel's unparalleled success, however, speaks volumes about the gullibility or cupidity of the U.S. governing elite.
4. George Washington, "Farewell Address, 1796," in W. B. Allen, ed., *George Washington: A Collection* (Indianapolis, Ind.: Liberty Fund, 1988), 523–24.
5. Daniel Robinson, *American Ideals: Founding a "Republic of Virtue"* (Chantilly, Va.: Teaching Company, 2004), disk 5, lecture 10, track 7.
6. Even as we are on the verge of losing wars in Afghanistan and Iraq, and are faced with instability that could ultimately require U.S. military intervention to protect oil production in Saudi Arabia and Nigeria, the don't-worry-be-happy oil experts continue to chatter away. "Regardless of the cause, rising oil prices during this decade have helped the national interest in the long term," wrote Philip Auerswald of George

Mason and Harvard universities. "Like the 'traveling pants' in the series of teen novels by the same name, the notion that oil imports lead to energy insecurity magically fits everyone who tries it on—environmentalists, military hawks, foreign policy idealists, subsidy-seeking oil executives, and even anti-U.S. propagandists. Yet while the energy insecurity argument fits an array of agendas, it does not fit the facts. Politicians and pundits alike would do well to put this treasured, but frayed notion aside." Clearly, protecting the "free market" is more important for Auerswald and his ideological colleagues than avoiding wars fought for access to oil. One wonders how eager he is to have his children or grandchildren fighting for oil in the Niger Delta or the eastern province of Saudi Arabia. See Philip E. Auerswald, "Calling an End to Oil Alarmism," *Boston Globe* (online version), January 23, 2007.

7. Allen, *George Washington*, 525.

8. George Washington to Bushrod Washington, January 15, 1783, quoted in Bruckner F. Melton Jr., *The Quotable Founding Fathers* (Washington, D.C.: Potomac Books, 2004), 23.

9. The words are, respectively, those of the Clinton administration's two top defense officials, General Hugh Shelton, Chairman, Joint Chiefs of Staff, and Secretary of Defense William Cohen. See Kean et al., *9/11 Commission Report*, 120.

10. Richard A. Clarke, *Against All Enemies: Inside America's War on Terror* (New York: Free Press, 2004), 224. The italics in the last sentence are mine. Mr. Clarke here, of course, is constructing another post hoc defense of President Clinton's failure to defend Americans by holding out the prospect of an Arab-Israeli settlement as a good reason for delaying retaliation for the *Cole*. Only a nuance-addled senior federal bureaucrat would have forgone the chance to smash al-Qaeda in favor of another iteration of Arab-Israeli talks that have a half-century record of unrelenting failure. One ought never to delay defending his country if what he is delaying for requires a certifiable act of God to achieve.

11. Although it is a bit of a macabre exercise, some of the documents and Islamist insurgents and terrorists we have captured since 9/11 have provided information about specific individuals who trained at specific camps that had long been on the IC's radar and that were described in the yearbooks mentioned in the text. We are thus learning the hard way that the camps were imparting effective, professional-level military training on a wide variety of weapons and explosives during the decades when U.S. and Western governments were allowing them to operate without interference.

12. Even the number one million should not be considered an upper limit. An unknown number of Islamists simply showed up at one or another of the Muslim world's jihads and insurgencies—Chechnya, Eritrea, Kashmir, Somalia, etc.—and learned how to fight in a kind of on-the-job way. Some of these men got killed before their cold start got very far, but others survived and lived not only to fight but also to train and inspire others. Between fighters produced in formal camps and those produced by on-the-job training, we are looking at very large numbers indeed. And today, in addition to the camps, some would-be insurgents are training at or near their homes using detailed instructional materials downloaded from the Internet.

13. For a fuller perspective on the threat to America these camps have produced, consider that the *Washington Post* published an article in late 2005 that claimed that the CIA's clandestine service then had about a thousand officers deployed worldwide. I have no idea whether this number is high, low, or accurate, as it is a figure that the

Agency must go to great pains to protect. But let us assume that the *Post*'s total is in the ballpark. It is then extremely likely—I would say it is certain—that since 1982 the training camps of al-Qaeda, and of other Sunni and Shia Islamist organizations, have been producing at least as many well-trained insurgents and terrorists *annually* as the CIA had officers deployed to chase them in 2005. In addition, and as Mr. Tenet has stated, U.S. national security also requires that the vast majority of CIA officers overseas collect intelligence on targets other than training camps, such as Russia, China, nuclear proliferation, and narcotics trafficking. They are also focused on gathering intelligence pertinent to the protection of U.S. forces deployed overseas; in an odd situation, the CIA—the folks who are unarmed—spend much of their time protecting the people who are armed to the teeth. Anyway, in this roughest of estimates in 2008 the trained Islamist fighters are very likely to outnumber the CIA officers available to track and capture them by about 25 to 1—a ratio that would greatly increase if the training camps around the world have since 1982 produced, as seems likely, more than twelve hundred fighters a year. These totals, as noted, would not include the Islamist fighters who have been trained at home by men returning from the formal camps, or those who have downloaded training manuals from the Internet and done their training at makeshift camps near their homes. For CIA overseas personnel totals, see Walter Pincus and Dana Priest, "Goss Reportedly Rebuffed Senior Officials at CIA," *Washington Post,* November 14, 2004, A-6.

14. Omar Nasiri, *Inside the Jihad: My Life With al-Qaeda. A Spy's Story* (New York: Basic Books, 2006), 142–44. Nasiri also notes that he was trained intensively on the enemy he would encounter. "Abu Suhail taught us about all the enemy weapons as well," Nasiri writes. "Abu Suhail would show us photographs of guns—guns from America like the M-16—and teach us all the same things we learned on other weapons, but this time only theoretically. He also taught us what made the enemy weapons distinct; how American mortars, for instance, fired different rounds from the Russian ones we were using." Ibid., 143. For additional analysis of the al-Qaeda camps and the general environment in which they operated, see the excellent, detailed, and ground-breaking book by Peter L. Bergen, *The Osama Bin Laden I Know* (New York: Free Press, 2006), xxxiv, and the lengthy firsthand account by bin Laden's former chief bodyguard, "Interview with Abu Jandal," *Al-Quds Al-Arabi* (online version), August 3, 2004, and March 18–29, 2005.

15. The summer 2006 dismantling by British authorities of an Islamist cell in the U.K. that was planning to destroy U.S. and British airliners flying west across the Atlantic Ocean stimulated a good deal of media reporting about the replacement of al-Qaeda's Afghanistan-based camps destroyed by the U.S.-led coalition with new camps built on the Pakistani side of the Durand Line. This reporting was then confirmed in a rare public speech by Dame Eliza Manningham Buller, director general of the British Security Service (DG/MI5). Dame Eliza said that MI5 and British police had identified at least sixteen hundred al-Qaeda–related individuals in the U.K. and expressed her confidence that many more had not yet been identified. (Her confidence was justified as MI5 announced in November 2007 that the total is now two thousand al-Qaeda–related individuals.) Many U.K.-based Islamists, Dame Eliza added, "often have links back to al-Qaeda in Pakistan and through these links al-Qaeda gives guidance and training to its largely British foot soldiers here on an extensive and growing scale." Perhaps we should not be surprised by Dame Eliza's

conclusions as, once again, al-Qaeda publicly announced in 2003 that its South Asia camps were again up and running. Writing in March 2003, senior al-Qaeda lieutenant Sayf al-Adl described a November 2001 action against U.S. forces near Khandahar. The Americans destroyed an al-Qaeda tank, al-Adl recounted: "The entire crew of the tank escaped. Shrapnel hit Khalid in the head, paralyzing the left side of his body. He recovered after four months, except for a slight effect in his left hand. He [has] now [March 2003] resumed training near the Afghan-Pakistani border in one of the secret camps of al-Qaeda." For solid reporting on the re-established and new camps see James Gordon Meek, "Qaeda Camps Surge," *New York Daily News,* August 13, 2006; "Five Suspects Learnt Bomb Skills at al-Qaeda Camps," *Daily Telegraph,* August 12, 2006; and Mohammed Khan and Carlotta Gall, "Accounts after 2005 London Bombings Point to al-Qaeda Role from Pakistan," *New York Times,* August 12, 2006. For DG/MI5's speech, see "Terrorist Threat to UK—MI5 Chief's Full Speech," *Times Online,* November 11, 2006, and "Full Text of MI5 Director's Speech," www.telegraph.co.uk, November 6, 2007. For al-Qaeda confirming the continued existence of its South Asia camps see Sayf al-Adl, "The al-Qaeda Organization Writes a Letter to the Iraqi People," www.alfji.com, March 5, 2003.

16. In the years between 9/11 and my resignation from the CIA in November 2004, I was not aware of an ongoing program to identify and track all the terrorist/insurgent training camps operating in the world. Indeed, after U.S. and NATO forces closed the well-known al-Qaeda and Taliban training camps in eastern and southeastern Afghanistan, the Bush administration often spoke as if there were no more al-Qaeda training camps operating. This, of course, is incorrect, as camps for al-Qaeda and other Islamist groups continue to operate without interference in Yemen, Sudan, Somalia, Lebanon, Mindanao, Chechnya, Kashmir, and elsewhere. In addition, al-Qaeda and the Taliban are not the kind of organizations to simply throw up their hands and say: "The Americans have closed our Afghan camps. Oh, woe is us! The infidels are stronger than Allah! Let's give up and go home." The odds greatly favor a situation where, after the Afghan camps were closed, the groups set up camps in Pakistan and unoccupied areas of Afghanistan; sent would-be fighters for training in some of the places just listed; and, for al-Qaeda, elsewhere in the world. If there was ever a task worth doing in the post-9/11 world, a worldwide inventory of all terrorist/insurgent training camps was it. Such a survey would at least have allowed the U.S. Intelligence Community to get a handle on the pace at which Islamist groups were and are training additional forces.

17. Kean et al.: *9/11 Commission Report,* 213.

18. Peter L. Bergen systematically destroys this myth in both of his fine books, *The Osama Bin Laden I Know* (New York: Free Press, 2006) and *Holy War, Inc.: Inside the Secret World of Osama Bin Laden* (New York: Free Press, 2001), 63.

19. The indefatigable efforts of Ambassador Tomsen to help the Afghans are admirable, poignant, and relentlessly Western-centric. His advocacy of a U.S.-like federal system for Afghanistan has been consistent for nearly twenty years. See Peter Tomsen, "A Chance for Peace in Afghanistan," *Foreign Affairs* 79, no. 1 (January–February 2000), 179–83.

20. For a fine and comprehensive analysis of the Afghan and international milieus in which all of this took place see Steve Coll, *Ghost Wars: The Secret History of the CIA,*

Afghanistan, and Bin Laden, from the Soviet Invasion to September 10, 2001 (New York: Penguin, 2004).

21. The remarks regarding John Jay are quoted in McDougall, *Promised Land,* 29.
22. Statement of Secretary Madeleine Albright, http://secretary.state.gov, March 3, 1998.
23. *The New Yorker*'s Lawrence Wright has written a book that I believe to be one of the very best on the events preceding 9/11. I spoke to Mr. Wright on several occasions as he was writing and am satisfied that he quoted me accurately. My only criticism of the book is that it leans too far toward describing the FBI as a competent counterterrorist organization and toward making the FBI's John O'Neill a hero. To the contrary, on the basis of my own dealings, and those of my colleagues, with Mr. O'Neill and all senior FBI officers, I am forced to say that, in my opinion, they did more to ensure that 9/11 occurred than almost any other individuals in the U.S. government. In particular, Mr. O'Neill's actions poisoned relations between the FBI and the CIA; he withheld information from the FBI's partners in the Intelligence Community; he misled the congressional intelligence committees; and he disrupted anti–al-Qaeda intelligence operations overseas in Yemen, the Balkans, and Azerbaijan. Mr. O'Neill's death on 9/11 was a rare instance of almost biblical justice. See Lawrence Wright, *The Looming Tower: Al-Qaeda and the Road to 9/11* (New York: Alfred A. Knopf, 2006), viii.

    The incompetence of the FBI is perhaps best shown in its attempt to convict a Pakistani and his son—respectively, an ice-cream vendor and a sixth-grade dropout—in Lodi, California. FBI claims that the men were part of an al-Qaeda terrorist cell fell apart in court when the lies of the Bureau's main witness came to light. See Dan Thompson, "Trial of Father and Son Revealed no Evidence of Terrorist Cell," Associated Press, April 15, 2006; "Information from FBI Spy Questioned," www.recononet.com, March 30, 2006; Rone Tempest, "Al Qaeda in Lodi 'Unlikely,' " *Los Angeles Times*, March 30, 2006; and Andrew Maykuth, "California Terror Case Weakens in Court," State.com, April 5, 2006.
24. Abu-Ubayd al-Qurayshi, "The Fourth Generation of War," *Al-Ansar* (Internet), January 29, 2002.
25. For a good and detailed discussion of the Bojinka plot, see Simon Reeve, *The New Jackals: Ramzi Yousef, Osama Bin Laden and the Future of Terrorism* (Boston: Northeastern University Press, 1999), 77–91.
26. The exasperation of the senior FBI officer in this instance is attributable to several factors, but one of the most important is the simple and seldom-acknowledged fact that the FBI and CIA have very separate missions in terms of geographic responsibilities and the statutes that authorize their respective operations. The FBI works in the United States and is bound by U.S. law; overseas it generally works with local legal regimes and abides by local law; and its mission is to arrest, try, and convict criminals. The CIA, on the other hand, is authorized by statute to do very little in the United States, while overseas it is authorized to break any and every law to accomplish its mission of collecting foreign intelligence and of conducting, as authorized by the president, lethal and nonlethal covert-action operations. Overseas the CIA works harmoniously and legally with its liaison partners as much as possible, but legalities never stand in the way of suborning foreign nationals to commit treason or of breaking laws to steal information. These statutory missions are exceedingly different from one another, and perfect cooperation between the two

agencies is simply not in the cards. This is a hard, commonsense fact, and Congress, through its calls throughout the 1990s and since 9/11 for "seamless cooperation" and "complete sharing of information" among all Intelligence Community components, has misled Americans into believing such things are possible, indeed that they have already been put in place.

This much said, I must add that there is ample room at the margins for effective CIA-FBI-DoJ cooperation, especially against the transnational threats of terrorism, nuclear proliferation, narcotics trafficking, and organized crime. Between 1996 and 1999, for example, the CIA's bin Laden unit worked side by side with attorneys from the Southern District of New York—Mary Jo White, Patrick Fitzgerald, and Ken Karras—and FBI/New York special agent Daniel Coleman. Messrs. Fitzgerald, Karras, and Coleman worked routinely and regularly in the spaces housing the bin Laden unit and had access to every document acquired by CIA. The net result of the cooperation was that the first U.S. indictment of Osama bin Laden was based almost entirely on CIA-acquired information, which the Southern District's attorneys carefully and legally maneuvered through the legal "wall of separation." The same sort of cooperation helped yield other indictments and convictions of captured al-Qaeda fighters. If I may say as a parenthetical, the 9/11 Commission overemphasized the role of the "wall" in preventing effective CIA-FBI-DoJ cooperation. The "wall" was annoying but penetrable given good faith on all sides. What the commission should have told Americans was that when the wall was impenetrable, it was mostly because senior FBI officers like John O'Neill, Dale Watson, and Michael Rolenz wanted it to be—protecting bureaucratic turf, not Americans, was their goal.

27. Clarke, *Against All Enemies*, 81.
28. Machiavelli's discussion of the concept of "cruelty well-used" is in *Prince,* 29–32.
29. I do not want to make too much of the possibility of weakening Saddam by slaughtering a good part of his Baghdad-based intelligence service, but it would have been worth the effort and may have led to good things beyond the corpses of hundreds of Saddam's thugs. An intelligence headquarters in any country is a far more lucrative target than, say, the headquarters of an infantry or armored division. At the most basic level, nation-states have far more soldiers than they have intelligence officers. In striking a military target, therefore, the personnel killed are pretty easily replaced, as armies are usually overloaded with the generals, staff officers, and other categories of soldiers who man a division-level headquarters. In attacking an intelligence headquarters, however, you are likely to kill individuals who are more difficult to replace because of their analytic skills, linguistic talents, technical capabilities, overseas operational experience, and a range of other abilities that are unique to a clandestine service. In addition, intelligence service headquarters hold the vital records and databases on which operations, analysis, and (in dictatorships and police states) internal security and dissident-suppression are based.
30. One of the sad-but-true realities of intelligence collection in wartime or insurgency situations is that the steady application of military violence stimulates the collection of useful intelligence. People who are being bombed, strafed, shelled, or otherwise violently harassed have a strong sense of motivation to keep moving, and because of our array of observation tools, enemy fighters are in great danger of being detected when they are moving. In addition, people under military attack tend to become

excited and make communication mistakes, speaking on unencrypted telephones or talking in the clear on radios, giving our SIGINT-interception capabilities the chance to locate the speakers for elimination. One of the reasons Osama bin Laden and Ayman al-Zawahiri are alive today is because it is so difficult to use military power as a means of stimulating intelligence collection. Why is this the case? Because the U.S. government's rules of engagement for military and intelligence personnel are so restrictive—including, at times, the submission of a written memo to validate a target and ask permission to engage it—that by the time approval to fire is received by the officers assigned to find and kill bin Laden, al-Zawahiri, Mullah Omar, or their lieutenants, the target has often disappeared.

31. "I was initially disappointed that the retaliation had been so small," Clarke wrote. "My disappointment faded with time because it seemed that Saddam had gotten the message. Subsequent to that June 1993 retaliation, the U.S. intelligence and law enforcement communities never developed any evidence to further Iraqi support for terrorism against Americans." Clarke, *Against All Enemies,* 84.

32. On this point, one wonders if, in the years since 1914, any Great Power has deployed two armies abroad—as has the United States today—without having complete control over the oil supplies that make them viable.

33. See John Adams to the Officers of the First Brigade of the Third Division of the Massachusetts Militia, October 11, 1798, quoted in James H. Hutson, *The Founders on Religion: A Book of Quotations* (Princeton, N.J.: Princeton University Press, 2005), 76. It always has seemed odd to me that any educated American citizen can question the basic reality that America was founded as a Protestant Christian nation and that its founding documents were written to mirror, validate, and build on that reality. Long before the Declaration of Independence and the Constitution, American colonists had established that their goal in coming to America was to build a Christian community. The signers of the Mayflower Compact (November 11, 1620), for example, declared that they had come to America "for the glory of God, and the advancement of the Christian faith," while the representatives of the colonies of Plymouth, Massachusetts, and New Haven, Connecticut, in drawing articles of confederation in 1643, maintained that the colonists "all came into these parts of America with one and the same end and aim, namely, to advance the kingdom of our Lord Jesus Christ and to enjoy the liberties of the Gospel in purity with peace." It is ahistorical, therefore, to deny the Christian roots of American society and government, and an exercise in willful ignorance to refuse to acknowledge the pervasive role Christian beliefs continue to play in the workings of the contemporary American polity. While some Americans are zealously eager to prove John Adams wrong and show that the Constitution will serve an atheist America, the outcome of that test is still undecided. What is pertinent in regard to our war with the Islamists, and the argument that radical Islam can be defanged by the installation of secular democracy in the Muslim world, is to keep historical facts front and center: America was founded as a Christian nation, and its founding documents and machinery of government are to this day derived from and influenced by Christian scripture. To the extent that we forget or ignore this historical reality, we will tend to overestimate the chances of successfully transferring America's constitutional and democratic machinery to such non-Christian societies as Iraq and Afghanistan. For the 1620 and 1643 documents noted above, see Donald S. Lutz,

ed., *Colonial Origins of the American Constitution: A Documentary History* (Indianapolis, Ind.: Liberty Fund, 1998), 31–32, 365–66. I also want to acknowledge my debt to Daniel Robinson for helping me to understand the importance of Christianity in America's founding and in the drafting of the documents Americans live by. For a riveting and exciting introduction to the thought and beliefs of America's founders see Daniel Robinson, *American Ideals: Founding a Republic of Virtue*, 12 lectures (Chantilly, Va.: Teaching Company, 2004).

Chapter 2. Fighting Islamists with a Blinding Cold War Hangover, 1996–2001

1. Armstrong Williams, "Missing the Mark . . . Amid Self-Delusion," *Washington Times,* October 19, 2000, A-19.
2. Each administration I worked for also demonstrated exactly the same mind-permanently-made-up attitude toward Saudi Arabia. Although intelligence is collected on Saudi Arabia, senior IC and administration officials tend to shrug off any negative intelligence about the Saudis, whether it regards Riyadh's assistance to anti-U.S. Islamists around the world, involvement in corruption or other criminal activities, or other nefarious matters. In addition, both Israel and Saudi Arabia can head off any effort to get negative intelligence to senior policymakers because each country's ambassador in Washington has easy and immediate access to the White House.
3. Two instances of such protectiveness toward Moscow, although minor in the overall scheme of things, show how deeply ingrained this tendency was in the parts of the Intelligence Community that were focused on the USSR. The Afghan-Soviet war was a matter of intense interest to both houses of Congress, and so CIA officers were regularly called on to brief the members and staff of the two intelligence committees. On such an occasion one of the CIA's Soviet experts was asked by a congressman why the CIA had not told the committee about a recent massacre of Afghan civilians by the Red Army. The officer responded that the murders were relatively small in number and we did not want to make too much out of a "minor atrocity." The congressman was livid over the term "minor atrocity" and warned the officer to stop protecting the Soviets.

     On another occasion preparations for a congressional briefing were marked by an argument over trees. At the time the commander of a Soviet unit in northeastern Afghanistan was ordered to move a large portion of his command south along a road that was heavily forested on each side right up to the edge of the road. Before moving, therefore, the commander wisely sent his engineers to cut down a wide swath of trees on each side of the road to lessen the ability of the mujahedin to ambush the column from point-blank range. The briefing team's Soviet experts objected to describing the commander's action because they believed the "politicians" in Congress would use the information to defame the Soviets as destroyers of the Afghan environment. As ludicrous as this argument was, senior CIA managers agreed, and the information was deleted from the briefing.

     This, as I said, was low-level nonsense, but it increases the admiration one must have for President Reagan's tenacity in overcoming the much greater protectiveness toward the USSR displayed by senior Intelligence Community managers who had spent their careers as Soviet hands. It also, I think, explains much of the 1980s venom that was directed toward DCI William J. Casey and Deputy Director for Intelligence Robert Gates as they worked with Mr. Reagan to break the Bolsheviks and their apologists in the U.S. government.

4. Charles S. Maier, *Among Empires: America's Ascendancy and Its Predecessors* (Cambridge, Mass.: Harvard University Press, 2006), 152.

5. The subject of terrorist groups acquiring WMD was always met with deep skepticism at the CIA and in the Intelligence Community generally. This primarily is due the nation-state orientation of intelligence officers and managers and their view that only nation-states had the money, expertise, and safety capabilities necessary to handle WMD materials safely. This was fair enough during the Cold War, but the rise of transnational threats thereafter changed things drastically. In al-Qaeda's case, for example, the CIA had solid information by late 1996 that bin Laden had several years previously formed a unit to build, steal, or purchase WMD—preferably a nuclear device—and staffed it with hard scientists, technicians, and engineers. He had told the unit that money was no object, and of course personal health and safety were not issues for those willing and even eager to die as martyrs. This information was contained in a fifteen-to-twenty-paragraph intelligence report, which detailed what we had learned in excruciating detail. CIA senior managers, however, still did not believe that al-Qaeda or any other terrorist group was serious about getting and using WMD and so edited the report down to two short paragraphs. The full report was not released until a year later, after repeated appeals from the officers who had collected the information.

6. In all the post-9/11 investigations, analysis, and media commentary, no one seems to have posed the question that is most important in regard to how good the intelligence had to be before Washington could act to destroy an entity—al-Qaeda—that we believed was determined to detonate a mass-destruction weapon in the United States. Senior Clinton NSC officers Richard Clarke, Daniel Benjamin, Steven Simon, and unnamed senior CIA officers have said that (a) by 2000 the CIA had been reporting "for years" that al-Qaeda was seeking nuclear and chemical weapons; (b) President Clinton was fixated on the WMD issue since at least 1995; (c) the White House believed that al-Qaeda had been trying to acquire WMD "[b]y early 1994, if not earlier"; and (d) the Cabinet was advised by the CIA in early 1998 that "[s]ooner or later bin Laden will attack U.S. interests, perhaps using WMD." Note that all the reporting about al-Qaeda's WMD intentions was available before the ten chances to capture or kill were presented to President Clinton between May 1998 and May 1999. It is inexplicable, at least to me, how all the investigations, pundits, and journalists have let Clinton officials have it both ways; that is, the al-Qaeda WMD threat was clear, but the intelligence was never good enough to try to destroy al-Qaeda. Question: How definitive must the intelligence be before the U.S. government acts to prevent a nuclear explosion in a U.S. city? See Clarke, *Against All Enemies*, 162–63, 177; Daniel Benjamin and Steven Simon, *The Age of Sacred Terror* (New York: Random House, 2002), 128–29; and Kean et al., *9/11 Commission Report,* 112.

7. Many of the opportunities to capture or kill bin Laden are listed in *9/11 Commission Report*, 108–43. To the best of my memory, the chances were as follows:

- May 1998: Capture opportunity at bin Laden's compound south of Khandahar City
- September 1998: Capture opportunity north of Khandahar City
- December 1998: Military attack opportunity, governor's palace, Khandahar City
- February 1999: Military attack opportunity, governor's residence, Heart City
- March-April 1999: Multiple military attack opportunities, hunting camp, near Khandahar
- May 1999: Military attack opportunities on five consecutive nights, Khandahar City

8. For a stunningly misleading account of the number of occasions bin Laden's location was fixed by the CIA's clandestine service, and equally deceptive comments on the quality of the information available to President Clinton on opportunities that arose to eliminate bin Laden, see Clarke, *Against All Enemies,* 196–204.

   In the binder of documents I prepared for working with post-9/11 panels, there are memoranda from the seniormost officers of the CIA's Counterterrorist Center, as well as cables from the CIA's senior officer in Pakistan, that document that DCI Tenet was repeatedly told by his top advisers that the intelligence was not going to get better. In addition, DCI Tenet repeatedly told those of us involved in the ten opportunities to eliminate bin Laden that he had on each occasion informed Messrs. Clarke, Berger, and Clinton of this fact.

9. The best assessment of Moscow's side of a proxy war is the study prepared by the Soviet General Staff on Afghanistan. See Lester A. Grau and Michael A. Gress, eds. and trans., *The Soviet Afghan War: How a Superpower Fought and Lost* (Lawrence: University of Kansas Press, 2002), xiii.

10. See Mohammad Yousaf and Mark Adkin, *The Bear Trap: Afghanistan's Untold Story* (Lahore, Pakistan: Jang Publishers Press, 1992), 189–206.

11. From my perspective, the Afghans are the exception to this general conclusion about Cold War proxies. Afghans are a truly peculiar people—stubborn, courageous, and extraordinarily patient and independent. With or without U.S., Saudi, or Pakistani assistance the Afghan mujahedin would have continued to fight the Soviets with whatever arms they could gather until they were either victorious or wiped out.

12. Michael Abramowitz and Griff White, "Insurgent Activity Spurs Cheney Trip to Afghanistan," *Washington Post*, February 27, 2007, A-1; David E. Sanger, "Cheney Warns Pakistanis to Act Against Terror," *New York Times*, February 27, 2007, A-9; and Machiavelli, *Prince*, 40–41.

13. John McCain and Robert Dole, "Save Darfur Now," *Washington Post*, September 10, 2006, B-07. The conservative side of the U.S. political spectrum is likewise abundant with these private-sector champions of U.S. intervention. From the democracy-and-freedom peddlers at Freedom House, the American Enterprise Institute, and the National Endowment for Democracy, to the overseas Christian-conversion campaigns conducted under the guise of the evangelical humanitarian organizations led by Pat Robertson and Franklin Graham, the political right is just as obsessed with embroiling the United States in costly interventions abroad that serve their specific interests but not America's national ones. Indeed, some of the evangelicals—in the

same ways as the Israel-firsters—seem eager to involve their countrymen in other peoples' religious wars.

14. Gertrude Himmelfarb, "The Dark and Bloody Crossroads," *National Interest*, no. 32 (Summer 1993), 56.

15. It seems likely that economic interests also played a role in the Clinton administration's reluctance to upset the Taliban by trying to kill or capture bin Laden. As noted, the Clinton White House pushed hard in support of UNOCAL's effort to get Taliban permission to build a natural-gas pipeline through Afghanistan in the 1990s. In addition, President Clinton refused to kill Osama bin Laden in the spring of 1999 when he was visiting the hunting camp of a prince from the United Arab Emirates in the desert near Khandahar. Why? The prince's father was about to buy U.S.-made F-16 fighter planes valued at $8 billion. For the natural-gas deal see Kean et al., *9/11 Commission Report*, 111, and "The Great Game, Oil and Afghanistan: An Interview with Ahmed Rashid," *Multinational Monitor* 22, no. 11 (November 2001). For the hunting camp chance, see Clarke, *Against All Enemies*, 200; Kean et al., *9/11 Commission Report*, 137–39; Benjamin and Simon, *Age of Sacred Terror*, 281; and Tenet, *Center of the Storm*, 123. Together these three works provide a nifty cover-up of the reason Washington failed to attack bin Laden and the hunting camp of the UAE princes. In his book Clarke said the camp "looked a lot more like a luxury mobile home than a terrorist hideout. We feared that the target was not al-Qaeda, but a falcon hunting camp from a friendly state." The *9/11 Report* says Clarke told the commissioners that "the intelligence [about the camp] was dubious." Benjamin and Simon claim the attack was called off when the White House learned that "the camp belonged not to bin Laden but to a group of wealthy Emiratis who had flown to Afghanistan for a hunting trip." The Clinton-protecting Tenet simply and completely untruthfully adds, "Before a decision could be made [by the president] as to whether to launch a strike, we got word that bin Laden had moved on."

Each account sounds plausible, and each is untrue. The CIA knew and told the White House and the NSC from the moment of the camp's establishment that it belonged to the UAE princes and was complete with luxurious tents, dozens of four-by-four vehicles, and a plane parked near the facility. Likewise, it was common knowledge in Khandahar that the UAE princes were hiring locals as laborers and cooks. The camp itself served as a magnet that repeatedly drew bin Laden there to meet, dine, and pray with the princes; we knew this from human assets and technical means. The bottom line for this story is that the Clinton White House and NSC knew (a) from the first that the camp belonged to the UAE princes; (b) that bin Laden was going to the camp to visit the princes; and (c) that a variety of intelligence sources were telling us when he was in the camp on a timely basis. Why did President Clinton fail to attack? Because making money was more important than protecting Americans. Per Clinton NSC senior directors Benjamin and Simon: "At the moment the Tomahawks [cruise missiles] were being readied, the United States was in the final stages of negotiations to sell eighty Block 60 F-16s [to the Emiratis], America's most sophisticated export fighter jets."

The tools covered by the term "technical means" include all methods of intelligence collection that are not dependent on firsthand human observation. While not commenting on the bin Laden operation specifically, the reader can imagine how very useful is the work of CIA-based imagery analysts in helping to corroborate reporting

Notes

from human assets. This is particularly true when the assets are reporting on physical features—buildings, hills, road intersections, culverts, vehicles, bridges, etc.—in the immediate vicinity of an individual(s) being sought. The ability to validate reporting and thereby build confidence in asset reporting that cannot be confirmed by "U.S. eyes" via the at-times-astounding work of imagery analysts was one of the most important tools that were brought to bear in CIA efforts against bin Laden. For more information about the technical means used with CIA assets in Afghanistan than I could ever have gotten approved by CIA's Publication Review Board, see the information DCI Tenet apparently allowed to be disclosed for publication in Bob Woodward, *Bush at War* (New York: Simon & Schuster, 2002), 6–7.

16. See Kenneth Katzman, "Afghanistan: Current Issues and U.S. Policy Concerns," *Congressional Research Service Report* (Internet version), November 21, 2001. Richard Clarke also thought it better to bend to the will of the feminists than to protect all Americans. He told the 9/11 commissioners that he opposed a U.S. State Department proposal to ask the Saudis to give the Taliban $250 million in return for bin Laden because "the idea might not seem attractive to either Secretary [of State] Albright or First Lady Hillary Rodham Clinton—both critics of the Taliban's record on women's rights." Kean et al., *9/11 Commission Report*, 125.

17. John Quincy Adams, "Speech on July 4, 1821," Future of Freedom Foundation, www.fff.com.

18. Maier, *Among Empires,* 242.

19. Joseph Nye, *Soft Power: The Means to Success in World Politics* (New York: Public Affairs, 2005), and more recently, Joseph Nye, "Our Impoverished Discourse," www.huffingtonpost.com, November 1, 2006. To be fair to Dr. Nye, it should be noted that Washington's feeble use of hard power over the past decade has perhaps created too much of a task for soft power to achieve. Our enemies no longer believe America will use its hard power in full measure, and so soft power does not have the hard power partner—either in fact or in the foe's expectations—that fueled its success during the Cold War. Today, as Mark Steyn has written, " 'Soft power' is wielded by soft cultures, usually because they lack the will to maintain hard power." See Mark Steyn, *America Alone: The End of the World as We Know It* (Washington, D.C.: Regnery Publishing, 2006), 46.

20. Adams, "Speech on July 4, 1821."

21. Joseph S. Nye, "Propaganda Isn't the Way: Soft Power," *International Herald Tribune*, January 10, 2003.

22. The CIA's bin Laden unit—known as "Alec Station" at its inception—was given a charter of five tasks in late 1995.

    a. To review on-hand information about bin Laden, collect as much new intelligence as possible, and determine if bin Laden and al-Qaeda were a national security threat to the United States.

    b. Disseminate bin Laden and al-Qaeda–related intelligence to the Intelligence Community as expeditiously as possible.

    c. Develop a set of covert-action operations designed to erode al-Qaeda's military capabilities.

    d. Assist U.S. federal law-enforcement authorities to indict bin Laden.

    e. Prepare a covert operation to capture bin Laden.

These tasks were fully accomplished by mid-May 1998, although the federal indictment of bin Laden was not publicly announced until the following November. The bottom line here is that the CIA's clandestine service delivered splendidly on all counts, and the Clinton administration did not act on the product it received.

23. The consistent effort of senior U.S. government officials to prevent Americans from learning of Saudi perfidy is common under Democrats and Republicans. In September 2002, for example, Prince Turki al-Faisal wrote in a *Washington Post* op-ed: "In 1996 . . . at the instruction of the Saudi leadership, I shared all the intelligence we had collected on bin Laden and al-Qaeda with the CIA." Having been on the scene at the time, I can categorically say that this is untrue. The response of the Bush administration to criticism of the Saudis, moreover, continued the don't-worry-they're-our-pals mantra of President Clinton's team. In November 2004 White House press spokesman Ari Fleischer told reporters, "I see no reason to believe that Saudi Arabia is not committed to the campaign against terrorism," and Secretary of State Colin Powell followed by reminding critics of Riyadh "that Saudi Arabia has been a great friend to the United States for many, many years, and is a strategic partner." See Prince Turki al-Faisal, "Allied Against Terrorism," *Washington Post,* September 17, 2002, 21, and David E. Sanger, "Bush Officials Praise Saudis for Aiding Terror Fight," *New York Times,* November 27, 2002. For Prince Bandar's statement see "Ex-Saudi Ambassador: Kingdom could have helped U.S. prevent 9/11," www.cnn.com, November 2, 2007. In a larger sense, Bandar's November statement probably means that the Saudi rulers have decided the Democrats are likely to win the next presidential election and so are throwing them a few bones to help beat up both the Bush administration and the CIA—which the Democrats, of course, thrive on. Bandar is doing what the Saudis always do: They cozy up to the U.S. political party they think will win the White House. Soon after the next U.S. president is inaugurated you will see pictures of him or her holding hands with the Saudi king and walking around the Camp David grounds. This groveling will occur no matter which party wins; because America is so dependent on Saudi oil, neither party can afford to hold a grudge against America's energy masters in Riyadh.

24. Shaykh Nasir bin Hamd al-Fahd, "A Treatise on the Legal Status of Using Weapons of Mass Destruction against Infidels," May 1, 2003.

25. For an excellent analysis of the dimensions of the threat posed to the United States by the unsecured nuclear arsenal of the Former Soviet Union, and of the dereliction of the Clinton and George W. Bush administrations in allowing that threat to fester, see Graham Allison, *Nuclear Terrorism: The Ultimate Preventable Catastrophe* (New York: Times Books, 2004).

26. "The two keys in bello requirements," just-war scholar Jean Bethke Elshtain has written,

> are proportionality and discrimination. Proportionality refers to the need to use the level of force commensurate with the nature of the threat . . . Discrimination refers to the need to differentiate between combatants and noncombatants . . .
>
> Knowing and intentionally placing noncombatants in jeopardy and putting in place strategies that bring the greatest suffering and harm to noncombatants rather than combatants is unacceptable on just war grounds. According to just war think-

ing, it is better to risk the lives of one's own combatants than those of enemy non-combatants . . . It is always suspect to destroy the infrastructure of civilian life.

See Jean Bethke Elshtain, *Just War Against Terror: The Burden of American Power in a Violent World* (New York: Basic Books, 2003), 65–66.

27. Machiavelli, *Prince,* 10, 32.
28. Quoted in Tsouras, *Civil War Quotations,* 235.
29. "Interview with Abu Jandal," *Al-Quds Al-Arabi,* March 28, 2005. "One night before the [August 20, 2007] bombing," Abu Jandal recalled, "Shaykh Usama bin Laden decided to go to the Khowst camps . . . I remember that when we reached a cross-roads between Khowst and Kabul in Wardak Province, Shaykh Usama bin Ladin said: 'Where do you think, my friends, where should we go, to Khowst or to Kabul?' We said we should go to Kabul in order to visit our comrades at the front there. He said: 'With God's help, let us go to Kabul.' "
30. On August 19, 1998, the day before the attack, I was told by one of the top officials in the CIA's Counterterrorist Center that the White House had told the DCI that it was adjusting the timing of the cruise-missile strike so as not to attack at the time of evening prayers. Killing bin Laden and other insurgent chiefs at prayer, the White House had decided, carried too much risk of offending the Muslim world. Interest-ingly, the missiles did hit the main mosque, but it was empty because prayers were over.
31. Joshua Mitchell, "Not All Yearn to be Free," *Washington Post,* August 10, 2003, B-7.
32. For a discussion of this supposed need for "imagination" and even for "institutional-izing" it, see Kean et al., *9/11 Commission Report,* 339–48.
33. Abdel Bari Atwan, "Saudi Incidents: Causes and Results," *Al-Quds Al-Arabi,* June 1, 2004, 1.
34. George Washington to Marquis de Malmedy, May 16, 1777, quoted in Melton, *Quotable Founding Fathers,* 63.
35. David Brooks, "Among the Bourgeoisophobes," *Weekly Standard,* April 15, 2002, 25.
36. *The 9/11 Commission Report* quotes an officer from the Joint Chiefs of Staff as say-ing that "Bin Laden had left his quarters before the strike would have occurred." I was running this operation from the CIA side in Washington, and I have no recollection of ever learning that bin Laden had departed before we could have launched an attack. Even if this is true, however, it was unknown before the decision was made not to shoot, and we were operating on that Sunday on the basis of first-hand, eyewitness information that bin Laden had entered the building for the night. If he left before the missiles would have hit the target, it was because the NSC had taken many hours from the time the targeting data arrived in Washington before reaching any kind of deci-sion. And they made a negative decision, at a moment when our best data said bin Laden was still in the targeted building. Thus, the Clinton team's decision not to attack amounted to a conscious decision to forgo an opportunity to protect Americans. See Kean et. al., *9/11 Commission Report,* 131.
37. For the stark and substantive differences between Shias and Sunnis not only on the importance and appropriateness of shrines but on myriad other issues, see the excel-lent and wonderfully informative Vali Nasr, *The Shia Revival: How Conflicts Within Islam Will Shape the Future* (New York: W.W. Norton and Co., 2006), esp. 31–61.

38. Andrew J. Bacevich, "A Less than Splendid Little War," *Wilson Quarterly* (Winter 2001), 83.
39. Ernest Hemingway, *Islands in the Stream* (New York: Charles Scribner's Sons, 1970), 41–42.
40. Ibid., 42.
41. Ralph Peters, *New Glory: Expanding America's Global Supremacy* (New York: Sentinel, 2005), 30.
42. Colonel Thomas X. Hammes, USMC (Ret.), *The Sling and the Stone: On War in the 21st Century* (St. Paul, Minn.: Zenith Press, 2004), xi.
43. Perhaps a good deal of blood and treasure could have been saved if Secretary Rumsfeld, his military transformers, and the RMA'ers had read a little history. The folly of depending on relatively few soldiers and specialized modern weaponry, as well as the reality that man-to-man combat would remain the central feature of war, was explained by Machiavelli in the sixteenth century. Writing to dismiss the reliance of Italian princes on artillery and cavalry—the specialized modern weaponry of the era—Machiavelli argued "that it suits whoever wishes to make a good army to accustom his men with exercises either feigned or true to get close to the enemy, to come at him wielding the sword, and to stand chest to chest with him. And one ought to found oneself more on infantry than on horse for the reasons that will be said below [He argues: "Ordered infantry can easily break a horse, and only with difficulty be defeated by them."] If one found oneself on infantrymen and on the modes said before, artillery becomes all together useless. For in getting close to the enemy, infantry can flee the blows of artillery . . . [T]he foundation and the sinew of the army, and that which should be esteemed more, should be the infantry." See Niccolò Machiavelli, *Discourses on Livy,* trans. Harvey C. Mansfield and Nathan Tarcov (Chicago: University of Chicago Press, 1996), 166–69.
44. Kean et al., *9/11 Commission Report,* 126–43.
45. See Benjamin and Simon, *Age of Sacred Terror*, 282, and Clarke, *Against All Enemies,* 200.
46. The problem with SIGINT collection against al-Qaeda in Khandahar and the other issues that are the focus of the documents in my report are described in general terms in a letter I sent to the two congressional intelligence committees in September 2004. Neither committee responded to my letter. The letter was acquired by and much of it printed in *The Atlantic* in December 2004. See "Verbatim: How Not to Catch a Terrorist," *Atlantic Online,* December 2004. In addition *The 9/11 Commission Report* notes that the NSA was responsible for "maintaining capability against older [communications] systems, such as high-frequency radios and ultra-high and very-high frequency (line-of-sight systems) that work like old-style television antennas." The commissioners, needless to say, do not reveal that the NSA failed utterly—indeed, refused to try—to fulfill this responsibility in 1996–99 regarding bin Laden–related communications in Afghanistan. See Kean et al., *9/11 Commission Report,* 93.
47. Of the period when I was managing CIA operations against bin Laden, Richard Clarke has written: "I still to this day do not understand why it was impossible for the United States to find a competent group of Afghans, Americans, third-party country nationals or some combination who could locate bin Laden in Afghanistan and kill him. Some have claimed that the [U.S.] lethal authorizations were convoluted or the

294

'people in the field' did not know what they could do . . . but the President's [Clinton] intent was very clear: kill bin Laden. I believe that those who in the CIA claim the authorizations were insufficient or unclear are throwing up the claim to excuse the fact that they were pathetically unable to accomplish the mission." This, like much else in Mr. Clarke's book and post-9/11 statements, is misleading. At no time in this period did the CIA have legal authorization to kill bin Laden; if we had, as I told Mr. Clarke to his face in spring 1998, bin Laden would have been long dead. What Mr. Clarke is doing in this statement is throwing up a claim to disguise the obvious: he, Mr. Berger, and President Clinton cared little about protecting Americans and were not manly enough to order such an attack, and their moral cowardice resulted in three thousand deaths on 9/11. See Clarke, *Against All Enemies,* 204.

48. Alexander F.C. Webster and Darrell Cole, *The Virtue of War. Reclaiming the Classic Traditions East and West* (Salisbury, Mass: Regina Orthodox Press, 2004), 210.

Part II: Six Years of War, 2001–2007

Chapter 3. Afghanistan—A Final Chance to Learn
History Applies to America

1. For a recent, excellent study of Paine, see Craig Nelson, *Thomas Paine: Enlightenment, Revolution, and the Birth of Modern Nations* (New York: Viking Penguin, 2006).
2. Washington Journal, C-SPAN TV/Radio, October 22, 2006.
3. Scheuer, *Through Our Enemies' Eyes,* 275–86, and *Imperial Hubris,* 21–58.
4. Sir John Keegan, "How America Can Wreak Revenge," *Daily Telegraph,* September 14, 2001, and "If America Decides to Take on the Afghans, This Is How to Do It," *Daily Telegraph,* September 20, 2001.
5. Milt Bearden, "As the War Turns," *Los Angeles Times,* November 18, 2001, and "Afghanistan, Graveyard of Empires," *Foreign Affairs* 80, no. 6 (November–December 2001).
6. Woodward, *Bush at War.*
7. al-Adl, "The al-Qaeda Organization Writes a Letter."
8. Richard K. Betts, "The Soft Under-Belly of American Primacy: Tactical Advantages of Terror," *Political Science Quarterly* 117, no. 1 (Spring 2002), 22.
9. Osama bin Laden, "Declaration of Jihad Against the Americans," *al-Islah* (Internet), September 2, 1996, and "Text of the World Islamic Front's Statement Urging Jihad Against Jews and Crusaders," *Al-Quds Al-Arabi* (Internet), February 23, 1998.
10. If the U.S. military had been prepared to attack Afghanistan immediately after 9/11, it is likely that only minimal damage could have been done to al-Qaeda, but that heavy human and material damage could have been inflicted on the Taliban. Bin Laden and his lieutenants, of course, knew the attack was coming, and bin Laden has said that they learned of the precise attack date six days before the advent. Taken together these facts suggest that al-Qaeda's personnel and matériel were well dispersed by 9/11. On the other hand, I have seen no indication that bin Laden tipped off Mullah Omar to the timing of the attack, and so Taliban manpower and material resources probably would have been sitting ducks immediately after 9/11.
11. Like the good Republican multiculturalists they are, the Bush team quailed at the

thought of offending Muslim opinion and removed the word *justice* from its operational name for the invasion of Afghanistan. Likewise, Woodward's book *Bush at War* shows that President Bush and his Cabinet officers were committed to victory in Afghanistan as long as it could be done in a politically correct manner—that is, with little or no "collateral damage." See, for example, Woodward, *Bush at War,* 166, 208, 210.

12. Ibid., 65.

13. Since Woodward's book was published, President Musharraf has claimed that soon after 9/11 Washington sent Deputy Secretary of State Richard Armitage to Pakistan to threaten a U.S. military attack on the country if Islamabad did not do everything the United States wanted done against bin Laden. Mr. Armitage has denied the story. See "U.S. Threatened to Bomb Pakistan," BBCNEWS.com.uk, September 22, 2006, and "Armitage Denies Threatening Pakistan after 9/11," MSNBC.MSN.com, September 22, 2006.

14. The downside of this savagery-limiting and time-wasting zeal for coalition-building can be seen in the run-up to the Afghan invasion. On September 30, 2001, for example, Secretary of State Powell advised his cabinet colleagues that the U.S. military should be assigned to "[g]o after some targets that won't get us into trouble with either the Arabs or Europeans." Here we have the secretary of state recommending attacks on politically correct targets—not the targets most worth destroying—in order to avoid offending current or potential coalition partners. Then on October 3, 2001—three-plus weeks after 9/11—General Richard Meyers (USAF), then chairman of the Joint Chiefs of Staff, informed the cabinet that "they [his staff] are still trying to find a role [in the coming Afghan war] for key allies." Apparently finding a role for "key allies" was more important than annihilating as much of Taliban and al-Qaeda forces as possible before they could fully disperse. See Woodward, *Bush at War,* 181, 191.

15. Chris Wallace, "Interview with President Clinton," www.foxnews.com, September 26, 2006.

16. For the chances to kill or capture bin Laden that Mr. Clinton said he did not have, see Kean et al., *9/11 Commission Report,* 126–43.

17. Wallace, "Interview with Clinton."

18. Mr. Clinton seems to have been referring to a follow-on plan to an earlier one called Delenda Est—"[al-Qaeda] Must be destroyed"—which was put together by Richard Clarke after the 1998 East Africa bombings. Clarke's Delenda Est was a plan (like the one Mr. Clinton described to Chris Wallace) that was meant to be a comprehensive and ongoing campaign against al-Qaeda until it was destroyed. In 1998 Delenda Est started and ended with the August 20, 1998, cruise-missile strikes on Afghanistan and Sudan. If Mr. Clinton did leave a plan for the Bush team—which I never heard of or saw—it was most likely a revision of Delenda Est. While working with Mr. Clarke in the 1990s, I found that he was very fond of planning large-scale, protracted counterterrorism campaigns. Each was grand in design, minimal in execution, and ultimately ephemeral in duration. For the Delenda Est plan, see Clarke, *Against All Enemies,* 181–204.

19. The perpetually adolescent quality of Mr. Clinton's leadership shone through in his interview with Chris Wallace. When asked why he did not attack al-Qaeda after the bombing of the U.S. destroyer *Cole,* Mr. Clinton responded that the "CIA and FBI

refused to certify that bin Laden was responsible while I was there." That is, "I am commander-in-chief, but it is my subordinates' fault that I did not defend America." See Wallace, "Interview with Clinton."

20. The term *heroin factories* might be foreign to American readers, as I know it was to me when I became chief for CIA operations against Afghan heroin producers in February 2000. The term is not an exaggeration, however. The Afghans who cultivate poppies for heroin production in southern Afghanistan are first and foremost modern and efficient businessmen; they are not nickel-and-dime entrepreneurs hustling dope in their spare time. Rather than small refining facilities, the major producers in southern Afghanistan—particularly in Khandahar and Helmand provinces—have either taken over or built towns dedicated to heroin production. Outdoor racks for drying, laboratory buildings for refining procedures, barracks for the workforce, motor pools, well-armed checkpoints and fighting positions, and warehousing for precursor chemicals and final product are located in the towns. These heroin-factory towns make easily locatable targets for air strikes.

21. Almost all the heroin consumed in the U.K. comes from Afghanistan, and in turn, the heroin trade drives most of the crimes in the U.K.'s cities. In an effort to destroy its heroin problem at the source, British troops assigned to Afghanistan have been deployed in the southern provinces of Khandahar, Oruzgan, and Helmand. See Declan Walsh, "In Afghanistan, Taliban Turning to the Drug Trade," *Boston Globe* (online version), December 18, 2005; Toby Hamden, "British Troops 'Will Be Targets in Afghanistan,' " *Sunday Telegraph* (online version), January 29, 2006; Christina Lamb, "British Face 20-Year War to Tame Taleban," *Times Online,* March 19, 2006; Mark Townsend, "Drugs Fuel Big Rise in Organized Crime," *Observer,* July 30, 2006; and Paul Kelbie, "Cheap, Pure Heroin Set to Flood Britain, Say Police," *Independent,* February 5, 2007. For Afghan heroin entering the United States, see Marisa Taylor, "Surge in Afghan Heroin hits United States," www.contracostatimes.com, January 7, 2007.

22. The failure to appreciate Afghanistan as part of the Islamic whole (beyond the ephemeral sense of limiting collateral damage to avoid offending Muslims) helped Washington misjudge how long its welcome would last in the eyes of non-Afghan Muslims. Just after 9/11, in fact, the United States had some room for acting with savagery even in the eyes of Muslims. The Muslim world was stunned by the surprise, ferocity, and brazenness of the 9/11 attacks and spent the next year debating whether al-Qaeda had staged the attacks or whether the Israelis had done so in cooperation with the CIA. In addition, bin Laden received a good deal of criticism from his Islamist peers for not preceding the attacks with the Prophet-mandated warnings to Americans, offers of chances to convert to Islam, and offers of a truce. He also was criticized for not securing religious approval before the attack to kill so many people. The leaders of other Islamist groups also condemned him for bringing the superpower's military wrath down on the Islamist movement, an event they considered fatal to the movement. These intra-Islamic debates and confusions—together with the Islamic religion's deeply held belief in the righteousness of exacting an eye for an eye—gave America an operational period that, while still limited, was longer than it would have been had it invaded Afghanistan without the 9/11 predicate. For the Koran and hadith-based criticisms of bin Laden by other Islamists, see Scheuer, *Imperial Hubris*, 152–61. For the Islamists' criticisms of bin Laden's strategy of attacking the

United States—the "far enemy"—and their belief that the U.S. military response would destroy the Islamist movement, see Fawwaz Gerges, *The Far Enemy: Why Jihad Went Global* (New York: Cambridge University Press, 2005). Dr. Gerges's book argues that bin Laden destroyed the Islamist movement via the 9/11 attacks and the devastating U.S. military retribution they engendered. This argument is based mostly on his conversations with Egyptian and a few other Islamists, the commonality among whom is their dislike of bin Laden. Gerges's thesis (and that of his sources) now lies in shreds and tatters as the United States edges toward final defeat in Afghanistan and Iraq. When that occurs, bin Laden's strategy of attacking the American far enemy and then being patient until the U.S. administration of the day suffered more pain than it could stand and threw in the towel will have been vindicated, giving the then-victorious Islamist movement a new birth and bin Laden enormously enhanced stature.

23. See Philip Smucker, *Al-Qaeda's Great Escape: The Military and Media on Terror's Trail* (Dulles, Va.: Brassey's, 2004), xxv.

24. Condoleezza Rice, President Bush's then-national security adviser, manifested the ignorance about Afghanistan that was present across the nation's highest councils. On Kabul, Ms. Rice felt the rejoicing of the city's populace as the Northern Alliance and the U.S.-led coalition occupied the city meant that Washington "had underestimated the pent-up desire of the Afghan people to take on the Taliban." Ms. Rice, in addition, had earlier told President Bush and Secretary Powell, "You know, the Russians never took Kabul." As striking as is Ms. Rice's lack of knowledge about Afghanistan—she is a Soviet expert, after all—even more striking is that no one in the Executive Branch seemed to correct her mistakes. See Woodward, *Bush at War,* 219, 313.

25. The Western influence in Kabul is angering conservative Afghans. Afghan teens are wearing jeans, listening to Indian pop music, watching Hollywood movies, and gathering in mixed-sex groups. In addition, the presence of Western diplomats, military personnel, and Europeans working for more than six hundred Kabul-based Western NGOs has stimulated the establishment of hotels, bars, restaurants, stores selling alcohol, and brothels to flourish in the city. As much as the lack of law and order, these perceived Western perversions make Afghans recall the Taliban regime's Islamic rule fondly. "Afghanistan is an Islamic country," a senior Kabul cleric warned, "and it should be following the laws of Sharia. In the previous regimes there were no shops where they clearly sold alcohol. There were no houses of hotels where they had prostitutes. Now we do have these things." See Ben Arnoldy, "Kabul Must-see TV Heats Up Culture War in Afghanistan," ABCNEWS.com, May 10, 2005; Kim Barker, "In Afghanistan, Cultural Struggle Turns Dangerous," *Chicago Tribune,* May 22, 2005; and Chris Sands, "Kabul Clerics Rally Behind Taliban," *Toronto Star,* May 22, 2006.

26. One of the greatest post-9/11 disservices done to both America and the U.S. Intelligence Community is to be found in the testimony on HUMINT collection from then-DCI George Tenet and then-CIA deputy director for operations James Pavitt to the congressional Intelligence Oversight Committee and the 9/11 investigatory panels. The gist of that testimony was that if Congress had supplied more money and more positions to the clandestine service before 9/11, the quantity and quality of human intelligence would have been better and perhaps the attack might have been stopped.

The implication was that a massive investment of money and new personnel would improve HUMINT immediately. This of course is not the case. Collecting HUMINT is difficult—you are, after all, trying to persuade someone to commit treason—and dangerous and cannot be counted on in the short term for more and better information simply because Congress allocates a large amount of money and positions. Such growth, over a good many years, is likely to produce better HUMINT, but there is no quick fix for the HUMINT problem. On this issue, Mr. Tenet's testimony was particularly interesting, as in the decade or more before 9/11 (as chief of staff for the Senate Select Committee on Intelligence, NSC Director for Intelligence Programs, the Deputy Director of Central Intelligence, and then DCI) he was not known for an eagerness to expand the clandestine service.

The post-9/11 hunt for bin Laden offers an excellent example of how hard it is to collect reliable HUMINT against the Afghan and Islamist targets. For the CIA and other U.S. and foreign intelligence services, the Pashtun tribes residing along both sides of the Pakistan-Afghanistan border present a formidable obstacle to the collection of intelligence, let alone the capture of major al-Qaeda and Taliban figures. The Pashtun people are divided into tribes, subtribes, and clans. These groupings are often at odds with each other, at times violently so, but they do form a relatively homogenous and strongly insular society. While Muslim non-Pashtuns are today more welcomed than they were a decade ago—occasionally to the point of intermarrying and becoming permanent residents—Westerners are not and, even when disguised, stick out like the proverbial sore thumb. Even small U.S. Special Forces units are not likely to operate for long without being discovered. Clandestine HUMINT collection in the tribal regions, therefore, has to be done through surrogates (Pashtuns willing to work for us) or by close-in SIGINT collection against local radios, telephones, cell phones, walkie-talkies, etc.

CIA HUMINT-collection operations in the tribal regions since 1979 demonstrate that it is not hard to recruit Pashtun assets, but that it is almost impossible to recruit one who will betray a brother Pashtun or (because of tribal mores guaranteeing that, once accepted, guests be protected) a non-Afghan Muslim. As always, Afghans will take your money and tell you what you want to hear, but they generally will not provide actionable intelligence, and like those the U.S. military hired to capture bin Laden at Tora Bora, they always show up a few hours too late. This is a lesson that the CIA learned well during the Afghan jihad, that a new generation of clandestine officers is learning today, and that military officers and senior policymakers apparently will never learn.

Collecting reliable HUMINT among the Pashtuns, moreover, has become more difficult because the conservative nature of Afghan Islam has deepened since the Soviet invasion of 1979. The pressures and sacrifices of war, the pride and sense of solidarity derived from the reality that Muslims had defeated the Soviet superpower, and the unrelenting proselytizing activities of the Pakistani religious parties and the money- and faith-dispensing Islamic NGOs sponsored by Arabian Peninsula regimes have all moved the Pashtuns' brand of Islam much closer to the standard of the Middle East. While there are still significant differences between the two, the tribes' development of an increasingly conservative faith adds another layer of resistance to whatever recruitment enticements Western intelligence services can offer.

Each of the points above applies in almost equal measure to the Pakistani intelligence and military services. The army and ISID are not much more welcomed than Westerners or unvouched-for Arabs in the border region. Tribal leaders usually tolerate the Pakistanis, but experience has demonstrated that their ability to collect reliable HUMINT in the Pashtun regions is limited, as is their willingness to share all of what they do collect. In addition, both the military and intelligence services consider themselves under constant threat, move only in well-armed, multivehicle convoys, and seldom venture out of their compounds at night. The situation for Pakistani military and intelligence units in the tribal regions has, of course, become much less tenable and much more dangerous in the wake of unprecedented, prolonged, and bloody Pakistani Army operations in the region since 2003.

27. Keegan, "If America Decides to Take On the Afghans."
28. Keegan, "How America Can Wreak Vengeance."
29. Lord Roberts is quoted in Frank L. Holt, *Into the Land of Bones: Alexander the Great in Afghanistan* (Berkeley: University of California Press, 2005), 5. Dr. Holt is a distinguished classicist whose extraordinarily pertinent book should be mandatory reading for all hands in the executive and legislative branches of the U.S. government, as well as for every Afghanistan-bound military and intelligence officer. In addition, Ralph Peters, one of America's preeminent and most prophetic strategists, has seconded the importance of both Keegan and Lord Roberts for contemporary U.S. leaders. "We need to relearn the usefulness of punitive expeditions," Peters wrote in 2005. There will be times in the future when "we simply will need to send in our military on a punitive expedition to exact a price that discourages further attacks on our homeland or on our interests, and then leave with our guns still smoking . . . Punitive expeditions are not described anywhere in our current military doctrine. That isn't proof of our moral enlightenment but of the benighted state of our strategic thinking." To date, sadly, the American governing elite has paid little attention to Colonel Peters's always-acute insights. See Ralph Peters, *New Glory: Expanding America's Global Supremacy* (New York: Sentinel, 2005), 83.
30. Emphasizing his group's long and close ties with al-Qaeda, Hekmatyar told a Pakistani television interviewer in January 2007 that his fighters had been among those who helped bin Laden and his lieutenants to escape from Tora Bora in December 2001. See "Rebel: We Aided Bin Laden Escape," Associated Press, January 11, 2007. For the best account of the disaster the U.S. generals inflicted on U.S. national security by letting bin Laden escape, see Gary Bernsten and Ralph Pezzulo, *Jawbreaker: The Attack on Bin Laden and al-Qaeda: A Personal Account by CIA's Key Field Commander* (New York: Three Rivers Press, 2006).
31. In Woodward's nearly four-hundred-page book one of the few hints that the Bush administration even momentarily focused on solving the border problem using U.S. resources comes on page 237: "There was some talk [at an October 7, 2001, meeting of NSC principals] of sealing the border." Woodward writes that the NSC concluded that "it seemed an impossible idea, not practical given the hundreds of miles of mountainous and rough terrain, some of the most formidable in the world." Well, there is no denying that closing that border was a hard job, but if the NSC did not believe the best military in the world could close the border and trap bin Laden, why did it decide that the task could be safely allotted to the poorly armed and trained and generally anti-U.S. Pakistani border forces? The ingrained tendency of U.S. officials to look for proxies to do U.S. dirty work prevailed again, and so bin Laden remains alive and free

as this is written. In addition, an effort to close the border to snare bin Laden would have required large amounts of U.S. military manpower and so would have played havoc with the plans of Defense Secretary Rumsfeld (the dean of the RMA'ers) and would have proven that his concept of "military transformation" ensured only that America had the wrong weapons and not enough soldiers and Marines to do the job. See Woodward, *Bush at War*, 237.

32. For excellent discussions of the U.S.-vs.-al-Qaeda combat at Shahi Kowt and elsewhere in Afghanistan, see Sean Naylor, *Not a Good Day to Die: The Untold Story of Operation Anaconda* (New York: Berkeley Books, 2005), and Stephen Biddle, *Afghanistan and the Future of Warfare: Implications for Army and Defense Policy* (Carlisle, Penn.: U.S. Army War College, Strategic Studies Institute, 2002).

33. By not abandoning the Cold War practice of finding foreigners to do America's dirty work, we have blithely assumed that Musharraf's Pakistan is an American proxy, with national-security interests that mirror those of the United States. The truth is that virtually none of the many things Musharraf has done to assist the United States in Afghanistan have been in Pakistan's national interest. Indeed, by supporting the installation of Karzai's pro-India, minimally Pashtun regime, Musharraf weakened security on his country's western border, and by sending the Pakistani army into the Pashtun regions, he diverted nearly a corps-size military organization from the Indian border and brought his country to the brink of civil war. He even tolerated Washington's clearly destabilizing demand that former Prime Minister Benazir Bhutto—whose government was manned by kleptomaniacs of epic avarice—be allowed to return to the country and reinvolve herself in Pakistan's political mix. Musharraf's accommodation of Washington's wishes vis. Mrs. Bhutto brought such chaos to the country's politics that he had to declare a near-martial-law "state of emergency" in early November 2007. History will show, I believe, that America has seldom if ever had an ally more willing than President Musharraf's Pakistan to take actions to further U.S. interests, actions that in no way served its own. Musharraf, however, drew the line at risking complete political collapse in Pakistan; he was not going to play the role of Taliban leader Mullah Omar, the only national leader in memory who knowingly sacrificed his country for a friend. In future years, when America's defeat in Afghanistan is apparent, and if he survives, Musharraf will be able to reflect on his relationship with President Bush and lament (as President Lincoln said about his relationship with General George McClellan), "Poor George . . . I did all I could for him, but he could do nothing for himself."

34. Holt, *Into the Land of Bones*, 19–20, 76–77.

Chapter 4. Iraq—America Bled White by History Unlearned

1. Bernard Lewis, "License to Kill: Osama bin Laden's Declaration of Jihad," *Foreign Affairs* 77, no. 6 (November–December 1998), 14–19.
2. See, for example, Osama bin Laden, "Message to Our Brothers in Iraq," Al-Jazirah Satellite Television, February 11, 2003.
3. In one of those only-in-historically-ignorant-America moments, the Clinton administration was confident that it had pulled the rug out from under bin Laden and negated this issue when most U.S. forces were moved from Saudi Arabia to Kuwait

and Qatar. If administration officials had known a bit of Islamic history, they would
have known that the Prophet Muhammad had said that all infidels should be evicted
from the Arabian Peninsula, not from Saudi Arabia, as the latter had not yet been
founded in the seventh century. So on this issue Washington managed to pull its own
hair over its own eyes, spending large sums to relocate U.S. forces but leaving bin
Laden's grievance as relevant as ever.

4. Jeff Stein, "Can You Tell a Shia from a Sunni?" *New York Times,* October 18, 2006.
5. Ibid.
6. Ibid. Not wanting to be outconfused by a member of the House Intelligence Committee he chairs, Representative Silvester Reyes (D-Texas) told reporters he believed
al-Qaeda was "predominantly, probably Shia," and added that "it is hard to keep
things in perspective and in categories." See "Queries Vex New Chair of Intelligence,"
Reuters, December 12, 2006.
7. Robert D. Kaplan, *Warrior Politics: Why Leadership Demands a Pagan Ethos* (New
York: Vintage Books, 2002), 39.
8. Stephen Hayes, *The Connection: How al-Qaeda's Collaboration with Saddam Hussein Has Endangered America* (New York: HarperCollins, 2004).
9. After grossly exaggerating the terrorist potential of Iraq, the Bush administration has
not said nearly enough about the genuine terrorist threat posed by Iran inside the
United States. Yes, the White House and the American Enterprise Institute are always
warning that Tehran sponsors terrorism, but they focus on Iran's terrorist activities in
the Middle East and against Israel. They seldom mention the continental United
States as a target. Why? Because Washington does not want to admit that the real terrorist threat posed by Iran and its Lebanese Hezbollah partner is inside the United
States. Iran's intelligence service and Hezbollah's cadre have built terror-supporting
infrastructures inside the United States and across Canada over the past twenty
years, thanks to the U.S. governing elite's refusal to enforce immigration laws and
impose border controls. U.S. law-enforcement agencies know Iran and Hezbollah are
here, but they have no precise handle on total numbers or locations. It is extremely
unlikely that either Iran or Hezbollah would stage an unprovoked terrorist attack
inside the United States—both have the fatal handicap of having known return
addresses—but if Washington attacks Iran, all bets would be off.
10. Not long after destroying the Iraqi bulwark against the westward movement of
Sunni jihadists, Washington, with bipartisan congressional support, took a strong step
toward accelerating the fall of the Syrian anti-Islamist bulwark by forcing Bashir
al-Assad to withdraw Syrian military and intelligence forces from Lebanon. Washington's public humiliation of al-Assad emboldened his domestic Islamist militants,
while the Syrian withdrawal inaugurated—with the key summer 2006 assistance of
the Israeli Defense Force—the disintegration of Lebanon's political stability that we
are now witnessing. The White House and the Congress both deserve thank-you notes
from bin Laden for their successful efforts on al-Qaeda's behalf.
11. See Scheuer, *Imperial Hubris,* 7, 229–30.
12. While there is nothing funny about the Bush administration not destroying
al-Qaeda–related WMD experiments when that option was available, al-Zarqawi's
chemical-weapons team once found themselves in an unusual position. They had designated a horse to be used as the subject for one of their experiments and walked him
into one of the camp's buildings. The Islamists stood the horse in a large metal tub

and then applied the chemical substance being tested. The experiment worked like a charm, and the horse quickly died. Now, however, Allah's would-be chemical warriors had the horse lying dead in a metal tub. Obviously, he could not exit the way he entered. This caused some consternation, and the now-contaminated horse eventually had to be removed piece by piece.

13. The first two categories of Iraqi fighters, dispersed regulars and the *fedayeen,* were described by the Bush administration from the outset as either "remnants of Iraqi forces" or more opaquely by the Pentagon as "Former Regime Elements" or FREs. The same sort of terminology also was used in Afghanistan after the capture of the Taliban's capital in Khandahar; thereafter the forces of the U.S.-led coalition were described as "mopping up" Taliban and al-Qaeda "remnants." Both cases were nothing more than blatant attempts to deceive Americans about the enemies' remaining strength, and another example of how U.S. leaders still believed in the possibility of conducting "bloodless wars." In Iraq, U.S. decision-makers let between 400,000 and 500,000 Iraqis go home with their guns (and later kept them angry and at home by formally disbanding the Iraqi army) and earlier had permitted probably a bit more than 60,000 Taliban and al-Qaeda fighters to similarly melt away with their weapons. What the White House and the Pentagon termed "remnants" were basically the entire enemy force in both countries that had fled from a head-on confrontation with America's unbeatable conventional military prowess to hide and fight again another day in circumstances more favorable to themselves. When both Iraqi and Afghan insurgents reemerged to engage U.S.-led forces in guerrilla-style warfare, the administration continued to misinform the American people by describing these virtually bottomless pools of military manpower as "remnants." At one point, in fact, CIA officers were told that Deputy Secretary of Defense Wolfowitz had decreed that the term "insurgents" would not be used in the Pentagon's intelligence analysis because it gave "legitimacy to terrorists." Even at this late date the Cold War belief that the United States was the master of the international political ballet still prevailed; the insurgents simply could have no legitimacy in any American mind, or Muslim mind, for that matter, unless the U.S. government awarded it to them.

14. There are two classic works, one very short and one longer, on the post–Great War British disaster in Iraq, or Mesopotamia as it was then called. The shorter work is T. E. Lawrence, "Report on Mesopotamia," *Sunday Times,* August 2, 1920. The longer and much more recent work is David Fromkin, *A Peace to End All Peace: Creating the Modern Middle East* (New York: Henry Holt and Co., 1989). Lawrence's report and the sections of Fromkin's book on Iraq (especially pages 449–54) are both unnerving and eerily familiar for the contemporary American reader. Lawrence's report begins: "The people of England have been led in Mesopotamia into a trap from which it will be hard to escape with dignity and honor." Sound familiar?

15. Machiavelli, *Prince,* 28

16. This is not to say that the Iranian and Sunni services are not involved in getting would-be mujahedin to Iraq. They certainly are, but with the open borders all around Iraq, entry to the battlefield is relatively easy. As in Afghanistan, the provision of cash, ordnance, identity and travel documents, and some paramilitary training by these services suffices. The services are going with the flow more than directing it.

17. The many routes traveled and sponsors available for the young Arabs intent on going to Afghanistan in the 1980s to fight the Red Army are excellently covered in

Bergen, *The Osama bin Laden I Know.* A fine and extensive firsthand account of how one European Muslim got to the Afghan arena after the Soviet retreat is Nasiri, *Inside the Jihad,* 3–100.

18. For the impact of prison on Ayman al-Zawahiri, see the exceptional, groundbreaking essay by Lawrence Wright, "The Man Behind Bin Laden," *New Yorker,* September 16, 2002. The impact of al-Zarqawi's prison experience is described in two articles featuring al-Zarqawi's religious mentor, the famed Islamist scholar Abu Muhammad al-Maqdisis; see Luqman Iskandar, "Calling for the Formation of a Global Body of Sunni Ulemas . . . ," *Al-Arab al-Yawm,* July 5, 2005, and Yasir Abu-Hilalah, "Interview with Abu Muhammad al-Maqdisis," Al-Jazirah Satellite Television, July 5, 2005.

19. On the role of Afghan war veterans in Bangladesh and Thailand, see, for example, David Mantero, "How Extremism Came to Bangladesh," *Christian Science Monitor,* September 6, 2005, and "Southern Thailand: Insurgency, not Jihad," *International Crisis Group,* Asia Report No. 98, May 18, 2006.

20. "92 al-Qaeda Suspects Freed in Amnesty," *Los Angeles Times,* November 17, 2003.

21. "Algeria Pardons 5,065 Prisoners to Mark Muslim Feast," www.deepikaglobal.com, January 18, 2005.

22. "Mauritania: Junta Declares General Amnesty for Political Prisoners," Reuters, September 5, 2005.

23. Said Moumni, "One-hundred and sixty-four Detainees Belonging to the Salfia Jiahdia Group Are Pardoned," *Annahar al-Maghribiyah*, November 5, 2005.

24. "Morocco Pardons 10,000 to Mark Independence," Reuters, November 17, 2005.

25. "Saudi Arabia: Almost 400 Prisoners Released," www.adnki.com, December 19, 2005.

26. "Algeria to Pardon or Reduce Sentences for 3,000 Terrorists," www.evening echo.ie/news, February 2006.

27. "Over 2,000 Algerians to be Released Under Reconciliation Charter," Radio Algiers/Channel 3, March 1, 2006.

28. "Ben Ali Frees 1,600 Tunisian Prisoners," www.middle-east-online.com, February 27, 2006.

29. "Yemen Frees 627 Zaidi Rebels," www.middle-east-online.com, March 3, 2006.

30. Human Rights Watch, "Libya: Hopeful Sign as 132 Political Prisoners are Freed," www.yubanet.com, March 3, 2006. Not surprisingly, the U.S. military announced in November 2007 that among foreign insurgents in Iraq, Libyans formed the second-largest contingent. See Richard A. Oppel Jr., "Foreign Fighters in Iraq Are Tied to U.S. Allies," *New York Times,* November 22, 2007.

31. Lee Harris, "Terror in Egypt: It Isn't Going to Stop Anytime Soon," *Weekly Standard* (Internet version), April 27, 2006.

32. "5 Ex-Guantanamo Detainees Freed in Kuwait," Associated Press, May 22, 2006.

33. "Yemen Acquits 19 Men in al-Qaeda-linked Trial," Reuters, July 8, 2006.

34. "Seven Security Detainees Escape Saudi Jail," Reuters, July 8, 2006.

35. "Mauritania Frees Suspected Islamist After Fourteen Months," Reuters, July 28, 2006, and "Mauritania: Three al-Qaeda-linked Suspects Escaped from Jail," Associated Press, April 27, 2006.

36. Morocco: Huge Amnesty Signals Historic Day," www.africa-interactive .net/index.php? PageID=3580, March 12, 2007, and "Fighters infiltrate from

Morocco to Iraq," www.alsumaria.tv/en/print-news-1-1896.html, March 22, 2007. None of the releases described account for the large numbers of Islamist fighters—including some captured on battlefields in Iraq and Afghanistan—that such regimes as Saudi Arabia and Yemen are cycling through what they describe as religious rehabilitation camps. The authorities in both countries claim that camp graduates are cured of jihadist tendencies, but there is no way to know whether these camps are anything more than part of a process that provides eyewash for Western governments prone to believe in such psychological rehabilitation and allows captured fighters to return to the wars. The Saudi regime is the highest volume rehabilitator, releasing 1,500 former al-Qaeda fighters from prison in November 2007. Perhaps not coincidentally, Saudis form the largest group of foreign insurgents in Iraq. See Eli Lake, "1,500 Qaeda Members Freed After Counseling," *New York Sun,* November 27, 2007; Talal Malik, "1,500 'Extremists' Released by Saudi," www.Arabianbusiness .com, November 26, 2007; Richard A. Oppel Jr., "Foreign Fighters in Iraq Are Tied to U.S. Allies," op cit.; "Saudi to Temporarily Release 55 Former Guantanamo Detainees; Give Them Money," Associated Press, October 6, 2007; and Kathy Gannon, "Yemen Coddling Terrorists," Associated Press, July 5, 2007.

37. Arab and Muslim regimes also derive an international-opinion benefit from releasing these prisoners: they win the applause of politically influential Western human-rights groups for releasing "prisoners of conscience." When in 2006 the Libyan regime of Colonel Qaddafi, for example, released 132 political prisoners, among them 86 Muslim Brotherhood members, the Middle East and North Africa director for Human Rights Watch Sarah Leah Whitson overflowed with praise for the Libyans. "The release of these longtime prisoners is a welcome step," Ms. Whitson said. "It is wonderful that 132 political prisoners are free. The Libyan government should now allow these people to express their views and engage in peaceful political activity." That Colonel Qaddafi might have released some of these men on the condition they travel to Iraq or Afghanistan to kill American soldiers seems never to have occurred to Ms. Whitson, and it probably would not have mattered to her if it did. Efforts by Washington to prevent Libya and other Arab regimes from freeing "prisoners of conscience" are not in the cards, as U.S. political leaders are cowed, as they were during the Cold War, by human-rights groups and are very unlikely to court the groups' condemnation or their own depiction by the media as foes of religious freedom. In the case of Libya, moreover, U.S. leaders would not want to alienate the authoritarian Qaddafi regime, with which they are planning to further increase American dependence on Arab oil. For Ms. Whitson's comments see "Libya: Hopeful Sign as 132 Political Prisoners Freed," March 3, 2006.

38. Since 2001 Islamists have made strong gains in elections in Egypt, Palestine, Saudi Arabia, Lebanon, Turkey, Pakistan, Kuwait, Iraq, and Bahrain. For summary articles on this trend, see Roula Khalaf and William Wallis, "Rising Islamist Tide Redefines Middle East's Political Canvas," *Financial Times,* January 27, 2006; Jonathan Last, "One Last Thing—Democracy, of Itself, Is Not a Solution to All Problems," *Philadelphia Inquirer,* August 6, 2006; Hassan M. Fattah, "Democracy in the Arab World, a U.S. Goal, Falters," *New York Times,* April 10, 2006; and Dan Murphy and Joshua Mitnick, "In Mideast Elections, Militants Gain," *Christian Science Monitor,* June 8, 2005.

39. Ironically, America's wartime allies and U.S. officials also authorize prisoner releases that contribute to the Islamists' manpower. Afghan president Karzai and Iraqi prime

minister al-Maliki have both been forced by domestic political pressures to release large numbers of men captured on the battlefield. Karzai, for example, has been attacked by the Afghan media for declaring an amnesty for "thousands of Taliban and their terrorist guests" who almost immediately "regrouped against the government and security of Afghanistan. They have mocked the good will of the Afghan government and have made efforts to expand and aggravate aggression and warfare in Afghanistan." On the American side, the U.S. military has released Saudi, Pakistani, Chinese, Yemeni, European, and Afghan Islamist fighters. The release of Afghan Pakistani prisoners from Guantanamo Bay, in particular, has repeatedly backfired. Many of the freed Afghans and Pakistanis have rejoined the Taliban-led jihad in Afghanistan, and some have been subsequently killed or recaptured by U.S. forces in Afghanistan. See "The Son of a Wolf Will Be a Wolf," *Cheragh,* October 24, 2004; Fayiz al-Maliki, "Mazhar: Saudi-U.S. Talks for the Release of 124 Saudi Detainees in Guantanamo," *Al-Watan* (online version), October 18, 2004; James Gordon Meek, "Freed, Many Rejoin Taliban," *New York Daily News,* February 13, 2004; "Ex-Detainee Leading Pakistani Militants," *Washington Post,* October 13, 2004, A-14; and John Mintz, "Released Detainees Rejoining the Fight," *Washington Post,* October 22, 2004, A-1.

40. Elizabeth Fox-Genovese, "Multiculturalism in History: Ideologies and Realities," *Orbis* 43, no. 4 (Fall 1999), 538. Those in American political life who ahistorically insist that U.S. society and culture is no better than any others and that it is exportable to the world at large despite immense cultural differences, would do well to consider Dr. Fox-Genovese's conclusion that "the United States ranks as the primary example of a democratic multicultural society, and it has owed its success to distinctly Western values and institutions, including individualism and democracy."

41. Fouad Ajami, "Where U.S. Power is Beside the Point," *New York Times,* October 17, 2000.

42. Since leaving the CIA, I have been involved in teaching intelligence analysis to junior U.S. military personnel—lieutenants, captains, and NCOs. Most of these men and women are on their way to Iraq or Afghanistan, many of them for the second or even third time. In late 2006 one young sergeant offered me an example of how difficult it is for U.S. soldiers and Marines to eliminate the threat they face. This sergeant said that his unit's camp came under mortar fire from Iraqi insurgents, and his squad was sent out of the camp to try to find and destroy the mortar and its crew. The squad worked around to the flank of the mortar position and found that its insurgent crew had fired the last of its rounds and was breaking down the mortar to leave the area. The squad leader radioed this information back to his unit and asked permission to attack. His request was denied because the insurgents were no longer in the act of attacking Americans, and so they were allowed to move off with their mortar, presumably to attack U.S. forces again another day.

43. "A recent conference of British and American experts at Ditchley Park in England," Dr. Nye wrote in early 2007, "concluded that while a hard-power response is necessary against the identified hard core of terrorism, this might not amount to more than 10 or 20 percent of the whole defense effort [against militant Islamism]. A larger effort should be devoted to public communication with mainstream Muslims." Nye suggests that using soft power and dropping the term "war on terrorism"

are keys to winning "the generational struggle to win hearts and minds of mainstream Muslims and hinder al-Qaeda recruiting." Again, Dr. Nye and the soft-power advocates press ahead with their advocacy despite polls that show that "mainstream Muslims" hate U.S. foreign policy as much as al-Qaeda does, and that while they are attracted to America's values, they are increasingly repelled by its neopagan popular culture. In this context, a complete reversal of U.S. foreign policy toward the Islamic world and the re-Christianization of America would be needed to enable U.S. soft power. Harvard would never approve. See Joseph S. Nye, "Just Don't Mention the War on Terrorism," *International Herald Tribune*, February 8, 2007.

44. Quoted in Wright, *Oxford Dictionary of Civil War Quotations*, 368, 372.
45. Quoted in Fred Anderson and Andrew Cayton, *The Dominion of War: Empire and Liberty in North America, 1500–2000* (New York: Viking, 2005), 336.
46. Fareed Zakaria, "Why the War Was Right," *Newsweek,* October 20, 2003.
47. Fareed Zakaria, "The Radicals Are Desperate," *Newsweek,* March 15, 2004.
48. Fawaz Gerges, "A Change of Arab Hearts and Minds," *Christian Science Monitor,* February 4, 2004, and "Al-Qaeda Represents a Security Nuisance, Not a Strategic Threat," www.bruneitimes.com.bn, November 17, 2006.
49. Three recent books suggest that the Islamists, Sunni and Shia, are attracting many of the Muslim world's educated young. See Robert A. Pape, *Dying to Win: The Strategic Logic of Suicide Terrorism* (New York: Random House, 2005); Alan B. Krueger, *What Makes a Terrorist: Economics and the Roots of Terrorism* (Princeton, N.J.: Princeton University Press, 2007); and Marc Sageman, *Understanding Terror Networks* (Philadelphia: University of Pennsylvania Press, 2004). Dr. Sageman is particularly good in using statistical research to deflate the West's inexplicably durable myth that terrorists are bred by poverty, unemployment, and illiteracy. On the issue of employment, for example, Dr. Sageman writes:

> The popular wisdom on terrorists suggests that they were desperate people, with little economic opportunity or without a decent occupation. In this sample, I collected occupational information on 134 people [identified as Islamist terrorists]. At the time they joined the jihad, 57 were professionals (physicians, architects, preachers, teachers), 44 had semi-skilled positions (police, military, mechanics, civil service, small business, students) and 33 were considered unskilled. So only a quarter of the whole sample could be considered unskilled workers with few prospects before them. These unskilled terrorists were heavily concentrated in the Maghreb . . . The rest of the sample showed the same type of upward mobility found in terms of educational levels. An argument can be made that, far from being a product of falling expectations, the jihad was more a result of rising expectations among its members. (78)

50. Fareed Zakaria, "Terror and the War of Ideas," *Washington Post,* April 10, 2004, A-15.
51. Mansoor Ijaz, "Terrorism's New Operating System," *National Review Online,* September 17, 2005.
52. While there is no end of bad advice and guidance from individuals such as these, a good deal of sound advice from Muslim commentators in Europe and the Middle East

goes unheeded. An example comes from the pen of Rami G. Khouri, editor at large of Beirut's *Daily Star.* "My conclusion," Khouri wrote in 2005,

> after this rich week of travel and conversation [in the United States] is that sensible middle class Americans want to get on with the hard work of making a living in challenging times, while their federal government conducts a foreign policy based more on make believe perceptions and imaginary realities.
>
> Bush's speech at the National Endowment for Democracy last week reaffirmed to me that Washington's policy to fight terrorism is a mish mash of faulty analysis, historical confusions, emotional anger, foreign policy frustrations, worldly ignorance, and political deception all rolled into one.
>
> He completely ignores the impact of American, Israeli, and other foreign policies on the mindsets of hundreds of millions of people in the Arab-Asian region.

What Mr. Khouri misses is that President Bush's foreign policy is essentially the consensus foreign policy of the U.S. governing elite, spiced with more pungent rhetoric but plagued by the same self-inflicted failures and disasters. See Rami G. Khouri, "Bush's Fantasy Foreign Policy," www.tompaine.com, October 11, 2005.

53. Benjamin and Simon, *The Next Attack: The Failure of the War on Terror and a Strategy for Getting It Right* (New York: Times Books, 2005), 225.
54. Baker III and Hamilton, *The Iraq Study Group Report,* xvii. Like the 9/11 commissioners, the Study Group's members were served by an excellent and highly qualified staff. The published study seems to me to bear the same stamp of political expediency as the published *9/11 Report,* suggesting that the research and analysis done by the Study Group's staff was not fully exploited.

Chapter 5. And the Islamists' Fire Quietly Spreads

1. The only senior U.S. official who has urged Americans to take seriously what bin Laden et al. say has been President George W. Bush. Mr. Bush did so explicitly in the fall of 2006 and in the 2007 State of the Union Address. Not surprisingly, however, Mr. Bush told Americans that if they read bin Laden's words, they would learn that the Islamists hate Americans for who we are, not for what we do. To read, it seems, is not always to learn, but President Bush at least has taken the first step. See "Press Conference of the President," www.whitehouse.gov, September 15, 2006, and "Our Enemies Are Quite Explicit About Their Intentions," *Boston Globe,* January 24, 2007.
2. The distinguished scholar of Islamic law Khaled Abou El Fadl has explained that bin Laden and his allies are waging a defensive jihad, the justification for which is solidly based in Islamic jurisprudence, and he notes that they have not argued that they are waging an offensive jihad to reestablish the caliphate. "But it is important to note," Dr. El Fadl has written,

> that the notion of defensive jihad is well rooted in the classical juristic tradition, and that contemporary Islam has not had a problem adopting the idea of defensive jihad . . . Even Muslim fundamentalists insist that they are fighting either to defend the

integrity of Islamic sovereignty or to regain occupied territory. On no occasion in recent memory have Muslims pursued a jihad to convert the world.

    See Khaled Abou El Fadl, "Holy War versus Jihad," *Ethics and International Affairs,* 14 (2000), 138.

3. In an incisive essay that the neoconservatives must have forgotten to erase from the record, Dr. Lewis has suggested that the current Muslim dictatorships imported their fascism from Europe, and traditional Islam contains materials from which a form of democracy could be constructed.

> The kind of dictatorship that exists in the Middle East today has to no small extent been the result of modernization, more specifically of European influence and example. This included the only European political model that really worked in the Middle East—that of the one party state, either in the Nazi or communist version, which do not differ greatly from one another . . .
>
> The traditions of command and obedience are indeed deep-rooted, but there are other elements in Islamic tradition that could contribute to a more open and freer form of government: the rejection by the traditional jurists of despotic and arbitrary rule in favor of contract in the formation and consensus in the conduct of government; and their insistence that the mightiest of rulers, no less than the humblest of his servants, is bound by the law . . .
>
> The study of Islamic history and the vast and rich Islamic political literature encourages the belief that it may well be possible to develop democratic institutions—not necessarily in our Western tradition of that much misused term, but in one deriving from their own history and culture, and ensuring, in their way, limited government under law, consultation and openness, and a civilized and humane society. There is enough in the traditional culture of Islam on the one hand and the modern experiences of the Muslim people on the other to provide the basis for an advance towards freedom in the true sense of the word.

See Bernard Lewis, "Democracy and the Enemies of Freedom," *Wall Street Journal,* December 23, 2003. Interestingly, Osama bin Laden's critique of the al-Saud family's rule is consonant with Lewis's suggestion that there is an Islam-based alternative to the European fascism of Arab rulers. "Governing," bin Laden wrote in 2004, "is a contract between the Imam [ruler] and the people who will be ruled by him. This contract contains rights and obligations for both parties. It also has provisions for cancellation and making it null and void. One of the provisions which nullify the contract is betraying the Deen [religion] and the Ummah. And that is exactly what you [the al-Sauds] have done. This is of course if we assume that the contract was a valid one to begin with. But we all know that you have forced yourself upon people without consulation or acceptance." See "Osama bin Laden's December 16, 2004, Statement to the Saudi Rulers," http://jihadunspun.com.

4. Ian Buruma, "Ghosts of the Holocaust," *Los Angeles Times,* June 3, 2007. The Islamic world's historic lack of a fixed and consistent interest in "Christendom" is well and concisely discussed in Andrew Wheatcroft, *Infidels: A History of the Conflict Between Christendom and Islam* (New York: Random House, 2004), 36–55.

5. The urban legend that Osama bin Laden is a Muslim-come-lately in his focus on the

Palestine-Israel war is often stated but not supportable. In his 1996 declaration of war on the United States, for example, he refers to the Palestine-Israel war on seven different occasions, and throughout his public remarks he refers to the motivation he has derived to attack the United States from Israel's attack on Palestinian refugee camps at Sabra, Shatila, and Qana in Lebanon. See bin Laden, "Declaration of Jihad Against the Americans"; John Miller, "Talking to Terror's Banker," www.abcnews.com, May 28, 1998; Peter Arnett, "Osama bin Laden: The Interview," www.cnn.com, May 12, 1997; and "Mujahid Osama Bin Laden Talks Exclusively to *Nida'ul Islam* About the New Powderkeg in the Middle East," *Nida'ul Islam*, January 15, 1997.

6. Bin Laden, "Declaration of Jihad Against the Americans."

7. For bin Laden on the proper per-barrel price for oil, see "Osama Bin Laden's December 16, 2004, Statement to the Saudi Rulers," www.jihadunspun.com, and Hamid Mir, "Interview with Osama Bin Ladin," *Pakistan,* March 18, 1997.

8. " 'Islamists win' in key Saudi poll," www.new.bbc.co.uk, February 11, 2005; Steve Coll, "Islamic Activists Sweep Saudi Council Elections," *Washington Post*, April 24, 2005, A-17; and Faiza Seleh Ambah, "Saudi Crackdown on Dissenters," *Christian Science Monitor,* May 16, 2006.

9. Jordan is the linchpin of Washington's efforts to secure a Palestinian-Israeli settlement, and so rising Islamist militancy is a significant problem for its efforts. See Rana Sabbagh-Gargour, "Jordan Carefully Measures Its Democratic Openings," www.daily star.com.lb, December 12, 2006; "Jordan Turns Its Sights on Muslim Brotherhood," *Financial Times,* June 22, 2006; Suleiman al-Khalidi, "Jordan Says Islamist MPs Face Incitement Charges," Reuters, June 12, 2006; "Jordan Detains Islamist Deputies," Al-Jazirah Satellite Television, June 12, 2006; Borzou Daragahi, "Jordan's King Risks Shah's Fate, Critics Warn," www.latimes.com, October 1, 2006; and Jamal Halaby, "Jordanian Elections," Associated Press, August 1, 2007.

10. "Mubarak says Brotherhood Are Threat to Security," Reuters, January 11, 2007; Dina Abdel Mageed, "Analysis: Egypt's Cat and Mouse Game with the Brotherhood," www.metimes.com, January 28, 2007; and Jonathan Wright, "Egypt's Mubarak Defends Constitutional Changes," Reuters, March 24, 2007.

11. On the nationalist motivations of Hezbollah, see Pape, *Dying to Win,* 129–39.

12. Roger Hardy, "Thailand: The Riddle of the South," BBCNEWS.com, February 15, 2005.

13. William F. Buckley, "In Search of Anti-Semitism," *National Review*, December 30, 1991.

14. David Gergen, "There is No Israel 'Lobby,' " *New York Daily News*, March 26, 2006.

15. John Mearsheimer and Stephen Walt, "The Israel Lobby," *London Review of Books*, March 23, 2006, also available at www.imemc.org

16. Those in the West seeking to downplay the threat posed by bin Laden do so in the very Western way of pointing to results of personality polls, and there is no doubt that the al-Qaeda chief's personal popularity has dropped since 9/11. I would argue, however, that the truly telling polls are those that measure attitudes toward U.S. foreign policy across broad sections of the Muslim world, and those polls have consistently shown increased negatives for U.S. policy since 9/11, especially since the invasion of Iraq. I would speculate that another al-Qaeda attack in the United States would restore bin Laden's personal poll numbers—and then some—because of the deep

hatred of Muslims for U.S. government actions in their world. For details of the University of Maryland poll, see Tony Blankley, "A Rising Tide of Fury," www.Real ClearPolitics.com, May 3, 2007, and for the argument focused on bin Laden's personal popularity, see Ed Johnson, "Muslim Support for Osama bin Laden Is Falling, Researchers Say," www.bloomberg.com, July 25, 2007.

17. Michael F. Scheuer, "A Fine Rendition," *New York Times,* March 11, 2005.

18. In the hours after 9/11 CIA's bin Laden unit was tasked to define several operations that could be quickly run to strike back against al-Qaeda and its supporters. One of the most lucrative ideas suggested was to ask each country to raid an Islamist NGO on its territory and seize whatever electronic media and hard-copy data there was on hand. We were well aware that Islamist NGOs—especially those sponsored by Saudis and Kuwaitis—had been essential in the growth, disguise, and geographic dispersal of the international organization of al-Qaeda and other Islamist militant groups. The suggested raids would have netted far more relevant data on how the NGO-al-Qaeda-Islamist system worked than we ever had before. The raids, of course, could do nothing about 9/11, but the thought was that they might produce information allowing us to stop the next attack. The White House rejected the idea because they were concerned it would offend Muslim opinion.

19. Ayman al-Zawahiri, "The Zionist-Crusader aggressions on Gaza and Lebanon," www.muslim.net, July 28, 2006.

20. Quoted in Hamid Mir, "U.S. Using Chemical Weapons—Usama bin Laden," *Ausaf,* November 10, 2001, 1, 7.

21. "Statement by Shaykh Usama Bin Ladin, May God Protect Him [and] the al-Qaeda Organization," *al-Qal'ah* (online version), October 14, 2002.

22. Ibid.

23. Ibid.

24. Osama bin Laden, "Message to Muslims in Iraq," December 28, 2004, www.dazzled .com/soiraq'pdf/Iraq.zip.

25. Tariq Ramadan, *In the Footsteps of the Prophet: Lessons from the Life of Muhammad* (New York: Oxford University Press, 2007), ix–x.

26. This is absolutely not to say that bin Laden has replaced the ulema as the religious instructor and guide of Muslims. He has not. Bin Laden has never shown the least inclination to play such a role, and he has consistently said that the clerics who have been imprisoned in Muslim countries and the United States are the rightful leaders of jihad and reformation in the Islamic world. Just as some Westerners have claimed bin Laden "hijacked Islam," other Westerners incorrectly claim that bin Laden aspires to be the new "mahdi" or even the "caliph" of the Islamic world, claims that are made nowhere in the corpus of his rhetoric and writings.

27. Dr. Madawi al-Rashid, "Islam Today: From the Jurisprudence Scholars to the Men of the Cave," *Al-Quds Al-Arabi* (online version), February 6, 2006.

28. Ibid. Dr. al-Rashid's argument that senior Islamic scholars are being discredited and left behind may help to explain two recent high-profile efforts they have made to reassert their leadership. In the first, Shaykh Salman al-Awdah, renowned Saudi scholar and former mentor of bin Laden, published a public letter to the al-Qaeda chief beseeching him to reconsider his martial approach to rectifying the Muslim world's problems. Al-Awdah, however, was neither willing to attack bin Laden personally nor to claim that he was not a good Muslim; indeed, al-Awdah addressed him

as "My brother Usama." In the second effort, 138 prominent Islamic scholars—including the grand muftis of Egypt and Syria—addressed a letter to Pope Benedict VI and other Christian leaders in which they called for a dialogue between the leaders of the two faiths. Neither effort shows much confidence on the part of the Muslim scholars. Shaykh Awdah's noncombative letter to bin Laden testifies to the respect the latter continues to command among Saudis and to al-Awdah's fear of alienating his flock. The Muslim scholars' letter to the pope also had a pleading air to it, urging the need for Christian-Muslim dialogue, but strongly intimating that negating the bin Laden–inspired Islamist movement would be impossible if Christians continued to "wage war against Muslims on account of their religion, oppress them and drive them out of their homes." See Shaykh Salman Bin-Fahd al-Awdah, "Letter to Usama bin Ladin," *Islam Today WWW*, September 17, 2007; and "An Open Letter and Call From Muslim Religious Leaders to His Holiness Pope Benedict XVI, et al.: A Common Word Between You and Us," October 11, 2007, ww.brandeis.edu/offices/communications/muslimletter.pdf.

29. Reza Aslan, "A Coming Islamic Reformation," *Los Angeles Times* (online version), January 28, 2006.

30. For example: "The history of the present King of Great Britain is a history of repeated injuries and usurpations, all having in direct object the establishment of an absolute Tyranny over these States"; "He has refused to pass other laws for the accommodation of large districts of people, unless those people would relinquish the right of Representation in the Legislature, a right inestimable to them and formidable to tyrants only"; and, "He has obstructed the Administration of Justice, by refusing his Assent to Laws for establishing Judiciary Powers. He has made Judges dependent on his Will alone, for the tenure of their offices, and the amount and payment of their salaries. He has erected a multitude of New Offices, and sent hither swarms of Officers to harass our people, and eat out their substance." See John Rhodehamel, ed., *The American Revolution: Writings from the War of Independence* (New York: Literary Classics of the United States, 2001), 128.

31. Osama bin Ladin, "Declaration of Jihad Against the Americans Occupying the Land of the Two Holy Mosques: Expel the Heretics From the Arabian Peninsula," *Al-Islah* (online version), September 2, 1996. Like Jefferson's treatise, bin Ladin's also stressed (a) the burden of government-imposed taxes (in a tone that may resonate with American taxpayers today) and (b) that resort to arms came only after a long series of peaceful remonstrances by Saudi reformers to the king, each of which had been rejected.

> It [the Saudi reformers' slate of objections] pointed to the state's financial and economic situation and the terrible and frightful fate in store as a result of the debts of usury which have broken the state's back, and to the waste that has squandered the nation's wealth to satisfy personal wealth, resulting in taxes, duties, and excises imposed on the public. (a)
>
> Although the [reformers'] memorandum submitted all that [they proposed] leniently and gently, as a reminder of God and as good advice in a gentle, objective, and sincere way, despite the importance and necessity of advice for rulers in Islam, and despite the number and positions of the signatories of the memorandum and their sympathizers, it was of no avail. Its contents were rejected and its signa-

tories and sympathizers were humiliated, punished, and imprisoned. The preachers' and reformers' eagerness to pursue peaceful reform methods in the interest of the country's unity and to prevent bloodshed was clearly demonstrated. So why should the regime block all means of peaceful reform and drive the people toward armed action? That was the only door left open for the public for ending injustice and upholding right and justice. (b)

32. George W. Bush, Second Inaugural Address, http://whitehouse.gov, January 20, 2005. For all the scorn that has been launched in condemnation of President George W. Bush's supposedly inferior intellectual capabilities, it must be noted that Mr. Bush was absolutely right when he said that all human beings yearn for freedom and liberty. Like most Americans, however, Mr. Bush's accurate insight was boxed in by the "free society" we have established on the North American continent. The quote marks around the term "free society" are meant not to be demeaning but rather to denote ownership—as in "our" free society. When Mr. Bush and most Americans (with the notable exceptions of the Democratic party's core factions and most of the academy's social science faculties and law schools) use the term, they are talking about a republican form of mixed government, a constitution grounded in the British constitution, the common law, the philosophy of the Scottish Enlightenment, and a polity whose most enduring and protective mores are guided by Protestant Christianity. With these tools Americans have built history's freest, fairest, and most economically prosperous republic. Sadly, whether America turns out to be history's most durable and longest-lived republic is an open question.

The clear success of America's republican experiment rightly inculcates pride and a sense of accomplishment among most Americans, but it also induces an odd combination of Pollyanna-ishness and intolerance regarding the concept of freedom held by others in the world. The intolerance, not surprisingly, becomes most pronounced when we are examining the attitudes toward freedom of those outside the Anglo-American tradition. Born of a revolution meant to secure freedom and liberty for themselves and their posterity, Americans have a history of running hot and cold regarding the revolutions of others that are proclaimed to be efforts to attain freedom. And that is the way it should be. Revolutions, even if staged in the name of freedom, are not all by definition beneficial to the national-security interests of the United States, which must, of course, always be the deciding factor in determining the U.S. response to revolution.

Both ends of the Cold War provide a good glimpse of the dangers and promise inherent in supporting other peoples' revolutions. Woodrow Wilson (about whom not enough negative can ever be said) took a halfhearted swing at the Bolshevik Revolution but backed out almost as soon as he began, believing that any new Russian government had to be better than that of the evil, freedom-hating tsar. Today we may be standing squarely athwart an incipient revolution that may or may not benefit us if we succeed but that is surely damaging us mightily as we seek to suppress it. That revolution is the one being led and inspired by Osama bin Laden and that is meant, ultimately, to overthrow every authoritarian Muslim government in the world except for a restored Taliban rule in Afghanistan.

33. Even given this authoritarian record, however, the Islamists' governing philosophy is less despotic than that of most of the governments they intend to overthrow. The bril-

liant, commonsense American strategist Ralph Peters, who is not remotely a softy regarding America's Islamist enemies, has accurately assessed the Islamists' philosophy and found that reality does not mesh with the neoconservatives' iron rule that the destruction of the current U.S.-protected Muslim tyrannies will inevitably lead to Islamofascist regimes. "The power of Islamic fundamentalist regimes in power has been deplorable," Mr. Peters writes.

> They torture without remorse, imprison or execute without trial, and restrict basic freedoms to a degree intolerable to Westerners. Yet, after all the gore has been hosed into the sewer, there is a moral center to the greatest of the fundamentalists. It just isn't our moral center. Not many fundamentalist leaders share our taste for liberal democracy (which we acquired over the better part of a millennium), but some do share other ideals we profess. They are for mass education (although we might not agree with their curriculum and their exclusion of women). They desire to democratize their nation's wealth, if not its government. They seek to do [that] which social demagogues only promised. They have a sense of honor higher than that prevalent in the deathbed societies they seek to revitalize. And their reactions have yet to prove anywhere near as belligerent toward other states as their rhetoric.

See Ralph Peters, *Fighting for the Future: Will America Triumph?* (Mechanicsburg, Penn.: Stackpole Books, 1999), 127.

34. See Michael F. Scheuer, "Clueless into Kabul," *American Interest* 2, no. 1 (September–October 2006), 111–19, and Pamela Constable, "Afghan Leader Losing Support," *Washington Post*, June 26, 2006, A-1.

35. Helene Cooper, "Saudis Say They Might Back Sunnis If U.S. Leaves Iraq," *New York Times,* December 13, 2006, and Diana Ellis, "Saudi King: Spreading Shiism Won't Work," Associated Press, January 27, 2007.

36. For the strengthening authoritarian trend in constricting Islamist activities in Jordan, see Jamal Halaby, "Jordan's King Puts Constitutional Monarchy on the Back Burner for Now," Associated Press, August 26, 2005; "Jordan Blocks Muslim Militants from Pulpits," Agence France-Presse, September 4, 2006; Jamal Halaby, "Jordan Lawmakers Limit Religious Edicts," www.thestate.com, September 14, 2006; and Shafika Mattar, "Jordan Fears Growing Shiite Influence," www.washingtonpost.com, November 17, 2006.

37. Hamza Hendawi, "Syria Fears Spillover of Sectarian Strife," www.theday.com, January 22, 2007; Anthony Shadid, "Syria's Unpredictable Force," *Washington Post,* May 27, 2005; Ibrahim Hamidi, "Can Syria Keep Its Islamist Genie in the Bottle?," www.dailystar.com.lb, January 12, 2005; Neil MacFarquhar, "Syria, Long Ruthlessly Secular, Sees Fervent Islamic Resurgence," *New York Times,* October 24, 2003, A-1, and, Rime Allaf, "Fundamentalism No Benefit to Syria," www.metimes.com, July 24, 2007.

38. Uri Avnery, "The Next Crusades," Arabic Media Internet Network, March 5, 2005.

39. Judith Ingram, "Rebellion Spreads into Russia," *Washington Times*, May 8, 2005; Simon Saradzhyan, "Chechnya: Spreading the Insurgency," www.isn.ethz.ch, June 13, 2006; and "Chechen Rebel Chief Declares Islamic Emirate," Threat and Claim Monitor, Intel Center, November 29, 2007.

40. Fiona Hill, Anatol Lieven, and Thomas de Waal, "A Spiraling Danger. Time for a

New Policy Toward Chechnya," *CEPS Policy Brief*, no. 68 (online version), April 2005, and "Interview with Sergei Markedenov, Institute of Political and Military Analysis, Moscow," Radio Free Europe/Radio Liberty, May 5, 2006.

41. Sebastian Smith, "Islamic Rebels Tighten Grip on Dagestan," *Australian*, July 20, 2005; C. J. Chivers, "Russia Steps Up Anti-terror Drive as Chechen War Spreads," *New York Times,* October 23, 2004; "Soldier Causalities Exceed 6,600 in Chechnya Campaigns," *Novosti* (online), August 10, 2007; and "Near-Daily Violence Grips Ingushetia," Moscow Times.com, September 3, 2007.

42. Andrew MacGregor, "Islam, Jamaats and Implications for the North Caucasus, Part 1," *Terrorism Monitor* (www.Jamestown.org) 4, no. 11 (June 2, 2006), and Part 2, *Terrorism Monitor* no. 12 (June 15, 2006); and Svante Cornell, "The North Caucasus: Spiraling Out of Control?," *Terrorism Monitor* 3, no. 7 (April 7, 2005).

43. Hill, Lieven, and deWaal, "Spiraling Danger"; Jonah Hull, "Russia Sees Muslim Population Boom," Al-Jazeerah.net, January 7, 2007; and Oleg Petrovskiy, "Hired Jihad Fighters in No Hurry to Get to Iraq. They Are Quite Happy in Chechnya," www.utro.ru, July 27, 2004.

44. Lawrence Scott Sheets and William J. Brand, "Atomic Smugglers Pose New Hazard for Former Soviet Republics," *International Herald Tribune* (online version), January 25, 2007; Desmond Butler and Katherine Schraeder, "Georgia Sting Seizes Bomb Grade Uranium," Associated Press, January 25, 2007; Tenet, *Center of the Storm*, 279; Dr. Paul A. Goble, "The Islamization of Russia," Association of Former Intelligence Officers Conference, October 26, 2007.

45. Steyn, *America Alone,* 2, 27.

46. Joginder Singh, "Bangla Is Going the Pak Way," *Asian Age* (online version), January 13 2006, and Eliza Griswold, "Bangladesh for Beginners," www.slate.com. December 29, 2005.

47. "Drifting Toward Extremism," http://planetguru.com, February 6, 2005, and Griswold, "Bangladesh for Beginners."

48. Charles Tannock, "The World Cannot Afford Bangladesh's Going Taliban," *Daily Star,* July 21, 2005.

49. Alok Bonsai, "Terror: Bangladesh's Growing Export," *Asia Tribune* (online version), April 9, 2006; Rolana Buerk, "Bangladesh and Islamic Militants," BBCNEWS.com.uk, February 25, 2005; and Mamun-Ar-Rashid, "Countless Militant Networks like Spider's Net," *Dainik Janakantha,* July 19, 2005, 1, 11.

50. Chowdhry Manuf, "Islamic Militant Behind Deadly Bangladesh Blasts Surrenders," Agence France-Presse, March 2, 2006; Farid Hussain, "Bangladesh Attacks Bring Fear of Militancy," *Boston Globe* (online version), December 9, 2005; David Montero, "How Extremism Came to Bangladesh," *Christian Science Monitor* (online version), September 6, 2005; "Bangladesh Bombs Spotlight 'Holy Warriors,' " Reuters, September 2005; and Anjoli Aggarwal, "HUJI has Close Ties with ISI and Osama," *Times of India Online*, April 6, 2006.

51. Tannock, "World Cannot Afford"; Romananda Sengupta, "Bangladesh: Next Terror Frontier?" *Rediff India Abroad* (http://us.rediff.com), December 19, 2005; Paul Eckert, "Bangladesh Bomber Arrests Said Only the Beginning," Reuters, March 8, 2006; and Maneeza Hussain, "The world Can't Afford to Ignore Bangladesh," India Monitor.com, August 29, 2005.

52. Dan Morrison, " 'Bomb Culture' Threatens Bangladesh," *Washington Times,* January

Notes

15, 2005; Montero, "How Extremism Came to Bangladesh"; Sengupta, "Next Terror Frontier?"

53. "Bangladeshis Hail Capture of Top Militants," Reuters, March 7, 2006.
54. Mamun-Ar-Rashid, "Countless Militant Networks"; Griswold, "Bangladesh for Beginners."
55. Tannock, "World Cannot Afford"; Mizan Rahman, "Bangladesh Militant Leader 'Tied to al-Qaeda'," *Gulf Times* (online version), March 26, 2006; Brigadier General Showkat Hossain, "Operation Haluaghat—Security During the Next Election," *Protham Alo* (online version), July 17, 2006; and Mamun-Ar-Rashid, "Countless Militant Networks."
56. "Drifting Toward Extremism"; Bonsal, "Bangladesh's Growing Export;" Sengupta, "Next Terror Front?"; Mamun-Ar-Rashid, "Countless Militant Networks"; and Shahid Allam, "Spectre of Fundamentalism: Warning Bells Getting Louder," *New Nation* (online version), February 22, 2005.
57. "Bangladesh Declares Emergency, Imposes Curfew," Reuters, January 11, 2007; Matthew Rosenberg, "Rivalry Fuels Bangladeshi Political Crisis," Associated Press, December 24, 2006; "Presence of Afghan Veterans in Bangladesh Poll Flayed," www.indiannews.com/bangladesh, December 28, 2006; and Y. P. Rajesh, "Bangladesh Islamists Confident of Expanding Hold," Reuters, January 31, 2007. In 2006 the organization Transparency International named Bangladesh the most corrupt country in the world for the fifth consecutive year. See "Bangladesh Most Corrupt," *Daily Star*, January 1, 2006, and "Politicians Losing Respect of People for Corruption," *New Nation Online Edition*, January 27, 2007.
58. Princeton Lyman and Scott Allan, "Prevent the Rise of Another Taliban," *Baltimore Sun* (online version), October 19, 2004.
59. Edmund Blair, "Conservative Anglicans Warn Liberal Churches in the West," Reuters, October 31, 2005, and Edward Harris, "Nigerian Christians Burn Muslim Corpses," Associated Press, February 23, 2006.
60. George Thomas, "Terror Havens: al-Qaeda's Growing Sanctuary in Nigeria," www.cbn.com, May 2, 2005; Andrew McLaughlin, "Behind Rising Oil Cost: Nigeria," *Christian Science Monitor*, January 18, 2006; and "Nigerian Taliban plots comeback," Agence France-Presse, January 11, 2006.
61. "Shell Evacuates Oil Field After Attacks by Niger Delta Militants," Agence France-Presse, February 11, 2006; Jeffrey Tayler, "Nigeria's Troubles Could Become America's," www.allafrica.com, March 13, 2006; Erich Marquardt, "The Niger Delta Insurgency and Its Threat to Energy Security," *Terrorism Monitor* 4, no. 16 (August 10, 2006); and "Five Nigerians on Terror Charges," news.bbc.co.uk, November 23, 2007.
62. Tayler, "Nigeria's Troubles."
63. Ibid.
64. Dino Mahtari and Guy Dinsmore, "U.S. Upset with Nigeria over Warlord's Flight," *Financial Times,* March 28, 2006, and John C. K. Daly, "Nigeria Continues to Slide Toward Instability," *Terrorism Monitor* 4, no. 24 (December 14, 2006).
65. Dan Darling, "Nigeria's Oil War," http://threatwatch.org, February 21, 2006, and Marquardt, "Niger Delta Insurgency."
66. "Fueling the Niger Delta Crisis," International Crisis Group, Africa Report No. 118, September 28, 2006.

Notes

67. Marquardt, "Niger Delta Insurgency."
68. Ibid.; Sebastian Junger, "Blood Oil," *Vanity Fair,* February 2007, 112, 114; and Jad Mouawad, "Growing Unrest Posing a Threat to Nigerian Oil," *New York Times,* April 21, 2007.
69. Nigeria is an ideal al-Qaeda target because the flow of oil to the United States and the West can be disrupted without damaging the energy infrastructure of Arab oil-producers. In addition, bin Laden is always willing to work with the devil if it means striking a blow against the primary enemy of Islam, the United States. In the case of the Niger Delta, al-Qaeda would not even consider an effort that aimed at Islamicizing the overwhelmingly Christian insurgent movement there, but would simply and unobtrusively look for opportunities to assist the insurgents with cash and by upgrading their training, weaponry, and logistics networks.
70. Marquardt, "The Niger Delta Insurgency."
71. Ibid., and Junger, "Blood Oil," 114.
72. Christian Purefoy and Peter Koenig, "Nigeria Looms as Wild Card in Shell Recovery," www.timesonline.co.uk, February 5, 2005.
73. John Brandon, "In Thailand's South, Fertile Ground for Terrorism," *International Herald Tribune,* February 11, 2005; John M. Glionna, "In Thailand, a New Model for Insurgencies?" *Los Angeles Times,* October 1, 2006; and "Southern Thailand: Insurgency Not Jihad," International Crisis Group, Asia Report No. 98, May 18, 2005.
74. Suttin Wannabovorn, "Militants May Join Thailand Insurgency," Associated Press, September 24, 2005; Allan Dawson, "As Thailand Goes . . . ," www.techcentralstation.com, July 21, 2005; Sarah Stewart, "Thailand, Malaysia Row Exposes Rift over Muslim Rebellion," Agence France-Presse, November 3, 2005; and Bashkar Dasgupta, "Insurgency in Thailand," www.hindustantimes.com, March 11, 2005.
75. "Thai Foreign Minister Rules Out Autonomy for South, Says No al-Qaeda Link," www.todayonline.com, November 7, 2005; "Thaksin Rules Out Talks with PULO," *Nation,* January 26, 2006; "No End in Sight as Thailand's Forgotten War Drags On," *Taipei Times,* January 29, 2006; "Thailand's Emergency Decree: No Solution," International Crisis Group, Asia Report No. 105, September 18, 2005; and "Southern Thailand: Insurgency Not Jihad."
76. Dr. Alamgir Hussain, "Thailand Insurgency: It's Jihad But Experts Don't Get It," www.americanchronicle.com, December 4, 2006; Matthew B. Arnold, "Who Is Behind the Violence in the South?" *Bangkok Post,* December 13, 2006; "Thai Army Commander General Sonthi Cuts Short Haj Pilgrimage to Return Home," *Phuchatkan,* January 1, 2007; "Bangkok's Bombs," *Weekly Standard*, January 3, 2007; George Wehrfritz, "Thailand's Muslim Insurgency Is Spinning out of Control," www.msnbc.msn.com, August 12, 2007; "Rebels 'ready for long years of fighting,' " www.bangkokpost.com, August 29, 2007; and Ian Storey, "Thailand Cracks Down on Southern Militants," *Terrorism Monitor* 5, no. 17 (September 13, 2007).
77. "U.S. Voices Disappointment over Coup in Thailand," *International Herald Tribune,* September 20, 2006; "U.S.-Thailand Alliance," www.defenselink.mil; and Depart-ment of State, "Background Note: Thailand," www.state.gov, November, 2006.
78. "U.S. Involvement in Somalia," Reuters, January 9, 2007, and Salad Dahul, "Official: Bomb Suspect Killed in Somalia," Associated Press, January 10, 2007.

317

79. Abdulgarim Omar, a Somali intellectual living in Mogadishu, made the following comments on the Arabs' presence and purposes in Somalia in late 2003.

> No one helps us anymore, except the Arabs, who are here in droves with their money, their Koranic schools, and with their humanitarian organizations, which in reality conceal other objectives. They do not teach Islam, but Wahhabism, the state religion of Saudi Arabia . . . More than training, what the mosques offer is indoctrination, especially the new mosques that have been built with Saudi, Yemeni, and [United] Arab Emirate money, and portray portraits of bin Ladin, who by now in Mogadishu is almost considered a hero.

See Massimo A. Alberizzi, "Al-Qaeda Trains New Taliban in Somalia," *Corriere della Sera,* November 27, 2003.

80. Edmund Sanders, "Ethiopia's Intervention May Destabilize Region," *Los Angeles Times,* January 7, 2007; Martin Fletcher, "The Islamists Were the One Hope for Somalia," www.timesonline.co.uk, January 8, 2007; "U.S. Involvement in Somalia"; Eric S. Margolis, "The Crusade Moves On to Somalia," *Gulf Times,* December 30, 2006.

81. Moahmed Olad Hassan, "Ethiopia Openly Launches Offensive Against Somalia's Powerful Islamist Movement," Associated Press, December 24, 2006: "State Department: U.S. Supports Ethiopian Military," CNN.com, December 27, 2006; Guled Muhamed, "Somali Gov't Close to Taking Mogadishu," Reuters, December 28, 2006; and "Key Facts on Somali President Yusuf," Reuters, October 29, 2007.

82. The U.S. air strikes targeted three senior East Africa–based al-Qaeda fighters: Fazul Abdallah Muhammad, a Comoran involved in al-Qaeda's 1998 attacks on the U.S. embassies in Kenya and Tanzania; Abu Talha al-Sudani, al-Qaeda's chief in East Africa and an explosives expert; and Saleh Ali Saleh Nabhan, a Kenyan. See "America Intervenes in Somalia," www.telegraphyindia.com, January 10, 2007; John Donnelly, "U.S. Uses Somali Events to Press al-Qaeda," *Boston Globe,* January 10, 2007; and Karen DeYoung, "U.S. Strike in al-Qaeda Targets al-Qaeda Figure," *Washington Post,* January 8, 2007. None of the three were killed, but that failure does not invalidate the attempt. For the foreseeable future, this sort of preemptive attack will be indispensable and must become a mainstay of U.S. strategy against the Islamists. In order to continue protecting America in this manner, however, U.S. leaders will have to learn to ignore the complaints and criticisms of the EC, human-rights groups, and other antinational organizations. They also ought to learn to order the attacks and then keep their mouths shut.

83. Jonathan Clayton, "Raids Could Backfire on U.S.," *Australian,* January 10, 2007. Within days of Ethiopian forces occupying Mogadishu, Somali Islamists were attacking their convoys and foot patrols, and by mid-January 2007 the transitional government had declared a ninety-day state of emergency to deal with the violence. See "Mogadishu Fighting Escalates," www.hamiltonspectator.com, January 11, 2007; Hassan Yare, "Somali Parliament Declares 3-Month State of Emergency," Reuters, January 13, 2007; and Sahal Abdulle, "Somali Gunmen Attack Convoy of Ethiopian Troops," Reuters, January 15, 2007.

The always missing historical context for the U.S. decision to support the

Ethiopian invasion includes the following points, which together make it reasonable to anticipate the slow growth of an Islamist insurgency in the country and perhaps the region.

a. Ethiopia and Somalia have been rivals throughout their history, and Ethiopian interventions in Somalia have been common in the past and have caused lengthy wars. Somalis have traditionally viewed Ethiopia as an expansionist colonial power eager to ease its land-locked status by acquiring ports on the Somali coast.

b. Ethiopian invasions when backed by a non-Muslim power have encouraged the rapid growth of Islamic militancy and readiness for jihad in Somalia's traditionally moderate practice of the faith. Several British-backed Ethiopian invasions in the first decade of the twentieth century, for example, had exactly this effect in Somalia. If past is prologue, the U.S.-backed Ethiopian invasion may again prove "that foreign intervention is the fuel that allows political Islam to grow in an otherwise hostile [Somali] environment."

c. Christian Ethiopia's invasion of Muslim Somalia and its subsequent destruction of the ICU government is likely to make Ethiopia a more acceptable target for all Islamists. Traditionally, Ethiopia has held a place of respect and distinction in Islamic history and theology because it was a Christian nation whose ruler provided refuge and protection for Muslims who had to flee from persecution on the Arabian Peninsula during the first years of Islam. The Prophet Muhammad, in recognition of the Ethiopians' assistance to his brethren, said, "If you went to the country of the Abyssinians, ye would find there a king under whom none suffereth wrong. It is a land of sincerity in religion." The ruler who protected the Muslims later converted to Islam. Because of this history, contemporary Islamists have been reluctant to attack the interests of a country honored by their Prophet. The December 2006 Ethiopian invasion, however, may lessen the strength of the Prophet's injunction and result in attacks on Ethiopian targets. Indeed, Shaykh Sharif Shaykh Ahmed, a senior ICU leader, has said that the Somalis' response to the invasion would not be limited to Somali territory. "The war is entering a new phase," Shaykh Ahmed warned. "We will fight Ethiopia for a long, long time and we expect the war to go every place."

On the long history of Ethiopian-Somali hostilities, see Nicolla Nasser, "Commentary: Ethiopian Invasion to Spur Anti-U.S. Foment," *Middle East Times* (www.metimes.com), January 9, 2006, and "Somalia's Role in Horn of Africa Tensions," Reuters, December 24, 2006. For a fascinating examination of the jihad-producing impact of Great Power–backed Ethiopian invasions of Somalia, see Andrew McGregor, "Expelling the Infidel: Historical Look at Somali Resistance to Ethiopia," *Terrorism Monitor* 5, no. 1 (January 2007). On Ethiopia's historically privileged status in Islamic history and theology, see Lings, *Muhammad,* 77–84; Ramadan, *Footsteps of the Prophet,* 59–62; Scott Baldauf and Mike Pflanz, "U.S. Takes Hunt for al-Qaeda to Somalia," *Christian Science Monitor,* January 10, 2007; and Salad Dahul, "Islamic Forces Retreat in Somalia But Say They Expect War 'to Go Every Place,' " Associated Press, December 26, 2006.

84. For bin Laden's most recent statement on Somalia, see Osama bin Ladin, "To

the Nation, in General, and the Mujahedin in Iraq and Somalia, in Particular," Al-Sahab Media Organization (www.muslim.net), July 1, 2006. For al-Zawahiri's most recent statement on Somalia see Ayman al-Zawahiri, "Rise Up and Support Your Brothers in Somalia," Al-Sahab Media Organization (www.muslim.net), January 5, 2007.

85. For a useful, well-argued Muslim analysis that concludes that the Ethiopian and U.S. actions in Somalia in December 2006 and January 2007 might well spark an Islamist insurgency/jihad in the countries of East Africa, see Nasser, "Commentary."

86. There has been a crop of books depicting the political portents and terrorism threats posed by the Muslim populations of Europe, and the befuddled efforts of EC politicians trying to cope with the realities of demography and Islamist militants. See Bruce Bawer, *While Europe Slept: How Radical Islam Is Destroying the West from Within* (New York: Doubleday, 2006); Melanie Phillips, *Londonistan* (New York: Encounter Books, 2006); Bat Ye'or, *Eurabia: The Euro-Arab Crisis* (Madison, N.J.: Fairleigh Dickinson University Press, 2005); and Claire Berlinski, *Menace in Europe: Why the Continent's Crisis Is America's, Too* (New York: Crown Forum Books, 2007).

87. Joseph Cardinal Ratzinger, "On Europe's Crisis of Culture," www.zenit.org, July 26, 2005.

88. Mark Lilla, "Godless Europe," *New York Times,* April 2, 2006.

89. Niall Ferguson, "The March of Islam," *Daily Telegraph,* May 21, 2006, and Ferguson, "The Origins of the Great War of 2007—and How It Could Have Been Prevented," *Sunday Telegraph,* January 15, 2006.

90. Tony Blankley, *The West's Last Chance: Will We Win the Clash of Civilizations?* (Washington, D.C.: Regnery Publications, 2005), 147–48.

91. George Weigel, *The Cube and the Cathedral: Europe, America, and Politics Without God* (New York: Basic Books, 2005), 21–22.

92. Steyn, *America Alone,* 2, 32.

93. Mark Steyn, "Bicultural Europe Is Doomed," *Daily Telegraph,* November 15, 2005.

94. Before becoming Pope Benedict XVI, Cardinal Ratzinger warned Europe's leaders that their developing confrontation with their Muslim citizens was based not on them being the last vestiges of Christianity on the continent but on "the cynicism of a secularized culture that denies its own [Christian] foundations . . . It is not the mention of God that offends those who belong to other religions, but rather the attempt to build the human community absolutely without God." Needless to say, the leaders of the EC, who are if anything more viciously anticlerical than the French philosophes, took no heed of the cardinal's commonsense warning. Ratzinger, "Europe's Crisis of Culture."

95. Gertrude Himmelfarb, *The Roads to Modernity: The British, French, and American Enlightenments* (New York: Vintage Books, 2004), 150, 161.

96. Quoted in ibid., 166.

Chapter 6. "The bottom is out of the tub": Taking Stock for America in 2007

1. The Lincoln-Meigs conversation is recounted in Ethan S. Rafuse, *McClellan's War: The Failure of Moderation in the Stuggle for the Union* (Bloomington and Indianapolis: Indiana University Press, 2005), 170.

2. See the results of a Pew Research poll published in June 2006 and a BBC poll published in January 2007. Brian Knowlton, "Global Image of the U.S. Worsening, Survey Finds," *New York Times,* June 14, 2006; Jonathan Marcus, " 'Listen More' Is World's Message to U.S.," http://newsvote.bbc.co.uk, January 23, 2007; and "U.S. Image Sharply Worsens," Reuters, January 23, 2007.

3. Bin Laden and other al-Qaeda leaders have gone into great detail in instructing Islamists how to successfully defend themselves from initial U.S. "shock and awe" attacks, stressing that once that phase concludes, the U.S. forces are a far less formidable enemy than was the Soviet military. See "Statement by Usama Bin Ladin," Al-Jazirah Satellite Television, December 27, 2001; Osama Bin Laden, "Message to Our Brothers in Iraq," Al-Jazirah Satellite Television, February 11, 2003; and Sayf al-Adl, "The al-Qaeda Organization Writes a Letter to the Iraqi People," www.alfjr.com, March 5, 2003.

4. Writing in *Federalist 15,* Hamilton argued that when foreign powers looked upon the United States under the Articles of Confederation, they perceived not a strong sovereign power but rather "the imbecility of our government" that managed to produce ambassadors who are "mere pageants of mimic sovereignty." This situation, Hamilton concluded, endangered America's future as it strove to survive in the world. And so are we endangered today by Washington's pageants of mimic military power. See Alexander Hamilton, *Federalist 15,* in George W. Casey and James McClellan, *The Federalist: The Gideon Edition* (Indianapolis, Ind.: Liberty Fund, 2001), 68–75.

5. In addition to the August 20, 1998, cruise missile on the Khowst camps, another set of missiles simultaneously hit a drug-manufacturing facility in Khartoum that Washington believed was involved in producing chemical weapons.

6. It is worth worrying how Washington's unwillingness to use its military power to defeat insurgents armed with forty-year-old weaponry is perceived by nation-states that are deemed a threat to the United States, such as Russia, China, North Korea, Venezuela, and Iran. The willingness of U.S. leaders to let their country be defeated in two wars rather than risk international condemnation for using military power too brutally must surely make our nation-state rivals question how credible U.S. resolve is to hold them in check. Such questioning could lead to a bit of envelope-pushing by our rivals to see how far they can go in defying America.

7. Because I am one of the chief architects of the CIA's rendition program against al-Qaeda, I am often asked whether the program was worthwhile. My answer always is a most emphatic yes. Khalid Shaykh Muhammad, Abu Zubaydah, Kahlid bin Attash, and another twenty or so senior al-Qaeda leaders would be working to defeat America and kill its citizens if it were not for CIA rendition program operations. The program, I believe, is the single most successful U.S. counterterrorism program, and the men and women who have risked their lives to execute it deserve the thanks of their countrymen. I also would note (for those who are concerned with such things) that in my almost twenty years of managing CIA covert operations, the rendition program received the most intense scrutiny from lawyers, politicians, senior civil servants, and congressional overseers of any I was associated with.

That said, the program has never been properly understood by Americans or the media. When it was created, the program had only two goals: (1) to find, apprehend, and incarcerate Islamists involved in anti-U.S. operations, and (2) to seize from them at the time of their capture any paper or electronic documents they possessed;

on these documents was information never intended to be read by the U.S. clandestine service. Capturing senior al-Qaeda fighters was never predicated on what we might be able to learn from them via interrogation; to receive legal permission to execute an operation, the documentary evidence of terrorist activities had to be conclusive; no individual was ever picked up because someone had a hunch he would have something interesting to say. In addition, we did not think interrogation would produce much of worth because we knew al-Qaeda fighters were trained to respond to their questioners with fabricated information or a great deal of accurate information that was dated, would take long periods of time to exploit, and would ultimately lead to no follow-up operations.

Why, then, were captured al-Qaeda fighters taken to third countries, a practice the media have described as outsourcing torture? The answer lies in the decision that President Clinton, National Security Adviser Sandy Berger, and terrorism chief Richard Clarke made not to bring captured al-Qaeda fighters to the United States. The U.S. legal system, they argued, could not abide the manner in which these men were captured—no Miranda rights—or the fact that no U.S. law-enforcement official would be able to testify under oath that the individual had not been abused when arrested, or that his media had not been tampered with after his capture. On this assumption Mr. Clinton and his team approved taking the captured men to countries where there were already existing legal charges against them. In almost all cases the charges were terrorism-related, and some of those captured had been convicted of crimes in absentia. They were taken to third countries, therefore, because President Clinton had directed the CIA to take them there. At the time this reasoning seemed to me to accurately reflect the incompatibility between rendition and standard trial procedures in the U.S. court system. More important, it allowed the CIA to execute the president's program for getting senior al-Qaeda fighters who were threats to America off the street.

Notwithstanding this benefit, however, senior CIA officers repeatedly reminded the Clinton national security team that the Islamist fighters acquired via rendition operations were being taken to states that the U.S. State Department routinely cited as human-rights abusers. In response, the White House tasked the CIA to request assurance from each foreign government that received an al-Qaeda fighter that the prisoner would be treated according to that country's laws. In other words, State X would have to pledge that it would treat the al-Qaeda fighter according to the laws of State X. Needless to say, the prisoner-receiving government always made this assurance, and it was passed to the White House. At no time in my experience did the president or his advisers ever task the CIA to solicit from a prisoner-receiving country a guarantee that an al-Qaeda fighter would be treated according to U.S. legal standards or the norms of international law. Claims made by former Clinton administration officials to the contrary are lies.

The problem with the rendition program is that it has emerged as the major counterterrorism tool of the U.S. government. The program was never intended to be, or capable of being, the instrument through which al-Qaeda would be defeated. Al-Qaeda is far too large an organization to be defeated by what President Clinton and President George W. Bush have described as a process of "arresting them one man at a time and bringing them to justice." The CIA's rendition program was and is successful in picking off senior al-Qaeda leaders and thereby keeping al-Qaeda off

Notes

balance because of the need to replace talented leaders. It was not and is not the means to victory, and that it is now thought of as such speaks again to the pernicious effect of Cold War hangovers: the constant search for third-country proxies to handle captured rendition targets; the fear of applying strong military force even after it is clear that arresting Islamists one at a time does not adequately protect America; and the willingness of presidential administrations from both parties to be intimidated by human-rights groups and vote-seeking politicians like Senator McCain and Senator Carl Levin (D-Michigan) (Michigan is a large Muslim-population state) into neutering the one counterterrorism program that was producing positive and measurable results. My congressional testimony on the rendition program can be read in "Extraordinary Rendition in U.S. Counterterrorism Policy: The Impact on Trans Atlantic Relations," April 17, 2007, serial 110–28, http://foreignaffairs.house.gov/110/34712.pdf.

8. Quoted in Woodward, *Bush at War*, 65.
9. Ibid. In July 2007 the National Intelligence Estimate came close to officially recognizing General Powell's mistake in identifying the 9/11 raids as an attack on the entire Western community (rather than what it was, a direct attack only on the United States) by noting its concern that the "level of international cooperation [against al-Qaeda] may wane as 9/11 becomes a more distant memory and perceptions of the threat diverge." The term "perceptions of the threat diverge" appears to be a bureaucratic nicety that means that the Intelligence Community anticipates that our non-English-speaking allies will come to see that they are on al-Qaeda's bull's-eye list only as long as they are overtly aiding the United States. See "NIE: The Terrorist Threat to the U.S. Homeland," July 17, 2007.
10. Osama bin Laden, "Statement to the Peoples of Countries Allied to [the] Tyrannical U.S Government," *Alneda* (online), November 21, 2002.
11. Ibid.
12. Ibid.
13. Ibid.
14. Osama bin Laden, "Speech to the Peoples of Europe," Al-Arabiyah Television, April 15, 2004.
15. Ibid.
16. "Spanish Government Admits Defeat," http://news.bbc.co.uk., March 15, 2004; Isambard Wilkonson, "Election Blow of Bush's War on Terrorism," www.telegraph.co.uk, March 15, 2004; and Faye Bowers, "Do Terrorists Play Election Politics?" *Christian Science Monitor,* March 17, 2004.
17. "Official Results: Prodi Defeats Berlusconi," Associated Press, April 11, 2006.
18. Kevin Sullivan and Mary Jordan, "Blair Says He Will Step Down Within 12 Months," *Washington Post,* September 8, 2006, A-12.
19. Sebastian Berger, "Thailand Coup Raises Hope for a Deal with Muslim Insurgents," www.telegraph.co.uk, September 29, 2006, and Kim Barker, "Gleam Is off Thailand's Quiet Coup," *Chicago Tribune*, December 10, 2006.
20. Craig Gordon, "When Did Bush Know?" www.newsday.com, June 2, 2006; Ruxandra Adam, "Maliki Slams U.S. Military for Attack," http://news.softpedia.com, August 8, 2006; Fisnik Abrashi, "Karzai: Attacks Wearing Thin on Afghans," Associated Press, December 8, 2006; "Karzai Criticizes Foreign Tactics," www.newsvote.bbc.co.uk, June 22, 2006; Tim Abalone and Michael Evans, "Karzai

Wants Rethink on Terror War as al-Qaeda Urges Uprising," www.timesonline.co.uk, June 23, 2006.

21. "France Will Withdraw Some Forces from Afghanistan," *International Herald Tribune,* December 17, 2006, and Elaine Ganley, "French Pull Troops from Afghanistan," *Washington Post,* December 20, 2006.

22. Alan Cowell, "Britain to Pull 1,600 Troops out of Iraq, Blair Says," *New York Times,* February 21, 2007; Mark Rice-Oxley, "As U.S. Surges, British Start Exiting Iraq," *Christian Science Monitor,* February 22, 2007.

23. Ian Fisher, "Italian Prime Minister Resigns," *New York Times,* February 22, 2007, and Phil Stewart, "Italy's Prodi Quits After Foreign Policy Defeat," *Boston Globe,* February 21, 2007.

24. Kim Murphy, "New Polish Premier Pledges Iraq Pullout," *Los Angeles Times,* November 24, 2007; Tim Johnston, "Bush Ally Defeated in Australia," *New York Times,* November 25, 2007; and Rohan Sullivan, "Australian Troops Home from Iraq in 2008," Associated Press, November 30, 2007.

25. Sachiko Sakamaki, "Fukuda Fails to Renew Japan Deployment for Afghan War," www.bloomberg.com, November 1, 2007; Jung Sung-ki, "Troop Pullout from Afghanistan Starts," www.koreatimes.com, August 30, 2007; "Cost of Afghan War a 'biggie' for Dutch; not so much in Canada," www.canadianpress.google.com, October 30, 2007; "Sarkozy Favors French Afghan Withdrawal," news.brisbane times.com.au, April 27, 2007; and Thomas Walkom, "Memo for Minister McKay: The Hearts and Minds campaign Isn't Working. It's Time to Talk Peace with the Taliban," *Toronto Star* (online), August 18, 2007.

26. Pape, *Dying to Win,* 129–39.

27. For America's military, diplomatic, and intelligence services, this reality is new, unique, and profoundly disquieting. Historically all three services are assigned tasks to further the implementation and success of U.S. foreign policy. Now, however, a successful effort in support of any U.S. policy on which bin Laden has focused Muslim attention worsens America's problems. The U.S. military overthrows Saddam's regime and occupies Iraq; Muslims see the fulfillment of the Koran's guidelines for a defensive jihad. U.S. diplomats support Beijing's contention that Muslim Uighur separatists are terrorists; heretofore-neutral Uighurs become anti-American. Intelligence officers provide data to Saudi Arabia that allows the capture and incarceration of local mujahedin; Saudi Islamists harden their view that Riyadh is an un-Islamic, American agent. In reality, an event that U.S. leaders view as a success for their policies can often truly be a case of one step forward and two—or more—steps back.

28. Little should be made of the upticks in U.S. popularity that always occur after U.S. relief aid is delivered to the scene of natural disasters in the Muslim world, such as the post-9/11 tsunami in Indonesia and the earthquake in Pakistani Kashmir. This aid reinforces the admiration that Muslims already have for American generosity, but it does nothing to lessen their animosity toward our foreign policies. Muslims make a clear and broad separation between the two sets of issues.

29. Bernard Lewis, *What Went Wrong? Western Impact and Middle Eastern Response* (New York: Oxford University Press, 2002).

30. See, for example, "Christian Evangelist Franklin Graham Blasts Islam, Says Will Rebuild Churches in Sudan," Associated Press, October 9, 2006.

31. To be fair, some eminent scholars believe Christianity is growing as fast as or perhaps faster than Islam. See for example Philip Jenkins, "The Next Christianity," *Atlantic Monthly* (October 2002), 68. Perhaps deciding which estimate is precisely correct matters less than Jenkins' all-too-accurate conclusion. "But the twenty-first century," he warns, "will almost certainly be regarded by future historians as a century in which religion replaced ideology as the prime animating and destructive force in human affairs, guiding attitudes toward political liberty and obligation, concepts of nation-hood, and, of course, conflicts and wars."

32. William Dalrymple, "Islamophobia," *New Statesman* (online version), January 19, 2004.

33. Ibid.

34. Abid Mustafa, "Why the West Has Lost the Ideological War Against Muslims," *Media Monitors Network* (online version), March 11, 2005.

35. Kenneth S. Stampp, *And the War Came: The North and the Secession Crisis, 1860–1861* (Baton Rouge: Louisiana State University Press, 1970), 253.

36. Don E. Fehrenbacher, *Sectional Crisis and Southern Constitutionalism* (Baton Rouge: Louisiana State University Press, 1995), 31.

37. James F. Simon, *Lincoln and Chief Justice Taney: Slavery, Secession, and the President's War Powers* (New York: Simon & Schuster, 2006), 96, 112, 121, 271. In reviewing the cauldron of substantive issues debated in antebellum politics, as well as northern derision of the South, the analogy to contemporary American politics becomes troublingly and perhaps eerily apparent. In the current debate on culture, the genuine substantive issues are apparent: homosexuality, abortion, pornography, evolution-vs.-creationism, and so on. Also noticeable is the often condescending tone of superiority that those individuals who take the pro-side of the issues use toward their opponents. Not only are creationists said to be wrong, for example, but they are described as antimodern, unsophisticated, antiscience, parochial, and misogynist, and their pro-life arguments are ridiculed as quaint, mystical, or fanatically religious. Such rhetoric cannot help but hinder the search for common ground.

38. Fehrenbacher, *Sectional Crisis*, 31.

39. Since that speech, two anthologies of bin Laden's major speeches have been published, but together they only scratch the surface of the corpus of his materials and leave the work of al-Zawahiri and other al-Qaeda leaders untouched. The better, more complete of the two anthologies is Randall Hamud, ed., *Osama bin Laden: America's Enemy in His Own Words* (San Diego, Calif.: Nadeem Publishing, 2005). The other useful work is Bruce Lawrence, ed., *Messages to the World: The Statements of Osama bin Laden* (London: Verso, 2005). Finally, a third anthology—*The Al-Qaeda Reader*, published in 2007—claims to "prove once and for all" that al-Qaeda is waging an offensive vice defensive jihad, and that its true motivation is to destroy western civilization and establish a worldwide caliphate. The selection of documents from the enormous al-Qaeda archive is small and selective; meant to support neoconservative scare-mongering about the caliphate and the rising tide of Islamo-fascism; and introduced and endorsed by the Neocons' history-is-what-I-say-it-is spokesman, Victor Davis Hanson. While the neoconservatives have long identified the publication and wide-distribution of al-Qaeda documents in English as tantamount to supporting terrorism, Hanson now endorses their publication in an unscholarly form

Notes

that will mislead Americans about their enemies' intentions and motivations. The real tragedy in *The Al-Qaeda Reader* is that its compiler and editor, Raymond Ibrahim, is obviously a talented and knowledgeable man. His endnotes in the volume about the ins and outs of Islamic theology are extensive, clear, and very valuable to the average reader. Unfortunately, Mr. Ibrahim's status as an admirer and former student of Dr. Hanson has led him to produce a volume that supports his mentor's view, but does little to accurately inform Americans. See Raymond Ibrahim (ed.), *The Al-Qaeda Reader* (New York: Broadway Books, 2007).

40. It is impossible to conceive a rationale for why the U.S. government or some major foundation has not already sponsored the translation and publication of the full texts of speeches, letters, books, and interviews by bin Laden and Zawahiri. We learned a horrific lesson from failing to translate and publish Hitler's *Mein Kampf* in a timely manner, and we rectified it by making the works of Communist leaders accessible to all Americans who were interested. Given the threat that al-Qaeda poses to the United States, the approach we took to the words of Communist leaders seems appropriate for those of bin Laden et al. Although I disagree with the conclusions President George W. Bush draws from reading the words of al-Qaeda's leaders, his attitude toward them is exactly right. "The world ignored Hitler's words and paid a terrible price," Mr. Bush said in September, 2006. "Bin Laden and his allies have made their intentions as clear as Lenin and Hitler before them. The question is: Will we listen? Will we pay attention to what these evil men say?" See Ken Herman, "Bush: Pay Attention to Words of Evil," www.kentucky.com, September 6, 2006.

Chapter 7. "O enemy of God, I will give thee no respite": Al-Qaeda and Its Allies Take Stock

1. "Transcript of Republican Presidential Debate in South Carolina," www.nytimes.com, May 17, 2007.
2. Patrick J. Buchanan, "Who Was Right—Ron or Rudy," www.townhall.com, May 18, 2007.
3. "The Terrorist Threat to the Homeland: NIE Key Judgments," www.dni.gov, July 17, 2007.
4. Woodward, *Bush at War*, 45.
5. Jonathan Tobin, "That Old Standby—the Scapegoat," http://jewishworldreview.com, December 16, 2004.
6. Gabriel Schoenfeld, "What Became of the CIA?" *Commentary* (March 2005), online www.opinionjournal.com.
7. Morris J. Amitay, "Not Very Funny," www.washingtonpac.com, April 20, 2006. For my article (to which Mr. Amitay refers) praising the Israeli government's superb and utterly successful covert political-action campaign to suppress criticism of Israel in the United States, see Michael F. Scheuer, "Does Israel Conduct Covert Action in America? You Bet It Does," www.antiwar.com, April 8, 2006.
8. Mearsheimer and Walt, "Israel Lobby." The article was then developed into the authors' book, *The Israel Lobby and U.S. Foreign Policy* (New York: Farrar, Straus, and Giroux, 2007).
9. James Carroll, "The Thread of Anti-Semitism," *Boston Globe*, April 3, 2006; Max

326

Boot, "Attacking the Israeli Lobby," *Los Angeles Times*, April 3, 2006; "Paper on Israeli Lobby Draws Ire," United Press International, April 3, 2006; Christopher Hitchens, "Overstating Jewish Power," www.slate.com, March 27, 2006; David Gergen, "There Is No Israel 'Lobby.' " *New York Daily News*, March 26, 2006; Victor Davis Hanson, "When Cynicism Meets Fanaticism," www.nationalreview.com, March 31, 2006; Steven Simon, "Here's Where the 'Israel Lobby' Is Wrong," *Daily Star,* May 4, 2006; Jonathan Tobin, "View from America: The Paranoid Style of American Anti-Israel Politics," www.jpost.com, April 3, 2006; and Richard L. Cravatts, "Anti-Semitic Paranoia at Harvard," http://news.bostonherald.com, April 3, 2006.

10. Gergen, "No Israel 'Lobby.' "

11. In Islam, *takfir* is the process of excommunication: that is, declaring a person or a group of persons non-Muslim. *Takfiris* are those who take it upon themselves to judge whether an individual or group should be excommunicated. While living in the Sudan in the early 1990s, for example, bin Laden was twice attacked by *takfiris* who believed he was not a "good Muslim." Currently, there are small groups of Sunni Islamists who can legitimately be called *takfiris*, and these groups often take it upon themselves both to excommunicate and then kill those excommunicated. This is a small, unpopular trend within the Islamist militant movement because most Sunnis believe that the *takfiris*, in essence, illegitimately preempt Allah's final judgment on an individual. Some U.S. writers, like Mary Habeck and Fawaz Gerges, have identified al-Qaeda as a *takfiri* organization, but this is grossly inaccurate. Overall, the Israel-first *takfiris* of U.S. politics are much more dangerous to U.S. interests than are Islamist *takfiris*.

12. Quoted in Melton, *Quotable Founding Fathers*, 101.

13. Quoted in James MacGregor Burns, *Roosevelt: The Lion and the Fox* (New York: Harcourt, Brace, and World, 1956), 283.

14. William R. Cook, *Tocqueville and the American Experiment*, 24 lectures (Chantilly, Va.: Teaching Company, 2006).

15. Ibid., CD 5, lecture 10, and Alexis de Tocqueville, *Democracy in America*, ed. Harvey C. Mansfield and Debra Winthrop (Chicago: University of Chicago Press, 2000), 227.

16. McDougall, *Promised Land, Crusader State*, 6.

17. Tocqueville, *Democracy in America,* 243–45.

18. Bin Laden has repeatedly discussed al-Qaeda's goal of bankrupting the U.S. economy. See, for example, Taysir Alouni, "Interview with Usama Bin Ladin, 21 October 2001," www.qoqaz.com, May 23, 2002, and "Statement by al-Qaida leader Osama bin Ladin," Al-Jazirah Satellite Television, December 27, 2001. On spreading out U.S. forces, Zawahiri has written: "In this great battle . . . It is compulsory on the Muslim youth to spread the battle against the crusaders and Jews on the biggest space possible of land, and to threaten their interests in all places, and not to let them rest or find stability." See Ayman al-Zawahiri, "The Freeing of Humanity and Homelands Under the Banner of the Qur'an," www.jiahdunspun.com, March 8, 2005.

19. In the period since July 2006, there have been about thirty messages from bin Laden and al-Zawahiri. The great majority of them have been from the latter.

20. Osama bin Laden, "Message to the American People," Al-Jazirah Satellite Television, January 19, 2006, and Azzam al-Amriki, "Legitimate Demands," *As-Sahab*, May 29, 2007. For the best examination of this American mujahid, see Raffi Khatchadourian, "Azzam the American," *New Yorker,* January 22, 2007.

21. Although bin Laden has never publicly compared himself to Saladin, the latter's heroic legend in the Islamic world makes easy comparisons between him and bin Laden inevitable. Neither was a trained Islamic scholar or jurist; both were soldiers who shared the rigors of their fighters' lives; each led a defensive jihad against "Crusaders" when the established authorities in the Islamic world refused to do so; both labored successfully to build multiethnic military organizations: both excelled at using the media to build support for jihad among the masses; and each was renowned for his personal bravery, piety, humility, and aversion to opulence and luxury. For a good and concise look at Saladin's career, see Roy Jackson, *Fifty Key Figures in Islam* (London and New York: Routledge, 2006), 101–106.
22. "Press Briefing by Scott McClellan," www.whitehouse.gov, January 19, 2006.
23. Baker and Hamilton, *Iraq Study Group Report.*
24. The term "the blessed nineteen" is used by al-Qaeda leaders as a collective description of the nineteen fighters who conducted the attacks on Washington and New York on September 11, 2001.
25. Alan Fram, "Muslims in U.S. Split on Terrorism," Associated Press, May 23, 2007; Geneive Abdo, "America's Muslims Aren't as Assimilated as You Think," WashingtonPost.com, August 27, 2006.
26. "Transcript: Bush on London Bombings," www.washingtonpost.com, July 7, 2005; "Terrorists Strike London in Series of Blasts," www.foxnews.com, July 7, 2005; and "CNN Breaking News: London Bombings," http://transcriptscnn.com, July 7, 2005.
27. Allan Woods, "Alleged Terror Plot Shows Canadian Values under Attack, Prime Minister," *Ottawa Citizen,* June 4, 2006.
28. "Interview with Prime Minister John Howard," www.pm.gov.au, July 2, 2007.
29. On Washington cutting funding for the Hamas government, see "U.S. Senate Votes to Block aid to PA," Associated Press, June 24, 2006. For Netanyahu's remarks, see Netanyahu, "It's '38, and Iran is Germany," www.jpost.com, November 14, 2006, and quoted in Rick Richman, "Revisiting (and Reliving) 1938," http://american thinker.com, November 28, 2006. On Lieberman, see Peter Urban, "Lieberman Says Iran Is Waging War," *Connecticut Post Online*, July 3, 2007.
30. For a sampling of the American *takfiris'* attacks on President Carter for his book *Palestine: Peace Not Apartheid* (New York: Simon & Schuster, 2006), see Deborah Lipstadt, "Jimmy Carter's Jewish Problem," *Washington Post,* January 20, 2007, A-23; Mona Charen, "Brave Jimmy Carter?" www.nationalreviewonline.com, December 15, 2006; and Jacob Olidort, "Is 'Apartheid' the Right Word?: The Book Is Full of Falsities and Errors," www.thejusticeonline.com, January 24, 2007. The Baker-Hamilton report's comment is in *Iraq Study Group Report*, 55.
31. "Speech by Robert S. Mueller III at the Global Initiative Nuclear Terrorism Conference," www.fbi.gov, June 11, 2007, and Dipesh Gadher, "Al-Qaeda 'Planning Big British Attack,' " *Sunday Times,* April 22, 2007.
32. For bin Laden on these issues, see most recently "Statement by Osama Bin Laden," Al-Jazirah Satellite Television, April 23, 2006.
33. See "UK's 'Deep Concern' over Rushdie," BBC News, www.newsvote.bbc.co.uk, June 20, 2007, and "Britain's Rushdie Folly," *News*, www.the news.com.pk, June 20, 2007.
34. *Iraq Study Group Report* uses the words *Islam* and *Islamic* very sparingly and leaves the impression that the commissioners stayed as far away from the words as possible.

There is also some mention of "sectarian" violence. Nowhere in the report, however, is there a discussion of the problems that the United States and its allies now face because the U.S.-led invasion and occupation of Iraq fulfilled the Koran's requirement for a defensive jihad. This is, to say the least, an extraordinary oversight, one that amounts to negligence if it was not deliberate.

35. For the lecture by Pope Benedict XVI that caused the controversy, see Pope Benedict XVI, "Faith, Reason, and the University. Memories and Reflections," www.vatican.va, September 12, 2006, and Joseph Cardinal Ratzinger, "On Europe's Crisis of Culture," www.zenit.org, July 26, 2005.

36. For a sampling of the criticism directed at the pope, see "The Pope's Words," *New York Times,* September 16, 2006, and Ruth Gledhill, "Serious Errors of Both Fact and Judgment," www.timesonline.co.uk, September 16, 2006.

37. Jason Straziuso, "Taliban Undeterred After Death of Leader," Associated Press, May 14, 2007. For the growing numbers of mujahedin, see "NIE: Terrorist Threat to the U.S. Homeland."

38. "Terrorist Threat to UK—MI5 Chief's Full Speech," www.timesonline.uk.co, November 10, 2006; Alan Cowell, "Terrorist Threat to Last a Generation, Blair Says," *New York Times,* November 10, 2006; and "UK Spy Chief Fears Nuclear Attack," http://edition.cnn.com, November 10, 2006.

39. Preferring to spotlight liberty over enforcing the law for their international audience, the 9/11 commissioners said: "Our borders and immigration system, including law enforcement, ought to send a message of welcome, tolerance, and justice to members of immigrant communities in the United States and in their countries of origin." Kean et al., *9/11 Commission Report,* 390.

40. Eric Lipton, "Security Cuts for New York and Washington," *New York Times,* June 1, 2006; "U.S. Poorly Prepared for Attack, Says Report," *Washington Post,* A-13; Lara Jakes Jordan, "Homeland Security Faces Massive Overhaul," http://seattlepi.nwsource.com, June 17, 2005; and Siobhan Gorman, "U.S. Is Called Still Not Ready for a Disaster," *Baltimore Sun,* September 11, 2005.

41. John Solomon, "FBI Didn't Seek to Hire Experts," www.sfgate.com, June 19, 2005; William E. Odom, "Why the FBI Can't Be Reformed," *Washington Post,* June 29, 2005, A-21; John Solomon, "FBI Chief Won't Mandate Expertise," www.sfgate.com, June 20, 2005; Matthew Barakat, "[FBI] Supervsior: I Never Read Moussaoui Memo," www.thestate.com, March 22, 2006; Noah Shachtman, "The Federal Bureau of Luddites," www.slate.com, April 4, 2006; Lisa Myers et al., "Is the FBI Doing Its Best to Combat Terrorism?" www.msnbc.msn.com, December 5, 2006; and "Transcript of Interview with Admiral Mike McConnell," *Meet the Press,* www.msnbc.msn.com, July 22, 2007.

42. Baker and Hamilton, *Iraq Study Group Report,* 82.

43. Jeff Stein, "Can You Tell a Shia from a Sunni?" *New York Times,* October 18, 2006, and "Queries Vex New Chair of Intelligence," *Washington Post,* December 12, 2006, A-7.

44. Matthew Clarke, "Goss's Excellent Idea," *Christian Science Monitor,* June 21, 2005, and "Negroponte: Al-Qaeda Leaders Have 'Secure Hideout' in Pakistan," *USA Today,* January 18, 2007.

45. Al-Zawahiri's assessment is the only telling damage to al-Qaeda and the Taliban has been done by Pakistan's army. "[T]he real danger [to al-Qaeda]," al-Zawahiri told the late Abu Musab al-Zarqawi in July 2005, "comes from the agent Pakistani army that

is carrying out operations in the tribal areas looking for the mujahedin." See "Letter from al-Zawahiri to al-Zarqawi," www.dni.gov, October 11, 2005.

46. "India, U.S. reach landmark nuclear agreement," Associated Press, March 2, 2006.

47. Tom Regan, "U.S. Intel Chief: Al Qaeda Active, Strong in Pakistani Hideout," *Christian Science Monitor,* January 12, 2007; "Al-Qaeda Rebuilding in Pakistan," www.bbc.co.uk, January 12, 2007; and Mark Mazetti and David Rhode, "Al-Qaeda leaders rebuilding network in Pakistan," *International Herald Tribune*, February 19, 2007.

48. Kahlid Hassan, "Pakistan Polls Must Be Free: Burns," *Daily Times*, July 26, 2007; Anwar Iqbal, "Pakistan Better Off with Elected Government: Boucher," *Dawn,* July 14, 2007; and Amin Saikal, "Pakistan Will Survive This Crisis," Age, July 26, 2007.

49. See Jamie Glazov, "Interview with Ralph Peters," www.frontpagemag.com, September 7, 2005. Bin Laden's views regarding the importance of Fallujah are in Osama bin Laden, "Message to Muslims in Iraq," www.dazzled.com/soiraq/pdf/Iraq.zip, December 28, 2004. The Sunni insurgents at the first battle of Fallujah, bin Laden wrote, "stood firm before them [U.S. Marines] despite their small numbers and their inadequate gear, bare headed and with their chests uncovered . . . God sufficeth them. [They are] writing a new page of glory in the history of our nation with their blood and corpses."

50. Baker and Hamilton, *Iraq Study Group Report*, 70.

51. For a review and analysis of the disrupted August 2006 plot by Pakistani Islamists in England to down ten or more U.S. and U.K. airliners flying the Atlantic, see Michael F. Scheuer, "The London Plot: A Tactical Victory in an Eroding Strategic Environment," *Terrorism Focus* 3, no. 32 (August 15, 2006).

52. "Senate Passes $2.8 Trillion Spending Plan for 2007," Associated Press, March 17, 2007; "Ben Bernanke Warns U.S. Congress to Lower Budget deficit," www.market watch.com, January 19, 2007; and Robert D. Hormats, *The Price of Liberty: Paying for America's Wars* (New York: Times Books, 2007), p. 298. For a provocative speculative essay on how another major terrorist event could conceivably trigger an economic disaster, see Niall Ferguson, "The Next Meltdown," *Time,* January 4, 2007.

53. Baker and Hamilton, *Iraq Study Group Report*, 32. The Study Group may have underestimated the per-month cost; see "Iraq War to Cost $8.4 Billion per Month," Reuters, January 18, 2007. For the current and higher figures, see for example Regan E. Doherty, "The Costs of War: A Looming Crisis," *Medill Reports*, www.medill.northwestern.edu, May 23, 2007; Eric Margolis, "The Second Most Expensive War in American History," http://axisoflogic.com, July 17, 2007; Joseph A. Kechichian, "How Much Will Iraq Really Cost?," *Gulf News*, http://archive.gulfnews.com, July 16, 2007; and Tony Capaccio, "Iraq War Costs Approach $567 Billion, Congressional Report Says," www.bloomberg.com, July 19, 2007.

54. Bin Laden, "Message to the American People."

55. For the most recent flap over a civil liberties–related issue, see Michael J. Sniffen, "U.S. Gov't Terror Ratings Draw Outrage," Associated Press, December 2, 2006.

56. "Our silence is our real propaganda," bin Laden claimed in late September 2001. "Rejections, explanations, or corrigendum only waste your time, and through them, the enemy wants to engage you in things which are not of use to you. These things are pulling you away from your cause. The Western media is unleashing such a baseless propaganda, which makes us surpise[d] but it reflects on what is in their hearts and

gradually they themselves become captive of this propaganda. Terror is the most dreaded weapon in the modern age and the Western media is mercilessly using it against its own people. It can add fear and helplessness in the psyche of the people of Europe and the United States. It means what the enemies of the United States cannot do, its media is doing that. You can understand as to what will be the performance of the nation in a war, which suffers from fear and helplessness." See "Exclusive Interview with Usama Bin Ladin," *Ummat,* September 28, 2001, 1, 7.

57. Lewis, "License to Kill."
58. Daniel Byman, "Scoring the War on Terrorism," *National Interest,* no. 72 (Summer 2002), 75–84, and "Fatwa by 26 Saudi Ulema Urges 'Resistance' Against 'Occupation' Forces in Iraq," Al-Jazirah Satellite Television, November 6, 2004.
59. Dan Murphy, "Signs of Al Qaeda in Deadly Jordan Attacks," *Christian Science Monitor,* November 10, 2005; Simon Freeman, "Senior Palestinians Among 56 Dead in Jordan Hotel Bombs," www.timesonline.co.uk, November 10, 2005; "Al-Qaeda Claims Missile Attack on Israel," http://newsminemsn.com.au, December 29, 2005; Illene R. Prusher, "Al Qaeda Takes Aim at Israel," *Christian Science Monitor,* January 13, 2006; Abd al-Rahman al-Rashid, " 'Al-Qaida' in Syria," *Al Sharq Al-Awsat,* July 4, 2005, 11; and Thair Abbas, "Al-Qaeda in Lebanon," *Al-Sharq Al-Awsat,* March 18, 2006.
60. Howard Cincotta, "Freedom Will Prevail in 'Long War' Against Terror, Rumsfeld Says," http://usinfo.state.gov, February 4, 2006.
61. "Interview of the Vice President by John King, CNN," www.whitehouse.gov, June 22, 2006.
62. Baker and Hamilton, *Iraq Study Group Report,* 7, 39.
63. Ibid., 76–77.
64. "All that we have mentioned here," bin Laden said in October 2004, "has made it easy for us to provoke and bait this [George W. Bush] administration. All we have to do is send two mujahedin to the furtherest point East to raise a piece of cloth on which is written al-Qaida, in order to make the [U.S.] generals race there to cause America to suffer human, economic, and political losses without achieving for it anything of note other than some benefits for their private companies." See Osama bin Laden, "Message to the American People," Al-Jazirah Satellite Television, October 20, 2004.
65. Transcript of Republican Presidential Debate in South Carolina, May 15, 2007, and Buchanan, "But Who Was Right."
66. Quoted in Lings, *Muhammad,* 112.

Part IV. Where to from Here?

1. Mary Habeck, *Knowing the Enemy: Jihadist Ideology and the War on Terror* (New Haven, Conn.: Yale University Press), 173.
2. Sageman, *Understanding Terror Networks,* 182.
3. Walter Russell Mead, *Power, Terror, Peace, and War: America's Grand Strategy in a World at Risk* (New York: Alfred A. Knopf, 2004), 176.
4. Habeck, *Knowing the Enemy,* 174–75.

5. Louise Richardson, *What Terrorists Want: Understanding the Enemy, Containing the Threat* (New York: Random House, 2006), 206.
6. Ibid., 232.
7. Mead. *Power, Terror, Peace,* 172, 167.
8. Ibid., 188
9. Richardson, *What Terrorists Want,* 217.
10. Mead, *Power, Terror, Peace,* 201; Richardson. *What Terrorists Want,* 235; Elshtain, *Just War Against Terror,* 167.
11. Habeck, *Knowing the Enemy,* 176–77.
12. Sageman, *Understanding Terror Networks,* 182.
13. Elshtain, *Just War Against Terror,* 169.
14. Quoted in Steyn, *America Alone,* 79.
15. Richardson, *What Terrorists Want,* 237.
16. Jacob Dolson Cox, Military Reminiscences, www.sonofthesouth.com.

Chapter 8. A Humble Suggestion—America First

1. Quoted in Robinson, *American Ideals,* guidebook, 95–96; "George III's Letter on the Loss of America," www.nationalcenter.org.
2. Abdel Bari Atwan, *The Secret History of al-Qaeda* (Berkeley: University of California Press, 2006), 13.
3. Baker and Hamilton, *Iraq Study Group Report,* 55.
4. Elshtain, *Just War Against Terror,* 169.
5. Richardson, *What Terrorists Want,* 204.
6. Thomas Paine, *Common Sense* (1776), http://bartleby.com.
7. Casey and McClellan, *Federalist,* 355–62.
8. General Washington's words can be read at www.quotedb.com.
9. Daniel Yergin, "Energy Independence," *Wall Street Journal,* January 23, 2007.
10. Gal Luft, "An Energy Pearl Harbor," *Washington Post,* March 5, 2006.
11. Bush, Second Inaugural Address.
12. Martin van Creveld, *The Changing Face of War: Lessons of Combat, From the Marne to Iraq* (New York: Ballantine Books, 2006), pp. 269–270.

Epilogue: An Abiding Uniqueness

1. Quoted in Walter LaFeber, ed., *John Quincy Adams and American Continental Empire* (Chicago: Quadrangle Books, 1965), 42–46.
2. George F. Kennan, "On American Principles," *Foreign Affairs* 74, no. 2 (March–April, 1995).
3. Talbott, *Churchill on Courage.*

Bibliography

Books

Allen, W. B., ed. *George Washington: A Collection*. Indianapolis, Ind. Liberty Fund, 1988.

Allison, Graham. *Nuclear Terrorism: The Ultimate Preventable Catastrophe*. New York: Times Books, 2004.

Anderson, Fred, and Andrew Cayton. *The Dominion of War: Empire and Liberty in North America, 1500–2000*. New York: Viking, 2005.

Aslan, Reza. *No god but God: The Origin, Evolution, and Future of Islam*. New York: Random House, 2006.

Atwan, Abdel Bari. *The Secret History of al-Qaeda*. Berkeley: University of California Press, 2006.

Baker, James A., III and Lee H. Hamilton, Co-Chairs, *The Iraq Study Group Report: The Way Forward—A New Approach*. New York: Vintage Books, 2006.

Bawer, Bruce. *While Europe Slept: How Radical Islam Is Destroying the West from Within*. New York: Doubleday, 2006.

Belloc, Hilaire. *The Great Heresies*. Rockford, Ill.: Tan Books and Publishers, 1991.

Benjamin, Daniel, and Steven Simon. *The Age of Sacred Terror*. New York: Random House, 2002.

———. *The Next Attack: The Failure of the War on Terror and a Strategy for Getting It Right*. New York: Times Books, 2005.

Bergen, Peter L. *Holy War, Inc.: Inside the Secret World of Osama Bin Laden*. New York: Free Press, 2001.

———. *The Osama Bin Laden I Know*. New York: Free Press, 2006.

Berlinski, Claire. *Menace in Europe: Why the Continent's Crisis Is America's, Too*. New York: Crown Forum Books. 2007.

Bernsten, Gary, and Ralph Pezzulo. *Jawbreaker: The Attack on Bin Laden and al-Qaeda: A Personal Account by CIA's Key Field Commander*. New York: Three Rivers Press, 2006.

Biddle, Stephen. *Afghanistan and the Future of Warfare: Implications for Army and Defense Policy*. Carlisle, Penn.: U.S. Army War College, Strategic Studies Institute, 2002.

Blankley, Tony. *The West's Last Chance: Will We Win the Clash of Civilizations?* Washington, D.C.: Regnery Publications, 2005.

Burns, James MacGregor. *Roosevelt: The Lion and the Fox*. New York: Harcourt, Brace, and World, 1956.

Bibliography

Cappon, Lester J., ed. *The Adams-Jefferson Letters*. Chapel Hill, N.C.: University of North Carolina Press, 1959.

Carey, George W., and James McClellan. *The Federalist: The Gideon Edition*. Indianapolis, Ind.: Liberty Fund, 2001.

Clarke, Richard A. *Against All Enemies: Inside America's War on Terror*. New York: Free Press, 2004.

Coll, Steve. *Ghost Wars: The Secret History of the CIA, Afghanistan, and Bin Laden, from the Soviet Invasion to September 10, 2001*. New York: Penguin, 2004.

Conrad, Joseph. *Under Western Eyes*. New York: Penguin Books, 1980.

Cook, William R. *Machiavelli in Context: 12 Lectures*. Chantilly, VA: The Teaching Company, 2006.

Cox, Jacob Dolson. *Military Reminiscences*. www.sonofthesouth.com.

Elshtain, Jean Bethke. *Just War Against Terror: The Burden of American Power in a Violent World*. New York: Basic Books, 2003.

Fehrenbacher, Don E. *Abraham Lincoln: Selected Speeches and Writings, 1859–1865*. New York: Literary Classics of the U.S., 1989.

———. *Sectional Crisis and Southern Constitutionalism*. Baton Rouge: Louisiana State University Press, 1995.

Fromkin, David. *A Peace to End All Peace: Creating the Modern Middle East*. New York: Henry Holt and Co., 1989.

Fukuyama, Francis. *The End of History and the Last Man*. New York: Free Press, 2006.

Gerges, Fawwaz. *The Far Enemy: Why Jihad Went Global*. New York: Cambridge University Press, 2005.

Gramm, Kent. *Gettysburg: A Meditation on War and Values*. Bloomington: Indiana University Press, 1994.

Grau, Lester A., and Michael A. Gress, eds. and trans. *The Soviet Afghan War: How a Superpower Fought and Lost*. Lawrence: University of Kansas Press, 2002.

Habeck, Mary. *Knowing the Enemy: Jihadist Ideology and the War on Terror*. New Haven, Conn.: Yale University Press, 2006.

Hammes, Thomas X., USMC (ret.). *The Sling and the Stone: On War in the 21st Century*. St. Paul, Minn.: Zenith Press, 2004.

Hamud, Randall, ed. *Osama bin Laden: America's Enemy in His Own Words*. San Diego, Calif.: Nadeem Publishing, 2005.

Hayes, Rutherford B. *Diaries and Letters*. www.RutherfordBHayesPresidential Center.com.

Hemingway, Ernest. *Islands in the Stream*. New York: Charles Scribner's Sons, 1970.

Herndon, William H., and Jesse W. Weik. *Herndon's Life of Lincoln*. New York: Da Capo Press, 1983.

Himmelfarb, Gertrude. *The Roads to Modernity: The British, French, and American Enlightenments*. New York: Vintage Books, 2004.

Holt, Frank L. *Into the Land of Bones: Alexander the Great in Afghanistan*. Berkeley: University of California Press, 2005.

Hormats, Robert D. *The Price of Liberty: Paying for America's Wars*. New York: Times Books, 2007.

Hutson, James H. *The Founders on Religion: A Book of Quotations*. Princeton, N.J.: Princeton University Press, 2005.

Bibliography

Ibrahim, Raymond. *The Al-Qaeda Reader.* New York: Broadway Books, 2007.

Jackson, Roy. *Fifty Key Figures in Islam.* London and New York: Routledge, 2006.

Kaplan, Robert D. *Warrior Politics: Why Leadership Demands a Pagan Ethos.* New York: Vintage Books, 2002.

Kean, Thomas H., et al. *The 9/11 Commission Report.* New York: W.W. Norton and Co., 2003.

Krueger, Alan B. *What Makes a Terrorist: Economics and the Roots of Terrorism.* Princeton: Princeton University Press, 2007.

LaFeber, Walter, ed. *John Quincy Adams and American Continental Empire.* Chicago: Quadrangle Books, 1965.

Lawrence, Bruce, ed. *Messages to the World: The Statements of Osama bin Laden.* London: Verso, 2005.

Lewis, Bernard. *What Went Wrong? Western Impact and Middle Eastern Response.* New York: Oxford University Press, 2002.

Lings, Martin. *Muhammad, His Life Based on the Earliest Sources.* Rochester, Vt.: Inner Traditions International, 1983.

Lutz, Donald S., ed. *Colonial Origins of the American Constitution: A Documentary History.* Indianapolis, Ind.: Liberty Fund, 1998.

Machiavelli, Niccolò. *The Prince.* Translated by N. H. Thompson. New York: Barnes and Noble Books, 1999.

————. *Discourses on Livy.* Translated by Harvey C. Mansfield and Nathan Tarcov. Chicago: University of Chicago Press, 1996.

Maier, Charles S. *Among Empires: America's Ascendancy and Its Predecessors.* Cambridge, Mass.: Harvard University Press, 2006.

McDougall, Walter A. *Promised Land, Crusader State: The American Encounter with the World Since 1776.* New York: Houghton Mifflin, 1997.

Mead, Walter Russell. *Power, Terror, Peace, and War: America's Grand Strategy in a World at Risk.* New York: Alfred A. Knopf, 2004.

Mearsheimer, John J., and Stephen M. Walt. *The Israel Lobby and U.S. Foreign Policy.* New York: Farrar, Straus, and Giroux, 2007.

Melton, Buckner F., Jr. *The Quotable Founding Fathers.* Washington, D.C.: Potomac Books, 2004.

Nasiri, Omar. *Inside the Jihad: My Life With al-Qaeda: A Spy's Story.* New York: Basic Books, 2006.

Nasr, Vali. *The Shia Revival: How Conflicts Within Islam Will Shape the Future.* New York: W.W. Norton and Co., 2006.

Naylor, Sean. *Not a Good Day to Die: The Untold Story of Operation Anaconda.* New York: Berkeley Books, 2005.

Nye, Joseph. *Soft Power: The Means to Success in World Politics.* New York: Public Affairs, 2005.

Pape, Robert A. *Dying to Win: The Strategic Logic of Suicide Terrorism.* New York: Random House, 2005.

Peter, Ralph. *Fighting for the Future: Will America Triumph?* Mechanicsburg, Penn.: Stackpole Books, 1999.

————. *New Glory: Expanding America's Global Supremacy.* New York: Sentinel, 2005.

Phillips, Melanie. *Londonistan.* New York: Encounter Books, 2006.

Bibliography

Rafuse, Ethan S., *McClellan's War: The Failure of Moderation in the Stuggle for the Union*. Bloomington and Indianapolis: Indiana University Press, 2005.

Ramadan, Tariq. *In the Footsteps of the Prophet: Lessons from the Life of Muhammad*. New York: Oxford University Press, 2007.

Reeve, Simon. *The New Jackals: Ramzi Yousef, Osama Bin Laden, and the Future of Terrorism*. Boston: Northeastern University Press, 1999.

Rhodehamel, John, ed. *The American Revolution: Writings from the War of Independence*. New York: Literary Classics of the United States, 2001.

Richardson, Louise. *What Terrorists Want: Understanding the Enemy, Containing the Threat*. New York: Random House, 2006.

Risen, James. *State of War: The Secret History of the CIA and the Bush Administration*. New York: Free Press, 2006.

Robinson, Daniel. *American Ideals: Founding a "Republic of Virtue."* 12 lectures. Chantilly, Va.: Teaching Company, 2004.

Sageman, Marc. *Understanding Terror Networks*. Philadelphia, Penn.: University of Pennsylvania Press, 2004.

Santayana, George. *Life of Reason*. Teddington, U.K.: Echo Library, 2006.

Scheuer, Michael F. *Imperial Hubris: Why the West Is Losing the War on Terrorism*. Dulles, Va.: Potomac Books, 2004.

———. *Through Our Enemies' Eyes: Osama bin Laden, Radical Islam, and the Future of America*, rev. ed. Dulles, Va.: Potomac Books, 2005.

Simon, James F. *Lincoln and Chief Justice Taney: Slavery, Secession, and the President's War Powers*. New York: Simon & Schuster, 2006.

Stampp, Kenneth S. *And the War Came: The North and the Secession Crisis, 1860–1861*. Baton Rouge: Louisiana State University Press, 1970.

Steyn, Mark. *America Alone: The End of the World as We Know It*. Washington, D.C.: Regnery Publishers, 2006.

Strauss, Leo. *Thoughts on Machiavelli*. Chicago: University of Chicago Press, 1958.

Sun Tzu. *The Art of War*, trans. Samuel B. Griffith. London: Oxford University Press, 1963.

Tenet, George. *At the Center of the Storm: My Years at the CIA*. New York: HarperCollins, 2007.

Tsouras, Peter G., ed. *Civil War Quotations: In the Words of the Commanders*. New York: Sterling Publishing Co., 1998.

Van Creveld, Martin. *The Changing Face of War: Lessons of Combat From The Marne to Iraq*. New York: Ballantine Books, 2006.

Webster, Alexander F. C., and Darrell Cole. *The Virtue of War: Reclaiming the Classic Traditions East and West*. Salisbury, Mass: Regina Orthodox Press, 2004.

Weigel, George. *The Cube and the Cathedral: Europe, America, and Politics Without God*. New York: Basic Books, 2005.

Wheatcroft, Andrew. *Infidels: A History of the Conflict Between Christendom and Islam*. New York: Random House, 2004.

Woodward, Bob. *Bush at War*. New York: Simon and Schuster, 2002.

Wright, John D., ed. *The Oxford Dictionary of Civil War Quotations*. New York: Oxford University Press, 2006.

Wright, Lawrence. *The Looming Tower: Al-Qaeda and the Road to 9/11*. New York: Alfred A. Knopf, 2006.

Ye'or, Bat. *Eurabia: The Euro-Arab Axis*. Madison, N.J.: Fairleigh Dickinson University Press, 2005.

Bibliography

Yousaf, Mohammad, and Mark Adkin. *The Bear Trap: Afghanistan's Untold Story.* Lahore, Pakistan: Jang Publishers Press, 1992.

Articles, Essays, and Statements.

Abalone, Tim, and Michael Evans. "Karzai Wants Rethink on Terror War as al-Qaeda Urges Uprising." www.timesonline.co.uk, June 23, 2006.

Abbas, Thair. "Al-Qaeda in Lebanon." *Al-Sharq Al-Awsat*, March 18, 2006.

Abdo, Geneive. "America's Muslims Aren't as Assimilated as You Think." Washington post.com, August 27, 2006.

Abdulle, Sahal. "Somali Gunmen Attack Convoy of Ethiopian Troops." Reuters, January 15, 2007.

Abramowitz, Michael, and Griff White. "Insurgent Activity Spurs Cheney Trip to Afghanistan." *Washington Post,* February 27, 2007, A-1.

Abrashi, Fisnik. "Karzai: Attacks Wearing Thin on Afghans." Associated Press, December 8, 2006.

Adam, Ruxandra. "Maliki Slams U.S. Military for Attack." *http://news.softpedia.com*, August 8, 2006.

al-Adl, Sayf. "The al-Qaeda Organization Writes a Letter to the Iraqi People." www.alfjr.com, March 5, 2003.

Aggarwal, Anjoli. "HUJI Has Close Ties with ISI and Osama." *Times of India Online*, April 6, 2006.

Ajami, Fouad. "Where U.S. Power Is Beside the Point." *New York Times*, October 17, 2000.

Al Awdah, Shaykh Salman Bin Fahd. "Letter to Usama Bin Ladin." Islam Today (online), September 17, 2007.

Alberizzi, Massimo A. "Al-Qaeda Trains New Taliban in Somalia." *Corriere della Sera*, November 27, 2003.

Albright, Madeleine. "Statement of Secretary Albright." http://secretary.state.gov, March 3, 1998.

"Algeria Pardons 5,065 Prisoners to Mark Muslim Feast." www.deepikaglobal.com, January 18, 2005.

"Algeria to Pardon or Reduce Sentences for 3,000 Terrorists." www.eveningecho.ie/news, February 2006.

Allaf, Rime. "Fundamentalism No Benefit to Syria." www.metimes.com, July 24, 2007.

Allam, Shahid. "Spectre of Fundamentalism: Warning Bells Getting Louder." *New Nation* (online version), February 22, 2005.

Alouni, Taysir. "Interview with Usama Bin Ladin, 21 October 2001." www.qoqaz.com, May 23, 2002.

"Al-Qaeda Claims Missile Attack on Israel." www.newsmine.msn.com.au, December 29, 2005.

"Al-Qaeda Rebuilding in Pakistan." www.bbc.co.uk, January 12, 2007.

Ambah, Faiza Seleh. "Saudi Crackdown on Dissenters." *Christian Science Monitor,* May 16, 2006.

"America Intervenes in Somalia," www.telegraphindia.com, January 10, 2007.

Amitay, Morris J. "Not Very Funny." www.washingtonpac.com, April 20, 2006.

Bibliography

"An Open Letter and Call From Muslim Religious Leaders to Pope Benedict XVI, et al: A Common Word Between You and Us." www.brandeis.edu/offices/communications/muslimletter.pdf, October 11, 2007.

"Armitage Denies Threatening Pakistan after 9/11." MSNBC.MSN.com, September 22, 2006.

Arnett, Peter. "Osama bin Laden: The Interview." www.cnn.com, May 12, 1997.

Arnold, Matthew B. "Who Is Behind the Violence in the South?" *Bangkok Post*, December 13, 2006.

Arnoldy, Ben. "Kabul Must-see TV Heats Up Culture War in Afghanistan." ABCNEWS.com, May 10, 2005.

Ar-Rashid, Mamun. "Countless Militant Networks like Spider's Net," *Dainik Janakantha,* July 19, 2005.

Aslan, Reza. "A Coming Islamic Reformation." *Los Angeles Times* (online version), January 28, 2006.

Atwan, Abdel Bari. "Saudi Incidents: Causes and Results," *Al-Quds Al-Arabi*, June 1, 2004.

Auerswald, Philip E. "Calling an End to Oil Alarmism," *Boston Globe* (online version), January 23, 2007.

Avnery, Uri. "The Next Crusades." Arabic Media Internet Network, March 5, 2005.

Azoulay, Orly. "Obama's Israel Advisor: Next White House Chief of Staff," http://www.ynetnews.com, November 2, 2008.

Bacevich, Andrew J. "A Less Than Splendid Little War," *Wilson Quarterly* (Winter 2001).

———. "Fighting a War in Name Only." *Los Angeles Times*, June 21, 2004.

Baldauf, Scott, and Mike Pflanz. "U.S. Takes Hunt for al-Qaeda to Somalia." *Christian Science Monitor*, January 10, 2007.

"Bangkok's Bombs." *Weekly Standard*, January 3, 2007.

"Bangladesh Bombs Spotlight 'Holy Warriors.' " Reuters, September 27, 2005.

"Bangladesh Declares Emergency, Imposes Curfew." Reuters, January 11, 2007.

"Bangladesh Most Corrupt," *Daily Star,* January 1, 2006.

"Bangladeshis Hail Capture of Top Militants." *Reuters*, March 7, 2006.

Barakat, Matthew. "[FBI] Supervisor: I Never Read Moussaoui Memo." www.thestate.com, March 22, 2006.

Barker, Kim. "In Afghanistan, Cultural Struggle Turns Dangerous." *Chicago Tribune,* May 22, 2005.

———. "Gleam Is off Thailand's Quiet Coup." *Chicago Tribune,* December 10, 2006.

Bearden, Milt. "As the War Turns." *Los Angeles Times*, November 18, 2001.

———. "Afghanistan, Graveyard of Empires." *Foreign Affairs* (November–December, 2001).

——— and Larry Johnson. "Don't Exaggerate the Terrorist Threat." *Wall Street Journal,* June 15, 2000.

"Ben Ali frees 1,600 Tunisian prisoners," www.middle-east-online.com, February 27, 2006.

"Ben Bernanke Warns U.S. Congress to Lower Budget Deficit," www.marketwatch.com, January 19, 2007.

"Berger Mystery Deepens," *Boston Herald*, January 21, 2007.

Bibliography

Berger, Sebastian. "Thailand Coup Raises Hope for a Deal with Muslim Insurgents," http://telegraph.co.uk, September 29, 2006.

Betts, Richard K. "The Soft Under-Belly of American Primacy: Tactical Advantages of Terror." *Political Science Quarterly* 117, no. 1 (Spring 2002).

Bin Laden, Osama. "Declaration of Jihad Against the Americans Occupying the Land of the Two Holy Mosques: Expel the Heretics From the Arabian Peninsula." *Al-Islah* (online), September 2, 1996.

———. "Statement by Osama Bin Ladin." Al-Jazirah Satellite Television, December 27, 2001.

———. "Statement by Shaykh Usama Bin Ladin, May God Protect Him [and] the al-Qaeda Organization." *al-Qal'ah* (online), October 14, 2002.

———. "Statement to the Peoples of Countries Allied to [the] Tyrannical U.S. Government." *Alneda* (Internet), November 21, 2002.

———. "Message to Our Brothers in Iraq." Al-Jazirah Satellite Televsion, February 11, 2003.

———. "Speech to the Peoples of Europe." Al-Arabiyah Television, April 15, 2004.

———. "Message to the American People." Al-Jazirah Satellite Television, October 20, 2004.

———. "Message to Muslims in Iraq." www.dazzled.com/soiraq/pdf/Iraq.zip, December 28, 2004.

———. "Message to the American People." Al-Jazirah Satellite Television, January 19, 2006.

———. "Statement by Osama Bin Laden." Al-Jazirah Satellite Televsion, April 23, 2006.

———. "To the Nation, in General, and the Mujahedin in Iraq and Somlia, in Particular," Al-Sahab Media Organization, www.muslim.net, July 1, 2006.

Blair, Edmund. "Conservative Anglicans Warn Liberal Churches in the West." Reuters, October 31, 2005.

Bonsal, Alok. "Terror: Bangladesh's Growing Export." *Asia Tribune* (online version), April 9, 2006.

Boot, Max. "Attacking the Israeli Lobby." *Los Angeles Times*, April 3, 2006.

Bowers, Faye. "Do Terrorists Play Election Politics?" *Christian Science Monitor*, March 17, 2004.

Brandon, John. "In Thailand's South, Fertile Ground for Terrorism." *International Herald Tribune*, February 11, 2005.

"Britain's Rushdie Folly." *News,* www.thenews.pk, June 20, 2007.

Brooks, David. "Among the Bourgeoisophobes." *Weekly Standard,* April 15, 2002.

Buchanan, Patrick J. "But Who Was Right—Ron or Rudy?" www.townhall.com, May 18, 2007.

Buckley, William F. "In Search of Anti-Semitism." *National Review*, December 30, 1991.

Buerk, Rolana. "Bangladesh and Islamic Militants." BBCNEWS.com.uk, February 25, 2005.

Buruma, Ian. "Ghosts of the Holocaust." *Los Angeles Times*, June 3, 2007.

Bush, George W. Second Inaugural Address. http://whitehouse.gov, January 20, 2005.

Butler, Desmond, and Katherine Schraeder. "Georgia Sting Seizes Bomb Grade Uranium." Associated Press, January 25, 2007.

Bibliography

Byman, Daniel. "Scoring the War on Terrorism." *National Interest*, no. 72 (Summer 2002).

Cappacio, Tony. "Iraq War Cost Approach $567 Billion, Congressional Report Says." www.bloomberg.com, July 19, 2007.

Carroll, James. "The Thread of Anti-Semitism." *Boston Globe*, April 3, 2006.

Charen, Mona. "Brave Jimmy Carter?" www.nationalreviewonline.com, December 15, 2006.

"Chechen Rebel Chief Declares Islamic Emirate." *Threat and Claim Monitor, Intel Center,* November 29, 2007.

Chivers, C. J. "Russia Steps Up Anti-terror Drive as Chechen War Spreads." *New York Times*, October 23, 2004.

Cincotta, Howard. "Freedom Will Prevail in 'Long War' Against Terror, Rumsfeld Says." http://usinfo.state.gov, February 4, 2006.

Clarke, Matthew. "Goss's Excellent Idea." *Christian Science Monitor*, June 21, 2005.

Clayton, Jonathan. "Raids Could Backfire on U.S." *Australian*, January 10, 2007.

"CNN Breaking News: London Bombings," http://transcriptscnn.com, July 7, 2005.

Coll, Steve. "Islamic Activists Sweep Saudi Council Elections." *Washington Post*, April 24, 2005, A-17.

Constable, Pamela. "Afghan Leader Losing Support." *Washington Post*, June 26, 2006.

Cooper, Helene. "Saudis Say They Might Back Sunnis If U.S. Leaves Iraq." *New York Times*, December 13, 2006.

Cornell, Svante. "The North Caucasus: Spiraling Out of Control?" *Terrorism Monitor* 3, no. 7 (April 7, 2005).

"Cost of Afghan War a 'biggie' for Dutch; not so much in Canada." canadian press.google.com, October 30, 2007.

Cowell, Alan. "Terrorist Threat to Last a Generation, Blair Says." *New York Times*, November 10, 2006.

Cravatts, Richard L. "Anti-Semitic Paranoia at Harvard." http://news.bostonherald.com, April 3, 2006.

Dahul, Salad. "Islamic Forces Retreat in Somalia But Say They Expect War 'to Go Every Place.' " Associated Press, December 26, 2006.

———. "Official: Bomb Suspect Killed in Somalia." Associated Press, January 10, 2007.

Dalrymple, William. "Islamophobia." *New Statesman* (online version), January 19, 2004.

Daly, John C. K. "Nigeria Continues to Slide Toward Instability." *Terrorism Monitor* 4, no. 24 (December 14, 2006).

Daragahi, Borzou. "Jordan's King Risks Shah's Fate, Critics Warn." www.latimes.com, October 1, 2006.

Darling, Dan. "Nigeria's Oil War." http://threatwatch.org, February 21, 2006.

Dasgupta, Bashkar. "Insurgency in Thailand." www.hindustantimes.com, March 11, 2005.

Dawson, Allan. "As Thailand Goes . . ." www.techcentralstation.com, July 21, 2005.

Department of State. "Background Note: Thailand." www.state.gov, November 2006.

DeYoung, Karen. "U.S. Strike in Somalia Targets al-Qaeda Figure." *Washington Post,* January 8, 2007.

Bibliography

Doherty, Regan E. "The Costs of War: A Looming Crisis." *Medill Reports,* http://medill.northwestern.edu, May 24, 2007.

Donnelly, John. "U.S. Uses Somali Events to Press al-Qaeda." *Boston Globe*, January 10, 2007.

"Drifting Toward Extremism." http://planetguru.com, February 6, 2005.

Eckert, Paul. "Bangladesh Bomber Arrests Said Only the Beginning." Reuters, March 8, 2006.

El-Fadl, Khaled Abou. "Holy War Versus Jihad." *Ethics and International Affairs* 14 (2000), 133–40.

Ellis, Diana. "Saudi King: Spreading Shiism Won't Work." Associated Press, January 27, 2007.

"Exclusive Interview with Usama Bin Ladin." *Ummat*, September 28, 2001.

"Ex-Detainee Leading Pakistani Militants." *Washington Post,* October 13, 2004.

"Key Facts on Somali President Yusuf." Reuters, October 29, 2007.

al-Fahd, Shaykh Nasir bin Hamd. "A Treatise on the Legal Status of Using Weapons of Mass Destruction against Infidels," May 1, 2003.

al-Faisal, Prince Turki. "Allied Against Terrorism." *Washington Post*, September 17, 2002, 21.

Fattah, Hassan M. "Democracy in the Arab World, a U.S. Goal, Falters." *New York Times*, April 10, 2006.

"Fatwa by 26 Saudi Ulema Urges 'Resistance' Against 'Occupation' Forces in Iraq." Al-Jazirah Satellite Television, November 6, 2004.

Ferguson, Niall. "The Origins of the Great War of 2007—and How It Could Have Been Prevented." *Sunday Telegraph*, January 15, 2006.

———. "The March of Islam." *Daily Telegraph*, May 21, 2006.

———. "The Next Meltdown." *Time*, January 4, 2007.

"Five Ex-Guantanamo Detainees Freed in Kuwait." Associated Press, May 22, 2006.

"Five Nigerians on Terror Charges." news.bbc.co.uk, November 23, 2007.

"Five Suspects Learnt Bomb Skills at al-Qaeda Camps." *Daily Telegraph*, August 12, 2006.

Fletcher, Martin. "The Islamists Were the One Hope for Somalia." www.timesonline.co.uk, January 8, 2007.

Fox-Genovese, Elizabeth. "Multiculturalism in History: Ideologies and Realities." *Orbis* 43, no. 4 (Fall 1999).

Fram, Alan. "Muslims in U.S. Split on Terrorism." Associated Press, May 23, 2007.

"France Will Withdraw Some Forces from Afghanistan." *International Herald Tribune*, December 17, 2006.

Freeman, Simon. "Senior Palestinians Among 56 Dead in Jordan Hotel Bombs." www.timesonline.co.uk, November 10, 2005.

"Fueling the Niger Delta Crisis." *International Crisis Group, Africa Report No. 118*, September 28, 2006.

"Full Text of MI5 Director General's Speech." www.telegraph.co.uk, November 6, 2007.

Gadher, Dipesh. "Al-Qaeda 'Planning Big British Attack.'" *Sunday Times*, April 22, 2007.

Ganley, Elaine. "French Pull Troops from Afghanistan." *Washington Post*, December 20, 2006.

Bibliography

Gergen, David. "There Is No Israel 'Lobby.' " *New York Daily News*, March 26, 2006.

Gerges, Fawaz. "A Change of Arab Hearts and Minds." *Christian Science Monitor*, February 4, 2004.

———. "Al-Qaeda Represents a Security Nuisance, Not a Strategic Threat." www.bruneitimes.com.bn, November 17, 2006.

Giraldi, Philip. "AIPAC's Man in the Obama Camp," http://www.antiwar.com, November 18, 2008.

Gledhill, Ruth. "Serious Errors of Both Fact and Judgment." www.timesonline.co.uk, September 16, 2006.

Glionna, John M. "In Thailand, a New Model for Insurgencies?" *Los Angeles Times*, October 1, 2006.

Goble, Paul A. "The Islamization of Russia." Conference of Association of Former Intelligence Officers, October 26, 2007.

Gordon, Craig. "When Did Bush Know?" www.newsday.com, June 2, 2006.

Gorman, Siobhan. "U.S. Is Called Still Not Ready for a Disaster." *Baltimore Sun*, September 11, 2005.

Griswold, Eliza. "Bangladesh for Beginners." www.slate.com, December 29, 2005.

Halaby, Jamal. "Jordan's King Puts Constitutional Monarchy on the Back Burner for Now." *Associated Press*, August 26, 2005.

———. "Jordan Lawmakers Limit Religious Edicts." www.thestate.com, September 14, 2006.

———. "Jordanian Elections." Associated Press, July 31, 2007.

Hamden, Toby. "British Troops 'Will Be Targets in Afghanistan.' " *Sunday Telegraph* (online version), January 29, 2006.

Hamidi, Ibrahim. "Can Syria Keep Its Islamist Genie in the Bottle?" www.dailystar.com.lb, January 12, 2005.

Hanson, Victor Davis. "When Cynicism Meets Fanaticism." www.nationalreview.com, March 31, 2006.

Hardy, Roger. "Thailand: The Riddle of the South." BBCNEWS.com, February 15, 2005.

Harris, Edward. "Nigerian Christians Burn Muslim Corpses." Associated Press, February 23, 2006.

Harris, Lee. "Terror in Egypt: It Isn't Going to Stop Anytime Soon." *Weekly Standard* (online version), April 27, 2006.

Hassan, Moahmed Olad. "Ethiopia Openly Launches Offensive Against Somalia's Powerful Islamist Movement." Associated Press, December 24, 2006.

Hendawi, Hamza. "Syria Fears Spillover of Sectarian Strife." www.theday.com, January 22, 2007.

Herman, Ken. "Bush: Pay Attention to Words of Evil." www.kentucky.com, September 6, 2006.

Abu-Hilalah, Yasir. "Interview with Abu-Muhammad al-Maqdisi." Al-Jazirah Satellite Television, July 5, 2005.

Hill, Fiona, Anatol Lieven, and Thomas de Waal. "A Spiraling Danger: Time for a New Policy Toward Chechnya." *CEPS Policy Brief*, no. 68 (online version), April 2005.

Himmelfarb, Gertrude. "The Dark and Bloody Crossroads." *National Interest*, no. 32 (Summer 1993).

Hitchens, Christopher. "Overstating Jewish Power." www.slate.com, March 27, 2006.

Bibliography

Hossain, Brigadier General Showkat. "Operation Haluaghat—Security During the Next Election." *Protham Alo* (online version), July 17, 2006.

Hull, Jonah. "Russia Sees Muslim Population Boom." Al-Jazeerah.net, January 7, 2007.

Human Rights Watch. "Libya: Hopeful Sign as 132 Political Prisoners are Freed." www.yubanet.com, March 3, 2006.

Hussain, Dr. Alamgir. "Thailand Insurgency: It's Jihad But Experts Don't Get It." www.americanchronicle.com, December 4, 2006.

Hussain, Farid. "Bangladesh Attacks Bring Fear of Militancy." *Boston Globe* (online version), December 9, 2005.

Hussain, Maneeza. "The World Can't Afford to Ignore Bangladesh." India Monitor.com, August 29, 2005.

Ijaz, Mansoor. "Terrorism's New Operating System." *National Review Online*, September 17, 2005.

"India, U.S. Reach Landmark Nuclear Agreement." Associated Press, March 2, 2006.

Ingram, Judith. "Rebellion Spreads into Russia." *Washington Times*, May 8, 2005.

"Interview with Abu Jandal." *Al-Quds Al-Arabi* (online version) August 3, 2004, and March 18–29, 2005.

"Interview with Prime Minister John Howard." www.pm.gov.au, July 2, 2007.

"Interview with Sergei Markedenov, Institute of Political and Military Analysis, Moscow." Radio Free Europe/Radio Liberty, May 5, 2006.

"Interview of the Vice President by John King, CNN." www.whitehouse.gov, June 22, 2006.

Iqbal, Anwar. "Pakistan Better Off with Elected Government: Boucher." *Dawn*, July 14, 2007.

"Iraq War to Cost $8.4 Billion a Month." Reuters, January 19, 2007.

Iskandar, Luqman. "Calling for the Formation of a Global Body of Sunni Ulemas" *Al-Arab al-Yawm*, July 5, 2005.

" 'Islamists Win' in Key Saudi Poll." new.bbc.co.uk, February 11, 2005.

Jenkins, Philip. "The Next Christianity." *Atlantic Monthly* (October 2002).

Johnston, Tim. "Bush Ally Defeated in Australia." *New York Times*, November 25, 2007.

"Jordan Blocks Muslim Militants from Pulpits." Agence France-Presse, September 4, 2006.

"Jordan detains Islamist deputies." Al-Jazirah Satellite Television, June 12, 2006.

Jordan, Lara Jakes. "Homeland Security Faces Massive Overhaul." http://seattlepi.nwsource.com, June 17, 2005.

"Jordan Turns Its Sights on Muslim Brotherhood." *Financial Times*, June 22, 2006.

Junger, Sebastian. "Blood Oil." *Vanity Fair*, February 2007.

"Karzai Criticizes Foreign Tactics." www.newsvote.bbc.co.uk, June 22, 2006.

Katzman, Kenneth. "Afghanistan: Current Issues and U.S. Policy Concerns." *Congressional Research Service Report* (online version), November 21, 2001.

Kechichian, Joseph A. "How Much Will Iraq Really Cost?" *Gulf News*, http://archive.gulfnews.com, July 16, 2007.

Keegan, John. "How America Can Wreak Revenge." *Daily Telegraph*, September 14, 2001.

———. "If America Decides to Take on the Afghans, This Is How to Do It." *Daily Telegraph*, September 20, 2001.

Bibliography

Kelbie, Paul. "Cheap, Pure Heroin Set to Flood Britain, Say Police." *Independent,* February 5, 2007.

Kennan, George F. "On American Principles." *Foreign Affairs* 74, no.2 (March–April 1995).

Kennedy, Elizabeth A. "Somali Government Fails to Tame Capital." www.latimes.com, August 30, 2007.

Khalaf, Roula, and William Wallis. "Rising Islamist Tide Redefines Middle East's Political Canvas." *Financial Times*, January 27, 2006.

al-Khalidi, Suleiman. "Jordan Says Islamist MPs Face Incitement Charges." Reuters, June 12, 2006.

Khan, Mohammed, and Carlotta Gall. "Accounts After 2005 London Bombings Point to al-Qaeda Role from Pakistan." *New York Times*, August 12, 2006.

Khouri, Rami G. "Bush's Fantasy Foreign Policy." www.tompaine.com, October 11, 2005.

Kuttler, Hillel. "The View from the Top," *Jerusalem Post,* (Internet version), July 1, 1997.

Lake, Eli. "1,500 Qaeda Members Freed After Counseling." *New York Sun,* November 27, 2007.

Lamb, Christina. "British Face 20-year War to Tame Taliban." *TimesOnline*, March 19, 2006.

Last, Jonathan. "One Last Thing—Democracy, of Itself, Is Not a Solution to All Problems." *Philadelphia Inquirer*, August 6, 2006.

Lawrence, T. E. "Report on Mesopotamia." *Sunday Times*, August 2, 1920.

"Letter from al-Zawahiri to al-Zarqawi." www.dni.gov, October 11, 2005.

Lewis, Bernard. "License to Kill: Usama Bin Laden's Declaration of Jihad." *Foreign Affairs* 77, no. 6 (November–December 1998).

———. "Democracy and the Enemies of Freedom." *Wall Street Journal*, December 23, 2003.

Lilla, Mark. "Godless Europe." *New York Times*, April 2, 2006.

Lipstadt, Deborah. "Jimmy Carter's Jewish Problem." *Washington Post*, January 20, 2007.

Lipton, Eric. "Security Cuts for New York and Washington." *New York Times*, June 1, 2006.

Lyman, Princeton, and Scott Allan. "Prevent the Rise of Another Taliban." *Baltimore Sun* (online version), October 19, 2004.

MacFarquhar, Neil. "Syria, Long Ruthlessly Secular, Sees Fervent Islamic Resurgence." *New York Times*, October 24, 2003.

MacGregor, Andrew. "Islam, Jamaats and Implications for the North Caucasus, Part 1." *Terrorism Monitor* 4, no. 11 (June 2, 2006), www.Jamestown.org.

———. "Islam, Jamaats and Implications for the North Caucasus, Part 2." *Terrorism Monitor* 4, no. 12 (June 15, 2006).

———. "Expelling the Infidel: Historical Look at Somali Resistance to Ethiopia." *Terrorism Monitor* 5, no. 1 (January 2007).

Mahtari, Dino, and Guy Dinsmore. "U.S. Upset with Nigeria over Warlord's Flight." *Financial Times*, March 28, 2006.

Malik, Talal. "1,500 'Extremists' Released by Saudi." www.Arabianbusiness.com, November 26, 2007.

Bibliography

al-Maliki, Fayiz. "Mazhar: Saudi-U.S. Talks for the Release of 124 Saudi Detainees in Guantanamo." *Al-Watan* (online version), October 18, 2004.

Manuf, Chowdhry. "Islamic Militant Behind Deadly Bangladesh Blasts Surrenders." Agence France-Presse, March 2, 2006.

Margasak, Larry. "Clinton Aide Stashed Classified Documents Under a Trailer." *Associated Press*, December 21, 2006.

Margolis, Eric S. "The Crusade Moves on to Somalia." *Gulf Times*, December 30, 2006.

———. "The Second Most Expensive War in American History." http://axisoflogic.com, July 17, 2007.

Marquardt, Erich. "The Niger Delta Insurgency and Its Threat to Energy Security." *Terrorism Monitor* 4, no. 16 (August 10, 2006).

Mattar, Shafika. "Jordan Fears Growing Shiite Influence." www.washingtonpost.com, November 17, 2006.

"Mauritania: Junta Declares General Amnesty for Political Prisoners." Reuters, September 5, 2005.

"Mauritania: Three al-Qaeda-linked Suspects Escaped from Jail." Associated Press, April 27, 2006.

"Mauritania Frees Suspected Islamist After Fourteen Months." Reuters, July 28, 2006.

Mazetti, Mark, and David Rhode. "Al-Qaeda Leaders Rebuilding Network in Pakistan." *International Herald Tribune*, February 19, 2007.

McCain, John, and Robert Dole. "Save Darfur Now." *Washington Post*, September 10, 2006.

McLaughlin, Andrew. "Behind Rising Oil Cost: Nigeria." *Christian Science Monitor*, January 18, 2006.

McNicol, Alva. "NATO Hits Chinese Embassy." BBCNEWS.com, May 8, 1999.

Mearsheimer, John, and Stephen Walt. "The Israel Lobby." *London Review of Books*, March 23, 2006.

Meek, James Gordon. "Freed, Many Rejoin Taliban." *New York Daily News*, February 13, 2004.

———. "Qaeda Camps Surge." *New York Daily News*, August 13, 2006.

Miller, John. "Talking to Terror's Banker." www.abcnews.com, May 28, 1998.

Mintz, John. "Released Detainees Rejoining the Fight." *Washington Post*, October 22, 2004.

Mir, Hamid. "U.S. Using Chemical Weapons—Usama bin Laden." *Ausaf*, November 10, 2001.

———. "Interview with Osama Bin Ladin." *Pakistan*, March 18, 1997.

Mitchell, Joshua. "Not All Yearn to be Free." *Washington Post*, August 10, 2003.

"Mogadishu fighting escalates." www.hamiltonspectator.com, January 11, 2007.

Montero, David. "How Extremism Came to Bangladesh." *Christian Science Monitor* (online version), September 6, 2005.

"Morocco Pardons 10,000 to Mark Independence." Reuters, November 17, 2005.

Morrison, Dan. " 'Bomb Culture' Threatens Bangladesh." *Washington Times*, January 15, 2005.

Mouawad, Jad. "Growing Unrest Posing a Threat to Nigerian Oil." *New York Times*, April 21, 2007.

Moumni, Siad. "One-hundred and Sixty-four Detainees Belonging to the Salfia Jiahdia Group Are Pardoned." *Annahar al-Maghribiyah*, November 5, 2005.

Bibliography

Mozgovaya, Natasha. "U.S. Jews Laud Obama's Pick of Rahm Emanuel for Chief of Staff," *Haaretz* (Internet edition), November 9, 2008.

Muhamed, Guled. "Somali Gov't Close to Taking Mogadishu." Reuters, December 28, 2006.

"Mujahid Osama Bin Laden Talks Exclusively to *Nida'ul Isalm* About the New Powderkeg in the Middle East." *Nida'ul Isalm*, January 15, 1997.

Murphy, Dan. "Signs of Al Qaeda in Deadly Jordan Attacks." *Christian Science Monitor*, November 10, 2005.

Murphy, Dan, and Joshua Mitnick. "In Mideast Elections, Militants Gain." *Christian Science Monitor*, June 8, 2005.

Murphy, Kim. "New Polish Premier Promises Iraq Pullout." *Los Angeles Times,* November 24, 2007.

Mustafa, Abid. "Why the West Has Lost the Ideological War Against Muslims." Media Monitors Network (online), March 11, 2005.

Myers, Lisa. "Is the FBI Doing Its Best to Combat Terrorism?" www.msnbc.msn.com, December 5, 2006.

Nasser, Nicolla. "Commentary: Ethiopian Invasion to Spur Anti-U.S. Foment." *Middle East Times* (www.metimes.com), January 9, 2006.

"Near-Daily Violence Grips Inqushetia." MoscowTimes.com, September 4, 2007.

"Negroponte: Al-Qaeda Leaders Have 'Secure Hideout' in Pakistan." *USA Today*, January 18, 2007.

"Netanyahu, 'It's '38, and Iran Is Germany.' " www.jpost.com, November 14, 2006.

"Nigerian Taliban Plots Comeback." Agence France-Presse, January 11, 2006.

"92 al-Qaeda Suspects Freed in Amnesty." *Los Angeles Times*, November 17, 2003.

"No End in Sight as Thailand's Forgotten War Drags On." *Taipei Times*, January 29, 2006.

Nye, Joseph S. "Propaganda Isn't the Way: Soft Power." *International Herald Tribune*, January 10, 2003.

———. "Our Impoverished Discourse." www.huffingtonpost.com, November 1, 2006.

———. "Just Don't Mention the War On Terrorism." *International Herald Tribune*, February 8, 2008.

Odom, William E. "Why the FBI Can't Be Reformed." *Washington Post*, June 29, 2005.

"Official Results: Prodi Defeats Berlusconi." Associated Press, April 11, 2006.

Olidort, Jacob. "Is 'Apartheid' the Right Word?: The Book Is Full of Falsities and Errors." www.thejusticeonline.com, January 24, 2007.

Oppel, Richard A., Jr. "Foreign Fighters in Iraq Are Tied to U.S. Allies." *New York Times,* November 22, 2007.

"Our Enemies Are Quite Explicit About Their Intentions." *Boston Globe*, January 24, 2007.

"Over 2,000 Algerians to Be Released Under Reconciliation Charter." Radio Algiers/Channel 3, March 1, 2006.

"Paper on Israeli Lobby Draws Ire." United Press International, April 3, 2006.

Petrovskiy, Oleg. "Hired Jihad Fighters in No Hurry to Get to Iraq. They Are Quite Happy in Chechnya." www.utro.ru, July 27, 2004.

Pincus, Walter, and Dana Priest. "Goss Reportedly Rebuffed Senior Officials at CIA." *Washington Post,* November 14, 2004.

"Politicians Losing Respect of People for Corruption." *New Nation Online Edition*, January 27, 2007.

Bibliography

Pope Benedict XVI. "Faith, Reason, and the University. Memories and Reflections." www.vatican.va, September 12, 2006.

"Presence of Afghan Veterans in Bangladesh Poll Flayed." www.indiannews.com/bangladesh, December 28, 2006.

"Press Briefing by Scott McClellan." www.whitehouse.gov, January 19, 2006.

"Press Conference of the President." www.whitehouse.gov, September 15, 2006.

Prusher, Illene R. "Al Qaeda Takes Aim at Israel." *Christian Science Monitor*, January 13, 2006.

Purefoy, Christian, and Peter Koenig. "Nigeria Looms as Wild Card in Shell Recovery." www.timesonline.co.uk, February 5, 2005.

"Queries Vex New Chair of Intelligence." Reuters, December 12, 2006.

al-Qurayshi, Abu-Ubayd. "The Fourth Generation of War." *Al-Ansar* (Internet), January 29, 2002.

Rahman, Mizan. "Bangladesh Militant Leader 'Tied to al-Qaeda.' " Gulf Times (online version), March 26, 2006.

Rajesh, Y. P. "Bangladesh Islamists Confident of Expanding Hold." Reuters, January 31, 2007.

al-Rashid, Abd al-Rahman. " 'Al-Qaida' in Syria," *Al-Sharq Al-Awsat*, July 4, 2005.

al-Rashid, Dr. Madawi. "Islam Today: From the Jurisprudence Scholars to the Men of the Cave." *Al-Ouds Al-Arabi* (online version), February 6, 2006.

Ratzinger, Joseph Cardinal. "On Europe's Crisis of Culture." www.zenit.org, July 26, 2005.

"Rebel: We Aided Bin Laden Escape." *Associated Press*, January 11, 2007.

"Rebels 'ready for long years of fighting,' " www.bangkokpost.com, August 29, 2007.

Regan, Tom. "U.S. Intel Chief: Al Qaeda Active, Strong in Pakistani Hideout." *Christian Science Monitor*, January 12, 2007.

Richman, Rick. "Revisiting (and Reliving) 1938." http://americanthinker.com, November 28, 2006.

Rosenberg, Matthew. "Rivalry Fuels Bangladeshi Political Crisis." Associated Press, December 24, 2006.

Sabbagh-Gargour, Rana. "Jordan Carefully Measures Its Democratic Openings." www.dailystar.com.lb, December 12, 2006.

Sakamaki Sachiko. "Fukuda Fails to Renew Japan Deployment for Afghan War." www.bloomberg.com, November 1, 2007.

Saikal, Amin. "Pakistan Will Survive This Crisis." *Age*, July 13, 2007.

Sanders, Edmund. "Ethiopia's Intervention May Destabilize Region." *Los Angeles Times*, January 7, 2007.

Sands, Chris. "Kabul Clerics Rally Behind Taliban." *Toronto Star*, May 22, 2006.

Sanger, David E. "Bush Officials Praise Saudis for Aiding Terror Fight." *New York Times*, November 27, 2002.

———. "Cheney Warns Pakistanis to Act Against Terror." *New York Times*, February 27, 2007.

Saradzhyan, Simon. "Chechnya: Spreading the Insurgency." www.isn.ethz.ch, June 13, 2006.

"Sarkozy Favors French Afghan Withdrawal." new.brisbanetimes.com.au, April 27, 2007.

Bibliography

"Saudi Arabia: Almost 400 Prisoners Released." www.adnki.com, December 19, 2005.

Scheuer, Michael F. "A Fine Rendition." *New York Times*, March 1, 2005.

———. "Does Israel Conduct Covert Action in America? You Bet It Does." www.anti war.com, April 8, 2006.

———. "The London Plot: A Tactical Victory in an Eroding Strategic Environment." *Terrorism Focus* 3, no. 32 (August 15, 2006).

———. "Clueless into Kabul." *American Interest* 2, no. 1 (September–October 2006).

Schoenfeld, Gabriel. "What Became of the CIA?" *Commentary* (March 2005), www.opinionjournal.com.

"Senate Passes $2.8 Trillion Spending Plan for 2007." Associated Press, March 17, 2007.

Sengupta, Romananda. "Bangladesh: Next Terror Frontier?" *Rediff India Abroad* (http://us.rediff.com), December 19, 2005.

"Seven Security Detainees Escape Saudi Jail." Reuters, July 8, 2006.

Smith, Sebastian. "Islamic Rebels Tighten Grip on Dagestan." *Australian,* July 20, 2005.

Shachtman, Noah. "The Federal Bureau of Luddites." www.slate.com, April 4, 2006.

Shadid, Anthony. "Syria's Unpredictable Force." *Washington Post*, May 27, 2005.

Sheets, Lawrence Scott, and William J. Brand. "Atomic Smugglers Pose New Hazard for Former Soviet Republics." *International Herald Tribune* (online version), January 25, 2007.

Sheikh, Abdi. "Battles Rock Mogadishu for Second Day." Reuters, October 28, 2007.

"Shell Evacuates Oil Field After Attacks by Niger Delta Militants." Agence France-Presse, February 18, 2006.

Simon, Steven. "Here's Where the 'Israel Lobby' Is Wrong." *Daily Star*, May 4, 2006.

Singh, Joginder. "Bangla Is Going the Pak Way." *Asian Age* (online version), January 13, 2006.

Smith, R. Jeffrey. "Document-theft Probe Criticized." *Washington Post*, January 10, 2007.

Sniffen, Michael J. "U.S. Gov't Terror Ratings Draw Outrage." Associated Press, December 2, 2006.

"Soldier Casualties Exceed 6,660 in Chechnya Campaigns." *Novosti*, August 10, 2007.

Solomon, John. "FBI Didn't Seek to Hire Experts." www.sfgate.com, June 19, 2005.

———. "FBI Chief Won't Mandate Expertise." www.sfgate.com, June 20, 2005.

"Somalia's Role in Horn of Africa Tensions." Reuters, December 24, 2006.

"Son of Israeli Immigrant Accepts Obama Offer to Serve as Chief of Staff," http://www.ynetnews.com, November 5, 2008.

"Southern Thailand: Insurgency Not Jihad." *International Crisis Group, Asia Report No. 98*, May 18, 2005.

"Spanish Government Admits Defeat." http://news.bbc.uk.co, March 15, 2004.

"Speech by Robert S. Mueller, III, Global Initiative on Nuclear Terrorism," www.fbi.gov, June 11, 2007.

"State Department: U.S. Supports Ethiopian Military." CNN.com, December 27, 2006.

Stein, Jeff. "Can You Tell a Shia from a Sunni?" *New York Times*, October 18, 2006.

Steyn, Mark. "Bicultural Europe Is Doomed." *Daily Telegraph*, November 15, 2005.

Stewart, Sarah. "Thailand, Malaysia Row Exposes Rift over Muslim Rebellion." Agence France-Presse, November 3, 2005.

Storey, Ian. "Thailand Cracks Down on Southern Militants." *Terrorism Monitor* 5, no. 17 (September 13, 2007).

Bibliography

Straziuso, Jason. "Taliban Undeterred after Death of Leader." Associated Press, May 14, 2007.

Sullivan, Eileen. "21,000 Slipped Past Borders Illegally." Associated Press, November 6, 2007.

Sullivan, Kevin, and Mary Jordan. "Blair Says He Will Step Down Within 12 Months." *Washington Post*, September 8, 2006.

Sullivan, Rohan. "Australian Troops Home from Iraq in 2008." Associated Press, November 30, 2007.

Sung-ki, Jung. "Troop Pullout from Afghanistan Starts." www.Koreatimes.co.kr, August 29, 2007.

Tannock, Charles. "The World Cannot Afford Bangladesh's Going Taliban." *Daily Star*, July 21, 2005.

Tayler, Jeffrey. "Nigeria's Troubles Could Become America's." www.allafrica.com, March 13, 2006.

Taylor, Marisa. "Surge in Afghan Heroin Hits United States." www.contracostatimes.com, January 7, 2007.

"Terrorist Threat to UK—MI5 Chief's Full Speech," *Times Online*, November 11, 2006.

"Terrorists Strike London in Series of Blasts." www.foxnews.com, July 7, 2005.

"Text of the World Islamic Front's Statement Urging Jihad Against Jews and Crusaders." *Al-Quds Al-Arabi* (online), February 23, 1998.

"Thai Army Commander General Sonthi Cuts Short Haj Pilgrimage to Return Home." *Phuchatkan*, January 1, 2007.

"Thai Foreign Minister Rules Out Autonomy for South, Says No al-Qaeda Link." www.todayonline.com, November 7, 2005.

"Thailand's Emergency Decree: No Solution." *International Crisis Group. Asia Report, No. 105*, September 18, 2005.

"Thaksin rules out talks with PULO." *Nation*, January 26, 2006.

"The Pope's Words." *New York Times*, September 16, 2006.

"The Son of a Wolf Will Be a Wolf." *Cheragh*, October 24, 2004.

"The Terrorist Threat to the Homeland: NIE Key Judgments," www.dni.gov, July 17, 2007.

Thomas, George. "Terror Havens: al-Qaeda's Growing Sanctuary in Nigeria." www.cbn.com, May 2, 2005.

Tobin, Jonathan. "That Old Standby—The Scapegoat." http:jewishworldreview.com, December 16, 2004.

———. "View from America: The Paranoid Style of American Anti-Israel Politics." www.jpost.com, April 3, 2006.

Tomsen, Peter. "A Chance for Peace in Afghanistan." *Foreign Affairs* 79, no. 1 (January–February 2000).

Townsend, Mark. "Drugs Fuel Big Rise in Organized Crime." *Observer*, July 30, 2006.

"Transcript: Bush on London Bombings." www.washingtonpost.com, July 7, 2005.

"Transcript of Interview with Admiral Mike McConnell," *Meet the Press*. www.msnbc.msn.com, July 22, 2007.

"Transcript of Republican Presidential Debate in South Carolina, May 15, 2007." www.nytimes.com, May 17, 2007.

Bibliography

Urban, Peter. "Lieberman Says Iran Is Waging War." *Connecticut Post Online*, July 3, 2007.

"U.K. Spy Chief Fears Nuclear Attack." http://edition.cnn.com, November 10, 2006.

"U.K.'s 'Deep Concern' over Rushdie." BBC News, http://newsvote.bbc.co.uk, June 20, 2007.

"U.S. Involvement in Somalia." Reuters, January 9, 2007.

"U.S. Poorly Prepared for Attack, Says Report." *Washington Post*, December 3, 2005.

"U.S. Senate Votes to Block Aid to PA." Associated Press, June 24, 2006.

"U.S.-Thailand Alliance." www.defenselink.mil.

"U.S. Threatened to Bomb Pakistan." bbcnews.com.uk, September 22, 2006.

"U.S. Voices Disappointment over Coup in Thailand." *International Herald Tribune*, September 20, 2006.

Walkom, Thomas. "Memo to Minister McKay: The Hearts-and-Minds Campaign Isn't Working. It's Time to Talk Peace With the Taliban." *Toronto Star*, August 18, 2007.

Wallace, Chris. "Interview with President Clinton." www.foxnews.com, September 26, 2006.

Walsh, Declan. "In Afghanistan, Taliban Turning to the Drug Trade." *Boston Globe* (online version), December 18, 2005.

Wannabovorn, Suttin. "Militants May Join Thailand Insurgency." Associated Press, September 24, 2005.

Wehrfritz, George. "Thailand's Muslim Insurgency Is Spinning Out of Control." www.msnbc.msn.com, August 12, 2007.

Wilkonson, Isambard. "Election Blow of Bush's War on Terrorism." www.telegraph.co.uk, March 15, 2004.

Woods, Allan. "Alleged Terror Plot Shows Canadian Values Under Attack, Prime Minister." *Ottawa Citizen*, June 4, 2006.

Wright, Jonathan. "Egypt's Mubarak Defends Constitutional Changes." Reuters, March 24, 2007.

Wright, Lawrence. "The Man Behind Bin Laden." *New Yorker*, September 16, 2002.

Yare, Hassan. "Somali Parliament Declares 3-month State of Emergency." Reuters, January 13, 2007.

"Yemen Acquits 19 Men in al-Qaeda-linked Trial." Reuters, July 8, 2006.

"Yemen Frees 627 Zaidi Rebels." www.middle-east-online.com, March 3, 2006.

Zakaria, Fareed. "Why the War Was Right." *Newsweek*, October 20, 2003.

———. "The Radicals Are Desperate." *Newsweek*, March 15, 2004.

———. "The Best Ways to Beat Terror." *Newsweek*, April 12, 2004.

al-Zawahiri, Ayman. "The Freeing of Humanity and Homelands, Under the Banner of the Qur'an." www.jihadunspun.com, March 8, 2005.

———. "The Zionist-Crusader Aggressions on Gaza and Lebanon." www.muslim.net, July 28, 2006.

———. "Rise Up and Support Your Brothers in Somalia." *Al-Sahab Media Productions* (online), January 5, 2007.

Index

Index

Index

Index

Index

Index

Index

Index

Index

Protestant Reformation, 163, 268
Provincial Reconstruction Teams, 108
Pulaski, Casimir, 79
Putin, Vladimir, 62, 195–96, 230–31

Qaddafi, Muammar al-, 81, 231, 300n
Qatar, 123

Rains, Claude, 103
Ramadan, Tariq, 161
Rashid, Madawi al-, 161–63, 307n
Reagan, Ronald, 21, 42, 43, 55, 56–57,
    75, 80, 84, 92, 214, 247, 283n
  Cold War and, 5–6
Reid, Harry, 214
religion, 66, 70, 94, 269
  in Europe, 179–80
  U.S.'s roots in, 281n–82n
rendition program, 207, 316n–18n
Republican Party, U.S., 4, 17, 29,
    70–71, 72, 74, 109, 139, 142, 186,
    203, 216, 219
Reuters, 173
Revolution in Military Affairs (RMA),
    87–94, 185, 289n
  insurgents' weapons and, 88–89
  Peters's analysis of, 87–88
  targeting of bin Laden and, 90–91
Reyes, Silvester, 297n
Reykjavik Summit, 6
Rice, Condoleezza, 101, 102, 128, 197,
    269, 293n
Roberts, Lord Frederick, 110–11,
    295n
Robertson, Pat, 285n
Robinson, Daniel, 27
Rolenz, Michael, 280n
Roman Catholic Church, 163
Roosevelt, Franklin D., 214, 222, 239
Roosevelt, Theodore, 214
Rumsfeld, Donald, xiii, 101, 105, 137,
    138–39, 197, 238, 269, 289n, 296n
Rushdie, Salman, 156, 234

Russia, 62, 73, 98, 111, 181, 230, 316n
  Chechnya conflict of, xvi, 150,
    168–69, 207, 230
  Islamic NGOs and missionaries in,
    169–70
  North Caucasus region of, 168–70
  nuclear arsenal of, 169, 259
  see also Soviet Union

Sada Military Academy, 112
Sageman, Marc, 301n–2n
Sakharov, Andrei, 79–80
Saladin, 165, 226, 241, 323n
Salafi Group for Call and Combat,
    135
Salafism, 113, 171, 178, 185
Samaritan's Purse, 184
Santayana, George, 187
Saud family, 71, 261
Saudia (airline), 133
Saudi Arabia, 1, 10, 13, 15, 17, 23, 28,
    31, 51–52, 53, 60, 73, 74, 118,
    122, 123, 124, 125, 151, 153, 158,
    163, 167, 169, 171, 172, 175, 178,
    193, 205, 217, 222, 232, 241, 251,
    260, 274n, 276n, 282n, 287n–88n,
    297n, 300n, 301n, 319n
  Afghan War and, 111
  Gulf War and, 41
  oil embargo of 1973 and, 19–20,
    28–29, 132, 231
  September 11 attacks and, 72
  and spread of militant Islam, 185–86
  U.S.'s alliance with, 71–72
  Yom Kippur war and, 24
Sayyaf, Abdur Rasul, 112
Schoenfeld, Gabriel, 219–20
Schwarzkopf, Norman, 42
Scowcroft, Brent, 43
SEATO (Southeast Asia Treaty
    Organization), 92
Second Iraq War, see Iraq War
Senate, U.S., 69, 203

Index

Index

About the Author

Michael Scheuer is the former head of the CIA's Bin Laden Unit and Rendition Program. He resigned in November 2004 after nearly two decades of experience in covert action and national-security issues related to Afghanistan, South Asia, and the Middle East. He is the author of *Imperial Hubris: Why the West Is Losing the War on Terrorism* and *Through Our Enemies' Eyes: Osama bin Laden, Radical Islam, and the Future of America.* Scheuer holds a B.A., two M.A.'s, and a Ph.D. He is an Adjunct Professor of Security Studies at Georgetown University and a Senior Fellow and regular contributor to the Jamestown Foundation's Terrorism Focus (www.Jamestown.org/Terrorism). He lives in northern Virginia.